TOWARDS
MODERN
NATIONHOOD

TOWARDS MODERN NATIONHOOD

WALES AND SLOVENIA IN COMPARISON, *c.*1750–1918

ROBIN OKEY

UNIVERSITY OF WALES PRESS
2023

www.uwp.co.uk

British Library Cataloguing-in-Publication Data
A catalogue record for this book is available from the British Library.

ISBN   978-1-78683-931-2
eISBN   978-1-78683-932-9

The University of Wales Press gratefully acknowledges the funding support of the Books Council of Wales in publication of this book.

Typeset by Marie Doherty
Printed by CPI Antony Rowe, Melksham, United Kingdom

CONTENTS

Map 1: Slovene ethnic territory in the nineteenth century   vi

Map 2: The traditional counties of Wales until 1973   vii

Introduction   1

PART ONE

1   Wales and the Slovene Lands: The Background   21

2   Awakenings, c.1750–1815   44

3   Towards a Turning Point, Wales and Slovenia c.1815–1847   79

4   The Parting of the Ways: 1847–1848   123

PART TWO

5   The Picture Takes Shape, 1848–c.1880   147

6   The National Movements Mature: Success and Shortfall   186

7   Culture, Consciousness and Challenge, 1880–1914   222

8   New Directions and Dénouement   260

Retrospect and Prospect   295

Bibliography   317

Index   335

Map 1: Slovene ethnic territory in the nineteenth century

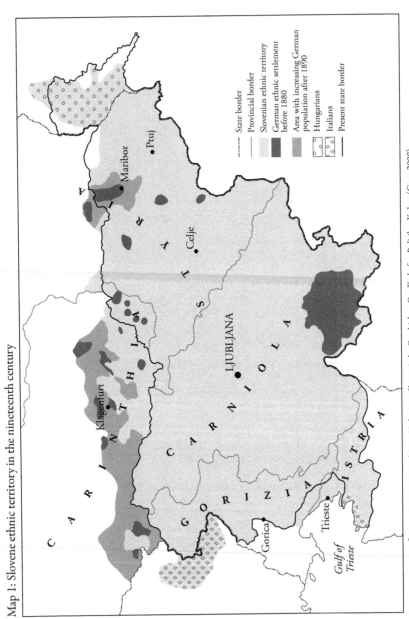

Map based on Peter Štih, Vasko Simoniti and Peter Vodopivec, Slowenische Geschichte. Gesellschaft – Politik – Kultur (Graz, 2008).

State border
Provincial border
Slovenian ethnic territory
German ethnic settlement before 1880
Area with increasing German population after 1890
Hungarians
Italians
Present state border

Map 2: The traditional counties of Wales until 1973

INTRODUCTION

A book on an unusual topic requires more than a perfunctory introduction. To compare two countries little known to the world and hardly at all to each other may savour of eccentricity and has so seemed to some academic colleagues. They have all the more justification when the author is a specialist in neither Welsh nor Slovene history and the period under discussion, crucial in the modern history of both countries, is one where their development diverged widely. What is now Slovenia was torn from its moorings in the ancient Habsburg Empire on the latter's break-up in 1918, and found a new home in the newly created state of Yugoslavia (the 'land of the South Slavs'). When Yugoslavia in turn collapsed in the early 1990s she became for the first time an independent country, joining the European Union in 2004. Wales by contrast has remained throughout part of the British state, itself imperial until well into the twentieth century though much more stable than its Habsburg counterpart. Both countries are the subjects of sophisticated historiographies, but whereas Slovenia's reflects a preoccupation with nationhood and a small nation's complex position in a shifting international landscape, modern Welsh history has been pre-eminently social, the experience of a Welsh common people in a largely unquestioned British framework. Indeed, it is hard to persuade Slovenes of Wales's credentials as a nation at all. Perhaps the best way to explain my choice of topic, then, is to describe briefly the background that led to it.

I am by origin an English-speaking south Walian brought up on the outskirts of Cardiff, since incorporated into the city. My family roots, the only ones I know anything significant about, go back to the upper Rhondda valley, in the pre-industrial and industrial period, which gave me a keen interest in the Welsh side of my A-level course in the 1950s, essentially as presented in David Williams's *History of Modern Wales*. Later on this interest played some role in my decision to make an aspect of the multinational Habsburg Monarchy the subject of my doctorate, leading to a career specialisation in east-central European history. On the way I acquired a thorough grounding in the Habsburg nationality question, particularly as concerned the Slavs, in the first place Serbs and Croats but also the culturally more developed Czechs. My education and my own inclination added to this some familiarity with modern British history, taught in terms of the evolution of the English constitutional state into the global British Empire. I gained in this process an appreciation of three quite different kinds of national story and of two empires, the British and the Habsburg. This drew me to problems of modernisation and in particular the challenge modernity posed to small peoples living in larger, imperial, state frameworks. Accelerating changes forced these to respond, either by redefining their identity in terms of a 'modern' nationhood or by assimilating more fully into the traditionally dominant culture of the respective empire. My line of study therefore offered ample potential material for the kind of comparison, taking up the Welsh connection and the question of Wales as nation, which I have now tried to write in retirement.

I ask the many who will think this a marginal issue in the sweep of world history to consider two facts relating to the twin poles of my topic. One is that in 1750, when my narrative begins, the world contained well short of a billion inhabitants. It now has seven and a half billion. The epochal reorganisation of every sphere of human society needed to spur and accommodate these changes is what the term modernisation addresses. Second, in 1750 there were about a score of sovereign states in the world which had some kind of ethno-national core. Most of these were in Europe, some of which also controlled the Americas and great swathes of Africa and Asia. Add to these Abyssinia, Persia, the Moghul empire, the ancient civilisations of East and south-east Asia and you have at most twenty-two. Now there are some two hundred independent states claiming nationhood under the United Nations. Together, these figures point to an intimate connection between the modern process and the building of nations. As to nationhood itself, this study will limit theoretical discussion to the strictly necessary. In the European context its most relevant aspect is the relationship between modern nations and the ethno-national structures from which they emerged, where views vary on the importance of the pre-modern legacy. I am sympathetic to the approach of the sociologist Anthony D. Smith, who gives due weight to preconditions of nation-building.[1] Where an ethnic group had developed a written literary language and had some sense of a common history and territory medieval and early modern historians have been willing to speak of nationhood, if differing in cohesion and ideology from what followed. Long-standing Welsh nationhood in this sense is indubitably not 'invented'; the issue is the nature of its transition to modernity

Most of my academic life, however, I pursued such wider comparative perspectives only to a limited extent, while concentrating on my area specialism. In the aftermath of the Second World War preoccupation with building a post-imperial and less class-ridden Britain made 'national questions' seem for the wider British public peripheral to, indeed, out of keeping with progressive modern life. Meanwhile, the smaller nations of eastern Europe lived a shadow existence behind the Iron Curtain or absorbed into the Yugoslav socialist federation, which only reinforced this perception. The collapse of the Soviet bloc in 1989–91 and the growing salience of race and gender relations in western Europe demonstrated that national and ethnic difference remained a powerful factor in human affairs, but in ways which heightened British suspicions of an ill-defined 'nationalism' as a disruptive force alien to the liberal individualist values of a would-be global world. Here the inter-Yugoslav wars, developments in Putin's Russia, increased holocaust awareness and heart-searching over white imperialism played a role. Before setting the terms of my comparison it would be helpful to set out briefly how issues of nationality have been seen from three standpoints relevant to this study: the British, the Slovenes and the Welsh.

There is a complex and often difficult relationship between large-nation intellectuals and the national, shared in Britain or rather, here, England. Leading thinkers in modern times anticipated many features of the dawning future. Alexis de Tocqueville in the 1830s, for example, predicted the geopolitical emergence of Russia and the United States as rival great powers; Karl Marx foresaw the way in which the concentration of capital would reshape class structures and the nature of political conflict. But they largely ignored or were dismissive of nationalism and would have been astonished by the existence of a twenty-first century independent Slovene state and devolved Welsh government in Cardiff. British traditions as a constitutional state made her sympathetic to certain nationalist movements against authoritarian rule, as in the case of the Spanish American colonies in the 1820s and later the movement for Italian national unity. Yet such sympathy was conditional. It applied to large populations with historic traditions, and not then if British strategic interests might be adversely affected. Thus millions-strong Hungarians had some popular but no governmental support in Britain for their revolt against Habsburg rule in 1849 because Britain upheld dynastic Austria as a bulwark against Russia. A national role for smaller peoples like the Welsh did not come into consideration. The assumption was that the two great factors of 'hard power', politics and economics, excluded them from any role in an age of expanding government, commerce and industry but further assimilation to the dominant cultures under which they lived. The great English liberal John Stuart Mill (1806–73) wrote of Welsh and Bretons as 'sulk[ing] on [their] own rocks, the half-savage relic of past times, revolving in [their] own little mental orbit without participation and interest in the general movement of the world'. This judgement added a further dimension of backwardness, beyond political and economic impotence. It implied, importantly, a moral aspect: the inability of such a society to grasp the universal values which for the liberal Mill underpinned the advance of civilisation.[2] Relatedly, another English liberal, Lord Acton, at the same time (the early 1860s) condemned nationalism in a famous essay because it subordinated higher moral and civil factors to the brute accident of race.[3] The ground was prepared for a reflex merging of the national with the racial which demeaned the former.

Mill's words should be taken in historical context. He intended no insult and terms he used like 'inferior' and 'superior' peoples were commonplaces of his age. Many Welsh and Bretons followed his advice to assimilate to 'the ideas and feelings of a highly civilised and cultivated people'. But it is necessary to point out that the language of 'universalism' is notoriously slippery and selective, as witness feminists' justified raised eye-brows over the 'Rights of Man' in 1789 or the celebrated democrat Thomas Jefferson's slave-owning lifestyle. The use of such language and the claims it implies come most easily to members of imperial nations. Mill's argument plainly underestimated the capacity of smaller communities to access wider human values off their own account and was made in substantive ignorance of what he was talking about. However, his authority and the British climate of the time helped close down avenues. It set the ethno-national and the universal in opposition to each other in ways which have dominated the British mindset and arguably exaggerated the tension between them. Here a distinction can be made between the Whiggish Acton and the more radical Mill. Both believed in the benefit the presence of ruling nations could offer in multinational states, like the English in the British Isles and the Germans in the Habsburg Monarchy.[4] But Acton saw in the principle of nationality itself a tendency toward an illiberal assertion of collective will to an extent that Mill did not. Precisely because small nationhood was not a matter of systematic British concern, attitudes to it and its viability have not been uniform. One might speak of an underlying scepticism tempered by circumstance.

The comment above about Mill's dismissal of 'backward' cultures is based on my study of the Habsburg Monarchy. This central European dynastic state had over centuries acquired control over some dozen nationalities ranked hierarchically, with Germans (and in places Hungarians and Italians) dominating a majority of Slavs and Romanians. This sprawling polity only underwent a centralising process in the eighteenth century, the high point being Joseph II's declaration of German as the official language over almost all the empire in 1784. But since German speakers were just a quarter of the population this measure helped stimulate a reaction from the non-Germans. Traditional sentiment was stimulated by new ideas about the social role of language expressed most vividly by the German Lutheran pastor and philosopher Johann Gottfried Herder (1744–1803). Against the growing power of the absolutist state, which he hated, Herder opposed the concept of the Volk, or ethno-national group, to him a more natural kind of social organisation from which human beings derived their deepest values, transmitted through the mother tongue. Herder's key concept of 'Humanity' saw this as incorporating and being enriched by the individual peoples, in a synthesis of individual, Volk and mankind which has earned him the title of father of cultural nationalism. It was a heady brew for non-dominant peoples since in Herder's eyes these all had a crucial contribution to make without which Humanity would be poorer. Linguistic revival proved a vital part of a programme which became common to numerous nationalities of the region, not only in the Monarchy. It helped to lubricate a drive for social reform of the largely feudal system and for political reform of absolute monarchy. It helped define the people who were encouraged by the example of the French revolution of 1789 and its democratic overthrow of the *ancien régime* to see themselves as a nation with potential political rights. Of course, all these factors did not come together at once but over many decades, if ever in the more sluggish cases. The winning of rights for public use of the reinvigorated national languages was in many ways the first and easiest line of advance because it posed a less overt threat to the material interests of entrenched elites. In these circumstances the adaptation of peasant tongues to modern norms proceeded surprisingly quickly as education provided dedicated cadres. Since Herderian concepts were common coin cultural nationalism became an international movement, through which individual peoples could access ideas and techniques and acquaint themselves with literary currents in a wider world.

These language movements were the most obvious aspects of what contemporaries called the renaissance or awakening of their peoples. In hindsight they can be seen as a struggle for what historians have dubbed 'cultural sovereignty': the equipping of the mother tongue to discuss all ideas and aspects of modern society, in principle, without having to resort to a foreign tongue.[5] In principle, because the ability to translate a play by Shakespeare into effective and understandable Slovene, say, was more important than that all Shakespeare's plays should be so translated, as they had been in German. Gradual also was the creation of institutions of one's own, like reading rooms, theatres, local banks and cooperatives, learned societies and the like with the mother tongue as medium, and the winning for it of a place in public institutions like schools, law courts and administration. Since these were goals shared by the most motivated sectors of an 'awakening' society they were increasingly achieved, just as the Nonconformists of Wales achieved their goal of building organisations with the developed infrastructure and ideological cohesion of the state church. As the achievements became more apparent, so a further goal came into view, unimaginable at the outset, namely, that the newly equipped languages, or in Wales the newly arisen Nonconformist churches, could challenge and displace old hegemonies, of the German language in Slovenia, or the Anglican Church in Wales. Effectively, that meant that alongside political and economic hard power the resources of 'soft power', like language or religion, could be mobilised into potent catalysts of social change. Round them the inchoate ethnic matter, the 'half-savages' of the unperceptive sociology of outside observers like Mill, could coalesce into self-conscious peoples. As such they could take advantage of the democratic message of the French revolution that gave the people, the 'third estate' of the Abbé Sieyès, the dignity and role of nationhood and become a political factor. This is what happened in the Habsburg Monarchy and, along a different path, in Wales.

The building of modern nations in the nineteenth-century Habsburg Monarchy (and also the Baltic lands) which this book will trace through the Slovene example, shows the positive side of the national idea. Rather than dividing, it united regions that had lived in parochial isolation. It gave the masses a voice in the marvel of literary language (too much taken for granted) bridging a medley of dialects and stimulating new creative literatures. It fostered civic spirit in a host of associations. The familiar negatives, from the petty egoisms of national contestation to the horrors of racist-tinged nationalism remain undeniable. But all major human impulses have their shadow side when taken to extremes. Are the positives of democratic nationalism more undermined by a Hitler than are those of socialism by Stalin and Pol Pot, or of religion by the Inquisition and fundamentalism? Suffice to say here that the break-up of the Habsburg Monarchy at the end of the First World War has played a major role in modern controversy over nationalism. Was the break-up the replacement of an outmoded dynastic system by the democratic nation-state, as largely thought at the time? Or was it, as has recently been argued by some American Habsburgists, a case of a multicultural model wrecked by the nationalist disease, pointing to Nazism and implicitly the holocaust? Resolution of these two propositions, exaggerated and questionable as put above, lies outside the scope of this book. Yet they point to a wider issue not irrelevant to its subject matter and will be returned to briefly in the Conclusion. The issue is the relationship between nationhood and democracy in international organisation. British responses to Habsburg break-up showed the potential for diversity on this matter in Britain's distinctive liberal imperial tradition. Winston Churchill expressed the most conservative standpoint. Viewing the inter-war difficulties of the nation-based succession states to the Habsburg Monarchy he commented that they had reaped the torments Hell reserved for the damned. During the First World War Liberals of the Acton School advocated internal reform of the Monarchy but opposed its break-up. Millsite liberals argued, by contrast, that the Czechs and South Slavs had now demonstrated their capacity for modern civilisation and led the way in pushing for a new international order, heralded in a 'New Europe' of nation states.

Critics of nationalism might note from this that a key issue in international politics has always been the relationship between large states (usually multiethnic) and small ones (often with an ethnic base). Historically, empires have competed among themselves for control of smaller states and control of their own constituent parts. Thus, the practical alternative to nation is empire, and to the national the imperial, not the universal. Aspiration to the universal belongs to all, a noble and necessary human trait, manifest in the spirit in which individuals and communities seek to achieve their particular practical goals. Empire and imperial are not intended here to have the negative connotations they have mostly acquired today. Historically speaking, such generalisation is not necessarily justified, any more than the negativity often associated with the terms nation and national. Modern progress has made a more democratic form of government possible, with its implications of devolution of power to ever broader strata. Yet the large unit, if less democratically close to the people, can be the more effective in practical organisational terms. The point here is to highlight how important the issue of the large–small relationship has been and still is historically, whether in the British Empire and Irish and Boer, Germany's relations with its smaller Slav neighbours, the United States and Latin America, or the great powers and their clients in the Middle East. Subaltern societies have often played key roles in international affairs.

Some will say this is a portentous framework in which to set Wales and its modern history. Perhaps it is. One is reminded of the expression 'little Wales' commonly and fondly used a century and more ago. Did not the ambitious and impressive Welsh-language youth movement, the Urdd, come into being in 1922 as 'Urdd Gobaith Cymru *Fach*'? But the fact that the 'Fach' was soon dropped from the title and that 'little Wales' now rings quaintly says something. Any community which claims to be a nation, as most Welsh people do, should take the term seriously; it is more than a courtesy title. At least there is a place for setting Welsh experience against that of other small nations. What does Welsh historiography have to say on the place of the nation in a wider framework, on which English and central European thinkers have spoken?

Older Welsh historians, like historians in most countries when rulers and battles were the central subject matter, concentrated on the ancient past, indeed, rarely ventured beyond 1282. This was true even of O. M. Edwards's *History of Wales* in the 'History of the Nations' series, which devoted only a few of its chapters to the post-conquest period. But by that time the outlines of a modern history were distinctly visible. It took on board the struggles of the common people for religious liberty in the Methodist and broader Nonconformist movement and their social engagement for education, against landlordism and in the burgeoning industrial society. The Welsh nation here was synonymous with the common people, given a special Welsh term, the *gwerin*. In the last half century this historiography has enjoyed a remarkable flowering. David Williams and David Jones set an agenda: the background that produced the Rebecca riots, the insurrections in Merthyr in 1831 and Newport in 1839 and ultimately the labour movement of iron workers, coal miners and quarrymen; Ieuan Gwynedd Jones and many others explored the social formation of nineteenth-century Nonconformist culture, whose religion and press have been well covered. The perspective has been widened to include women's history, urban history and the experience of minorities, religious and racial, and of emigration. Ieuan Gwynedd Jones has summed up the approach succinctly when he wrote that a Welsh historian had to be a social historian. In effect the emphasis has been on Wales as society rather than Wales as nation. Of course, these terms are not contradictory. All participants believed they were writing the history of a nation. It was Kenneth Morgan, the doyen of modern Welsh historians, who in 1981 addressed not just the political but the national implications of these social developments in a powerful synthesis. His *Rebirth of a Nation: Wales 1880–1980* argued that Welsh aspirations in the generations before 1914 should be seen as a successful bid for equal recognition in the broader British context of an emerging distinctive Wales, not, as in the Irish case, for separation from it.[6] This perspective acknowledged the reality that majority Welsh opinion never sought to raise a 'Welsh question' on Irish or other small nation lines, while offering grounds for the sense of achievement sought by any national community. The effect was to dissociate Welsh nationhood from the negative nationalism distrusted in the broader British context. Implicitly, Morgan presented Wales as a nation *sui generis*, so that comparison, except with Ireland in the common British setting, did not suggest itself.

All social phenomena are in a sense *sui generis* in that they arise in specific circumstances. Morgan skilfully drew out key specific features of the Welsh case. The value of comparison, however, is to throw up issues which one society took too for granted for serious debate but which the other viewed wholly differently, with significant results. Things which seem fundamental in one society can be quite secondary to another. Attitudes to language are a striking example in the present study. Welsh leaders to varying extents had reservations about the prospects for non-dominant languages in conditions of modernisation – and all the more so their later historians. These fears were initially shared in Central Europe, including Slovenia, but modern historians in the region take the view expressed already in the 1860s by a leader in the Finnish language movement: 'when in any country the educated people speak one language and the rest of the nation speak another the language of the educated class cannot survive'.[7] Such assumptions help account for the dramatic revival of the Slovene language and the relative indifference of nineteenth-century Welsh people to the fortunes of Welsh and the little attention paid to it – until very recently – by their historians. Such neglect, and the decline of Welsh, is a major reason for Slovene and east-central European reluctance to see the Welsh as a nation. Their attitude explains the bizarre figures to Welsh minds in a Soviet ethnographic handbook listing 700,000 for the Welsh 'ethnic group', as against more than 5,470,000 Irish. For the east European mindset only Welsh speakers could be considered Welsh. The Irish qualified as Irish, however, by virtue of their independent state.[8]

The blinkers in such calculations show that eastern Europeans too can learn from comparisons. Nationality is more flexible than their Herderian-derived dogmas. This book will argue with Kenneth Morgan and a host of others that the Welsh are a nation. But it will argue specifically that they became a nation in the modern sense – that is evolved from a traditional, if well-developed, ethnicity to a new form of self-consciousness in the formative nineteenth century – through a different process from that followed in central and eastern Europe. The process there among the smaller nations took linguistic form, in the development of a drive to cultural sovereignty in the sense described above. This is why the Czech historian of nationalism, Miroslav Hroch, famous for his three-stage paradigm of the process, explicitly rejected the idea of a Welsh nation.[9] He neglected the fact that there can be other forms of 'soft power' than the linguistic which the weak may exploit to sustain their identity vis-à-vis stronger neighbours. As already hinted, a powerful factor in ethnic maintenance can be religion. If the modern Slovene nation came to birth through language, Welsh identity owes much to the Nonconformist movement which moulded the mores and culture of the majority well into the succeeding labour-dominated era, and exercised influence outside its ranks. It was through it that the social mobilisation characteristic of modernity was achieved and a vision of a nation wedded to high things, with its own litany of struggles and heroes carrying emotive force, was successfully promoted. Mobilisation and vision are the two chief characteristics of the nineteenth-century European nation.

Naturally, several other factors were involved. Pre-modern Wales had a strong profile of pre-modern nationhood from the centuries of independence and the considerable literary heritage. The forms taken by industrialisation enabled the burgeoning religious movement of a rural society to embed itself in a more populous and dynamic environment. From another angle the strength of Nonconformity can be exaggerated. As social historians have shown, wide areas of traditional life were not transformed while the new life of the industrial valleys, still more so of the expanding ports, commercial centres and seaside resorts, was only partly won, and the pull of the wider British culture only fitfully held at bay.[10] The picture is one of a challenged national culture, comparatively speaking, but of an identifiable national culture all the same. This is the case which will be ventured for the Welsh side of the attempted comparison.

Why, of the various small peoples of the Habsburg Monarchy, have the Slovenes been taken for the other side of the comparison? Given the principle that like as far as possible should be compared with like, the choice is fairly obvious. Occasional references by Welsh historians to Welsh contacts with the Hungarian national leader Lajos Kossuth or to possible analogies with the Czechs are wide of the mark because Hungary was a large country which oppressed its own non-Magyar population, while the several million Czechs had had their own kingdom and operated on a different scale.[11] Slovenia, with a territory and population similar to Wales and similar social structure, is by far the most suitable counterpart. Of course, there are small peoples in western Europe, the Bretons and the Basques, who are still closer in that they like Wales have suffered linguistic erosion. However, I must work within my own competence, while hoping that as interest in comparisons of the Welsh experience grows these also may acquire case studies.

Comparison is not undertaken here in a social scientific sense. It does not use statistical method to test limited hypotheses like Michael Hechter's well-known work *Internal Colonialism* (1975), which argued that the figures could best be explained by Welsh experience as a 'periphery' of an Anglo-British centre in the English south east.[12] Perhaps comparison is not the appropriate word for what is attempted here. It takes basically chronological form, emphasising divergences in the two societies and differences of assumption or practice which call for particular explanation. A full comparison of two societies as a whole over an extended period is not really practicable. Even where the chosen societies share marked similarities at the starting point, in size, social structure and much past experience as with Welsh and Slovenes, this omits other shaping factors like religion and the nature of the empires they belonged to; fairly soon divergences emerge pointing to different scenarios. Better, then, to say that this study *juxtaposes* developments in Wales and Slovenia so that divergences can be more clearly focused and as far as possible explained. The distinctive patterns of the two societies as they take shape can thereby be more easily grasped and the logics which any two historical processes develop over time revealed. Any eventual Slovene readers are due apologies for the dilettante treatment of their country. The book's primary aim is to set Welsh history in a fresh context; its greater detail on the Welsh side of the story reflects the expected nature of the readership. For the book to perform its function, it is to be desired, however, that significant distortion of the Slovene material has been avoided. Hopefully, the story told of the other society will have interest for the majority who will be acquainted only with one. The Slovene experience seems to the outsider an admirable case of practical patriotism providing a relatively cohesive development towards the cultural sovereignty already described. The Welsh experience is more diffuse but has in a people's powerful aspiration towards successive goals of religious and then socio-political emancipation its own moving moments. Minor west European nationalities are little known in Slovenia. Given this background a Slovene reader might well be irritated to be set in such company and sceptical of perceived overhyping of Welsh national claims or the contradictions that might seem involved.

These problems confront Welsh people too. Indeed, the basic thesis advanced here of an alternative path to nationhood in the nineteenth century via religion rather than language runs up against many objections. One is that language figures the most prominently in modern Welsh appeals to nationhood, far more than an abandoned and often despised Nonconformity, though it does so in self-deluding statements about the 'vitality' of Welsh-language culture and official talk of 'creating' half a million more Welsh speakers by 2050. Another is that some of the most significant Welsh-speaking intellectuals of recent decades have themselves cast doubt on the official pretensions of modern Wales, men like J. R. Jones who pondered provocatively whether the Welsh were a 'people' (pobl) rather than a nation (cenedl),[13] and Simon Brooks whose brilliant polemic *Why Wales Never Was* excoriates the nineteenth-century linguistic failure and sees no future in Welsh speakers' attempts to work with English speakers for a 'civic' Welsh nationhood.[14] A third is a voice from English-speaking Welsh socialists, now, to be sure, no longer so clamant, who have attacked the 'Nonconformist Gaeltacht' Welsh speakers were accused of desiring.

These issues will be taken up with the weight of evidence meanwhile adduced in the Conclusion. The thesis of the soft power of language and religion will by then have been nuanced beyond the over-simplicities of an Introduction. The sharp distinction between these two forces needs to be revised. Adding to the interest of the comparison is that language played a great part in Wales and religion in Slovenia whose pious peasant majority accepted the language programme of Slovene liberals, while giving their votes to a conservative *kaisertreu* Catholic party. The cross currents are fascinating. Yet it is the very similarities amid difference which can make a comparison with the Slovene case painful for Welsh speakers especially. For members of an embattled minority who see a heritage endangered, it is potentially galling to see how another non-dominant community in many ways less well situated than themselves not too long ago has advanced to full cultural and political independence. There is a danger that comparison could evoke the kind of introspective recrimination to be found on the radical socialist left along the lines 'where did it all go wrong?' As successive chapters show Wales diverging ever further from the Slovene course of linguistic self-assertion there could be a danger too of a repetitive narrative lacking the freshness of the unknown that a previously untold story can offer. The present book seeks to avoid these dangers. One of its main arguments is that the national affirmation of small ethnicities is particularly dependent on external circumstances, like geopolitics and the local dominant power. Much internecine argument about native mistakes and missteps is therefore out of place. The aim here is a dispassionate analysis of a case of divergent development, whose inherent interest should stimulate curiosity. If the Welsh failure to follow one model, the Slovene, cannot but be one thread of the narrative, another thread is successively revealed, namely the distinctive model of nation-building that did occur in Wales. Words can be treacherous here. 'Failure' suggests a teleology, something that ought to have happened and didn't. Though I have a positive attitude to nationality, I do not think of it as highest value. There are many aspects of experience among which people's sense of nationhood is only one, if at certain conjunctions a very important one. Besides, the thesis of this book is that both the peoples it discusses did arrive at forms of nationhood, if by different paths.

It is the differences in the processes and their effects which are the chief subject matter of the book. What implications did social mobilisation have, primarily through language or primarily through religion, on what developed? Both entailed social activity, the founding and funding of schools, or chapels and churches. They carried different ideological and emotional charges, involved different kinds of social activity and implied different kinds of elite or intelligentsia. An elite educated in a secular school system potentially had easier access to a future process which had been in many ways set in train by the Enlightenment. On the other hand, the clergy had traditionally had the strongest ties with populations of peasants and workers. But there are many practical issues too. Welsh readers will ask how the Slovenes succeeded in adapting their languages to the needs of cultural sovereignty, in reducing the influence of dominant German upon it, in creating a popular literature at a competitive price in a tiny market: above all, how young Slovenes could get on in the world with only their language to offer. What would most hold back or inspire, the rough-hewn medium of the mother tongue or access to a rich world culture through an imperfectly understood alien speech? What effect would concentration on the mother or the foreign tongue have on relations with the dominant culture of the state and the local aristocracy, or political party structures? Which direction would the burgeoning middle class take, and which society would be the more outward-looking? Both saw themselves as children of the unprivileged, but would relations between farmer and tenant, master and worker differ as between the Welsh *gwerin* and incipiently 'nationally conscious' Slovenes? The Welsh had an older and richer literary culture to fall back on, but what of the Slovenes who were forced to build up a literature from scratch, effectively from foreign models? These questions are orientated to language and literary culture, but there are religious questions too. What consequences flowed from the fact that Slovenes belonged with Austrian Germans to an overwhelmingly dominant Church, effectively a state religion, while most Welsh were outside the church establishment in a religiously plural world? What impact did the organisation and ethos of the universal Catholic Church have on the situation as opposed to the nationally based Anglican Church? How did organised religion deal with developments like Darwinism or modernism in the church? A crucial question, finally, which rightly relativises an exclusive stress on two factors, religion and language: What was the role of the imperial state, the one with laissez-faire, the other with dirigiste traditions? How far did these shape the course Welsh and Slovene society took, rather than the motives and aspirations of the latter? What conduced more to national feeling and self-esteem, membership of a dynamic, successful monarchy or one with a venerable heritage that was increasingly felt to be struggling against the tide?

These are, I hope, interesting intellectual questions for my nineteenth- and early-twentieth-century comparison, in addition to pragmatic matters which may be mentioned here. Thus, in a notoriously multiethnic region, placenames will be given in the form now used by the state where they find themselves, with the caveat that Gorizia province will be given its Italian name and Slovene Gorica reserved for its capital. Full footnoting would overload the text, but enough is provided to give a sense of the sources used.

A further question suggests itself, though it has a presentist aspect. How strongly had the notion of Welsh and Slovene nationhood embedded itself in the popular consciousness by 1914? What legacy in each case had been left to the future? The crude opposition, language/religion, here appears relevant. A nationhood expressed in the language spoken, read and written by the entire population, as was nearly the case in Slovenia by that time, clearly was an ongoing factor for the foreseeable future. How far was this so in Wales where religion and religiosity had played a large role in its construction and been trumpeted as such in many quarters? Religion gradually lost its force in twentieth-century Wales. That need not mean that Welsh nationhood was correspondingly weakened. As has been said repeatedly above and will appear in what follows, many other factors, among the chief of them language, went into the making of Welsh nationhood by 1914. A plausible argument can be made that once nationhood has been rooted it acquires a sturdiness that can survive the disappearance of factors which helped shape it in the first place.

This has been abundantly tested in Slovenia's case during her experience as a minority nation in the two Yugoslavias, above all when Slovenia was divided between Germany and Italy in 1941–5 and the nation suppressed. It has not been similarly tested in Wales. There the British state provided a secure environment, an umbrella under which Welsh people could allow themselves a kind of dual nationality. Yet since Kenneth Morgan wrote *Rebirth of a Nation* in 1981, that Britain's solidity has been shaken. It is not impossible that within a couple of decades Scotland and Northern Ireland will have gone, leaving Wales tied to a nationalistic England with little inclination to use its threatened economic resources on subsidising Wales. At that time Welsh people will have to think politically about themselves as a nation. The resilience of the idea of a radical Wales born in Nonconformity and bequeathed to Welsh Labour will be put to the test. Hopefully, such a stark dénouement will not come about. But that Welsh people and Welsh scholars should become more used to thinking about themselves not just as a nation but as a nation among nations, aware of their traditions, strengths and weaknesses in a wider context, remains a salutary goal. That is not the major goal of this book, but making the point is an offshoot of the process of writing it.

It is a pleasure, finally, to thank Professor Robert Evans, Dr Simon Brooks and Dr Nigel Evans from Britain, and Professor Peter Vodopivec from Ljubljana for their interest in my work and assistance with corrections, the more so since the book was largely written under Covid restrictions. Gratitude is due also to my old friends and colleagues in the Warwick University History Department, Emeritus Professor Christopher Read and Honorary Professor Fred Reid for their support and comments, as also to Dr Dafydd Jones and the staff of the University of Wales Press for their kindly forbearance and, of course, to my family for their unstinting love and affection.

NOTES

1 For example, Anthony D. Smith, *The Ethnic Origin of Nations* (Oxford, New York, 1988).

2 John Stuart Mill, *Utilitarianism, Liberty, Representative Government* (London, Toronto and New York, 1910), pp. 359–66. (First published 1861.)

3 John E. E. Dalberg-Acton, First Baron Acton, *The History of Freedom and Other Essays*, ed. and intro. J. N. Figgis and R. Vere Laurence (London, 1907), pp. 270–300. (First published 1862.)

4 Dalberg-Acton, *Essays*, p. 299.

5 J. Chłebowczyk, *On Small and Young Nations in Europe* (Wrocław, 1980), p. 14.

6 Kenneth O. Morgan, *Rebirth of a Nation: Wales 1880–1980* (Oxford, 1981), p. 412.

7 E. Jutikkala, *A History of Finland* (London, 1962), p. 203. The writer's own mother tongue was Swedish.

8 S. I. Bruk (ed.), *Naselenie mira: etnodemograficheskii spravochnik* (World population, an ethnographic handbook) (Moscow, 1982), p. 255. Reflecting Soviet communist identification of language and nationality, the author's figure for Welsh people apparently adds together Welsh speakers according to the 1971 Welsh language census and an estimate of the number of Welsh speakers in the rest of Britain. His figure for Irish adds together the Irish in Britain and Ireland.

9 Miroslav Hroch, *Social Preconditions of National Revival in Europe* (Cambridge, 1985), p. 4.

10 Russell Davies's voluminous studies of Welsh social history, while paying due tribute to the contribution of Nonconformity, in particular expose the limitations of traditional presentations.

11 For Kossuth, see D. Williams, *A History of Modern Wales* (London, 1950), p. 274, and Kenneth O. Morgan, *Rebirth of a Nation: Wales 1880–1980* (Oxford, 1981), p. 91; for Czechs, Gwyn A. Williams, *When Was Wales?* (London, 1985), pp. 142–3, 206, 238.

12 M. Hechter, *Internal Colonialism: The Celtic Fringe in British national development, 1536–1966* (London, 1975).

13 J. R. Jones, *Ac onide. Ymdriniaeth mewn ysgrif a phregeth ar argyfwng y Gymru gyfoes* (And is it not so. A moral tale on the crisis of Wales today) (Llandybie, 1970), pp. 132–50. Jones added that if the Welsh were only a people, there had never been a people with greater potential for nationhood (p. 148).

14 Simon Brooks, *Why Wales Never Was: The Failure of Welsh Nationalism* (Cardiff, 2017), an adapted version of his original *Pam na fu Cymru: Methiant Cenedlaetholdeb Cymraeg* (Cardiff, 2015).

PART ONE

Chapter 1

WALES AND THE SLOVENE LANDS: THE BACKGROUND

Asked to name a small European country they thought might have something in common with Wales, few Welsh people would volunteer Slovenia. Yet arguably of the half dozen or so potential candidates with populations in 1750 of below a million, Slovenia is as plausible a choice as any. At roughly eight thousand square miles apiece in terms of traditional ethnic territory, with some 900,000 Slovenes and 600,000 Welsh inhabiting largely upland terrain long ruled by a stronger people, the fit is close indeed, if hilly Wales never reaches the heights of Alpine Slovenia. In each case the landowning elite had adopted the dominant language of the state, English in Great Britain, German in the Habsburg Monarchy. But the valleys cutting through Slovenia's ranges are often wider bottomed than their Welsh equivalents and flatter land stretches east and south towards the Hungarian and Croatian borders, while the heart of the country encloses a fair-sized plain containing the capital Ljubljana. Geography thus provides contrasts as well as parallels, for while Wales was bounded only by England and the sea, little Slovenia lay between Italians, Austro-Germans, Hungarians and Croats. Analogies cannot be pushed too far.

They appear even in certain fortuitous details, however. The modern homelands of Welsh and Slovenes both entered recorded history through incorporation into the Roman Empire in the first century AD, and Welsh and Slovene ethnic origins can be traced back to the period following that empire's fall, if in different ways. The Slovenes were one of a number of Slavonic tribes which migrated into the Balkan peninsula in the fifth and sixth centuries. The Welsh were descendants of an already present Celtic population (the 'ancient Britons') who took on a specific new identity with the evolution of the British language into Old Welsh during the Anglo-Saxon invasions of these years. Both Welsh and Slovenes retained a memory of a time when their ancestors had occupied much wider lands, the Welsh of ancient Britain and even earlier Celtic territories on the continent; the Slovenes, if more mistily, of Slav occupation of land as far north as Vienna before Germanic influx. The nineteenth-century national poet Prešeren invoked the name of the early seventh-century figure Samo as a Slovene hero. He actually ruled in Bohemia and Moravia. Slovene early history lacks the background of resistance to alien domination of the native Welsh principalities of Gwynedd, Powys and Dyfed, particularly the first-named, whose fall in 1282 proved to be the end of Welsh independence, but for Owain Glyndŵr's brief rule as 'Prince of Wales' in the early fifteenth century. Wales also shared with Ireland, England and Iceland the west European phenomenon of early literature in the mother tongue alongside Latin. The Welsh laws and chronicles, the courtly poetry of the princes and then of the nobles who maintained Welsh culture after the Conquest, the prose tales of the Mabinogi: all this was to provide a legacy which was being nurtured by an antiquarian reverence for old manuscripts as early as the thirteenth and succeeding centuries.

Slovene medieval experience causes Welsh observers something of the puzzlement Slovenes feel at the absence of Welsh national and linguistic consciousness, as they see it, in the modern period. Slovene-speaking Slavs arrived on the central European scene as camp followers of a ruling elite, the Avars, and then moved into the sphere of Germanic Franks migrating from the north. Three Germanic duchies – Carinthia, Styria and Carniola – formed within the framework of the Holy Roman Empire and more specifically of the emerging Habsburg dynasty, members of which came to monopolise the imperial crown. Slovene Slavs were the overwhelming majority in Carniola (named, incidentally, after the original Carians, of Celtic stock) and formed substantial minorities in the other two provinces. But they lived under German landowners, though Slav local elites remained for a time, in forms still debated by historians. Not till 1443 did the Emperor abolish the formal inauguration of Carinthian dukes in Slovene by Slav peasants sitting on chairs, an ancient ceremony going back to the period of a multi-ethnic 'Carantanian' entity – the term is from the Latin for Carinthia.[1] In smaller areas of modern Slovenia Slavs also lived under Italian or Magyar hegemony. Church organisation reflected subaltern status. While Wales's traditional four dioceses existed from ancient times and St David's later displacement by the metropolitan see of Canterbury was challenged by Gerald the Welshman (Giraldus Cambrensis) and by Owain Glyndŵr, no bishopric existed on Slovene soil till Ljubljana gained this status in 1461. Cultural life suffered from the lack of wealthy aristocratic courts. The one exception, that of the counts of Celje, fell with the last count's death in 1456. The Slovene language barely figured in public life in the Middle Ages, though its first documentation is quite early for the Slav world, in a tenth century source whose significance was not appreciated till much later. Technically, the very terms Slovene and Slovenian language are anachronisms for this period because they were not used in their modern sense till the national revival. Before then identity was either as Slav or more commonly regional, as Carniolan, Styrian, Carinthian, and so forth. Slovene folk traditions mingle Slavic strands with those of surrounding peoples. One of their most popular tales invokes the figure of the good ruler, who in time came to be associated with the fifteenth-century Hungarian king Matthias Corvinus and his battles with the Turks, whose frequent incursions were a menacing feature of late medieval and early modern Slovene life.

Slovene medieval anonymity can be overdone, however. There is a seeming paradox in the fact that the locus classicus of modern nationalism in the east-centre of the continent was the area where, earlier, ethno-national motifs had tended to be submerged in a composite of feudal lordship, multi-ethnic empire and dynastic rule. Yet the very pattern of Slav peasant masses working under German-speaking landlords came to serve as a trope in Slav national awakening for a self-image as peaceful, industrious, sturdily productive people over against Germanic marauding oppression. Most famously developed by the 'father of the Czech nation', the historian František Palacký (1798–1876), this became a substratum of Slovene consciousness as well. In a less aggressive formulation than Palacký's it featured in the story of the inauguration of Carinthian dukes mentioned above, which recalled the Carantanian tradition as part of Slovene identity. The later development of mother tongue literature to the east of Europe compared to the Welsh should not lead one to overlook the possibility of cultural and patriotic expression through Latin, as of course was true of Giraldus Cambrensis and Geoffrey of Monmouth in Wales. The funeral oration to the Hungarian and Bohemian king, Ladislas Posthumus by his chancellor Johannes Rot, has been called the first Slovene document of classical humanism, couched as it was in the Latin of that style and in honour of the nephew of the last Count of Celje, with that family's distinct Slovenian associations.[2] The first bishop of Ljubljana saw to it that his staff all received a thorough humanist training in Vienna University, usually followed by further study in northern Italy, notably Padua. Many Vienna University students in this period came from Slovene areas. A leading Vienna professor's identity is revealed when an enemy called him a perfidious Slav. We are living in the world of European humanism experienced also by William Salesbury, Gwilym Hiraethog, Bishop William Morgan and other figures of the Welsh Renaissance.

Members of small peoples had to seek learning outside their home-land. Jesus College, Oxford, was founded in 1571. The dual Vienna–north Italian axis is important to note in this connection. Slovenia's cen-tral European position opened it to external influence and even gave the Slovene language for the first time some cachet in the Renaissance period. Diplomacy had a special role in humanist culture. Nearly all Habsburg envoys to rising Muscovy came from Slovene lands. Sigismund von Herberstein, the most significant of them, stressed how valuable his knowledge of Slovene had been in Moscow. The leading humanist, Petrus Bonomi, Bishop of Trieste, is said to have expounded Virgil and Calvin to his students in Latin, German and Slovene.[3]

This background helps explain the otherwise barely comprehensible explosion of publishing in Slovene in the short-lived Slovene Reformation in the second half of the sixteenth century. The prime mover and organ-iser of the movement, Primus Trubar (1508–1586), had been part of Bonomi's audience in Trieste, but then absorbed the Lutheran message in many years' study in Germany. The literary language he devised, intended to be accessible to 'every genuine, ordinary Slav', in a few decades became the medium for a 'Slav Church' with its own creed and regulations (1562–64) and some fifty books, including the New Testament followed by the whole Bible (1582/1584) and a standard grammar, the latter procedure almost exactly mirroring events occurring contemporaneously in Wales. An energetic schooling policy was set in train to ensure the generalisation of Slovene in public life, steps supported by the noble diet of Carniola, the one Habsburg province where Slovene predominated and where Ljubljana lay. Yet Protestantism was the cause of the nobles and the urban burghers. It was less popular among the peasant masses and increasingly fiercely opposed by the Habsburg power. In an even shorter time than it rose it had been ruthlessly extirpated, together with its literature as far as possible. The Counter-Reformation set Slovenia's course for a century and a half.[4] Jesuits took over education and Capuchins led the way in a popular Catholicism of pilgrimage and processions. Attendance at the Jesuit college in Ljubljana rose in the seventeenth century from some 200 to over 650. A vigorous policy of church building, Baroque in spirit, changed the face of Slovenian towns. After the publication in Slovene of some New Testament texts and a catechism (1613–15) Slovene book production ceased for nearly sixty years, though interestingly Trubar's language and its script were retained. The Habsburg crushing of Protestantism entailed the defeat of the provincial Diets as well and the consolidation of that power in the system known as absolutism: a union of monarch, Church and duly loyal nobles overlaying the vast servile peasantry and an insignificant urban population.

Here a crucial divide in Welsh/Slovene experience occurred. In Wales the Reformation was less dramatic but more permanent. A small band of convinced Protestants supported Tudor religious policy. The Bible was translated into Welsh in 1588, four years after the Slovene Bible, on the basis of an Act of Parliament of 1563 which also ordered the holding of services in Welsh in Welsh-speaking areas. The provision that an English Bible should be placed alongside it in churches to aid the learning of English may have been a sop to critics of public endorsement of Welsh by those who advocated one language for the state.[5] This position had been earlier taken by the Act of Union of Wales with England of 1536/1543, which laid down that a knowledge of English was essential for the holding of public office in Wales. It has been plausibly argued that the notorious reference to 'sinister usages' which the Act aimed to remove was directed at attempts to stress differences between the King's subjects, rather than the Welsh language as such.[6] Yet the wording is minatory and shows the delicate position of a non-dominant group in a larger state, even if negligible contemporary evidence exists of Welsh opposition to the Act of Union's language clause. Welshmen who aspired to official employ or the office of Justice of the Peace (JP), the bulwark of the new administration at local level, were prepared to accept that this was conditional on a knowledge of English. This watered down notions that the Union offered a general equality before the law, however, since that law was to be operated in English, which ordinary people did not know. One provision put an end to use of Welsh law, written in that language. No formal provision was made for knowledge of Welsh on the part of court officials, a matter fateful in the longer term for the status of the mother tongue.

The laws of 1536 and 1563 made for a dualism between spheres of administration and law, conducted in English, and those of religion and culture, conducted in Welsh. The Elizabeth Church settlement required extensive translation of Anglican apologetics besides constant re-editions of the Welsh Bible (eight in the seventeenth, thirty in the eighteenth), which reshaped medieval norms into an elegant if linguistically conservative modern language, enabling the classic prose of the Puritan Morgan Llwyd and of Ellis Wynne. The homely verses of vicar Pritchard's *Cannwyll y Cymry* (The Welshman's Bible) and the many almanacs of Thomas Jones (1648–1713) represent influential uses of written Welsh at a popular level.[7] The latter preceded its Slovene equivalent, a peasant calendar, the first non-religious publication in Slovene, which appeared in 1725. All this Welsh activity, however, cannot disguise the fact of the language's decline in social status from the time recorded by Lord Herbert of Cherbury (1583–1648), when this scion of a distinguished Shropshire border family had been sent as a child to learn Welsh in a neighbouring gentry household.[8]

Nonetheless, through the fuller use of its literary language and the greater historicity of its traditions, Wales seems in the early eighteenth century to have the lead in proto-nationhood, at least to a Welsh observer. Yet the multi-volume work on the natural history, institutions and customs of his native Carniola by the polymath scholar-scientist, Baron Johann Weichard Valvasor (1641–93), shows a patriotic engagement with his province shared by many of the upper classes. He describes a *diglossia* in Ljubljana, where German and Slovene (which he calls Carniolan) were generally spoken though only German was written, a duality recognisable in the practice of the Anglesey squire William Bulkeley, whose diaries in English depict a conscientious member of an English-speaking ruling class, but whom we know to have been an avid participant in Welsh poetic circles. Valvasor also lets glimpse the ethnic reality that underlay the public German culture of Carniolan life. He cites a letter from the Vatican to the Carniolan estates asking for confirmation that pilgrims from the province should go to the Slav-orientated Saint Hieronimo hospice in Rome rather than its German equivalent. Many geographers, the letter went on, listed Carniola as Slav and visitors from there all commonly spoke the 'Illyrian' language among themselves. The

German-dominated estates replied that Carniola was German and part of the Reich; if language was taken as a criterion then Poles, Czechs, Macedonians and Bulgarians would be included too as the bounds of 'Illyrian' stretched into the unknown.[9] This answer illustrated a significant aspect of the Slovene position. As Slavs, Carniolans belonged to a vast group which was often treated by others as a unity, with a common language. Behind the apparent anonymity of a subordinate people in the status-conscious feudal world there was thus, as in Wales, a social reality which was recognised in practice, particularly by the Church, charged to minister to all manner of men.

Thus, by the mid-eighteenth century point at which the present comparison begins both Wales and the Slovene lands had become classic subaltern societies on the lines outlined in the introduction. Overwhelmingly, peasant populations lived out their lives under an order operating officially through a different language which the upper classes shared with their counterparts in a wider realm. These societies were not mere folk cultures because they were the product of the past experiences just described and variously remembered, in which the upper classes had also played a part and through which the two societies had evolved overall, looking both to indigenous traditions and the institutions of the wider realm in which they found themselves. This was true of upper classes and masses alike, if in different ways and degrees. The forms in which this process had resulted must now be described in more detail to ground the launching pad from which the two societies would take off into 'modernity'.

THE INSTITUTIONAL AND SOCIAL FRAMEWORK c.1750

Great Britain and the Habsburg Monarchy were recognised in the eighteenth century as societies almost at opposite poles, the one the only sizeable constitutional polity in the continent, the other the exemplar of the dynastic, absolutist state. Yet neither of the distinctions commonly made, between nation state and polyglot empire and between constitutionalism and absolutism, were clear-cut. Compared to today, the Europe of the time was everywhere a hierarchical place, where, apart from a few free but poor mountain communities, nobility dominated society in conjunction with monarchs and established churches. The British parliament was elected on an irregular and often bizarrely narrow franchise; it was not competent for Ireland, which had its own, and had only comparatively recently become so for Scotland, in 1707, while the Habsburg Monarchy included its own constitutional state: Hungary proudly claimed liberties preceding Magna Carta, in the Golden Bull of 1212. True, the Hungarian parliament was composed entirely of nobles and was called by Empress Maria Theresa just three times in her long reign (1740–80). But the obligation to summon parliament regularly had only been won in England by the Bill of Rights of 1689. Moreover, if modern constitutionalism is defined as a system of equal rights of citizens before the law, as opposed to the feudal practice of different legal status for different orders (nobles, clerics, burghers, peasants etc.) through separate courts, Hungary had its own legal codes as did several Austrian provinces, but then so did Scotland with its Roman, not common law. Church courts still existed in England together with a profusion of privileges attaching to universities, towns and other corporate bodies acquired in previous centuries pregnant with associations of feudal times.

Administratively, the Habsburg Monarchy evolved common instruments of governance for military and financial matters in the sixteenth century, and a Court Chancellery and State Council developed, flanked by Chancelleries to oversee relations between Vienna and the Hungarian and Bohemian lands. Slovenes and Welsh fell below such august forums. Some provision for Vienna's liaison with an 'inner Austria' including the Slovene lands was made from time to time with a seat in the Styrian capital Graz, but not as clearly or consistently as with Bohemia and Hungary. The absorption of the Bohemian Chancellery in the Court Chancellery in 1749 was a significant step towards centralisation. The Council of Wales and the Marches, abolished in 1689, offers a certain parallel. The only remaining institutional expression of Welsh identity became the Court of Great Sessions which continued to meet until 1830. A tentative conclusion from this survey might be that both the ways in which Great Britain and the Habsburg Monarchy have been contrasted do not wholly fit the eighteenth-century reality. Britain was not the nation state opposed to the multinational empire, nor the Monarchy the absolutist empire controlling the lives of its subject by royal fiat as old-fashioned notions of 'absolutism' implied. In foreign policy, it might be mentioned, Britain and Austria were actually allied against France for most of the 1689–1815 period.

To a fair extent, one might also relativise the differences in the more local operation of social power. True, the Habsburg system had much that was feudal about it. At a provincial level it rested on a governor, appointed by the monarch, and Diets dominated by a formally privileged nobility. Diets were ancient bodies, hedged round by widely varying prescription but always on the basis of separate 'orders' (in the Slovene lands usually clergy, lords, knights, with burghers in lesser numbers and less entitlement). Their significant financial functions, including the right to assent to new taxes and to apportion and collect direct taxation, allowed members considerable scope for mutual gain. 'Presents', made by diets to their own on occasions like marriage or for service deemed meritorious, were often substantial. Nobles themselves were exempt from taxation. The estates regularly maintained schools specifically for the education of young nobles, for whom the Carniolan Diet, for example, also employed a dancing master.[10] At the local level the holders of landed estates exercised direct 'patrimonial jurisdiction' over their peasants. The British system of JPs and county quarter sessions appeared more uniform and potentially less arbitrary in comparison.

Yet Welsh elites too enjoyed and abused wealth and power to an extraordinary extent in a poor country. The Fonmon estate owed £50,000 in the 1760s and Sir Watkyn Williams Wynn of Wynnstay £160,000 in 1779. In a vain attempt to compete with Wynnstay the Middletons of Chirk Castle had to raise new mortgages and squeeze their tenants who were in arrears. The game laws which supported the upper classes' hunting pastimes and the thirty-three new capital offences which protected their property under George II alone (1727–60) were eloquent testimony to warped social power. William Morris, one of the Morris brothers who will figure in this narrative, commented that the powers that be acted as if the killing of a horse were graver than the killing of a human being.[11] As to British parliamentary liberties, the huge sums spent by competing families on bribing the few electors – £4,000 for wine alone, amid £35,000 in all – in the Flint boroughs election of 1734 meant that elections were avoided altogether as far as possible. Only one county seat was contested in Montgomeryshire throughout the eighteenth century. The bulk of JPs showed little zeal for their important responsibilities; only a small number of those on the rolls regularly attended Quarter Sessions. Other similarities between the two societies can be found. Lesser nobles or gentry tended to lose out to fewer, more powerful families as wealth disparities increased, a process spurred in the Slovene lands by defeat of the mainly Protestant estates in the Counter-Reformation, and in both countries by the dying out of family lines.[12] The gap between the income of the Wynnstay estate or that of the Morgans of Tredegar – nearly £20,000 and £10,000 respectively in the 1730s – wealthy gentry at £1,000–2,000 and Caernarfonshire lesser gentry at a median range of £67 was plainly huge. It showed up regional differences too because Glamorgan had many more wealthy men than elsewhere in Wales, with incomes not far short of the English norm. In general Welsh estates earned little more than half their English counterparts.

For all these inequities in Wales, however, one feature of the Slovene experience cannot be easily glossed over. The great majority of Slovene peasants were not tenants of their landlord, as were the Welsh, but stood in relation to them as serf to lord. 'Serf', the conventional English translation, misleads if it conveys an image of Russian serfdom. Habsburg peasants were not chattels, whose Russian owners could freely sell them. They could sue their lord, only, of course, in the lord's own court. The key to the Austrian system was the distinction between dominical land, or the lord's demesne, worked by peasant labour (the *robota*), and rustical land, which the peasant held subject to the performance of *robota* and acquittal of various dues and often other services. The system was a patchwork of inherited obligations of almost infinite variety. Best off were peasants whose labour services were relatively light and/or who could bequeath their plot as they chose. All were, though, 'bound to the soil' in that they lacked freedom of movement or choice of occupation, though this was sometimes possible. They also had to have the lord's permission to marry. In the mid-eighteenth century 42 per cent of Styrians between twenty and forty years of age were unmarried.[13] From the seventeenth century these conditions worsened. Rising population and food prices, landlords' pressure to expand the dominical land at peasants' expense and a stepping up of *robota*, together with earlier state taxation, tolls and monopolies, led to a steady fall in the proportion of peasants with a 'full' or 'half' plot of land and the growth of 'cottars', holders of ever smaller fractions or even landless. In 1713 the last great Slovene peasant revolt broke out, when 720 peasant communities over a thousand square miles engaged the authorities and the military for over two months. This was on a wider scale than anything that followed or than the grain and other riots noted in eighteenth-century Wales. There too there was population pressure, however, and by mid-century a move began from the old 'three-life' system of peasant inheritance to shorter leases. One result was increased resort to the *tai unnos* or primitive dwelling thrown up in one night on waste land, securing a kind of squatters' right which the authorities recognised as a means of relieving the burden of the poor rates. Until *c.*1750 there was no essential change in peasant circumstances in either society. Slovene and Welsh homes continued to be in large majority made of wood and consist of one or two rooms, with the Slovene move to a second room a little later than in Wales. Diet was based on flummery and oat or barley cake with meat exceptional. White bread was rare, reserved in Slovenia for Fridays and holy days. 'You see hunger in their eyes' was one comment by a Slovene noble observer. 'The misery the poor here endure is not to be expressed', exclaimed a Powis Castle agent in 1741, admittedly the last time in which famine conditions struck Wales.[14]

One means by which some alleviation could be found was extra-agricultural activity, which expanded from the later seventeenth-century in both our countries. This was particularly taken up by those who could not live from their landholding, in Slovenia the cottars, for example. Mining and cloth production were the main branches, the former chiefly for iron, taking on a larger scale (Carniola and Carinthia; north-east Wales and Monmouthshire), though copper (Swansea), lead (Cardiganshire), coal (Neath) and quicksilver (Idrija) were also locally important. A big boost was given to trade in Slovenia by the opening of a free port in Trieste, on the rim of Slovene ethnic territory, and the steady improvement of the roads. The carting of trade goods, where salt was very important, became a significant work outlet for the rural population as did cattle droving in parts of Wales. Towns grew too, though not dramatically. There was an interesting difference in this respect. Town foundations had been much more common in medieval Wales than Slovenia, some eighty by the fourteenth century against a dozen. Of the fifty odd Welsh foundations which survived, however, the great majority had less than a thousand inhabitants in 1670 and the largest by 1750, Wrexham, Swansea and Carmarthen, still only some three thousand. The 1801 census shows 14 per cent only of the Welsh population living in towns of more than a thousand. In England and Wales together the figure for towns of over 2,500 inhabitants which in English circumstances more closely approximated to the definition of a town, was 30 per cent.[15] This is perhaps the most revealing example of Welsh backwardness vis-à-vis the English neighbour. Slovenia shows, by contrast, fewer but somewhat larger towns, in each respect less out of line with wider Austrian circumstances. Ljubljana's population grew from 7,500 to 9,000 between 1700 and 1750, Maribor, Klagenfurt and Gorica from 4,000–5,000 to 6,000–7,000. The three last-named towns were the largest settlements of Slovenes in Styria, Carinthia and Gorizia respectively, though dominated by Germans and (Gorica) Italians. Still in 1785, burghers (roughly equivalent to urban professionals) and workers together made up only 3.4 per cent of the population of Carniola and Gorizia, as opposed to 16.9 per cent in advanced Bohemia and 10 per cent in Austria as a whole.[16]

Yet modest urban growth could not adequately absorb the excess impoverished population. A tenth of the population of Ljubljana were beggars and Slovene paupers swelled the suburbs and surrounding villages of Trieste. According to a Welsh recollection of 1812 it was common fifty years earlier for groups of twenty youths to go begging together.[17] Wandering vagrants were an eighteenth-century preoccupation, haunting the contemporary imagination in ways foreign immigrants can do today and challenging observers to come up with new solutions. The English 1601 Poor Law envisaged treatment on a parochial level through the poor rate but this proved increasingly problematic as mobility grew with population. The number assessed as needy in Welsh counties was consistently about a third of the population, somewhat less in more prosperous Glamorgan. Welsh poor rates began to rise sharply, burdening some rural areas which had relied on traditional patriarchalism rather than apply them. Austrian legislation of 1552, mandating alms through religious bodies and parish based was found similarly wanting. Mercantilist schemes for workhouses and work schools for orphans were increasingly discussed, both in Britain and Austria, but were not implemented on any scale till after 1750. The societies which have been outlined here were, after all, remote from the centres of power.

From the standpoint of today these were poor, harshly hierarchical societies, whose people were ill-protected from the hazards of ignorance, disease and arbitrary justice. Their world was one of uncertainty and chance, where a diarist in the Vale of Glamorgan could record nineteen cases of drowning in his small locality, on coast, river, pond and lake.[18] Life expectancy at birth, at around thirty-five years, was less than half our own. What signs as yet were there of the intellectual, cultural and indeed moral resources which could sustain a claim to nationhood in succeeding generations?

CULTURE, INTELLECTUAL LIFE, IDENTITY

Small numbers, economic underdevelopment and political insignificance made it difficult for our subaltern peoples to match what may be termed the 'high culture' of major societies, in art and architecture, literature and thought. Alternative forms of folk culture and popular tradition, whose artistic value has been increasingly recognised in the modern world, had not yet received the validation of the romantic movement. High culture was associated with the dominant minority or with international bodies like the Catholic church, or foreign artists, builders and travelling theatre groups. Wales's four cathedrals were among the smallest in Britain, not helped by the non-residence of English bishops, which became the norm in the eighteenth century. Monasteries survived the Reformation only as ruins. The small scale of Welsh towns was not conducive to distinguished public buildings, though gentry town houses, post-primary schools and the regular appearance of assize courts lent a few of the 'county towns', like Brecon, a certain elegance as the century advanced. Swansea, with 6,000 inhabitants by 1800, and the beginnings of a resort culture as well as industry, has been compared to Southampton at about this time.[19] Slovenia fared better. There were five sculptors and ten painters, mainly Italian, in Ljubljana in 1730 who helped to beautify the town à la Baroque; foreign and native painters contributed to a Ljubljana style, which combined Italian influences with some indigenous features. Portraits of Carniolan nobles were an important aspect of this activity, as was the continued Counter-Reformation tradition of church building. With its Societas Operosum of 1701–25 (a kind of learned society, if short-lived), its Societas Philharmonica (1701) and its theatre in the Estates building (1735) Ljubljana offered a richer cultural life than any Welsh town offered, though none of this took place in Slovene. The capitals of Carinthia, Klagenfurt (Celovec), and of Italian-dominated Gorizia (Gorica), were similarly large towns with cultural institutions on the fringe of Slovene ethnic territory. Here and in wholly German Graz, the Styrian capital, a Slovene presence was much less evident than in Ljubljana; they offered Slovenes potential access to more sophisticated norms, like Shrewsbury and Bristol for Wales, but with a bigger Slovene flavour.

Unsurprisingly, the church was the chief organ in the spread of education. This took contrasting forms in the two countries. In the Slovene lands, where the Reformation had stressed the need for it, and in the mother tongue, the Counter-Reformation preferred to work through the pageantry of processions and visual effect. A ministry through the written word was hampered by the lack of teaching materials in the mother tongue. The scanty texts available were read basically by the clergy, though some of the laity, preserving them, became a nucleus for the so-called *bukovniki* (people of the book) of the eighteenth century. Still in the 1780s, no more than 3–4 per cent of the population of Carniola were literate, very few of them in the countryside. Secondary education was better organised, almost exclusively six-class Gymnasiums run by Jesuits in the major towns, following a classical curriculum taught in Latin. Diocesan seminaries complemented these, adding philosophy and sometimes theology, though students often took this up in institutions further afield, including Italy.

In Wales it was secondary education which was relatively neglected, remaining in the hands of the few 'grammar schools', usually from the Tudor period, where the sons of gentry and 'middling sorts' – well-to-do tradesmen and farmers – were taught Latin and some secular subjects through English. New initiatives went into primary education, where the Protestant aspiration to general education was reiterated successively in the Puritan 'free schools' of the 1650s, the Welsh Trust Schools of 1674–81 and those of the SPCK (Society for the Promotion of Christian Knowledge) from 1699. The repetition of the attempt shows the elusiveness of the goal, which failed to match the Scottish Presbyterian success in generalising a parochial school system. The difficulties were the dependence on benefactors' fluctuating funding but especially the insistence on the use of English as teaching medium. Only when the Revd Griffith Jones's circulating school movement, operating through itinerant instructors in the mother tongue, was launched in 1731 was it possible to pass from its predecessors' initial success in towns and more anglicised border areas to create a mass education movement through the whole country. The movement's flexibility, which enabled teaching to proceed when people were freer from agricultural duties – it was directed at adults as well as children – meant that 150 schools had been set up by 1740, when 8,767 attended. Between these schools and the distribution of Bibles, often free, which was the most effective side of the work of the Welsh Trust and the SPCK, a taste for Bible reading among the common people was created which was only deepened. Between 1731 and 1760 books published in Welsh numbered 452, an acceleration on the 545 appearing in the sixty years prior to this, which itself had represented a quintupling of production since the first Welsh printed book in 1546.[20] The lapsing of official restrictions on printing in 1695 played a part in all this. Thomas Jones the almanacist took the opportunity to move his press from London nearer to Wales in Shrewsbury, and in 1718 the first printing press in Wales itself began work. It quickly transplanted to Carmarthen, which became the country's first press centre, a century and a half after Ljubljana acquired a press in 1575. The absence of a substantial, centrally situated town in Wales to play Ljubljana's role will figure repeatedly in this comparative history.

The extent of Welsh-language publishing in these peripheral circumstances was all the more impressive and a sharp contrast with the paucity of the Slovenian equivalent. The five-volume sermons of the Capuchin friar Janez Svetokriški in 1672 were the first publication in Slovene since 1615. The book on the Baroque period in a leading series on Slovene literature largely amounts to a discussion of different aspects of Svetokriški's work. But as a comment on Slovene literary activity this would be slightly misleading as in line with other east-central European cultures more publication took place in Latin than in the West. Much of the material was topographic, cartographic or heraldic, remaining sometimes in manuscript, or was devoted to provincial histories or theology. This, however, plainly did not involve a mass readership. Valvasor's history of Carniola was the jewel of this genre. He earned a European reputation and membership of the Royal Society in London. His Welsh counterpart for scholarship was the famous botanist, antiquarian, father of Celtic studies and custodian of the Oxford Ashmolean Institution, the world's first modern museum, Edward Lhuyd (1660–1709). Lhuyd's chief work, the *Archaeologia Britannica*, anticipated some of the insights of later comparative linguists and boasted introductions to each of the Celtic languages in the tongue concerned.

The main distinguishing feature of Welsh literary culture was, however, the existence of a substantial body of poetry and prose in the mother tongue, dating from the early Middle Ages and continually added to thereafter. The golden age of Welsh poetry in the classical 'strict metres' had ended with the death of Tudur Aled, its last great master, in 1526. With the gradual accommodation of the Welsh noble society on which it rested to English norms, successive minor exponents were mourned on their passing as being the last in the old professional bardic tradition, till the death of Owen Gruffydd in 1730. Yet the craft itself was still fostered by farmers, craftsmen, clergymen and publishers alongside the freer metres of the Renaissance. Anglican clerics maintained an interest in intellectual matters and Welsh historical tradition. Two names may be singled out from several lexicographers and antiquarians which collectively testify to a rise of interest in these themes on the eve of the Enlightenment.

Moses Williams (1685–1742), an Anglican clergyman from the Teifi valley, Cardiganshire, came from an area of strong cultural traditions where fellow clerics and interested lay people copied manuscripts, planned translations and nurtured patriotic hopes for Welsh literature. Some had wider contacts with Oxford and London, like Williams himself whose acquaintance included specialists in Anglo-Saxon and Arabic, and a Welsh fellow of the Royal Society as well as Edward Lhuyd. Williams, the secretary of the Royal Society, had ambitious plans for a university-type forum for Welsh studies and Welsh manuscript publication but suffered frustration at lack of support. His main works, a new Bible edition and pioneer Welsh-language bibliography of Welsh books, fell short of his hopes for a Wales he thought as bountiful as Canaan but which could be still better if its upper classes applied the knowledge they gained in England to the development of their own country.[21] Theophilus Evans, likewise Anglican minister, published probably the most reprinted ever book on Welsh history, *Drych y Prif Oesoedd* (Mirror of Earliest Times, 1716). Its popularity was due to its vigorous style and whole-hearted endorsement of the patriotic myths of the Welsh classical past as the descendants of Brutus of Troy. It reproduced essentially the themes of the twelfth-century *Historia Regum Britanniae* (History of the Kings of Britain) which the author, Geoffrey of Monmouth, claimed to have translated from a book 'in the British tongue' (i.e. Welsh). Geoffrey's account has been called 'the most famous work of nationalistic historiography in the Middle Ages,'[22] and Evans's unblinking acceptance of it – for he knew of Lhuyd and others' soberer assessments – reflected pique at perceived English denigration of the Welsh national story. The issue is important. Geoffrey's work was a foundation text of what became known as 'the matter of Britain', the corpus of material dealing with King Arthur and his court at Camelot, Sir Galahad, Sir Lancelot and the search for the Holy Grail, the tragic love and death of Tristan and Isolde. All this together, endlessly delved into and recycled by writers, most prominently Chrétien de Troyes (*c*.1130–*c*.1191), evolved into a key theme of medieval European literature, whose influence and narrative power has survived into the present. Several of the characters involved figure in the Welsh medieval masterpiece, the prose tales of the Mabinogi. As literature and myth, the Arthurian sagas are a rare legacy of a small people to wider European culture.

With men like Moses Williams and Theophilus Evans we draw closer to the underlying themes this book will explore, of nationality and cultural identity. This is a wide-ranging subject which has been complicated more than it need be by ideological heat. Reaction against modern nationalist excesses has led to suspicion of nationhood itself, so that conceding a role for this in the past is seen as unhealthy 'primordialism'. Plainly, neither Wales nor the Slovene lands were nations in a modern sense in 1750, but logically speaking they could not be; too much recent discussion amounts to saying that there were no modern nations before modern times. The assumption of this book is that such collective identities emerged fully only after the period so far outlined. But it is reasonable to ask what inheritance from the past may have influenced this process and to assume that an ethnic element played a role in it, along with other factors. It is a matter of degree. Shakespeare's England was already more than an ethnic group, or the nationality of an elite that characterised medieval nationhood where it existed, as it did in Wales. Weaker groups often defined themselves pluralistically, like Valvasor's equivalent in northern Hungary, the polymath Mátyás Bel (1684–1749) who called himself 'by language a Slav, by nation a Hungarian, by education a German'. He was in no doubt what his reference group was, which made him what we would call a Slovak. The point is that identities were not quite as fluid or arbitrary as they seem to modern sceptics of nationhood. The national movements which followed assumed the existence of others felt to be nations and sought to emulate them. This applied to cultural (but divided) nations like nineteenth-century Germans and Italians which sought political unity and to smaller peoples in the Habsburg Monarchy which wanted to acquire full cultural nationhood in the first place. Culture was defined by language because it was the obvious means to communicate the message that the dawning Enlightenment was about to spread. It was this definition of culture by language which meant that a Bel's descendants in the great majority of cases became Slovaks and a Carniolan's Slovenes. This is the context in which this book situates Slovene and Welsh history, in the category of smaller, subaltern societies about to awaken.

There is a good case for saying that Welsh people entered this process of awakening with a clearer historical profile than Slovenes or other small peoples of east-central Europe. The many centuries of resistance to Anglo-Saxon and Norman invasion helped to shape a common awareness vis-à-vis the outsider, expressed linguistically in the Welsh laws, with their categories of 'Cymro mamtad', or Welshman descended from a Welsh mother and father, and the 'anghyfiaith' or those who spoke another language. In this period a powerful poetic tradition flourished, including a body of patriotic poetry along heroic martial lines, though this was only one aspect. The finest of Welsh medieval poets, Dafydd ap Gwilym, was a troubadour of love and nature and one of his most popular poems 'Trouble in a Tavern' handled the ethnic theme comically. Ethnic boundaries were often more sharply delineated in western Europe than further east where both in Germanic and Slavic speech areas dialects merged confusedly into each other. Welsh experience and literature led to a sharper awareness of their origins than Slovenes had. People thought of themselves in terms of their German-dominated provinces or more vaguely as Slavs. Among the learned because of its classical associations a claim to be Illyrians had some vogue. Illyria was the former Roman province in which southern Slavs settled, but the ancient Illyrians were probably Albanians. By contrast, old Welsh records often related, in however garbled a form, to real historical processes. For example, knowledge of the legend of the Treason of the Long Knives in which Saxons treacherously slaughtered their British hosts was and remains widespread among Welsh speakers; it plainly relates to the fifth-century Britons' loss of Kent.

That said, it is possible that such stories did as much to inculcate a sense in the Welsh of being historic losers as champions of freedom. The cleric Theophilus Evans repeated ancient writers' morality tale that British defeats were due to their sins. Once the Welsh had been decisively defeated the defiant spirit which had survived the Edwardian conquest till the fifteenth-century Glyndŵr revolt of 1400–12 yielded to a docility remarked on by eighteenth-century commentators. Or better perhaps to a distrustful resentment that eighteenth-century German travellers discerned in monoglot Czech speakers in Bohemia, who were also accused of being passive but sly, like Taffy the thief of the English nursery rhyme. One English observer remarked that the only Englishman whom the Welsh really accepted was the King.[23] Vague invocations of a nebulous but vast Slavdom may have been more comforting. It should also be remembered that the Protestant leader Trubar's successful creation of a standard literary for Slovene depended on awareness of the cultural commonality of those who spoke it. It is difficult to penetrate the multi-layered consciousness of traditional societies, until recently overwhelmingly peasant and illiterate, nor need we assume everyone thought alike.

What is fairly clear, though, and different from modern European experience, is that people could live together over long periods without fusing in any melting pot. Language borders offer a fascinating story. They may remain stable for many centuries, like that between Germanic and Romance speech in western Europe, Belgium for instance, or shift markedly, like the German–Slav divide to the east. In Wales, the 'landsker' separating Welsh and English-speaking Pembrokeshire fits the former pattern, but with some advance of Welsh between 1600 and 1900. Welsh also regained Flintshire in the twelfth century, advanced markedly along Offa's Dyke in the fifteenth, and largely submerged the Englishries of the Vale of Glamorgan between the Middle Ages and the nineteenth century. The English-speaking enclaves of south Pembrokeshire and south Gower held their ground, like the Gottschee German settlement in otherwise Slovene Carniola. A reverse set in during the eighteenth century in mid- and south Wales, starting in Radnorshire. The pattern shows that the social advantages of speaking a dominant language, of which modern society has become very aware, often had no effect at the local level in earlier times. The remarkable tenacity of custom at the level of small towns is registered in the early modern period both in Wales and Slovenia. The proportion of German and Slovene speakers in Ptuj changed little (slightly in Slovene's favour) between the mid-sixteenth and mid-eighteenth centuries, as appears to have been the case in Cardiff. Not till the second half of the eighteenth century is a switch to German explicable by perceived German superiority discernible in Slovenian towns, and it is likely that the same mindset operated in Wales too. The major long-term movement in Welsh towns, nearly all English foundations, was the absorption of the medieval English-speaking burgesses of medieval times.

Overall, the pattern in spoken use in the two countries showed common features: a prevalent monolinguism of the rural population and a fair measure of bilingualism of upper classes and townsfolk. There may be variations in detail here which can be significant. It seems likely that monoglottism was greater in Slovenia than in Wales, and the bilingualism of landowners greater, at least in Carniola, the Slovenian Gwynedd. Geraint Jenkins estimates monoglot Welsh at probably 90 per cent of the population even at the end of the early modern period (1536–1776).[24]

Slovene historians assume near universal rural monoglottism. A prima facie case can be made that Habsburg neo-feudalism, with restrictions on schooling and the free movement of peasants, reduced the opportunity for even the superficial acquaintance with the dominant tongue which could occur in Wales. But hard information is lacking and hindsight affects the two historiographies differently, with the Welsh alert to signs of linguistic erosion and the Slovenes less so. An 1812 survey in a border area of Carinthia gives a population 99 per cent Slovene, of whom 14 per cent were heads of households who also knew German.[25] By that time there was certainly some language shift in parts of the Welsh border counties but little before 1750.[26] More intriguing perhaps is the question of upper-class diglossia. In Carniola it appears that a fair number of nobles did know some Slovene, though their own conversation was in German. A case is recorded of young nobles at the theatre resorting to it to comment on a pretty girl in the audience.[27] Was there perhaps a touch of affection in the Carniolan nobles' use of the vernacular, as well as a sense that this is what it was for, rather than anything serious? Probably. Carniolan identity could clearly take on a strong patriotic colouring. The situation was similar in Gwynedd, though the gentry's identity there was explicitly Welsh and took literary form, as could be the case to a lesser extent throughout Wales. But interestingly, provision was made for pro formas in 'Carniolan' for lesser gentry to use in taking oaths. This went beyond Welsh practice for English was de rigueur in official contexts. When Norman French was replaced by English in certain legal processes in 1730/1, the archaic forms were replaced with Welsh ones in Merthyr Tydfil. This was disallowed and remained a unique initiative. The emerging British Empire took a national English form which prescribed the English language officially not just out of convenience but as a matter of principle.

It is not easy to bring together the diverse material of this opening chapter. In many ways, the pattern was not too different in our two societies: a large majority of poor peasants with still static technology, burdened by obligations to under-capitalised landlords, seeking increasingly to help themselves out through a role in a widely dispersed non-agricultural sector; persistent and mounting pauperism, for which traditional methods were inadequate; a small urban class, very thin in educated professionals relative to the rest of the state; dominant landowners, some one to two per cent of the population, in great majority speaking a different home language from their peasants or tenants, the latter being left to their own devices in a mental world circumscribed by subsistence, ancestral custom and snatches of religion: this was the situation. Yet this reality was mediated through quite different state structures. Still feudal Austria lagged behind a Britain getting into its commercial stride, but Wales lagged far behind the British average. Employment and output in Slovene mining were substantially lower than in Wales and the proportion of people on the land even higher. Changes in the number of rooms in peasant homes, and in new products like potatoes, seem to have been slower than in Wales but not by much. The result was a harsh relationship between the privileged and unprivileged but one harsher in the Slovene lands than in Wales. The major peasant revolts of 1573, 1635 and 1713 did not have Welsh equivalents. Philip Jenkins's finding of rising tension between landowner and tenant in Glamorgan is not backed up by David Howell in south-west Wales, who relates discontent more to intra-tenant rivalries. The cultural life of the Slovene masses was closer to the world of Vicar Pritchard than that of Griffith Jones and his step towards mass literacy. But living standards in Wales were probably little higher than in Slovenia. In his history of Monmouthshire (1796) the Enlightenment philosopher David Williams paints a dispiriting picture of the life of the monoglot Welshman as largely outside the pale of modern civilisation as he envisaged it. 'The feudal ideas and habits of an oppressed and degraded peasantry are not wholly abolished, and the use of the Cambro-British language is a perpetual impediment to instruction.'[28] This was a continuation of the failure of reality to match the visions of patriotism we have seen in Moses Williams. How should this situation be remedied and could such a creature as the monoglot Welshman or Slovene play a role in the process?

Phrasing the question in this way recalls what has been said above about the linguistic definition of culture in the national movements of eastern Europe. Could monoglots be saved from their backwardness only by giving them another language or could their language become transformed to meet new purposes? If the former, could they progress only by shedding their inherited identity or could other cultural paths to modernity open up which would allow them to embrace the future without repudiating their past? Real life usually does not fit such neat either/ors. Plainly, Welsh people have in majority become English speaking without abandoning a Welsh identity or a pride in language. This has been a more complicated process than the Slovene course, a typical case of European linguistic nationhood. Illuminating the Welsh pattern – because it was never a formal decision and so remains to be explored – is the purpose of the rest of this book.

NOTES

1 P. Štih, V. Simoniti and P. Vodopivec, *Slowenische Geschichte. Gesellschaft-Politik-Kultur* (A History of Slovenia, Society, Politics. Culture) (Graz, 2008), pp. 74–5, 36–8.

2 P. Simoniti, *Humanizam na Slovenskem i slovenski humanisti do XVI stoletja* (Humanism in Slovenia and Slovenian Humanists to the Sixteenth Century) (Ljubljana, 1979), pp. 21–4, 30.

3 Ibid., pp. 217–18 (Herberstein), 230 (Bonomi).

4 For the Slovene Reformation and Counter-Reformation, Štih et al., *Slowenische Geschichte*, pp. 142–50, 154–60. For the Ljubljana Jesuit college, p. 159.

5 P. R. Roberts, 'Tudor Legislation and the Political Status of "the British Tongue"', in Geraint H. Jenkins (ed.), *The Welsh Language before the Industrial Revolution* (Cardiff, 1997), pp. 123–52 (144).

6 Roberts, 'Tudor Legislation', p. 129.

7 *Cannwyll y Cymry* was not published till well after the author's death, in parts (1659–72) and in full (1681).

8 *The Life of Edward, First Lord Herbert of Cherbury, written by himself*, edited with an Introduction by J. N. Shuttleworth (London, 1976), pp. 14–15.

9 J. W. Valvasor, *Die Ehre dess Hertzogthums Crain* (Ljubljana, 1689), 4. Theil, Kapitel 33, pp. 598–601. (The Renowned Duchy of Carniola.) 'Illyrian' was a common term for south Slav speech, sometimes for Slavonic in general in the early modern period. Interestingly, the Vatican letter spoke of Styria and Carinthia too as Slav-inhabited provinces.

10 August Dimitz, *Geschichte Krains von den ältesten Zeiten bis auf dem Jahr 1813* (History of Carniola from the Earliest Times to the Year 1813), 4. Teil (Ljubljana, 1876), p. 62 (dancing master).

11 Geraint H. Jenkins, *The Foundations of Modern Wales: Wales 1642–1780* (Cardiff, 1987), p. 335.

12 *Slowenische Geschichte*, p. 158; D. W. Howell, *Patriarchs and Parasites: The Gentry of South-West Wales in the Eighteenth Century* (Cardiff, 1986, p. 213); Jenkins, *Foundations*, p. 264.

13 Štih et al., *Slowenische Geschichte*, p. 186.

14 *Historija naroda Jugoslavije* (History of the Nations of Yugoslavia), vol. 2 (Zagreb, 1959), p. 899; Jenkins, *Foundations*, p. 260.

15 For town sizes, D. W. Howell, *The Rural Poor in Eighteenth-century Wales* (Cardiff, 2000), pp. 26–7.

16 P. G. M. Dickson, *Finance and Government under Maria Theresa 1740–1780*, 2 vols (Oxford, 1987), vol. 1, p. 46.

17 Howell, *Rural Poor*, p. 109.

18 *The Diary of William Thomas of Michaelston-super-Ely near St. Fagans, Glamorgan 1762–1795*, ed. by R. T. W. Denning (Cardiff, 1995), p. 469.

19 L. Miskell, *'Intelligent Town': An Urban History of Swansea 1780–1855* (Cardiff, 2006), p. 6.

20 G. Jenkins, *Foundations*, pp. 204, 409.

21 J. Davies, *Bywyd a Gwaith Moses Williams 1685–1742* (The Life and Work of Moses Williams 1685–1742) (Cardiff, 1937), p. 124.

22 Halvdan Koht, 'The Dawn of Nationalism in Europe', *American Historical Review*, 52/2 (1947), 266–80 (270).

23 B. H. Malkin, *The Scenery, Antiquities and Biographies of South Wales* (2nd edn, 2 vols, London, 1807), vol. 1, p. 78.

24 Geraint Jenkins, *A Concise History of Wales* (Cambridge, 2007), p. 136.

25 J. Pleterski, *Narodna in politična zavest na Koroškem* (National and Political Consciousness in Carinthia) (Ljubljana, 1965), p. 12.

26 Maps based on the language of church services are too ready to take Anglican practice as an accurate reflection of the situation. That titled 'Principal Language Zones in Wales, *c*.1750', in Jenkins, *Foundations of Modern Wales*, p. 398 appears to be based on Eryn M. White, 'The Established Church, Dissent and the Welsh Language, *c*.1660–1811', in Geraint M. Jenkins (ed.), *The Welsh Language before the Industrial Revolution* (Cardiff, 1997), pp. 235–87. But this map does not seem to take into account frequent evidence in White's text that provision was regularly made for handfuls of English speakers but not vice versa: e.g. pp. 244, 259–61.

27 Marko Štuhec, 'Iz Lesc v Ljubljano po francosko. K poznavanju jezikove rabe krajnskega plemstva v prvi polovici osemnajstega stoletja' (From Lesec to Ljubljana in French. Towards an understanding of the linguistic usage of Carniolan nobles in the first half of the eighteenth century), *Zgodovinski časopis*, 20/3–4 (2006), 327–44 (340).

28 D. Williams, *The History of Monmouthshire* (London, 1796), pp. 345, 349.

Chapter 2

AWAKENINGS, c.1750–1815

Sometime in the middle of the eighteenth century the transition from early to later modern society began to accelerate in Europe, opening up new possibilities for our two societies. The Age of Reason, or Enlightenment, brought a heightened sense of mankind's ability to alter circumstances previously held to be subject to Providence and tradition. The intellectual energy this imparted led to greatly increased print production, offering forums for the wider circulation of new knowledge in what historians have called an emerging 'civic society' of public debate. Ideas gained ground that government could and should concern itself with a common good going beyond the maintenance of order and prescriptive rights. The 'scientific revolution' of the previous century had helped prepare the way, and the decline in religious strife opened space for new preoccupations.

The word 'accelerate' above acknowledges that all this was a matter of degree. Intellectual curiosity and opening to reason in social affairs were not inventions of the Enlightenment. But a few details, some weightier than others, may help illustrate new attitudes and how they interlinked in this period. Slovenia's highest peak, Triglav at 2,864 metres was first climbed in 1778, by three local villagers, navigating the narrow saddle between its two chief peaks on their bottoms where now an iron rail helps the intrepid. They were responding to the vogue for mountain exploration by foreign scholars drawn to Slovenia's terrain by their interest in the rising sciences of geology, volcanology and botany. A number of them came to involve themselves in wider issues of Slovenian folklore and culture. These were years when upland heights began to attract awe rather than horror and Snowdonia became an object of the romantic spirit in Wales. It was a time when famine, plague and major rural revolt (previously recurrent in Slovenia) came to an end. The announcement of the kinship of Indo-European languages in 1786 signalled the birth of modern linguistics, important to both our peoples, particularly the Slovenes – though it was made by William Jones, an Anglesey squire's son who was once introduced to the King of France as a man who knew every language but his own.

'Enlightenment' was a rolling process, which struck root in Britain and France and was successively emulated in central and southern Europe, first in Protestant Prussia, then in Catholic Austria and from there east and south-east into Hungary and the Slavic lands. With each shift it took a somewhat simpler and more formulaic guise, though it was never a revolutionary movement. Voltaire advocated enlightened absolutism, which became the norm in central Europe. Atheism was confined to a handful of philosophers. Indeed, everywhere the clergy played a large role, constituting as they did the largest body of educated people. Their version advocated a rational faith, cleansed of Baroque excess, and stressing the need for popular education to aid a better, less superstitious understanding of the faith, very much on Griffith Jones's lines. A certain earnestness entered the spirit of the times, both for Protestant and Catholic countries, helped by the spread of basic education. A notion of European superiority to other cultures strengthened. Where the early modern period had seen European discovery and conquest of the New World and its stone- or bronze-age peoples, the 'first imperial age' (1760–1830) ushered in an era of dominance of Christian Europe over other developed civilisations too in the Middle East, India and China.

With European power and knowledge grew the confidence and cohesion of the great European states and their elites. Britain was a conspicuous example. The loss of the American colonies was well compensated by commercial hegemony and the dawn of a new empire in India, Canada, the West Indies and the Cape. The disbanding of the Scottish parliament at the beginning of the eighteenth century was flanked by that of the Irish at the end, a centralising process mirrored in miniature by abolition of the Court of Great Sessions in Wales in 1830. Central power in Austria, Britain's chief partner against French ambitions in these years, also emerged strengthened, albeit after a more troubled course, which saw its survival threatened by Frederick the Great of Prussia and Napoleon. The

'Austrian Enlightenment' pursued under Maria Theresa (1740–80) and her son Joseph II (1780–90) reshaped a dynastic amalgam of territories into something closer to a united state, with a bureaucracy cutting back nobles' powers over their peasants and a standing army more independent of provincial funding. Peasants gained freedom of movement (1781); religious tolerance was granted to non-Catholics, censorship was eased and the principle of general primary education formally proclaimed. The need to make Austria competitive vis-à-vis Protestant Prussia lay behind much of this. Centralising tendencies threatened to curtail further the autonomous development of subaltern societies, yet also offered them expanding horizons.

This was probably more so in Austria than Britain. The reforming Habsburg state impinged on the traditional power of nobility and church and to an extent on existing social hierarchies. In more developed Britain social control lay less in the laissez-faire inclined state and more in a denser pattern of squire, JP and parson, whose stability helped preserve continuity. The Habsburg polyglot realm had to mobilise agents from populations outside these hierarchies and the dominant German-speakers, who were far fewer proportionally than the English in Britain. In the discussion below of the actions and motives of Welsh people and Slovenes the imperial contexts in which they operated must always be kept in sight. This presentation will plunge into the heart of the matter with the Slovene case, hoping that the novelty of a contrasting development will prove stimulating and provide a sharper basis for comparison. As implied at the end of the last chapter, Slovene evolution followed a more unidirectional pattern than the Welsh. All the three main interacting factors that shape history – the socio-economic, the political and the cultural – can be intimately related to the Slovene language revival. Language was a key factor in Welsh development too but its role was not so central. The Welsh experience had an intriguing logic of its own. This chapter begins the broaching of the distinction.

NATIONAL AWAKENING IN THE SLOVENE LANDS

Convention provides a precise date for the start of the Slovene national movement. In 1768 the Augustinian friar Marko Pohlin published in German his *Grammatik der crainerischen Sprache* (A Grammar of the Carniolan Language), stimulating a succession of grammars and dictionaries in following decades, in print or manuscript. He is the first of some half dozen language champions among many who will be picked out here for simplicity of presentation. In terms echoing Welsh complaints, Pohlin's preface lamented indifference to his 'almost entirely ruined' mother tongue and the denial of its right, clear to all 'reasonable' people, to be considered a 'useful' language for its speakers. The terminology – 'reasonable' and 'useful' – echoed enlightened preoccupations. Pohlin invoked Carniolan's inherent qualities, historical roots and the wide territories in which similar (Slav) languages were spoken, urging in the name of patriotism a grammar and dictionary to fix its norms and for it to be taught in the schools.[1] At least half the cohort of grammarians and etymologists who followed Pohlin's call were also clergymen. The Austrian Enlightenment in Austria marked a deliberate shift away from Counter-Reformation attitudes, reflected not only in regime policies but in a movement of 'Reform Catholicism' in the Church itself, in the curtailing of Baroque church practices and ideas. Mid-eighteenth-century manuscripts (still in Latin!) in a leading Slovene monastery show the influence of French rationalist thought (Descartes), even Newton. The dissolution of the Jesuit order in Habsburg lands in 1773 was a significant step, given their dominance in education and censorship. Other orders, like Pohlin's Augustinians, took up their role with more openness to new thought. Clerical language enthusiasts in Slovenia often sympathised with the simplicity of worship and moral rigour advocated by Jansenists, the Jesuits' arch enemies in the Catholic Church, though officially banned. Aims to raise the religious life, part of the earnestness of the age, went with greater attention to the common people, including their speech. New economic theory (physiocracy), which saw a productive peasantry as the basis of economic progress, worked in the same direction, as did notions of patriotism, a key word of the Austrian enlightenment, denoting concern for the common good which government should serve. While parishioners often disliked reduction of the number of saints' days and religious processions and bishops could resent state interference, there was much to align thoughtful clerics with state policies which historians have dubbed 'Josephinism', after the emperor Joseph II. Joseph himself used profits gained from monastic closures to fund the creation of new parishes. Slovene language enthusiasts dreamt of a network of parish priests as a means of inculcating incipient patriotism. Modern historians increasingly credit the activities of grass roots clergymen rather than the great names of the 'philosophes' for the gradual change in mentalities which took place in humbler locales than the salons of Enlightenment Paris.[2] It is important that their Slovene counterparts enjoyed support from the Jansenist-inclined Bishop of Ljubljana, Johann Karl von Herberstein. The importance of the religious background in both our societies cannot be overestimated. It was less conflicted in Slovene territory than in Wales. The Catholic hierarchy was non-native as in Wales but as befitted an international Church it was less concerned to push the dominant language than the Church of England. In other ways it reflected some of the worldly realism of the Anglicans. If its monopoly excluded the stimulus of nonconformity its internal structure allowed for different traditions between orders and its scientific contribution was not trivial. The Gruber brothers, all Jesuits who spent much of their life in Slovenia and taught in Ljubljana's quite impressive *lycée*, had notable hydrological, physical and mathematical interests which included draining the marshes around the town. The *lycée* with its school of mechanical engineering also produced the internationally famous writer of trigonometrical tables, son of a poor Slovene peasant, Georg Vega (Jurij Veha).

This helps explain the central European atmosphere from which Pohlin and the Slovene revival emerged. Many of the forerunners matured in the second third of the eighteenth century, before either the radical materialist turn further to the west or the writings of Johann Gottfried Herder, so often seen as the father of cultural nationalism. State reform of education opened a more public sphere for language activity than lexicography. In a memorandum of 1772 another clergyman, Blaž Kumerdej, stated that outside the towns hardly a hundred of the common people of Carniola were literate, though they were intelligent and ready for inclusion in the ongoing political and social process. He proposed a system of schools for this class, teaching in the mother tongue. Kumerdej (1738–1805), a philologist highly educated in Vienna, had been seized with an interest in Slovene at the age of twenty-four, a symptom of the tendency in this direction which marked the age. His proposal met with no response, but an all-Austrian edict of 1774 laid down the principle of compulsory primary education, nearly a hundred years before this was enacted in Britain. In 1775 Kumerdej became director of the 'normal school' in Ljubljana, the pinnacle of the triple system created by the 1774 edict, of rural, so called trivial, schools, urban schools and one in each province with a teacher training function. It is not clear why he did not do more in this position to advance his cause of Slovene as a language of instruction. The dictionary on which he laboured till his death, which was to underpin the project to make the language a fit instrument for modern life, remained unpublished. Kumerdej's life illustrated the frustration and falling short which have so often dogged the revival movements of small nations, particularly in their early stages.[3] Nonetheless, by 1790 there were some 160 schools of the lowest level in Carniola.

The man who took over responsibility for Carniolan education in 1787, Anton Tomaž Linhart (1756–95), was the most complex and certainly the most radical figure of the early Slovene revival. His bilingualism (he was town-born) and metropolitan ambitions recall Iolo Morganwg. Abandoning a Cistercian monastery, he threw himself into the life of Vienna with aspirations as a writer in German expressing much of the emotional turbulence of the *Sturm und Drang* phase of German literature. With joy he greeted a friend's similar escape from the 'unworthy prison' of monasticism for 'free air … life's happiness and the world's beauty'.[4] His volume of poetry *Blumen aus Krain* (Flowers from Carniola, 1781) was far more ambitious in range than the first ever publications of Slovene verse appearing around the same time, while a youthful play was a German tragedy inspired by Shakespeare and the contemporary vogue for 'titanism' – the clash of powerful characters. In an essay based on Alexander Pope's 'Essay on Man' Linhart went beyond Pope's Deist view of God to present a science-based picture of existence.[5] As a twenty-two-year-old he boldly told a short-lived Academy of educated Carniolans to put aside their prejudices and hasten ardently on the tireless search for truth. Yet between exaltation and depression Linhart was not happy. Back in Ljubljana from Vienna he told a friend that their fatherland (Carniola) was a street-walker who alternately enticed and rebuffed; he might do better to seek his bread in America.[6] In the same year, however, that Immanuel Kant famously asked 'What is Enlightenment?' he put to himself a crucial question: What are we Carniolans? Linhart resolved his dilemmas by devoting his energies to the budding cause of his mother tongue. Joseph II's edict making German the universal official language of his empire drew from him the comment that to take away a people's language and substitute another was not a matter of individual edicts but only of political revolutions or the imperceptible influence of long centuries.[7] He proposed not only to reverse the abolition of philosophy as a subject of the Ljubljana Lyceum or high school, which he achieved, but to add further branches of knowledge, making it akin to a university. One aspect of his programme, a central library in Ljubljana, was realised in the institution of the Lycean library in 1791. In addition, in 1789–91 Linhart published the first history of Carniola 'and the other south Slavs of Austria', organising the structure deliberately around the land and its inhabitants rather than the reigns of rulers in the spirit of the enlightenment goal of the history of civilisation. Here the Karantanian state briefly mentioned in Pohlin's preface was filled out with reference to the positive peasant role and the freedom-loving 'national character' of its people emphasised, without ignoring negatives of vengefulness and ignorance. The critique of feudalism and the dove-tailing of Slovene and wider south Slav history which were to be features of Slovene historiography thus received a first airing.[8] The radical note was struck also in Linhart's two Slovene-language comedies, another first – though only one was performed. In both, sturdy representatives of the common people outwit noble machinations, a common enough theme. There was a boldness in its handling, however, in that one of the plays was an adaptation for a Carniolan locale of Pierre Beaumarchais's notoriously anti-noble *The Marriage of Figaro*, which Joseph II had forbidden to be performed.

All told, Linhart's short life is noteworthy not just for the variety of his engagement but for the way he combined the concerns of the individual, the cosmopolitan and the patriot. The key to this was his passionate belief in freedom, necessary to the individual person and the collectivity. It seems Linhart was willing in his desire for the elevation of the Slovene language to subordinate his personal opinion. He told his friend Kuralt that though he was not sure, as a religious sceptic, of the value of the second Slovene translation of the Bible 1786–1802, he welcomed it for its service to the Slovene language.[9] Interestingly, he sought out and destroyed all the copies of *Blumen aus Krain* he could find. This may not have been primarily because it was in German, but because he lacked confidence in it as poetry. The desire to emulate the best in European literature as a son of Carniola was his most vital legacy to Slovene culture and emblematic of Slovene strivings as a whole.

Linhart's idea of a Slovene library had actually been anticipated by the greatest patron of the revival, the remarkable baron Žiga Zois, 1747–1819. Son of a part Italian father and Slovene mother, from whom he learnt Slovene, he was the owner of extensive iron works and reputedly the richest man in Carniola. Confined prematurely to a wheelchair he made himself, he pursued botanical and geological studies in contact with European leaders in these fields and was increasingly drawn to literary interests. Through his circle he encouraged projects like Kumerdej's dictionary, Slovene versification and old Slav history, while aiding Slav-related publication. He also translated parts of visiting Italian theatre groups' repertoire (songs and arias) to give Slovene cachet with Ljubljana audiences. Perhaps his greatest literary influence was on the leading poet of the revival, the parish priest Valentin Vodnik (1758–1819), a different and in some ways more representative figure than Linhart. Vodnik was no rural ignoramus; he knew Latin, German, Italian and French. But his quiet life is reflected in simple metres on familiar themes bound up with loyalty to the customs and folklore of Carniola and to the Habsburg Monarchy. By the mid-1790s, however, Zois was sending him examples of Italian metres as a model. Discussion of metres was rife among emerging litterateurs, partly because there was no past of serious poetry in Slovene to go on. In Wales, Slovenia and elsewhere Latin and Greek was a staple of secondary education and young people's first poetic experiments were very often translations from the classics, some of it (in German) essaying classical hexameters. Having edited the chief Slovene calendars to appear after the Protestant era, Vodnik became editor of the first Slovene newspaper, the weekly *Lublanske Novice* from 1797 to 1800. The French wanted to counter Austrian propaganda but Zois provided the spur. As to Vodnik, a shift in his uncomplicated ideology first came in the second French occupation of 1809–13, in two major poems, 'Illyria Revived', addressed to Napoleon (1809), and 'Illyria Enhanced' (1813–17) on the Habsburg's return.

The French occupation is an important example of the power of external affairs to impact on a small people's life. Having defeated Austria, Napoleon wished to cut her off from the sea and ensure France easy access to the Balkans and beyond. As a result Ljubljana became the capital of a territory more than twice the size of modern Slovenia, containing Carniola and some further Slovene territory, but also swathes of Italian and Croatian land. Playing on local sensibilities, the French named their new possessions Illyria, an ancient Roman name revived in the Renaissance and available thereafter to feed south Slav dreams of unity. Usually, these were Croat dreams, but Vodnik's use of the term shows how Slovenes could also now see themselves in a wider context. His first poem saw Illyria's past as promising a European future, his second announced the dawning of her 'freedom'. These hopes were illusory. Austria, regaining control, retained the Illyrian idea, as a kingdom inside the Habsburg Monarchy, but this kingdom remained on paper until it was formally abolished in 1849. French promises to make Slovene the language of instruction in primary and lower secondary schools hardly got off the ground and the high French taxation made their occupation unpopular with the masses. Yet the episode opened intoxicating perspectives for small circles of Slovene patriots and the French declarations of social equality, reversed by the Austrians, at least showed how age-old dominance could be challenged. It was an extreme case of the Slovene lands' geographical openness to influence, which in smaller ways had brought in Zois's Italian ancestors, and other figures in the age of enlightenment, like the natural scientist Balthazar Hacquet, a scholar of European reputation who interested himself in ethnological and language matters too.

The last of Zois's major contacts was the man destined to become the great Slavist Jernej Kopitar (1780–1844). Of peasant stock, Kopitar spent his first nine years as a shepherd boy before his father asked him if he wanted to study. He sent him, ambitiously, to a town, not a village school, where he was fortunate to have in the first class a teacher who knew Slovene. But for his parents' early death the talented youngster would most likely have become a priest and maybe a bishop, but a small allowance and a post as private teacher to Zois's nephew led him on a different course, spurred by his gift for languages. He learnt English, for example, by reading Edward Gibbon. Kopitar's first major work was his *Grammar of the Slav language in Carniola, Carinthia and Styria* published in German in 1809, through whose scholarly credentials he sought to win international respect for his mother tongue. It also established definitively the wider unity of what writers had previously given provincial labels. (Though Slovenian as a term had had its place since Pohlin's day, Slovenia as territorial concept seems first to have been used in 1844, in print at least.) Kopitar's career shows he achieved his aim. He became court librarian to the emperor in Vienna, state censor for books published in Slav languages in the Monarchy and the confident of other philological giants like the Czech Jozef Dobrovský and the Serb Vuk Karadžić. Kopitar worked on many issues, some of them broached by Zois: the origins of non-Latin alphabets used to write Slav, Cyrillic and Glagolitic, the newly discovered Freising manuscripts (the first record of written Slovene), the relation of Slovenian to the common Old Slav language and also to Serbian and Croatian. All this may seem abstruse but it helped give historical significance to a speech wholly insignificant in the present, and it had political implications. The native dialect of Zagreb and north-west Croatia (and mother speech of the Yugoslav leader Tito) is closer to Slovene than to standard Serbo-Croat. Kopitar believed that the Slovenes should have cultural leadership of this dialect continuum, indeed that Slovene was closest to the original Old Slav speech and its location. Another view held later by some Slovenes was that Slovenes should follow Zagreb in dropping a literary language of their own and adopting what came to be known as Serbo-Croat for their written medium.[10] The plot for this little Alpine people was thickening, as the complexities of their ethno-geographical position came into play.

All the figures so far mentioned were Carniolans. National and linguistic movements often start from a centre and spread out from it as they strengthen. Carinthia, however, also had active revivalists. Two Catholic priests, Ožbalt Gutsman and Urban Jarnik, wrote influential grammars, the first in Pohlin's time, the second in Kopitar's. Carinthia, after all, was the centre of the Karantanian myth. In Styria, where Slovenes were as numerous as in Carniola but under a German majority, a stimulus was given by the establishment of a chair for Slovene in the German-speaking capital Graz in 1812, actually before the equivalent chair in Ljubljana. It owed its foundation to the higher profile Slovene matters had gained during the Napoleonic wars. Historians see a tendency for some consolidation of the Slovene movement as far as education is concerned in these post-1815 years. Against the mortal dangers the empire had passed through, indulging modest cultural aspirations of a loyal population no doubt seemed a sensible way to proceed.

As a tiny, socially subordinate minority both in the Monarchy and among their fellow Slavs Slovene patriots had gained a precarious foothold against formidable odds. What lends their movement interest is how aware they were of these odds. Modern Slovene historiography stresses the way in this period they became consciously the subject in their own history. This can seem portentous when applied to Pohlin's decision to write a grammar of his mother tongue. His preface has the hallmarks of its limited provincial background. He ascribes credit to his language for its three-lettered word for God, Boh, which points to the Trinity; he sees his countrymen arriving in their homeland under the leadership of Japhet, son of Noah.[11] This reminds a Welsh reader of Theophilus Evans and *Drych y Prif Oesoedd*. But the speed and coherence of development thereafter is impressive. The leaders came from both town and country and seem to have been aware throughout of the need for a balanced approach; on the one hand to raise the sophistication of their language and culture, approaching it closer to norms of more advanced countries, on the other to serve the interests of their lowly countrymen. Zois, who emerges as a key strategist on the cultural front, stressed that the raising of the rural population should always be the focal point. Vodnik held that in teaching boys Latin poetry the literary appreciation should not be swamped by grammatical exegesis. It should be remembered that rudimentary though their own fledgling culture was these revivalists knew several languages and were well versed in other cultures. Linhart was not the only poet to feel shame at how far his own efforts fell short of his models. The emulative, future-pointing aspiration remained uppermost. Linhart's question 'What are we Carniolans?' makes good the claim for a new self-awareness. In these years the simple present of Vodnik's early verses, exemplified in his poem 'The satisfied Carniolan', was filled out with a claim to a past (Karantanian/Illyrian) and corresponding prospect of a future.[12]

Of course, aspiration is not achievement, though it is an essential precondition. Linhart said once he and his comrades were fools, dreaming their life away.[13] Ljubljana contemporaries commented that they would be ashamed to speak Slovene in an academy. Most manuscripts never reached publication. Linhart's Beaumarchais play was not performed. Many of Kopitar's scholarly theories were not borne out and his comforting argument that the Habsburg Monarchy was really a Slav state because it had a Slav majority (the so-called Austro-Slav idea) overlooked the determination of ruling elements to keep the Slavs in their place. In some ways the movement was too undeveloped for potential divisions to come to a head. Thus Vodnik could say that Linhard died reconciled to the Church while Kopitar claimed he died a freethinker. Cultural crumbs could be gained when harder facts of political and economic power remained unchallenged. But the decision to make culture and specifically language the ground of national self-definition was clear sighted if ambitious. Most of the correspondence of the figures cited here took place in German, and occasionally in French and Italian. Kopitar never published in Slovene because he did not think the language was yet ready for it. After all, no standard language or orthography to update the old Protestant forms emerged in this period. In Miroslav Hroch's famous typology of national awakening the land remained in stage A, in which a tiny circle of self-conscious patriots forms with as yet minimal response from the people they posit. Many patriots like Kopitar, Pohlin and Vodnik came from peasant stock but the mass remained in semi-servile limbo untouched by any impulse of 'civil society', for all the natural abilities Kumerdej saw in them, not implausibly in view of this peasantry's later development.

FIRST STIRRINGS OF MODERN WALES

Welsh readers will recognise several features of this process. The emergence of a group of educated enthusiasts concerned to enhance the status of their native culture recalls the Morris brothers and their circle. The role of the imperial capital where Linhart's intellectual life began and Kopitar's was played out is obvious in Wales too. Welsh historians have long noted the role of the French revolutionary years in Welsh experience. Yet this experience is harder to bring into a single narrative than with the Slovenes. There, linguistic preoccupations and the French revolutionary experience were linked in a common pattern of language-based national revival which mirrored processes taking place among other small Slav Habsburg societies, if at different tempos. The Czechs were a particularly important model. There were no similar narratives in the British context to help shape a patterning role. Thus the Welsh development was more diffuse. Industrial revolution was already making its mark in parts of Wales; Trieste's development as an international port on the fringe of Slovene ethnic territory, faster than Merthyr's, was to become very important later but it was still peripheral to Slovene national life. The key complicating factor, however, was religion. While clerical engagement, as has been shown, largely dovetailed with language patriotism in early Slovene development, in Wales it played a distinctive role from the start, which requires separate treatment from that of cultural regeneration.

Indeed, the term 'awakening' common to Welsh and Slovene historiography of the eighteenth century came in Wales to be associated with the religious movement rather than that of the patriotic intellectuals of the Morris circle. The latter's role in fostering Welsh nationhood has always been recognised, culminating in successive publications of their voluminous correspondence in the early twentieth century. But it has been somewhat overshadowed by the development of Welsh society and the 'radical tradition', with the self-activation of the *gwerin* or common people at its core, a self-activation sprung ultimately in the popular imagination from the religious revival of the eighteenth century. Writing in 1931 when this tradition, in its nonconformist-inspired form, was at its most self-confident, R. T. Jenkins pays tribute to the Morrises and their friends, yes, but notes that they were a small group which he unflatteringly labels a 'clique'. His classic account of the eighteenth century devotes considerably more attention to humbler kinds of cultural activity, like the hundreds of ballads often published in four- or eight-page booklets and the dozens of 'interludes' – short plays with stock characters and frequent social satire – which were likewise hawked about the countryside, as well as acted. In the context of this study his verdict offers an obvious starting-point for comparison.[14]

The Morris brothers, Lewis (1701–65), Richard (1703–79) and William (1705–63), sons of an Anglesey carter and farmer, were the nucleus of a group of correspondents sharing similar interests in Welsh language and antiquities. Like their Slovene counterparts (except Zois) their circle were not of elite origin, though more solidly rural in background. The clergymen in their ranks had a grammar school education – one of them (Edward Richard) ran such a school himself – but the brothers seem to have acquired some Latin and French through their own efforts while gaining clerical and technical skills which led Lewis and Richard into various government employments. Someone of Linhart's philosophical awareness was not to be found among them. It must be remembered that Welsh stirrings began nearly a generation before Slovene, in the rational pragmatism of mid-eighteenth-century Britain with its sense of advance over past prejudices. Within this framework its enlightenment was genuine. The eldest brother, Lewis Morris, whose official work produced his *Plans of Harbours, Bays and Roads in St George's and the Bristol Channel* (1748), was a man of encyclopedic interests in the spirit of the time ranging from mathematics, music, horticulture, husbandry and botany to machines and instruments of all kinds. His passion, though, was language and history. His criticism of previous Welsh scholars – the lexicographer Dr Davies for lack of knowledge of 'natural philosophy' and the scientist Edward Lhuyd for lack of knowledge of literature – plainly showed his hope that the present progressive age should unveil the Welsh and old British achievement in its full glory, which he claimed English antiquarians like Camden, in ignorance of the Welsh sources, had misrepresented.[15] An assiduous collector of such manuscript sources himself like all the brothers, possessed of an acute mind and shrewd judgement, he saw in the Society of the Cymmrodorion founded in 1751 by London

Welshmen – prominent among them his brother Richard – an instrument for a national project aping the Académie Française. A good poet himself in youth, he had the literary acumen to recognise the talents of his protégé, the brilliant young curate Goronwy Owen, to whom he looked for the revival of the classic poetry of Dafydd ap Gwilym and the Middle Ages. The spirit of the 'age of reason' helped inform his classicism and his distaste for Methodist 'enthusiasm'. It can be found also in the pastoral poetry of Edward Richard, one of the 'School of Welsh Augustans' in Saunders Lewis's appraisal of the literature of the period.[16]

The patronage of Goronwy Owen exemplified the Cymmrodorion's role as it saw it to encourage talent and assist publication of Welsh literary achievement, both for domestic and foreign audiences. Three collections of seventeenth- and eighteenth-century poetry appeared between 1759 and 1767. Evan Evans's *Specimens of the Poetry of the Ancient Welsh Bards* came out in 1764, followed in 1773 by *Gorchestion Beirdd Cymru*, likewise based on medieval manuscripts. A periodical publication of 1770 was short-lived as had been the first of this kind in Welsh, launched by Lewis Morris in 1735. Indeed, the Cymmrodorion's achievements fell rather short of its high aspirations, given that the two collections of 1759 owed less to it than to the efforts of poet-publishers whose Welsh Lewis Morris snobbishly disparaged. He himself never published the *Celtic Remains*, the life's work of his antiquarian studies, which only appeared a century after his death. Goronwy Owen produced some poetic gems but ultimately disappointed his admirers, emigrating to America and dying there relatively young at forty-six. Like Evan Evans his fate was to move between successive poorly paid curacies far from his native land, his talents unrecognised by his superiors. Both succumbed to drink. Evan Evans's scathing attack on the negative role of English bishops in Wales was another work not published in its author's lifetime. The tendency for work of the early patriots to remain in manuscript is something noted above in the Slovene case, part no doubt of the burden of the non-dominant condition, at least in the first stages of cultural revival. In Wales such travails, allied with Lewis Morris's snobbery, can lend support to R. T. Jenkins's tepid assessment of his movement's role. In comparative context, however, the significance of the Morris circle's ambitions is not to be denied. Lewis Morris's excitement at the discovery of the manuscript of the Gododdin, the perhaps as early as the seventh-century heroic poem of resistance to the Anglo-Saxon invaders (equal to Columbus's discovery of America, and the poem itself to

Homer and Virgil!); the intensity of Goronwy Owen's concern that Welsh with its great traditions should lag behind 'such novices' in poetry as the English and French: all this speaks to a culture's legitimate right, indeed essential need, to take itself seriously, dare to set itself in high company and be intellectually stirred by its own potential.[17] Only so can it validate itself in other's eyes – and its own. The intellectual excitement of the Morris circle's activity and its relative success in forging links beyond Wales is justification of its fame.

The Cymmrodorion left a legacy. While its role lapsed into that of social club – it later revived and still flourishes – it was followed in 1770 by the Gwyneddigion Society with activist aims and despite its name contacts all over Wales. It was the Gwyneddigion who took an English vicar to court for breach of the 1563 Act requiring clergy in Welsh-speaking parishes to know Welsh;[18] the eisteddfods it sponsored stimulated the revival of the eisteddfodic institution; and its publications – of Dafydd ap Gwilym (1790), the elegies of Llywarch Hen (1792) and the three-volume Myvyrian Archaiology (1801–7) – substantially rounded off the Cymmrodorion goal to see the medieval poetic heritage in print. The achievement was doubly remarkable, in the magnificent originals and their laborious recapture. Few European literatures can boast such a record and certainly none of the small nations with which Wales might be compared, Icelandic and Irish prose no doubt excepted. The musical heritage was also being made available, for example, in Edward Jones's researches. Blind John Parry was harpist to the future George IV, part of a general rise of interest in Wales attested by a host of travelogues enthused for its scenery and story in a budding romantic age. Even the unromantic, and unimpressed, Dr Johnson made the journey. The two societies described above were only part of a wave of bodies literary, musical, antiquarian and charitable which reflected the changing climate of the time.

It is not surprising in these circumstances that Welsh patriots should have seen their country's cultural heritage as their trump card in restoring the name of a small, poor country increasingly marginalised in England's rise to great power status. Nationhood was to be vindicated through the past. This was the overriding concern of men like Lewis Morris. His passion for the Welsh language lies there, in its reputation rather than its present and future prospects. More than his brothers he corresponded very largely in English except to contacts who habitually used Welsh themselves, like Dafydd Jones, Trefriw, the plebeian publisher whom he despised. Anticipating criticism on this score he once excused himself on the grounds that his milieu was largely English, a weak argument when he was working at the time in rural Cardiganshire, and one belied by the different practice of his London-based brother Richard who made only one visit to Wales in the last forty years of his life. There is social vanity here. Lewis Morris enjoyed playing the Welsh in/outsider with privileged knowledge in correspondence with English antiquarians whom he privately ridiculed for ignorance of Welsh texts. Yet it was an English scholar from whom he took the idea that a seventh-century figure, one Tysilio, might be the author of a history of the Britons, whom he then adopted and championed vehemently, on negligible grounds, as the true native source for Geoffrey of Monmouth's history, denied by the English.[19] The combative concern for English people's opinion is all but obsessive in the brothers, and may have inhibited publication, for fear of English criticism. Richard's term for them (plant Alis, the children of Alice, Alice being the legendary sister of the Saxon invader Hengist through whom the British leader Vortigern was betrayed) reveals the ancient hurt at conquest at the heart of his and others' psyche. The relationship of Celt to Saxon was fully matched by that between German and Slav, but the Welsh case had a dimension not really present in the Slovene, rooted in Welsh memories of two peoples' unequal struggle for mastery in 'the matter of Britain' a thousand years before. Yet, and this is a crucial qualification, memory of the past had no bearing on the present. Throughout the Morris correspondence there is no hint of anything but loyalty to the current establishment, to Great Britain, the Monarchy, the Church of England: all was endorsed with the satisfaction of citizens of a prestigious state in an enlightened age. Ancient heart searchings over the loss of the 'sovereignty of Britain' to the Saxons, reaching on to the prophetic poetry of the fifteenth century, had been salved by the accession of the Tudor dynasty of Welsh origin to the English throne in 1485 and still more by the spiritual blessings of Protestantism. The consummation for enlightened spirits was now the constitutional freedom of the British state and the prospects for progress of the age. Here Welsh thinking was quite aligned with English perspectives. The influential *History of Wales* (1786) offered by the English author William Warrington spoke warmly of the bravery and suffering of the medieval Welsh in the face of English injustice but contrasted it with the unity and amity that now obtained.[20] The numerous tourists and guidebooks of the dawning romantic age followed suit. Thus J. J. Evans, seeing Wales truly as a 'historic country', could write feelingly of the 'oppression and cruelty' of the past but add that people now lived 'in a time when the nature of society is much better understood', so that 'the great mass of the people are admitted into the background of the national picture'.[21]

Confirmation of this lopsided relationship can be seen in a significant and in some ways more admirable figure than Lewis Morris, the enterprising Caernarfonshire estate steward and man of parts William Williams, Llandegai (1738–1817). Williams was a stonemason's son brought up in an area where several literary clergy and a number of minor poets were active and contacts existed with the Morrises. He himself was the virtual founder of the north Wales slate industry on the Penrhyn estate he served, author of English books on the Snowdon mountains and Caernarfonshire and a Welsh history of Wales after 1282, together with a voluminous body of passable Welsh verse original and translated, land surveys, genealogies, theological reflections, biography, topography and ethnography. This appeared in a large number of local journals and newspapers though the bulk remained in manuscript, where his notes could cover matters as various as seventeenth-century British population, European translations of the Bible, the identity of Homer and Luther's biography. Private comments on landowners' conduct and their tenants' difficulties were often severe; Williams feared current trends risked social unrest. But no hint of this attitude is to be found in his published English work and reports to his superiors, while his own enterprise contributed to the social changes he criticised. A similar disjuncture appears in his response to the cultural campaign against the monoglot English vicar Thomas Bowles mentioned above. 'There has been turmoil and conflict between us and the English in every age' was his comment, noting 'the laws to abolish our language since their first arrival in our kingdom' and the 'shameful lies' of 'the thieving English in our midst' – but all this had only helped preserve the language, as demonstrated by the 'well-organised, impeccable and scholarly' Welsh magazine just published (1770).[22] Williams saw the English as a 'new nation ... sprung from different invading depredators' with an unstable language and insipid music.[23] But Welsh people, considering the disorderly past under native princes, should not grumble at what they might sometimes feel as oppression, or react like the French who lacked Britain's sound laws and freedoms. If only the wealthy enjoyed this freedom and inequality reigned, how and where under a just providence could this inconsistency be righted? Posing the question confirmed the need for the other world religion offered.[24] Williams's own religion was one of rational tolerance and good will, but as a fair-minded observer he noted that the Methodists he criticised had made people more moral and provident.

Williams's multifarious concerns reveal an intellectually alert figure touched by the conservatism of his milieu and the caution of the subaltern who knew his place. He has been described as the type of Welshman who cloaks anti-English feeling in a British context, 'knocking the English and praising Great Britain'.[25] Certainly there is an austere diffidence in his Welsh patriotism characteristic of this position. 'If the preservation of the Welsh nation and their language from utter extinction may be deemed of any value' was how he prefaced his tribute to the role of Snowdonia and its inhabitants as a bulwark in Welsh history.[26] He had a lively distrust of the common people and their susceptibility to disorder and affray, which made the union with England under the Welsh Tudor dynasty ultimately a positive feature of his book on Welsh history for all the pride in the 'valour' shown in preceding centuries. That said, and reassurance given his contemporary readers that they were living in better times, he was free to describe in vivid terms English harshness and deceit and belabour members of the Welsh upper classes who betrayed their inheritance by marrying out and opening the way for alien values.

William Williams outlived the Napoleonic wars. He and the Morris brothers were the products of a rural society which did not experience the outer world with the directness of a Ljubljana, short-lived capital of French-ruled Illyria. Yet the wide-ranging Welsh response to the French Revolution showed how Wales had developed in the previous forty years and how far its literary and historical traditions still put it ahead of the Slovene lands in terms of autonomous activity. In the 1790s Welsh book publication was more than double that of the sixties, to nearly five hundred, but in political material exceeded it sixfold.[27] In just three years (1793–6), with Britain at war with France, three periodicals of radical tendencies appeared, two in south and one in north Wales, in which the origins of the French Revolution were traced, radical literature discussed, both political and religious (Deism) and a translation of the Marseillaise published. The influence – and financial support – of the Gwyneddigion in London remained strong, however. This was a period of vigorous literary publishing activity by them, aided by a London Welsh Maecenas, the successful businessman Owain Myfyr (Owen Jones), in financial terms a Welsh Zois. The radical Clerkenwell innkeeper John Jones (Jac Glan-y gors), author of Welsh pamphlets setting out the essentials of Tom Paine's message and in Wales Thomas Richards in his *Cwyn yn erbyn Gorthrymder* (A Charge against Oppression) detailed peasant resentment of church tithes, landlord exactions and the abuses of a legal system in an unknown language. The background was rising population pressure, increased pressure on small farmers (the shift to annual tenancies), recurrent dearths (1794–5, 1799–1801) and crisis in the mid-Wales cloth industry. Those affected were not only the very poor but farmers, artisans and skilled workers, a section of the population particularly open to radicalisation in times of unrest as these were Europe-wide. Gwyn Williams's vivid account of the 1790s posits that a revolutionary period is precisely one which can awake imaginations and heighten chords of popular sentiment.[28]

This speaks out in the most important of the radical periodicals, *Cylchgrawn Cynmraeg* (The Welsh Language Journal, 1793–4) and its editor, the Baptist minister Morgan John Rhys (1760–1804). Active in the valleys of Glamorgan and Monmouthshire on behalf of Sunday and day schools, Welsh-language education and opposition to the slave trade, Rees came from the area of incipient industrialisation which was to play so big a part in Welsh life thereafter. His enthusiasm for the French Revolution and expedition to Paris in 1791–2 where he distributed Bibles and sought to propagate his form of non-dogmatic Christianity reflects the ferment of ideas of political and religious freedom on the British nonconformist left and his own Welsh national background. Within a religious framework which identified the French Revolution with the overthrow of papal and monarchical tyranny the five numbers of *Cylchgrawn Cynmraeg* lambasted persecution and state-imposed establishment of religion; it made the case for press freedom, parliamentary reform and the people as the source of power; it asked (in no. 4) why the Welsh should be hewers of wood and drawers of water who alone of peoples learnt other languages before their own. In a private letter Rhys urged that it was no time for churches to squabble on incidentals, but 'to unite against the common enemy of mankind, ignorance and prejudice'.[29]

The *Cylchgrawn* was sailing close to the wind in a political climate rapidly veering to reaction, in which Gwyneddigion contacts with English radicals aroused anxiety in some London Welsh circles. Rhys himself criticised the direction taken by Robespierre; his ideal was actually America, 'the new world, the habitation of justice established by God on the earth'; he praised the young republic's aid in corn to the embattled French.[30] The

1790s saw moves for emigration by the discontented intertwine with inflation of the long-standing myth of a twelfth-century Welsh prince Madog discovering America. It had been adopted by English propaganda at the outset of English imperial visions in the Elizabethan age and fed by later reports of Spaniards and others of pale-skinned Indian tribes in America's interior who could be Madog's descendants, all the more so as they had been overheard by Welsh travellers to speak perfect Welsh! At a time of heightened competition between France, Spain and Britain to find a route from the prairies to the Pacific and control of the fur trade, Welsh spokespeople hoped for support from the American government for expeditions to locate the Madogions. Morgan John Rhys was involved; the profits of the *Cylchgrawn Cynmraeg* were to be dedicated to this quest. Though the *Cylchgrawn* folded for financial reasons, the movement led to the young John Evans's pioneering exploration of the whole length of the Mississippi and Missouri (1796–7), but no Welsh Indians. Ohio became a centre of nineteenth-century Welsh settlement, where a Madog museum exists today. Morgan John Rhys himself emigrated to America, with aspirations to found a Welsh settlement in Pennsylvania, which however foundered before he died there in 1804, bequeathing in his descendants a succession of American educationalists and college principals. Both he and Evans benefited from a network of prior Welsh nonconformist settlement in touch with the homeland. He had learnt hard lessons but not wholly lost the idealism of an address on American Independence Day in 1795, certainly not his passionate anti-slavery commitment: 'Invincible Frenchmen, go on! ... Combined sons of freedom, go on! ... Ancient Britons! Awake out of your sleep! ...Why are your tyrants great? Because you kneel down and cringe to them. Rise up – you are their equals. If you cannot rise, creep to the ocean and the friendly waves will waft you over the Atlantic. Quit the despotic little island which gave you birth and leave the tyrants and slaves of your country to live and die together.'[31]

A more direct inheritance to modern Wales, though also based on myth, was the Gorsedd of Bards, now central to the modern Welsh National Eisteddfod, but in the mind of its inventor Edward Williams (Iolo Morganwg) an institution of the ancient British druids. The first Gorsedd was held on Primrose Hill in London in 1792. Iolo Morganwg (1747–1826) is one of the most remarkable figures of modern Welsh history. Correspondent of the Morris brothers, key figure in the Gwyneddigion's publications, the eisteddfodic movement and the

Madog affair (on which he lectured to the Royal Society), he had a hand in all aspects of the cultural tale told here. His story echoes others in the romantic age but is in totality inimitable. In part it recalls Linhart. Both were fully bilingual – Iolo's childhood home in the Vale of Glamorgan was actually English-speaking – and at one point aspired to make their name as poets in the dominant language in the capital. Brissot, the French Girondin leader, was one of the subscribers for Iolo's *Poems, Lyric and Pastoral* (London, 1794). Both, too, combined political and religious radicalism. Iolo became a Unitarian. But education shows a characteristic difference. Whereas Linhart had conventional Gymnasium training, Iolo claimed to have learnt his letters from observation of his father who was, as he became, a stone mason. He built on this through the network of scholars and poets existing in his native Glamorgan, as in many parts of Wales, initially through a master of Welsh metres in his home village, then the distinguished lexicographer John Walters, vicar in nearby Cowbridge, and the poets of upland Glamorgan like John Bradfield, a correspondent of Lewis Morris. Spells in London in the 1770s and 1790s saw his cooperation with the Gwyneddigion. In another guise, Iolo Morganwg recalls the brilliant young forger-poet Chatterton, or, more appositely, the Czech Hanka whose patriotic forgeries of alleged Czech medieval poetry were revealed – by Hanka himself – in 1817. Iolo's own, extensive, medieval forgeries were meant to bear out his bardic theories and elevate Glamorgan as the fountain head of Welsh poetry. Their excellence owed much to his voluminous discoveries of real manuscripts in the course of extensive journeys through Wales. He took laudanum through his long life.[32]

Let Iolo be left now in his cottage in Flemingston, filled to the rafters with his notes and manuscripts, for the great part unpublished in his lifetime. Suffice to say here that the nascent radicalism of the Gwyneddigion and the journalism of the 1790s, never systematically formulated, did not survive the hardening official crackdown from the middle of that decade, any more than the far stronger ranks of English dissent. At the same time, in 1795, conspirators were put on trial in Vienna and some shot, including Baron Siegfried von Taufferer from the Slovene lands. In Wales the authorities' persecution of Baptists for alleged complicity in the failed French landing in Pembrokeshire in 1797 and the imprisonment in 1803 of Thomas Evans, Unitarian minister and former radical editor, were warning shots. But in both countries there was no support for insurrection. In Wales the leading Methodist Thomas Jones of Denbigh published 10,000 copies of *Gair yn ei Amser* (A Timely Word), his answer to Jac Glan-y-gors. Against some liberal voices of dissenting ministers, Baptists, Congregationalists and in particular Unitarians, was ranged the rising religious force in the land, Methodism, which Gwyn Williams sees as stifling the 'new and semi-political Welsh "nation" which had clawed itself into semi-existence' in the 1790s.[33] This must next be addressed.

THE RELIGIOUS TURN

For many Welsh readers, like the present writer, the Methodist revival may first have been evoked by the story of William Williams Pantycelyn's conversion in a Breconshire churchyard through a sermon by Howel Harris in 1738, the traditional date, though it may have been a year earlier. The scene introduces two of the three leading figures of the movement: its chief writer Williams and its best-known organiser Harris. The third, with Harris its most famous preacher whose vast audiences in open-air meetings came from far and wide, was Daniel Rowland, whom both men met around this time. All were in their early twenties. A fourth man, the already mentioned Griffith Jones, vicar and circulating schools organiser, aged fifty-five, may be added as an inspirational influence for these young men, but he soon dissociated from the budding movement, embarrassed by its slackening ties with the official Anglican Church. This was illustrated by the fact that Harris's sermon above was preached outside Talgarth church itself in Talgarth church graveyard; many clergymen were banning their pulpits to the new 'enthusiasts' dubbed 'Methodists' and like Rowland and Harris favoured open air preaching. The setting up of Methodist *seiadau* (societies) meeting in other places, even, already (in Rowland's case) new buildings of their own, was to be minutely documented by Welsh religious historians over following generations, as the split with the religious establishment became a major feature of Welsh life and Welsh nonconformity was viewed as something specifically Welsh. It is easy to overlook the extent to which the Methodist movement was part of a more general religious awakening in Protestant countries, not just in England, where John Wesley launched his campaigns a couple of years after Harris. The major revival in New England in the 1730s had been preceded by twelve more local ones between 1712 and 1732. Lutheran Pietism, starting from A. N. Francke's reforms in Halle, had enthused the SPCK; Francke is one of the few foreigners referred to in Lewis Morris's correspondence.[34] It is possible to see the tendencies as an extension of the Reformation seen over a longer term, as attempts to found comprehensive state churches foundered and perspectives opened for freer worship. The reaction of pious young men to an underlying groundswell of educated scepticism as 'enlightenment' gained strength should not be excluded either.

The dramatic nature of the revival, the twenty thousand claimed to have attended some of Rowlands's open-air sermons, have often been described. Only the bare bones of Welsh methodism's development are needed in this general survey: the institutional growth in the 1740s; leadership split between 1752 and 1763; and renewed advance till the end of the century. Doctrinal squabbles inherent in Protestantism and apparent in Welsh Methodism's Calvinism as opposed to Wesley's were a matter of emphasis rather than hostility: at crucial points, though, they impeded formal union out of fear that this would give controversialists in each camp more opportunity to make trouble. It was not specifically a Welsh–English issue; the English Calvinist leader George Whitefield lost out to Wesley.

What need immediate emphasis here are continuity of institutional success and Methodist achievement in training a population open to Protestant goals of biblical literacy in the mother tongue. Far better than the Morrises, eisteddfodic and radical circles religious revivalism survived the passage of generations and the revolutionary and Napoleonic inter-regnum. Harris died in 1773, Rowland and Williams at the start of the 1790s. In a second generation Thomas Charles (1755–1814) and Thomas Jones, Denbigh (1756–1820) both as writers and in Charles's case also as brilliant organiser, sustained the success. Between them they composed a series of manuals, translations, theological treatises and a massive diction-ary of all words in the Welsh Bible, founded a monthly journal, *Y Drysorfa* (1799–1801), instigated and were active in the British and Foreign Bible Society, and steered through the Welsh Methodists' formal break from the Church of England to become an independent denomination in 1811, a generation after Wesley's Methodists had taken this step in England. Till this point they and all those mentioned above had been ordained Anglican clergymen who performed no Church services except to baptise and marry their Methodist followers, to whom they confined their work. By 1811, their numbers were becoming too thin to perform these tasks for an expanding flock and the need to ordain their preachers became pressing for even conservative-minded people reluctant to see themselves

as 'nonconformists'. Charles's signal accomplishment was his reorganisation of Griffith Jones's Welsh circulating schools which had lapsed after
Jones's successor as patron had died in 1779. Now as permanent Sunday
schools, open to all ages, they were to become a fixture of Welsh cultural
life followed by all denominations, including Anglicans. Indeed, what is
called the Methodist revival had spread by 1800 in its essential features to
long-standing Baptist and Congregational bodies which had experienced
a great increase of membership on the same scale as the Methodists.

Thomas Charles's role as educator had been anticipated in unique
form by William Williams (1717–91), better known as Pantycelyn after
the Carmarthenshire home where he was born. Probably the most remarkable figure of the revival, Pantycelyn is today best remembered for the
thousand or more hymns he composed, which brilliantly expressed its
main themes in lyrical form. Their purpose was strictly educative: to depict
the sorrowful state of the common people in the desert of hardship and
want, the sufferings of the crucified Christ, the blood of the lamb by which
salvation might be won, the trials of the Christian pilgrim striving not to
stray, and the beauties of the heavenly prospect for which his soul yearned.
All this drew on vivid imagery reflecting Pantycelyn's consummate ability
to paint natural landscape and the music of the saints to correspond to
every facet of the believer's heightened consciousness, the whole tautly
expressed in simple yet eloquent language with apt attention to the movement's theology. Yet his hymns were only part of Pantycelyn's prodigious
output, which included two book-length poems outlining the Christian's
spiritual journey in epic terms and several extensive prose treatises on various aspects of the religious life, most notably *Drws y Society Profiad* (The
Door of the Society of Experience) detailing how skilled interlocutors in
the *seiadau* central to Methodist practice might probe the state of individual minds and hearts with a view to conversion and its maintenance.
The psychological insights displayed in these works Pantycelyn had gained
on his continual travels, on foot and horseback, throughout Wales all his
life. Yet from the point of view of this study Pantycelyn's most interesting
production was his ambitious large-scale work *Pantheologia: sef Hanes Holl
Grefyddau'r Byd* (Pantheologia: namely The History of All the Religions
of the World), published in 1762.

In *Pantheologia* we see that Pantycelyn, the educated Anglican clergyman, too, belongs to the Enlightenment and shares many of its values.
His introduction deplores Welsh ignorance, the fact that (here he uses a

familiar small nation trope) no other part of Europe has so few books in its own language on matters of church and state or the sciences studied by others. Ignorance is the source of partiality and prejudice, particularly in matters of religion. Monoglot Welsh people do not know that the only difference between themselves and the abhorred Turk is a matter of religious principle, or what country things they eat, drink and wear come from. His goal is to show that only God's grace operating on the inner man, not externals, leads to faith in Christ; should this not succeed, his task is more than worth-while if his book gets people to read Welsh and seek knowledge, perhaps leading them to consult books which will have more effect on their souls. Williams's work was based on extensive reading, sometimes of out-of-date sources; it is thinnest on Buddhism, with emphasis on Buddhist monks and nothing on the Buddha; Hinduism appears as Brahmism. Non-Christian, indeed non-Protestant, beliefs are routinely condemned in formal judgement but only after being set out with seeming objectivity and in considerable detail. It is the anthropological, geographical, economic and political copiousness which is most striking, in the text and often very lengthy footnotes. The author's curiosity is insatiable as he moves from west African pagan societies, pre-Columbian and north America, India and Indo-China, Indonesia and the Philippines to China, Japan and finally the Muslim world (including pre-Muslim Persia and Egypt) before turning to Judaism and Catholicism. To take one example, he discusses at length where the native peoples of America came from, showing awareness of scholarly theories that lands now separate may once have been joined together.[35] His comments on the slave trade are humane while he notes the role of African chiefs. He does not spare European settlers who do a disservice to Christianity. In view of the cool view taken of religious enthusiasm in modern secular society, including Wales, and the clichéd image of the Methodist movement, the fresh impression of a subtle, inquiring mind made by this book and by extension Pantycelyn's oeuvre in general needs to be recorded. Pantycelyn's own disappointment at its tepid reception by his intended audience needs all the more to be recorded too. He concluded that Welsh people were not interested in his attempt to widen their horizons. More, he resolved to confine himself to the direct work of salvation only, not, he made plain, out of lack of interest in the world of nature and secular things, but as a mark of his commitment to the ultimate cause of religion. This, in the context of the national comparison being attempted here, was a significant choice, made by a passionate man. It foreshadowed similar tendencies in Welsh publishing. Yet *Pantheologia* shows the great variety of Welsh mental activity in the Enlightenment period.

TOWARDS A COMPARISON

In the period covered in this chapter both societies under review had moved some way from the placid uneventfulness of the earlier eighteenth century. Cultural and associational activity quickened markedly, albeit in Slovenia from a low previous level; the Slovene lands were temporarily thrust onto a wider stage by the French and Napoleonic wars; industrialisation got under way in south-east Wales. It was only a start. Much of the work of would-be patriots did not find publication or performance and men like Vodnik readily enough reverted to Austrian norms. Two aspects stand out for special comment, both of which reflected native initiative but which owed something to the ambience of their respective states: the Slovene linguistic movement and the emergence of Methodism and wider religious dissent in Wales.

Welsh observers cannot but be struck by the speed and seeming cohesion of Slovene language development. In 1779, the first ever book of Slovene poetry was published and within a generation a modern Slovene play was performed in the Carniolan capital, some hundreds of governmental regulations translated, an official government newspaper published, posts for Slovene in leading educational institutions set up and a start made on school textbooks, giving the language a public role Welsh only attained much later.[36]

Of course, the extent of Welsh literary and publicistic activity still greatly exceeded Slovene. Popular literacy had advanced dramatically as a result of the circulating and later Sunday school movements. The pamphlets of Jac Glan-y-gors and Thomas Richards on land questions and Morgan John Rhys in the incipiently industrialising area, together with the spread of Methodism, had no parallels among a passive semi-servile Slovene rural population. The activities of the Cymmrodorion and Gwyneddigion societies in London went a long way to make good the absence in Wales of a natural cultural centre like Ljubljana. Against all this the greater attention to Slovene as a medium of public day-school education was a merely potential factor which one stresses only in hindsight. The Sunday schools taught vastly more pupils than attended day schools in the two countries, and they worked with the state-sanctioned power of religion as a public good behind them. They taught only the reading of the Welsh Bible, not secular subjects, but at this time state-sponsored primary education had a heavily religious flavour and was intended by the authorities and certainly Habsburg Josephinism to inculcate values of orderliness and obedience to the powers that be. Actually, parents in both Wales and Slovenia at this time mostly saw primary schools as means for their children to learn English or German to get on in the world. Reformers who wanted mother-tongue teaching for reasons of patriotism and/or practicality also existed in both countries, though more mutedly in Wales. Austria was one of the first countries to attempt mass primary education and its polyglot nature made the pattern favoured, initial education in the vernacular and the dominant language thereafter and in the larger towns, seem appropriate. It is still the pattern in many ex-colonies in Africa. Slovene advocates of mother tongue schooling on this basis – they asked little more than this as yet – therefore went with the grain of official policy to a large extent. Welshmen who inclined to similar views like Morgan John Rhys, Walter Davies and William Williams, Llandegai, faced on the other hand a British climate which was not multicultural and had no support. The association of Welsh with the Sunday school and English with the day school made the very success of the former ironically a barrier to changing the latter.

In these circumstances the emphasis among most Welsh patriots as opposed to Slovene was on cultural tradition rather than language as such. The greater historicity of Welsh tradition plainly played a role here. Welsh literary development meant that linguistic standardisation, already well advanced, did not provide the challenge which in Arnold Toynbee's famous model could provoke response, leading to Slovene aspirations to extend Slovene's public role. The Morris circle seem to have accepted totally the dominance of English in this sphere. They found history surer ground for an essentially defensive national pride. In this way, Welsh tradition could act as a block to forward-looking visions. Slovene adaptability once the idea of language revival had been mooted rested in part on the limited baggage from the past. Mother-tongue primary education proved to be a more potent tool than most people could imagine.

The historian Prys Morgan stresses likewise this theme of the negative potential of tradition in Welsh cultural remembering, the Welsh literati's debilitating sense of loss of moorings to a known past, the erosion of old ways and creeping absorption into a civilisation not their own. His vast knowledge of the exchanges of a host of forgotten figures shows the extent of this brooding on a national heritage, lacking a uniting focus. Morgan gives it, however, perhaps a rather generalised slant. Nostalgia for the past is a universal trait, as is the sense that one's age is seeing the disappearance of old customs. Linhart's history of Carniola opens with the latter trope.[37] Morgan's examples of cultural decline are drawn from a wide time span, from the late seventeenth into the nineteenth century so that, like the growth of the bourgeoisie, it is hard to pin-point their individual force; terms like 'tragedy', 'deep sense of loss' and 'decaying way of life' risk being overdrawn or applicable to any gentry class in the transition to modern society.[38] Actual figures of the renaissance like Lewis Morris and William Williams, Llandegai, were men of active temperament, positive towards the progress of the day.

Yet if the case is drawn comparatively, to consider the specific nature of the challenge the dominant culture posed Welsh society and of the Anglo-English relationship, then the role of Welsh tradition becomes more clear-cut. It weakened the emulative aspect which characterised not just the Slovene but other small east-central European peoples' response to their situation. These peoples faced dominant cultures – German, Russian (but also Swedish or Hungarian) – which were themselves consciously engaged, à la Frederick and Catherine the Great or Joseph II, in emulating west European models. Enlightenment was a regional modernising process, in opposition to patterns from which Germans and Russians wished to free themselves. The smaller nations could, albeit with a time-lag and great difficulty, adopt many of the attitudes and techniques of this forward-looking modernisation to themselves. English enlightenment, however, was a more diffuse phenomenon: England was already a modern society, with a richly embedded and developed culture sustained by a (in European terms) progressive aristocracy and large middle class. Any blueprint as to which aspects of its complexity might best be followed by subalterns was less clear. It is not surprising that a sparse Welsh intelligentsia should look to their past, not seeking emulation but even claiming, as in Iolo Morganwg's case, a would-be cultural superiority to the Anglo-Saxon late-comers. Welsh culture, as Lewis Morris presented it, framed its heritage in rather arcane terms which aroused some interest among historically minded, antiquarian-orientated coteries in the dominant culture, but at the cost of not being taken seriously by that culture as a whole.

This verdict is no doubt too sharp. The Welsh eighteenth-century cultural turn did establish a new profile for Wales in educated English eyes, different from that of the bucolic squire and primitive peasantry: William Owen Pughe was a friend of the poet Laureate Robert Southey and was awarded a doctorate by Oxford University for his translation of Milton's *Paradise Lost*. The foundation was laid for important features of later Welsh life, like the Eisteddfod institution and the Welsh engagement with music. The Welsh movement did adopt the centrepiece of Enlightenment civil society, the practice of association of all kinds, whose spread to Wales itself made Welsh society less dependent on London. Nor were other small nationalities taken too seriously by larger cultures. But two negatives must be upheld. The intellectual foundations of Welsh cultural claims were faulty. Tysilio's alleged sixth-century manuscript as corner-stone of Geoffrey of Monmouth and the 'matter of Britain' was a figment of Lewis Morris's fond dreams. His and his brother Richard's insistence on the unchanging nature of the Welsh language through history was philologically crude. Indeed, Welsh philology regressed over the century from Edward Lhuyd's insights. Mistaken notions like the Breton scholar Paul-Yves Pezron's theory of roots, Iolo Morganwg's fanciful conception of an ancient British alphabet and Pughe's wrong-headed understanding of language do not bear comparison with Kopitar's work, which stood in the classical tradition of modern linguistic science developing under German auspices. Pughe's Welsh grammar gave as a paradigm for comparison of adjectives Welsh words corresponding to 'good, gooder, goodest', though he did make a gesture to reality by adding the actual terms 'good, better, best' in brackets afterwards. Many of the coinages in his voluminous dic-tionary were happy contributions to what became part of modern Welsh vocabulary but others were pedantic follies, and his translation of *Paradise Lost* was so idiosyncratic it is widely considered unreadable.[39]

The second negative was the weight of the legacy of defeat at the heart of the English–Welsh relationship, as reflected in Richard Morris's references to 'plant Alis' mentioned above. It is hard not to see in this an ongoing sense of embattlement against heavy odds, a habit of pessimism repeated in eighteenth-century assessments of the linguistic situation which are out of line with what seems to have been the reality. Thus Lewis Morris speaks of the English environment of his work in Cardiganshire and derides the Welsh of John Bradfield's Glamorganshire, Williams Llandegai says that Anglesey is half English. Yet the affair of vicar Bowles in Anglesey shows only five of his five hundred parishioners as knowing English.[40] Admittedly this was the heartland, the Welsh Carniola. But English travelers found Welsh monoglots omnipresent in the south too and people who 'sedulously' kept up the language as a distinction from England, though they assumed that better roads would relatively soon reduce it to the state of Cornish.[41] What lay behind all this? There is certainly evidence of erosion of Welsh in border counties in the second half of the century, proceeding furthest in Radnorshire, but affecting parts of Breconshire, Montgomeryshire and Monmouthshire. Goronwy Owen raged against a young Montgomeryshire curate who said there was nothing worth reading in Welsh and it was daily losing ground.[42] The pioneer socialist Robert Owen, born in 1771 apparently without the language in Newtown where it had been spoken in 1732, suggests an advance of English along the upper Severn valley in the interval. Elsewhere, however, statements about the decline of Welsh can only have related to its decline among the educated classes from which these statements came rather than in the general population. Interesting social assumptions arise here. Historians of nationalism in eastern Europe emphasise the cult of the common people, particularly the peasantry, as part of its rhetoric. Mere rhetoric is what it often was, but even as rhetoric it is not prominent in the writings of eighteenth-century Welsh patriots. It is a sign of the Enlightenment that the romanticisation of the common man had not yet triumphed over the aspiration towards civility and urbanity. English opinion was very important to the Morris circle. Goronwy's half-jesting outburst over the curate just mentioned was because the 'young urchin ... a wicked Imp' had let him down before an Englishman who had introduced him to Goronwy as a fellow-countryman. Insecurity vis-à-vis the traditional overlord characterised all non-dominant European peoples, particularly early in the process of self-assertion, but it was especially strong in the Welsh case.

This analysis lends some support to R. T. Jenkins's lukewarm appraisal of the Morris circle's contribution to the emergence of modern Wales. By the same token it directs attention to Jenkins's own heroes, the common people of the Nonconformist *gwerin*. Religion, source of consolation in hardship for the masses and mediator of what ideas reached them, was almost certainly closer to the bulk of the population in both our societies. Its fortunes, as with language, reflect the wider circumstances of the two great states in which they lived. Uniformity was the pattern in Austria.

When the fervour of Counter-Reformation Catholicism declined in the eighteenth-century the habits of religious uniformity remained. Less than one per cent reverted to Protestantism when religious toleration was introduced under Joseph II and it had negligible effect in the Slovene lands. Protestantism existed only in the small Slovene minority in Hungary which developed its own literary language at this time and retained it till 1918. Under Austrian enlightened absolutism Slovene church politics meant chiefly a tussle between a regime anxious to get diocesan boundaries into line with administrative ones, and bishops jealous of their traditional rights. Josephinism effectively made the Church an instrument of state policy. A kind of bargain resulted in which the state closed down large numbers of 'contemplative' monasteries which lacked 'useful' educative or health functions in enlightened eyes, while using their revenues to fund many new parishes. This was a more efficient and principled system than that of the Anglican state church in Wales, whose defects like pluralism of non-resident clergy had much to do with the rise of Methodism. However, it weakened the missionary spirit of the Church, without the safety valve of dissent which Protestantism afforded. It is important for our comparison that the Slovene national movement developed at a time when Austrian Catholicism was closest in temper as a social force to middle-of-the-road Anglicanism. Anglicans naturally tended to look askance at the rise of Methodism both in England and Wales, but the habits of British constitutionalism prevailed and a slippage away from the established church took place unimaginable in Habsburg Austria.

Methodists were technically Anglican Church members till 1811 in Wales, so unlike Baptists and Congregationalists not 'dissenters'. But their de facto separate status was recognised well before that. Early hostility and persecution had softened, though it was not forgotten. The comment of the Revd John Evans, an Anglican, on north Wales in 1798 reflects a general impression: 'Religion appears among this people to be what it really is, the most important concern of man.'[43] William Williams, Llandegai, another Anglican, confirmed approval of dissent for its good effect on public morals and order. Though the term 'Methodist revival' has stuck, Methodism energised Baptists and Congregationalists in equal measure. These denominations had never been as insignificant as later historians made them in building up the Methodist revival as a national turning point, but in the earlier eighteenth century they had shown the alternation in Protestantism between evangelical fervour and rationalist quietude.

Previously dissenting congregations, particularly Presbyterians, had drifted towards prioritising Jesus's role in the trinity (Arianism) till some moved out of trinitarianism altogether to a Unitarian theology. This tendency was reversed under the impact of Methodist emotionalism. The surviving Unitarian stronghold in central Cardiganshire was to become known as 'the Black Spot' to pious orthodox believers. It has produced a disproportionate number of radical Welsh figures, including the nineteenth-century poet Gwilym Marles, great-uncle of Dylan Thomas who was given his middle name from him.

The improved social behaviour for which William Williams praised Methodism was to mark Welsh mores. Gone, largely, were the unruly popular customs associated with Sundays in the diary of William Bulkeley in the first half of the eighteenth century. Yet this process, so associated with a distinctive Welsh puritanism, was part of a general turn in the later eighteenth century towards public and self-discipline. The Czech peasant diarist František Jan Vavák (1741–1816) stressed these qualities. The transition to the modern era tended to increase workloads – Austrian statistics record a fall in military recruits' height in this period – and people worked harder to keep up living standards. Bishop Herberstein's Jansenist seriousness was part of the same syndrome. In Wales the Methodist movement proved crucial to the earnest climate of the nineteenth century which helped further the self-expression of the previously unheard. At its outset it had a good deal of support from members of the 'middling classes', artisans, farmers and tradesmen, even some in the upper classes, as did the older Nonconformists. But already stories were forming which helped to consolidate its appeal as a popular movement: the fifteen-year-old Mary Jones who walked barefoot twenty-six miles to buy a Bible from the Revd Thomas Charles; the similar long journeys Ann Griffiths (1776–1805) took from Bala prayer meetings to her Montgomeryshire home, which in the legend transformed a light-hearted girl into the deeply introspective composer of passionate hymns of Christian devotion. Ann's oeuvre, as slender as Pantycelyn's was vast, was memorised by her servant and copied down by the servant's literate husband after Ann's premature death in childbirth. The litany of faith, sacrifice and survival against persecution which was to fuel nineteenth-century contestation and martyrology was already being compiled.

Thus the lineaments were forming of a movement which would absorb the energies of the majority of the Welsh people, for whom it would become a badge of national identity. In the early nineteenth century this was still not the case, but it was already the largest social movement involving either the Welsh or Slovene peoples and habitually using the native language in its publications. Yet of all aspects of a Welsh activity more diffuse than its Slovene counterpart, it was the least Welsh in inspiration and goal. 'Here I know myself a stranger/And my native country lies/ Far beyond the ocean's danger/In the land of Paradise' wrote Pantycelyn, though his huge labours for his people's souls and Welsh literature must be set in the scales. Howel Harris was an enthusiastic organiser of military Breconshire volunteers in his native Breconshire at the outbreak of the Seven Years' War in 1757. This was hardly significant in itself because patriotism in Wales or Slovenia at this time involved no breath of disloyalty to the imperial state. But it was indicative of the climate within which patriotism operated. In the case of the Methodist leaders a further indication is that in their own correspondence, much more than the Morris circle, they used almost exclusively English. This was to change when the older ex-Anglican leaders were replaced by ministers of humbler stock, but many of these too tended to this pattern as they acquired more education.

The period discussed in this chapter already offers several interesting and attractive figures who have a place in their respective national stories. The shape of those stories can only be fully glimpsed from the vantage-point of hindsight. The working out of two paths to self-expression awaits the pages which follow. It is valuable here to re-emphasise the important part that the two framing imperial states have to play in the tale: the one Great Britain where the relative freedom the Welsh enjoyed was delivered via the full force of a self-confident national culture identifying progress with itself; the other the Habsburg Monarchy, dynastic, not national, but constrained by self-interest to relax its close rein on its subjects and balance the interests of its dominant peoples with some recognition of the others.

NOTES

1 Marko Pohlin, *Grammatik der crainerischen Sprache* (A Grammar of the Carniolan Language) (Ljubljana, 1768), pp. 5–18.
2 R. W. J. Evans, 'The Origins of Enlightenment in the Habsburg Lands', in Evans, *Austria, Hungary, and the Habsburgs: Essays on Central Europe c.1683–1867* (Oxford and New York, 2006), pp. 36–56 (50).
3 Branko Slanovič, *Blaž Kumerdej* (Kranj, 1997).

4 Boris Paternu, 'Francoska revolucija in slovenska literatura' (The French Revolution and Slovenian Literature), in M. Kmecl (ed.), *Obdobje slovenskega narodnega preporoda* (The Period of the Slovene National Revival) (Ljubljana, 1991), 53.

5 Paternu, 'Francoska revolucija', 56.

6 Paternu, 'Francoska revolucija', 58.

7 Jože Pogačnik, 'Pojem naroda v slovenskem razsvetljenstvu' (The Concept of the Nation in the Slovene Enlightenment), in Kmecl (ed.), *Obdobje preporoda*, pp. 87–96 (p. 94).

8 Anton Linhart, *Versuch einer Geschichte von Krain und den übrigen südlichen Slovenen Oesterreichs* (Towards a History of Carniola and the Other South Slavs of Austria) (Nuremberg, 1796), pp. 211–23.

9 Paternu, 'Francoska revolucija', 59.

10 For Kopitar, see J. Marn (ed.), *Kopitarjeva spomenica* (Festschrift for Kopitar) (Ljubljana, 1880).

11 Pohlin, *Grammatik*, pp. 10, 6.

12 Zlata Šunalić, 'Pojem naroda u Vodnikovi poeziji' (The Concept of the Nation in Vodnik's Poetry), in Kmecl (ed.), *Obdobje preporoda*, pp. 209–18.

13 Jože Pogačnik, 'Pojem naroda v slovenskem razsvetljenstvu' (The Concept of the Nation in Slovene Enlightenment), in Kmecl (ed.), *Obdobje preporoda*, pp. 87–98 (96).

14 R. T. Jenkins, *Hanes Cymru yn y Ddeunawfed Ganrif* (History of Wales in the Eighteenth Century) (Cardiff, 1972), p. 116, for 'clique': first published, 1931. For more on ballads and interludes, see E. Cynfael Lake, *Huw Jones o Langwm* (Caernarfon, 2009).

15 *Additional Letters of the Morrises of Anglesey*, transcribed and edited by Hugh Owen, in *Y Cymmrodor*, vol. XLIX (London, 1949), Part II, pp. 513–14.

16 J. Saunders Lewis, *A school of Welsh Augustans, being a study in English Influences on Welsh Literature during part of the eighteenth century* (Wrexham, 1924).

17 *Additional Letters* ... Part I (London, 1947), p. 349 (Lewis Morris); *The Letters of Goronwy Owen, 1723–1767*, ed. by J. H. Davies (Cardiff, 1924), for example, pp. 7, 74–5, 103–4; for 'novices' p. 75.

18 Geraint H. Jenkins, '"Horrid unintelligible jargon": the case of Dr Thomas Bowles', in *Welsh History Review*, 15 (1990–1), 494–523.

19 *Additional Letters*, Part I, pp. 146, 185; Part II, pp. 451–2, 469, 471. See also A. O. H. Jarman, 'Lewis Morris a Brut Tysilio' (Lewis Morris and Tysilio's Brut), *Llên Cymru*, 2 (1953), 161–83.

20 Dafydd Glyn Jones, *Agoriad yr Oes: Erthyglau ar Lên, Hanes a Gwleiddydiaeth Cymru* (Unto the Age: Articles on Welsh Literature, History and Politics) (Talybont, 2001), pp. 192–8.

21 The Revd J. Evans, *Letters written during a tour in South Wales in the year 1803* (London, 1804), p. 410.

22 Dafydd Glyn Jones, *Un o Wŷr y Medra: Bywyd a Gwaith William Williams, Llandegai 1738–1817* (One of the Men of the Medra. Life and Work of William Williams, Llandegai) (Denbigh, 1999), p. 184.

23 Jones, *William Williams, Llandegai*, p. 299. Actually, Williams's many translations from English poetry testify to a considerable interest in English literature.
24 Jones, *William Williams, Llandegai*, pp. 178–9.
25 Jones, *William Williams, Llandegai*, p. 296.
26 Jones, *William Williams, Llandegai*, p. 283.
27 J. J. Evans, *Morgan John Rhys a'i amserau* (Morgan John Rhys and his times) (Cardiff, 1935), pp. 122–3. This made eighty political publications in the decade.
28 G. A. Williams, *The Search for Beulah Land* (London, 1980).
29 Evans, *Morgan John Rhys*, p. 136.
30 Evans, *Morgan John Rhys*, pp. 128–9; Williams, *Beulah Land*, p. 65.
31 Evans, *Morgan John Rhys*, pp. 137–8. The bulk of detail on the Madog issue comes from Williams, *Beulah Land*.
32 Of much on this remarkable character, see Geraint H. Jenkins (ed.), *A Rattleskull Genius: the many faces of Iolo Morganwg* (Cardiff, 2005).
33 Williams, *Beulah Land*, p. 12.
34 For the international background to and influences on Methodism, see D. Ceri Jones, Boyd Schlenther, Eryn White, *The Elect Methodists: Calvinistic Methodism in England and Wales, 1735–1811* (Cardiff, 2012).
35 *Pantheologia, sef Hanes Holl Grefyddau'r Byd*, in *Holl Weithiau, Prydyddawl a Rhyddiethol, y diweddar Parch. William Williams, Pantycelyn*, ed. by J. R. Kilsy Jones (London, n.d.), p. 529. (*Pantheologia, namely, A History of All the World's Religions*, in *The Complete Works, Poetic and Prose, of the late Revd William Williams, Pantycelyn*)
36 For official use of Slovene in the Enlightenment, see M. Orožen, 'Uredovalna slovenščina v drugi polovici osemnajstega stoletja'(Official use of Slovene in the second half of the eighteenth century), in *Obdobje razsvetljenstva v slovenskem jeziku, književnosti in kulturi* (Slovene Language, Literature and Culture in the Period of the Enlightenment), ed. Boris Paternu (Ljubljana, 1979), pp. 155–82.
37 Linhart, *Versuch einer Geschichte*, Vorrede (unpaginated).
38 Morgan, *The Eighteenth Century Renaissance*, p. 38.
39 For the linguistic theme: Catherine Glyn Davies, *Adfeilion Babel, Agweddau ar syniadaeth ieithyddol y ddeunawfed ganrif* (The Ruins of Babel. Aspects of Linguistic Thought in the eighteenth century) (Cardiff, 2000); Glenda Carr, *William Owen Pughe* (Cardiff, 1983).
40 Geraint H. Jenkins, *The Foundations of Modern Wales: Wales 1642–1780* (Cardiff, 1987), p. 346.
41 *The Torrington Diaries containing the tour through England and Wales of the Hon. John Bynge between the years 1781 and 1795*, vol. 1 (London, 1807), pp. 283, 293; Benjamin Malkin, *The scenery, antiquities and biography of South Wales: collected during two tours in South Wales in the year 1803*, 2nd edn with additions (London, 1807), p. 323 (sedulously).
42 *Letters of Goronwy Owen*, p. 67. This was 1753, when Goronwy was himself a curate serving in England.
43 The Revd J. Evans, *Letters written during a tour in North Wales in the year 1798, and at other times* (London, 1804), p. 410.

Chapter 3

TOWARDS A TURNING POINT: WALES
AND SLOVENIA c.1815–1847

The title of this chapter indicates that it will stop short of the year 1848 in which Slovenia, with the rest of the Habsburg Monarchy, was taken up in a revolutionary process posing central issues of liberalism and nationalism. In that year the emancipation of serfdom was proclaimed for the whole empire and the first calls were made for an autonomous Slovenia to be created, with equality of the native language with German. Yet the end date has deep significance for Wales also as the year of the publication of the notorious 'Blue Books' on Welsh education in which the Welsh language was accused of 'evil effects' and Welsh society criticised in terms which mobilised a majoritarian Nonconformist people along new political lines. The first half of the nineteenth century prepared the ground for these developments. The second half and then on to 1914 would be dominated by the working out of their implications. The events of the turning point, 1847–8, deserve a chapter in themselves.

The context was one of rapid progress for parliamentary, industrialising Britain and more sluggish circumstances in the Habsburg Empire. Emerging victorious from the wars with France which its mercantile wealth had helped finance Europe-wide, Britain's economic sinews were strengthened further by the industrial pre-eminence on display in the Great Exhibition of 1851, the first and greatest of such events to mark the increasingly bourgeois age. The census of that year recorded more people living in British towns than in the countryside. After the loss of the American colonies a new empire was rising in India, Australasia, Canada and the Cape. With the Great Reform Act (1832) which overhauled parliamentary representation and the repeal of the Corn Laws (1846) which consolidated free trade, Britain moved closer towards the modern pattern of government for which it has been widely admired.

A little noticed feature of the period is that the share of the UK population with Celtic mother tongue fell from at least one-fifth in 1800 to less than 8 per cent in 1851. This might seem to imply a rise in homogeneity in the state, but it was due almost entirely to the decline of Irish, itself a symptom of emigration and a deeper Irish malaise under direct rule from London. True, Daniel O'Connell, leader of campaigns for Catholic emancipation and home rule, was not exercised about his mother tongue's 'gradual abandonment',[1] and worked within the British liberal constitutional system he accepted. Yet that system's inability to deliver prosperity for Ireland posed a question for the state's English majority and its sensitivity to minorities – illuminated, not wholly reassuringly, by Benjamin Disraeli's witty summary in 1844:

> I want to see a public man come forward and say what the Irish question is. One says it is a physical question, another a spiritual. Now it is the absence of the Aristocracy. Now it is the absence of railways. It is the Pope one day and potatoes the next.[2]

In the case of Scotland and Wales, population growth and industrialisation matched England's. The greatest Scottish writer of the day, Sir Walter Scott, combined Scottish patriotism with strong loyalty to the Union. The general importance of religion in British state and society appears in arguably the leading affair in Scottish nineteenth-century public life, the Great Disruption of 1843 when Thomas Chalmers led a third of Scotland's Presbyterian ministers out of the national into the Free Church on an issue of religious freedom. Chalmers was the admired mentor at Edinburgh of the Revd Lewis Edwards, probably the leading intellectual figure of Victorian Wales and the first Welsh Nonconformist peasant son to attend University, a fact redolent of his community's remoteness from wider British life. The decline of the Irish language only enhanced the distinctiveness and marginality of the compact block of Welsh monoglots in the state, since the large majority of Ireland's remaining Gaelic speakers could also speak English in 1851. This distinctiveness was to combine with rural and industrial volatility towards the end of the period to spur government's rare attention to the smallest of the four countries under its rule. For Britain's economic dynamism was reflected in Wales. The Principality's population doubled in the first half of the century to some 1,163,000, undergoing a remarkable redistribution, as the share of industrialising Glamorgan and Monmouthshire rose from one-sixth to two-thirds of the whole. Laissez-faire policies produced the characteristic features of early industrial society, great wealth alongside great poverty in overcrowded, poorly built, unhealthy townships, and consequent social unrest. Yet communal disruption also unleashed communal energies, a shifting pattern of social movements and initiatives taking place beneath the gaze of an indifferent authority, until the fear arose that Wales might be another Ireland in the making.

Austria had been Britain's most consistent ally against France and earned a generation of security as a result. Her population rose to thirty million by 1850, against only eighteen million in England and Wales. But four-fifths of these lived on the land and Vienna was one-fifth the size of London. After the shock of the revolutionary and Napoleonic wars, Habsburg statesmen abandoned Joseph II's policy of radical reform from above, both with regards to peasant reform and his attempts at centralisation. The latter decision was sensible. Chancellor Clemenz Metternich realised that a dominance like that of the English in the United Kingdom was impossible for the proportionally far fewer German speakers in Austria. The Hungarian parliament and the provincial Diets elsewhere were thus restored, though like the English parliament under Charles I Hungary's was not called for long periods. Attempts to invoke a kind of supranational patriotism against Napoleon, as through a people's militia accompanied by patriotic songs translated into Slovene among other Habsburg languages, had some success. All-empire journals in German for politics and the arts, founded as forums for writers from different parts of the empire, gained less purchase, while a specifically German-orientated periodical launched in 1812 without official support soon closed. Kopitar was one of the intellectuals who looked askance at its statements that the non-Germans of Austria partook of a 'Germanic spirit'.[3] The abandonment of land reform came with a general aversion to change and over Metternich's long tenure (1809–48) a sense of drift settled at the top. Absolutism was not as draconian as contemporaries claimed. There was modest economic growth and a lively musical and theatrical life in the towns. Meanwhile, the creative initiative passed to the Monarchy's peoples who concentrated on building up their individual cultures. German remained the *lingua franca* of the empire's intelligentsia and the medium of commerce and of most schooling beyond primary level. It was the language in which the 'father of the Czech nation' František Palacký began to publish his epochal history of the Czech people in 1836 and which the Hungarian leader István Széchenyi used in his private diary. Hungarians and Poles, with a proud nobility of their own, became politically restless, however, while predominantly peasant peoples like the Czechs kept their heads down and concentrated on building up their language. How much more so then the humble Slovenes? This is the background to the (limited) use of Slovene as teaching medium in Slovene primary schools before 1848.

Here there was a parallel with the Welsh case of non-dominant groups' self-activation in the face of dominant indifference. Unlike the Welsh, though, Slovenes had models to follow in the other 'national revivals' of Slavs in the Habsburg Monarchy. The six million or so Czechs provided the paradigm case but Croats and Serbs also responded to similar impulses, as did Romanians, and Finns and Balts later in more backward Tsarist Russia. This was a collective experience of emulation through a vast region of east-central Europe and the Balkans, transmitted with inevitable lags from west to east and from larger groups to smaller. It shared with Wales the perspectives offered by the Enlightenment and the French revolution. Yet besides these were the ideas of the German Lutheran pastor-philosopher Johann Gottfried Herder, whose role as father of cultural nationalism has already been mentioned. Herder anticipated modern understandings of culture as something wider than the concerns of educated elites. It was the way of life and traditions of whole communities passed on through the mother tongue. His insights had taken shape in observations of Latvian folk song during his stay in then German-dominated Riga. They were naturally attractive to non-dominant groups which lacked the powerful elites of ruling nations. The contrast between a British society shaped in a self-confident English image and a Habsburg *ancien régime* where Herderian ideas bubbled beneath the surface is key to the story that this chapter will tell.

SLOVENE CULTURAL REVIVAL

The Slovene lands offer an example of just such a non-dominant group in early 'revival'. Politically and economically they shared the tendency to sluggishness imposed from the top. The maintenance of serfdom (peasant labour services – *robota* – and judicial subordination to their lords), ruled out significant structural change. A falling death rate brought by better health increased population – the last symptoms of famine conditions came in 1816–17 – but larger numbers swelled the ranks of poor and dwarf peasants and began a movement from the land which was to grow through the century. State-supervised primary education improved and was no doubt better than the 'dame schools' of contemporary Wales, but its spread was held back by overall backwardness, which limited resources for investment. School attendance rose from one-seventh to one-third of the school age population in the period, being lowest in eastern and southern Carniola. Iron and textiles remained the chief non-agricultural branches but were losing out to larger production units elsewhere. There were only twenty-five steam engines on the territory of modern Slovenia in 1847. The regime was suspicious of freedom of thought. It was in Ljubljana in 1821 that Emperor Francis put this most strongly, commenting on patriotism: 'is it patriotism for me?' The biggest single development was the Southern Railway from Vienna to the Adriatic which reached Ljubljana in 1849 and Trieste in 1857, through difficult terrain. It brought an end to the ancient carting trade which had been an important auxiliary source of peasant income.

In these restricted circumstances the growth of Ljubljana becomes all the more significant. Its population increased from ten to seventeen thousand between 1817 and 1847, keeping it a bigger potential centre of national life than any equivalent town in Wales. The Carniolan Agricultural Society, a savings bank (the second in the empire, 1820), a provincial museum (1821) and the Lycée, with its medical-surgical school and two-year pre-University philosophy course, together with theatre, soirées, journals, printing presses and frequent visitors and residents from other parts of the empire, made it a centre for the nobility, clergy, bureaucrats, professional people, wealthier bourgeois and students who constituted the typical intelligentsia of a central European provincial capital. If it was far behind an Innsbruck or Prague, it gained the march on other towns in the Slovene-speaking area like Klagenfurt, helped further by its position at the heart of the most Slovene-speaking province. In 1821, for some months it played host to a Congress of the European Powers, part of Metternich's programme to lock them into his defence of the status quo against revolutionary forces. Graz, capital of Styria, with its restored University (1827) and its Johanneum, a cultural institute founded by the reform-minded Archduke Johann (1811), had considerable appeal for Styrian Slovene students. But wherever Slovenes congregated in an urban atmosphere it remained one where the traditional use of German (or Italian) as language of higher cultural intercourse was unchallenged. Knowledge of Slovene by many in the educated classes also remained common, as did a kind of unproblematic diglossia in the towns, where both languages might be spoken according to the context. Memories of childhood by writers who later developed into Slovene patriots show this urban Slovene as a slipshod affair, heavily influenced by German, in an environment where issues of 'nationality' simply did not arise. One reminiscence about a Styrian married couple showed this could be true also for some village folk, for each spoke their own language and the husband's understanding of his wife's Slovene was eased because half the words were German anyway.[4]

Yet in this period the Enlightenment aspiration to shape a mother tongue fit for polite society began to make progress. Though few in numbers its advocates had certain factors on their side. Even conservative administrators saw a case for basic mother tongue literacy in the interests of state efficiency in a changing Europe. Linguistic hierarchy would be preserved by the use of the elite language as medium of instruction in the handful of secondary schools and in urban primary schools. We have seen how this operated to give Slovene a small rung at the bottom of the linguistic ladder, particularly in Carniola, the Slovene heartland. For it required official support for textbooks, teacher training and a modicum of linguistic standardisation, offering employment for members of a potential Slovene intelligentsia. Yet Slovenes still had no standard language amid competing dialects. In the 1820s this got worse when the traditional alphabet inherited from the sixteenth-century Protestants was challenged from two directions. One proposed replacing the Protestant 'diagraphs' (like the English 'th' 'sh', 'ch') by accents as Czechs and Croats had done: thus č for English 'ch' and so forth; another proposed new Cyrillic-like letters for such sounds. What with this and regional grammar differences, simple readers and catechisms were being printed in four different versions by the 1830s. Welsh readers may be surprised that the authorities were prepared to provide such books and in quite large runs (cumulatively fifty thousand in the 1820s), when Welsh had no place in day schools in liberal Britain. It was not as if there was any marked pressure from the population. Enquiries showed that almost half the parents of schoolchildren wanted education to take them out of the peasant class, with a knowledge of German.[5] In fact much of official opinion did wish pupils to acquire such knowledge and catechisms were also printed bilingually. However, since rural teachers were usually parish clerks, often with inadequate German, such instruction was not really practicable (though that often applied in Wales too). Poor results led the emperor himself to order a definitive consultation and to accept its conclusions that instruction in Carniolan 'trivial' (village) schools should be in Slovene with Slovene texts, as well as being bilingual in the urban schools and four 'normal schools' in Slovene areas. The consultation had involved the consistorial boards of the dioceses with Slovene population. Many there, like many landlords, were wary of teaching German because it would unsettle simple peasants, opening horizons which could threaten respect for traditional authority.[6] Griffith Jones had used as one argument for holding his schools in Welsh that it would prevent the circulation of potentially dangerous English books in the Welsh countryside.

This decision of 1829 was to have momentous consequences, no less than the development of mass education in the mother tongue, rather than the pattern in Wales. But in the shorter turn these were not so obvious. Provision remained inadequate. In 1847 when some 680 schools had been opened in Slovene areas, these were only 40 per cent of those estimated to be required.[7] Progress was slow in the secondary sphere too. What teaching of Slovene there was at this level in the provincial capitals was aimed only at prospective priests, who combined their parochial functions with teaching at the village school. Primary education was heavily orientated to religion and inculcation of obedience to the authorities. Maintaining this system was also the least expensive option, important for government.

Advocates of Slovene were fortunate that such motives gave them a limited base of operation at a humble popular level. Yet successful promotion of a minor language requires, besides this, its promotion as a medium of intellectual culture. Slovene in the 1820s faced difficulties at both levels. It was hard to visualise a serious cultural role for Slovene while the way to write it remained so unsettled. Bureaucrats wanted to know where, in terms of alphabet, to direct publication grants for school readers, particularly after two influential challenges to the old system published in 1824–5. From this arose the energy-sapping 'ABC war' of 1830–3 between language enthusiasts, which will raise a sigh for anyone aware of Breton and Cornish language spats. But the Slovene case belies the stereotypes. It shows the sophistication which language debates in our region could involve. The winners in the language war were two exceptional figures, who between them transposed the dispute onto another plane. Matija Čop (1797–1835) argued that the key issue was not orthography but the context in which Slovene should develop. For Čop, librarian of the Ljubljana *lycée*, and thoroughly versed in eight literatures ancient and modern, Slovene literature should aspire to the highest international models. He was inspired by the German romantic Friedrich von Schlegel's ideal of a literature universal in content if national in form. As yet the undeveloped Slovene language could not hope to match the achievements of mature cultures except possibly in poetry, thought Čop, but the goal was to forge a literary instrument which could hold its own in the world of modern bourgeois culture.[8] In France Prešeren (1800–1849) Čop believed Slovenes had a poet of potentially the highest quality. The *Slovene Bee*, four volumes of which were published between 1830 and 1834, was the first poetry anthology to appear in Slovene since the venture of 1779–81. Prešeren's contributions showed the great leap forward since Vodnik's day.

Prešeren epitomised the unhappy artistic genius. Born of well-to-do peasant stock and holding a doctorate in law from Vienna university he spent his life in minor legal employment, being five times rejected as candidate for a solicitor's independent licence. His search for personal fulfilment was equally frustrating, though he bore three children with an intermittent partner he refused to marry. This relationship tells something of language conditions in the capital. Prešeren's partner spoke urban Slovene but of such poor quality that he preferred to speak to her in German. Life-long heavy drinking led to dropsy and premature death. His most famous work, 'A wreath of sonnets' identified his rejected love for a Germanised Ljubljana burgher's daughter with his people's indifference to their language and their unhappy fate, while allowing a prophetic glimpse of better things. It is remarkable for its technical virtuosity as much as its lyrical beauty. Just a few years since the first ever Slovene sonnet had been written, it was made up of fifteen sonnets in which the last line of each opened the next and the fourteen repeated lines together composed the last, the 'magistrale'. In addition, the first letter of each line of the magistrale spelt out the name of Prešeren's would-be flame. Such sophistication fitted Čop's prescription perfectly; he was particularly interested in international varieties of metrical form and drew Prešeren's attention to their possibilities.

Prešeren himself mirrored Čop's learning and combination of Slavic and international interests. He met Mácha and corresponded with Čelakovský, the two leading poets of the Czech revival and he first read the epic of the Slovak Panslav, Jan Kollár, in John Bowring's English translation. It was the combination of the personal, the national and the universal in Prešeren's work which led Slovene activists quite quickly to see him as standard-bearer of their claim to nationhood. Called to give account before the judgment seat, they could proudly appear bearing a copy of his poems to show their part in 'the universe of human culture': thus the nineteenth century's leading Slovene literary critic in 1866.[9]

But this came too late for Prešeren. Life as lived is messy. When he died in 1849 his collected poems were selling badly and his and Čop's views had not gone uncontested. He quarrelled heatedly with the grand old man of Slovene linguistics, Jernej Kopitar, who had been on different sides in the ABC debate and had another view of the trajectory of Slovene. Kopitar, a proud, prickly figure, favoured a development from below, based on peasant speech, rather than the urbanity with which Čop and Prešeren hoped to win bilingual speakers in the towns for linguistic self-respect. His perspective was for a natural development, whereby gradually the different dialects of Slovene could converge as had the dialects of ancient Greece, to become the common koine of the New Testament.[10] As with William Owen Pughe in Wales language patriots in a small language context were driven back to speculate on first principles. Such discussion was rife in east-central Europe and could reach a high level in surprising contexts. In remote Finland, then little more populous than Wales or Slovenia, within a few years after 1815 at least four young scholars in the country's sole institute of higher education presented different views of how the native peasant tongue could become a literary language, involving sophisticated debate of the relation between language and nationality, the language of the peasants and the Swedish-speaking elite, the role of folk poetry, every-day speech, dialect varieties and the like.[11] References to Herder usually convey a misty romanticism to western readers. This of course existed and its sheer emotional power must be grasped. 'There is no rapture on earth like patriotism', wrote a young enthusiast to the Styrian poet Stanko Vraz, for it gave the power to scorn worldly things and strength-ened the will to undertake anything for the motherland; a nation which bred such sons, small as it might be, was worthy to claim its place among other nations.[12] In fact, at stake were hard intellectual problems with huge practical implications as the Slovene and Finnish examples showed. Slovenia itself was confronted with a complex situation where the issue was not only relations between Slovene dialects but to similar languages in the region. The 1830s saw the rise of the 'Illyrian' movement in nearby Croatia which aimed to unite Croatian dialects and bring them into alignment with Serbian. It was germane for Slovenes because some Slovene Styrians could find Prešeren's Carniolan speech as hard to understand as their neighbours in north-west Croatia. Since these Croats were prepared to give up their own dialect for the sake of a common Illyrian literary language (later to be known as Serbo-Croat) might not Slovenes do the same? Stanko Vraz urged Prešeren, a close friend, to follow him in taking this course. Literature, Vraz believed, could not be written in Slovene, the 'domestic dialect of a mere million people'. Linguistic union with Croats and Serbs could better enable Slovenes to survive as Slavs. Prešeren, however, disagreed. The fate of Slovene's 'dwarf literature' as he put it, should be left to judgment day.[13] Yet Prešeren once said himself that, if he had known Croatian better, ambition for broader literary pastures might have tempted him to adopt it.[14] There is irony in this. A short story by a leading Croatian writer in the 1870s describes how a young Germanised Slovene student, enthused with German poetry, is converted to patriotism by a pretty girl who knows no German but is reading Prešeren.[15] It is an example of the way in which budding literary movements influenced and encouraged each other in the atmosphere of romantic nationalism which was spreading in east-central Europe at this time.

The Illyrian movement lost much of its influence on Slovenes in the 1840s, partly because the use of this term was banned by the Habsburg authorities, suspicious of 'Panslavism' or in general closer ties between the various Slav peoples. Slovene made progress under its own right. An ambitious multi-volume collection of folk poetry (*Slovene poems of the Carniolan People*) was published between 1839 and 1844 on the initiative of a young Habsburg Pole who found in Ljubljana refuge from official displeasure in his native province. This was one of several instances where Slav residents from other parts of the Monarchy contributed to the Slovene cause. The term Slovene itself was winning out over provincial tags among the educated. In 1843, a weekly newspaper in Slovene, for which permission had previously been repeatedly refused by suspicious bureaucrats, began publication in Ljubljana, edited by a vet, Janez Bleiweis, on condition of avoiding politics. The paper *Kmetijske in rokodelske Novice* (News for Peasants and Craftsmen, hereafter *Novice*) appeared under the auspices of the Carniolan Agricultural Society as a four-page broadsheet offering its readers practical advice and titbits of information, in terms evoking the thirst for 'useful knowledge' of the age. No Welsh county agricultural society sponsored native journalism in this way. In fact, nearly half of the 1,512 subscribers as of 1847 were clergymen; nearly one-fifth officials, institutions and substantial householders (urban and rural), with teachers and students 8 per cent. Craftsmen numbered one in eleven and peasants just over one in twenty.[16]

Novice regularly carried articles on technical agricultural matters, fire insurance and the like, not to speak of favourite titbits of the time in all European journalism, like a report on rats born to a cat in France. But plainly Bleiweis's message, which was that those who did not change in a changing age lost out, had a wider purport and appeal. His paper addressed 'Slovenes' and sometimes 'Illyrians' but not 'Carniolans'; nearly 30 per cent of subscribers lived outside Carniola. It carried frequent references to Slavic books and activities in other parts of the Monarchy and its stress on the importance of schooling – in Slovene – for peasants and craftsmen chimed with the aspirations of language revivalists. All this was conducted in an upbeat, patriotic and loyalist style. An account of a visit by Montenegrins was used to stress how the humble local speech was actually a language of wide dimensions, the differences between Slovene and Serb-Croat being air-brushed out. The history of Illyrians was conveyed with brief vagueness in which ancient serfdom and Turkish attacks quickly passed to the beneficent improvements of successive Habsburg monarchs (for which grateful memory was due) and the promise of 'new happiness' to come.[17]

Bleiweis was far from Prešeren in temperament, a cautious, pragmatic Habsburgophile where the melancholic poet bore no love for the Habsburgs and was touched by the spirit of protest of the romantic age. In some Slovene historiography the distinction drawn has been one between the opportunistic conservative and the radical democrat. This has advantages for national history in dramatising the issues and highlighting different pathways through clearly identifiable individuals. It can also differentiate too sharply. Prešeren was a poet, not a politician. It has been plausibly said that the 'Sonnet Wreathe' ultimately prioritises the role of poetry rather than love or patriotism in his concerns. Prospective nations and their historians need individual figures to enthuse their members with a sense of high things done in their name. The German historian Joachim Hösler has criticised Slovene historiography for a tendency to exaggerate the strength of a Slovene national movement at this time and underplay the extent to which the loyalties of the majority remained essentially Carniolan. Insofar as they went wider, he sees this as towards a generalised Slavophilia, not later concepts of Slovenian unity. Language activism need not be evidence of a drive for self-conscious national affirmation when many other motives could have taken precedence: educational or scholarly or antiquarian interests, or in the case of the so prominent clergy, the desire for more informed and devout, less merely superstitious congregations.[18] The great mass of the population was untouched. A letter of Čop's brother, discovered only a century later, recounted how students hoping to enthuse peasants for the patriotic cause found themselves suspected of being spies of the regime.[19] The key differentiation in the population was not national but social, between peasants on the one hand and landlords and urbanites on the other.

There is much to be said for this interpretation, which has particular interest for Welsh observers of a period in which the Slovene scene had still not diverged so far from that in Wales. As has been seen, the decision to use Slovene as teaching medium can be explained by Habsburg practice and clerical-landlord conservatism without invoking patriotic agitation. Historians' claims that Prešeren sharply criticised unpatriotic Slovenes for writing in German sit oddly with the fact that 20 per cent of his own collected poems too were German; rather, Prešeren was annoyed when people neglected their mother tongue to write German badly. As an urbanite he moved in bilingual circles and contributed poems in both languages to the German literary review *Carniola*. The cohabitation of two language groups in larger towns, many members being bilingual, applied in Swansea, Cardiff and Newport at this time, not to speak of Carmarthen. The situation was one where societies in both countries operated in the dominant language but had members with both mother tongues. Bodies like the Ljubljana Casino, Shooting Society and Carniolan Historical Association were not the exclusive representatives of the non-national elite they have been presented but contained many members of Slovene origin, the distinction drawn at the time rather being between native Carniolans and incomers. Prešeren was asked to contribute a poem to the Shooting Society on three ceremonial occasions, 1834, 1837 and 1845, the last time composing in Slovene.

There are, though, problems with Hösler's position. It fits a current tendency to tar 'nationalism' with the brush of 'ethnicism'. Hösler regrets the adoption of Slovene-only instruction in Carniolan primary schools as preventing the emergence of a bilingual society into which the monoglot peasantry could have been assimilated. The trouble is that this would not have been the equal society of modern ideals but assimilation into the uneven cultural pluralism of Habsburg society, which involved the existence of dominant classes and their languages. In nineteenth-century circumstances of the growth of democracy and self-awareness it would have meant in Slovene areas an unsustainable dominance of German speakers over others, such as German nationalists and racists eventually aspired to. In the same context as John Stuart Mill dismissed the Welsh and Bretons as decaying ethnicities (see the Introduction) he argued that free institutions are impossible in a country made up of different nationalities, especially with different languages, because the 'united public opinion' necessary for representative government cannot exist.[20] He would doubtless have seen Slovenes in the same light as Welsh and there is little evidence that German democrats – or German socialists like Marx and Engels – looked beyond Poles and Hungarians as fully worthy of nationhood at this time. Multiculturalism in modern west European states where the minorities are mainly incomers is largely about race or religion – and assumes a common language. The Habsburg Monarchy could not do this. Its politics came to revolve around arrangements to solve this problem. Pre-existing coexistence rested on hierarchy which went against the dawning democratic spirit. In modern circumstances resentment of masters who spoke German led quite quickly to resentment of the German language and Germanness. Hösler is not wrong to say that division in the Slovene lands was social rather than consciously national. But to call this social factor the 'objective' one and to treat the transposition of social into ethnic resentment as somehow lesser is to ignore psychological realities and play down the fact that the problem was both ethnic and social.[21] Of course not all Slovenes were poor and German speakers better off but human reason judges by averages. Our society is very sensitive to differences in income, respect and promotion between men and women. Ethnic relations in Slovenian towns followed similar deeply entrenched patterns but with language as focus. Prešeren's own thwarted career path can be interpreted in these terms.

Active mobilisation against grievance was, true, very much a minority affair. Yet the Slovenian 'revivalists' made the most of limited opportunities offered by Austrian absolutism. The profusion of school texts they made available in Slovene helped put this option firmly in officialdom's mind and influenced their decision. Their education, strategic sense and acquaintance with European cultural trends are impressive. Though the foremost leaders were laymen, the key supporting role played by the clergy should not be overlooked, as writers of grammars and orthographical studies but particularly as far as the peasant masses were concerned. The parish priest had great influence over an uneducated peasant people as in Catholic Ireland. What handbooks in Slovene there were for improvements in agriculture, wine production, home economics and simple chemistry were written by clergy, a function little taken up by Welsh Nonconformist ministers. Slovene Catholicism was still influenced by 'Josephinian' goals of opposing order and morality to traditional superstition and ignorance, with the clergy as God's disciples, empowered to instruct the people how to reason and learn God's will, rejecting false thinking and living industrious lives.[22] This was a conservative version of enlightenment, stressing hierarchy and obedience in the family and the state, and the importance of distinguishing between what was valuable in the new and what should be retained from the old. It played a stabilising role and helped enhance peasants' self-reliance with its tale of their role as the bulwark of state and society. Its orientation was to the upper and middle peasantry, however, because it presupposed the maintenance of the family farm, which smallholders and the landless lacked.

The clergy's role was not only matter of pastoral care, however. That priests could be moved by patriotic motives and passionately so appears from a sermon delivered in 1834 by the young Anton Martin Slomšek, later a bishop, on St John's teaching on the Word, and the divine injunction to gratitude for every language: 'the mother tongue is the dearest gift we have received from our forefathers under the obligation to preserve and embellish and pass on to our children ... God will require that all those who deny the honour of their language should be cast into outer darkness ... Love your people, respect your language.' Slomšek added that he argued for the priest's responsibility in this regard not just for ecclesiastical reasons but primarily as an act of national cultural enlightenment.[23] As a seminarist in a hotbed of patriotic fervour in Croatia he had been deeply imbued with Herderian ideas. Herder's appeal to the Slavs 'now sunk so low', to wake from their long slumber and inscribe their name 'in the book of mankind' had a resonant effect on Habsburg Slavs and was translated into several Slav languages before 1848, if not yet Slovene, though well known. Contacts like Slomšek's with fellow Slavs in the common state, particularly Croats and Czechs, naturally strengthened linguistic consciousness. Career paths, whether bureaucratic or commercial brought Slav speakers quite frequently to Ljubljana in particular in this period, a source of inspiration lacking in Wales.

Slomšek was a Styrian, another sign of the expansion of the Slovene movement beyond Carniola. The first historical work in Slovene was a history of Styria, 'with particular regard to the Slovenes' published in the provincial capital, Graz in 1845. The rapidity with which a national consciousness could develop can be seen in the young Davorin Trstenjak who fell in love with the Slovene language in secondary school in 1839 and was writing in 1842 of the need to build it up so as 'to save what is to be saved' to escape the fate of the people of Alsace 'who are neither Germans nor French'. Social conditions were the same as in Carniola. An observer recorded how Slav peasants doffed their hats to everyone who looked urban, while their children ran up to kiss their hand.[24] Trstenjak sought to persuade Germans that the Styrian Slovenes were not the dangerous threat they feared. In this he had some success. A former enemy came to the view that the best solution was to educate the Slovenes so that the unbalanced relation of dominant and subordinate language would be replaced by one of equal bilingualism. This little point suggests something of the range of possibilities the Slovene revival had opened up.

Yet the advancement of Slovene as a language of culture had as yet minimal interest for the great peasant majority. Their overriding preoccupation was the Austrian regime's continuing refusal to address the land question. Joseph's grant of freedom of movement, the only part of his land reforms to survive the reaction after his death, increased the tendency for social differentiation in their ranks. A minority of better-off peasants was created who might be more accessible to Bleiweis's programme – interestingly, *Novice* assumed its peasant readers would themselves be employing farm labourers – but squeezing increasing numbers into ever smaller plots. The Church's preferred perspective, orientated round the maintenance of the family farm, had less relevance to these. Peasants retained the traditional visceral suspicion of landlords of a rural underclass. The Carniolan Agricultural Society sponsored agricultural innovation and an ambitious overhaul of land registration by the Society, but this had the effect of increasing tax burdens for some of the rural population. There were extensive threats of unrest in the countryside in 1844. Even the normally passive Carniolan Diet responded to the growing sense of drift and malaise of the regime in the 1840s with petitions for relaxation of censorship and some reform on the toxic land issue. It echoed palely the swelling mood of discontent at conservative regimes and economic difficulties, which were to precipitate the upheavals of 1848.

Rural overpopulation and anti-landlordism were also powerful forces in Wales. Of course, not everything in the Slovene story is equally relevant to the Welsh case. Some issues touched on, like the relations between the Slav languages, and the South Slav languages in particular, had no real Welsh counterpart, or are included only to illustrate the weakness of a 'Celtic' factor and Wales's relative isolation. Hopefully, these are still worth mentioning to round off a story which is interesting in itself and, if so seen, may increase willingness to follow the comparison in general. For the shape of the ground covered here necessarily has a bearing for any small non-dominant people entering modernity: the role of the national language in education and as instrument of literature and press; the kind of people who supported patriotic activity, and how far one can speak of them as an intelligentsia; the relationship of these to the urban middle classes associated with modernity and to the traditional intelligentsia, the clergy; the role of religion; the extent of engagement with the popular masses; the attitude to them of government, and the place of the minority people in the state. These will be kept in mind, if not mechanically followed, in the discussion of Wales below.

LANGUAGE AND CULTURE
IN EARLY NINETEENTH-CENTURY WALES

Wales in 1848 was still more active on many counts on the language front than Slovenia. In all, 145 periodicals appeared in Welsh or bilingually in the period 1800–50, and ten weekly papers (1814–54).[25] Language activism ranged somewhat wider than its predominantly cleric, professional or scholar base in Slovenia: in eisteddfodic circles, including aristocratic ones (that of Lady Llanover), among the Anglican clergy (y personiaid llengar/the literary parsons), in the variously named Welsh societies (provincial, Cymreigyddol), in working-class friendly societies (the Gwir Iforiaid), around the Baptist editor Joseph Harris, in movements for publication of 'useful knowledge' in Welsh, for establishing

Welsh-language 'academies', for Welsh-speaking judges, for Celtic cultural contacts, as well as in the London Welsh and the Association of Welsh Clergy in the West Riding of Yorkshire, who campaigned along with others against anglicisation in the state church. As in the Slovene case, the 1840s marks some acceleration of advance. What ultimately became the first commercially successful Welsh weekly paper, *Yr Amserau* of the Congregational minister Gwilym Hiraethog (William Rees, 1802–81), was published in 1843, quickly achieving a sale of 9,000 copies, depressing further the much lower sale of existing English-language weeklies. In 1845 the Calvinistic Methodist minister Lewis Edwards (1809–87) launched *Y Traethodydd* (The Essayist), an ambitious quarterly, modelled on the *Edinburgh Review*, whose substantial format and articles would not have been possible in Slovene at this time. Equally venturous was the translation in 1851 of volume one of *Chamber's Encyclopedia*, a formidable compendium of contemporary scientific and technical knowledge and the leading English-language publication of the day in this genre.

It is worth saying a little more about some of these activities. The eisteddfodic movement was closest in spirit to the Morris Circle of the eighteenth-century Welsh revival, a mixture of enlightened rationality and implicitly defensive patriotism based on pride in a perceived past. There was personal continuity in the Revd Walter Davies (Gwallter Mechain, 1761–1848), whose geological studies led him on a walk in Radnorshire to try to trace a seam linking the north-east and south-east coalfields.[26] He won the chair for poetry at the first of the Gwyneddigion's eisteddfods in 1789 and the first of a new series of biennial eisteddfods organised provincially from 1819. Davies scornfully rejected Welsh traditional patriotic myths. Prince Madog's discovery of America was a fit subject for poetry but not for an essay, he opined. He was the leading figure in the setting of eisteddfodic subjects and adjudications, with prizes, largely but not exclusively on Welsh themes which made the core of eisteddfodic gatherings. A typical 'literary parson' and stout churchman he nonetheless rejoiced at collaboration with 'Dissenters' for Christian mission abroad in 'this dawn of Gospel splendour'.[27] Other denominations were 'rivals' in a correspondent's phrase; they were not yet enemies. Likewise, Davies's patriotism was tempered. Offa's dyke preserved in Welsh minds memory of the Saxons' 'oppressive yoke',[28] yet this cowper's apprentice talent-spotted by the gentry and sent to Oxford resembled Slovene parish priests of his generation in his adaptation to the established order. The peripatetic provincial eisteddfods, along with mutual correspondence, were substitutes for clergymen living in tiny places, mainly in border counties, for an institutional centre like Ljubljana. When they came to an end the baton passed to the Abergavenny Welsh society in central Monmouthshire where the remarkable wife of the local MP was the main force for the next twenty years.

Lady Llanover was an example of the upper-class champion of a small nation cause more common in eastern Europe than in Wales, only a minor version of Baron Zois to be sure, but more than the English eccentric she has often been considered. She and her father were actually Welsh-born. With her supportive husband and her main collaborator, the Breconshire clergyman Thomas Price (Carnhuanawc, 1787–1848), another literary parson, a series of eisteddfods was organised from 1834 on a major scale, with balls, spectacular processions and distinguished guests including royalty, the future Prussian ambassador to Britain, Baron Bunsen, German Celticists, leading Bretons and a Czartoryski from this most famous of Polish noble families. The little Princess Victoria, brought by her mother, had herself patronised and presented prizes at previous eisteddfods, such acts of upper-class complaisance towards minority ethnicities being part of the fabric of traditional rule in multi-ethnic states. Similar *noblesse oblige* meant that subscription lists for Welsh-language publications common at this time always began with the aristocracy and the local gentry. One-fifth of the subscribers to Jane Williams's collection of Welsh tunes (1842), an eminently national project of the age, belonged to the latter group. Carnhuanawc himself was a substantial figure, an eloquent speaker and learned scholar, whose massive *Hanes Cymru* (History of Wales, 1842) was not matched by a history of Slovenia in Slovene for over half a century. He was a member of the Welsh Manuscripts Society founded in 1837.

In Carnhuanawc and Lady Llanover the transition was made to a full-blooded romantic view of the social function of nationality. A people's engagement with its culture, its poetry, its music, in collective activity like eisteddfodau and a vibrant vernacular press made for a happy people, Carnhuanawc believed: 'Show me another language in the world in which such a body of knowledge is found in the hands of the common people'.[29] The Welsh language promoted nationality, a virtuous feeling innate from birth and the parent of patriotism, argued Lady Llanover. Language loss made for a broken spirited people.[30] Her campaign for the revival of the Welsh triple harp attracted interest in music circles beyond Wales and like her advocacy of a Welsh national costume was in line with contemporary international interest in music and dress as ethnic markers. She was perfectly aware of regional costume variations. Nor was her support for the Welsh woollen industry a mere costume fad, but a practical measure backed up by a factory on the estate which worked till the 1950s. No doubt she did think her policies would help bolster the established church and the landed interest, as she has been accused, but these were not exclusively conservative positions most of her lifetime. Her husband was a liberal MP (who, incidentally, as Benjamin Hall, gave his name to Big Ben, built while he was Commissioner of Works at Westminster) and was also grandson of one of the founders of the Merthyr iron industry, so that the family had an industrial as well as rural hinterland. He built for his Abercarn iron workers the only day school in Wales at the time to teach through the medium of Welsh, fought with his wife against the appointment of English vicars to Welsh parishes and maintained a Welsh chapel for their Nonconformist tenants. Lady Llanover was a trustee of St David's Anglican theological college in Lampeter and Llandovery public school in both cases because of their initial commitment to teaching Welsh. The idea that she did not really know Welsh seems unfounded.[31] Knowledge of or interest in it by members of the upper classes was not so exceptional. Her mother's much-loved friend Elizabeth Greenly spoke it fluently. Lady Charlotte Guest, wife of another Merthyr industrialist, and a genuine English woman, made the first translation of the medieval tales of the Mabinogi at just this time. The second marquis of Bute, pioneer of the Welsh coal industry, shared the Llanovers' views about the importance of Welsh in school and parish church and the third and fourth marquisses spoke and wrote it, as indeed Lady Llanover's grandson was still doing in the 1930s.[32]

That said, the strident element in some of Carnhuanawc's praise of Welsh reflects the fact that he, Walter Davies and Lady Llanover all lived in border areas where it was weakening. Carnhuanawc's patriotic effusion above was a response to those who said that Welsh was a useless language.[33] A certain embattledness also reflected the literary parsons' concern at a specifically Anglican decline.[34] 'Our country is poor', commented Walter Davies himself on the difficulties of financing publication; but 'other persuasions', with their itinerant preachers, had ample means of spreading their literature: *Y Gwyliedydd* (an Anglican journal), seemed to be almost unknown compared to *Y Gwladgarwr* (Nonconformist), he commented.[35] The dynamic in Welsh society was passing into new hands. The link with conservative 'establishment' which helped Slav patriotic movements in the Habsburg Monarchy, where both had an interest in opposing German national liberalism, as in 1848, was breaking down in Wales as Nonconformists became the majority. Yet this is far from saying that interest in the language was ebbing. Nonconformists were taking up its cause and included many participants in eisteddfods.

The best example of this was the Baptist minister Joseph Harris (Gomer, 1773–1825), whose pseudonym evoked Welsh claims to a Biblical ancestry. The energies released by Nonconformity built the pillars of the new Welsh journalism. Harris launched the first Welsh weekly and long only non-denominational paper, *Seren Gomer* (1814–15), a bold, short-lived experiment, doomed by the swinging state tax on print of 6d a number, for all its circulation of two thousand, as compared to the initial eight hundred of Bleiweis's *Novice* thirty years later. Harris revived it as a Baptist monthly (1818–37) still effectively open to all shades of opinion. He is a crucial figure for comparison because a glowing language patriotism was as important to him as his sturdy Protestantism, and because he operated in Swansea, a flourishing industrial and mercantile centre and then the largest town in Wales. Announcing in his Address to the Welsh people his 'General Weekly Herald for the whole Principality of Wales' he invited his readers to enjoy the pleasures of knowledge; *Seren Gomer* stood 'in the breach between the dear Welsh language and its enemies', needing contributions which would 'tend to its purification and reform'.[36] A sense of a time of progress, a moving on from the limited matter available to Welsh readers in the last century, animated the whole venture, in the spirit of Slovenes who sought to induce patriotism in their own mixed, wavering urban population. Harris's attacks on the English language as a 'mishmash', patently inferior to Welsh, fell below his elevated rhetoric. He died shattered by the early death through TB of his only son, a brilliant multilingual young writer, urban-raised where his father had been a farmworker, but who shared his ideals. Interestingly the son had initially been influenced by the Swansea youth he mixed with who customarily spoke English. An aspiration to reverse this trend can be sensed in the young man, a sound instinct relevant to an important aspect of language maintenance. Gomer himself combined his journalistic activities with enthusiastic support of the eisteddfodic movement. Following him, his combination of attitudes was not found in most Nonconformist clergy, whose religion was more important to them than their mother tongue and journalism primarily a vehicle for their evangelism.

The 'cause célèbre' of Gomer's editorship was the controversy sparked by an attack on the Welsh language by a Welshman himself, David Owen (Brutus), taking advantage of *Seren Gomer*'s boasted openness to all shades of national opinion. Portraying the *Cymro uniaith* (monoglot Welshman) as the most ignorant creature under the sun and the glorification of Welsh as self-praise induced by the outside world's disregard, Brutus, a Nonconformist on the way to Anglicanism, condemned prejudice against English as a barrier to progress.[37] A number joined him, arguing for Welsh's practical uselessness and accusing the Welsh societies of being organs of a bardic conspiracy to maintain their hold on the people, perpetuating alleged slack morality and xenophobia.[38] Some of the expostulations which followed in defence of Welsh showed a narrow frame of intellectual and cultural reference, resorting to pathos – Brutus as guilty of matricide against his mother tongue and dancing before a bonfire of Welsh books – or to the kind of empty hyperbole in its praise he had mocked. Many pro-Welsh correspondents, however, argued sensibly that the learning of English did not need the abandonment of Welsh and concentrated on education, supporting Carnhuanawc's call for Welsh language schools, increase of Welsh language publication and textbooks, at the least separate provision for teaching both languages.[39] Most effective, as usually for an outraged non-dominant group, was satire, from editor Joseph Harris himself, in a sustained display of argument and wit. If knowledge of English turned the Welsh people into the Milton-reading, philosophy and astronomy-cultivating sophisticates Brutus associated with English culture, who would be left to plough, sow, reap, thresh, grind and bake bread for the English, or would their loaves grow on leafy trees and wine flow into their cups without the need for servitors to carry it?[40] Behind the mockery was the strongest sociological argument available for the Welsh language, that the charge one could not 'get on' with it alone might be valid for a number of individuals, but was more problematic for a whole community. Harris also made most clearly the case for the value of knowing Welsh for commercial and professional people in Wales, and enthusing monoglot pupils. With this he closed further discussion in his journal unless significant new material turned up. It is interesting, then, that the two most pro-Brutus articles in *Seren Gomer* appeared after his death. It boded ill for Welsh that they were tinged with some distaste in the new religious climate for the traditional bardic culture associated with pubs and by extension with the eisteddfods and Cymreigyddol (Welsh) societies at this time often held in them.

Nonetheless, *Seren Gomer* continued after its founder's death to be a journal dedicated to linguistic renewal on lines not dissimilar to the Slovene journalism that *Novice* later developed. It greeted 1828, the tenth anniversary of its renewal as a monthly, with the boast that now three Welsh books appeared for every one previously, Welsh readers were no longer so dependent on translation from English-language sources. The monoglot Welshman, it claimed at the start of 1831, had benefited from its services in his struggles with estate stewards, extortioners and arrogant gentry.[41] Reports on the 'Welsh societies' which mushroomed in the 1820s in the south Wales valleys and elsewhere were a staple feature, as was the call for Welsh-language education and textbooks; the paper called for Welsh speaking judges and bishops. It ascribed its success to its denominational impartiality; Carnhuanawc was a frequent correspondent. Most interesting from the late 1820s was the advocacy of colleges ('athrofeydd', the traditional term for denominational academies) for the systematic study of all sciences through Welsh. One proposal, calling for cooperation of the London Welsh with Welsh societies in the homeland and contacts with all Welsh MPs, envisaged something on the lines of London University college, with a member of the royal family as patron.[42] In Eiddil Ifor's view from Blaenafon in Monmouthshire, funding workshops operating in Welsh and keeping their accounts in it could lead to the Welsh people acquiring ownership of the mineral wealth around them.[43] Briefly and uniquely, some Welsh people saw the empowerment of their mother tongue in an economic context. The friendly society of the True Ivorites (Y Gwir Iforiaid), who conducted all their affairs in Welsh, flourished in the same industrialising milieu.

Attention has been paid to *Seren Gomer* because it is the closest parallel in Welsh experience to what became the dominant mode in Slovene journalism. It was also the accepted leading organ of its day. Yet it had many partners in its enthusiasm for 'gwybodaeth fuddiol', the term corresponding to English 'useful knowledge' and Slovene 'uporabno znanje'. At least a dozen were dedicated specifically to self-education in various forms in these years. Most were short-lived, like the journal of a society for spreading 'useful knowledge', offshoot of an English society of that name, founded in 1834, testifying to a felt need of an awakening society but one whose eyes were frequently bigger than its belly or financial capacity in a competitive, free-wheeling, not to say disorganised milieu. A feature of this activity was the attempt to discuss scientific matters in Welsh. Examples are *Y Brud a Sylwydd* (1828), a periodical set up specifically for this purpose; John William Thomas (Arfonwyson)'s *Elfennau Rhifyddiaeth* (Elements of Arithmetic, 1831–2), the most ambitious of half a dozen ventures in this field; the lectures on such topics as pneumatics and hydrostatics of Griffith Davies, Fellow of the Royal Society, delivered to London Welshmen and subsequently published. Altogether 181 works on scientific and related matters were published between 1800 and 1859, the most popular fields being astronomy, geography, botany, agricultural science and the fad of the age, phrenology or belief that the shape of the skull reveals mental faculties – source of the common phrase that someone has a 'bump for direction'.[44] As to periodicals the longest-lasting publications nearly always had denominational allegiances, like the Congregational *Dysgedydd* and *Diwygiwr*, the Methodist *Drysorfa*, and the Anglican *Haul*. Their pattern was common: a sermon or other religious matter; an 'essay' or article; domestic, parliamentary and foreign news; and snippets of information, in turn instructive or piquant. The mixture of idealism and excitement is well caught in the first Address to the reader of the eventually most successful, *Yr Amserau* (The Times) of William Rees (Gwilym Hiraethog), published in 1843 in Liverpool, burgeoning metropolis for north Walians. Glad like a giant to run its race, despite the grievous expiry, mostly swift, of a host of predecessors, as it phrased it, the paper placed its hopes in the fact that 'present circumstances have matured our nation's thinking in general to the point of giving it a joyful welcome', understanding at last that the time had come 'to wake from her sleep, open ... her eyes and look about her, observe, enquire and demand to know what is happening and is likely to happen on the earth'.[45] Hiraethog (1802–83) was a talented man, one of the archetypal figures of nineteenth-century Nonconformist Wales. From remote rural origins, limited village schooling and peasant and shepherd youth, he had risen as a young man through Cymreigyddol society influence and a local bard's tuition to some fame as an eisteddfodic poet before entering the ministry. At first the *Amserau* languished with a mere four hundred subscribers, facing the loss of its financial patron, before Hiraethog turned it round with letters in dialect by a purported Welsh hill farmer relating his trials from landlord and Church injustice. He pledged with no little self-confidence that, unlike its London namesake which had betrayed its reformist principles, his paper would make the press an instrument of truth, justice and peace, purified by Christian principle.

Perhaps the chief achievement of Welsh publishing was the appearance in 1845 of a high-quality quarterly, *Y Traethodydd* (The Essayist), intended by its editor, the Calvinistic Methodist minister Lewis Edwards, to be a means to raise the 'taste' of Welsh readers and the level of public debate in the Welsh language. Modelled on the *Edinburgh Review*, and specialising in substantial articles on a wide variety of themes, the *Traethodydd* would not have been possible in Slovene at this time. Early issues covered topics like the Corn Laws, Tea-Totalism, political economy (touching on socialism and Louis Blanc) and Hungary; Welsh literary matters: Welsh bibliography, Williams Pantycelyn, patriotism and the institution of the Eisteddfod; and Welsh religious leaders like John Elias and Joseph Harris. Later Edwards was to contribute extensive translations of Goethe's *Faust* and Kant's *Critique of Pure Reason*. Its initial concentration above all was on the importance of education for Wales, including the linguistic aspect. Writers showed pride in the progress in literacy and consciousness brought about by the rise of Nonconformity, but acknowledged Welsh people's lack of general, secular knowledge; they sought consciously to free their country from its intellectual isolation at a time of increasing change and commercial contacts with England. The principle was that education was a matter for everyone, not merely an elite, which was defended both against apathy in the masses and upper-class fears of disruption from below. The solvent of these fears was the spirit of religion which ensured both individual freedom and respect for authority. The key was to establish the cooperation lacking between 'the most intelligent class' and the 'ignorant *gwerin*' so as to remove the age-old 'disadvantage' under which the latter suffered.[46] A comparably bold venture to the *Traethodydd* followed in 1851, the publication of a Welsh translation of the first volume of *Chamber's Encyclopædia*, the most comprehensive English compendium of scientific knowledge of the time. The Welsh edition's introduction claimed that the flexibility and 'copious' vocabulary of Welsh meant that scientific terminology could be conveyed entirely through Welsh roots, dispensing with the Latinate and Greek approach of English.[47] It was by far the most ambitious Welsh exercise in useful knowledge.

This excursus shows a considerable range of activity on behalf of and in the Welsh language. Yet, for comparison, weaknesses must be noted too. Complaints about public apathy to the mother tongue were as rife as in Slovenia. There were parts of Wales where *Seren Gomer* was quite unknown and others where reading a periodical or indeed anything but the Bible was considered pointless, commented the paper.[48] David Rees, editor of the *Diwygiwr* (The Reformer) wrote of the 'inertness' of the *gwerin*, 'the misers' with their fists their wallets, 'the drunkards' in the corner of the pub.[49] Circulations were of course low in a poor society, though surprisingly high compared to figures in far more populous England.[50] More disturbing were doubts that a breakthrough had been achieved in changing the status of the Welsh language. A *Seren Gomer* leading article in May 1831 stated it was disappointing after all the enthusiasm about Welsh societies that the English and their language still held the upper hand. An exile noticed how fearful Welsh people were of their masters, avoiding encounter with any well-dressed man because of their ignorance of English.[51] For all the journal talk of Welsh schools and textbooks, little if anything seems to have been done concretely. The 1847 educational report noted only three day schools in the Principality where Welsh was used in instruction. The impressive sounding plans for a Welsh language college for which royal patronage was to be sought came to nought, as did the calls for Welsh judges and bishops. Mark Jones has recorded the legal issue through the century, a saga of frustration.[52] R. Elwyn Hughes concludes that, despite the considerable efforts made, a convincing vocabulary for discussing Welsh in science was not established. He quotes an eisteddfod attender in 1840 pronouncing it 'an astonishing fact, that there was not in the Welsh language a single work connected with the sciences'.[53] This suggests an 'astonishing' lack of impact, at least as far as this individual was concerned. It is noteworthy that in this very period patterns of urban diglossia that had subsisted for centuries seem to have broken down in some important growing towns, like Cardiff and Swansea. The 1847 educational reports noted that in the former Welsh was not spoken by the children, except those of recent migrants from the countryside. A mixture of grumbling at 'humiliation' and 'oppression' mixed with ineffectual protest can be detected in Welsh discourse on the language question. How are these uncertainties to be explained?

Many of them are part of the syndrome of non-dominance and occurred also in ultimately successful language revivals: social embarrassment and conflicted attitudes towards a disregarded and to this extent disempowering mother tongue; tentativeness, false starts and lack of confidence. It can be seen in Slovenia. Indeed, even Czech could appear to a Bohemian aristocrat in 1842 to be a language written by small groups of patriots more from 'an obscure sense of national honour' than any real hope or plan; this was sixty years after historians date its first stirrings.[54] The position of Welsh speakers in their own milieu was especially difficult because of the lack of salience of language as an issue for their rulers, depriving them of a framework where a coherent approach could be articulated with which people could become familiar. Bringing a minority language into the schools or expanding its vocabulary for modern purposes benefited greatly from some outside spur or official necessity. Austrian acceptance of mother tongue education and resultant textbook provision was a huge boon for Slovene patriots. The drive to develop vocabulary in specific fields came in the Monarchy when German ceased to be the only language of law courts or when new institutions were called for with the end of absolutism. The successful British state functioned unilingually and had no need to change its ways, which rested on a laissez-faire individualism assuming its values would spread over time to a receding Celtic fringe.

Yet official assumptions are not enough to explain Welsh development. Britain was a liberal society and language revival flourished elsewhere even in the autocratic terrain of Tsarist Russia among Finns and Balts. Other factors came into play. Wales lacked the sort of language-driven intelligentsia which sustained such movements and of which Slovenia is an example. Second, for all the loyalty and emotion the Welsh language evoked, the driving force in Wales was not linguistic, but religious revival. This second factor is simpler to grasp and will be addressed shortly. The first needs some initial commentary.

The term 'intelligentsia' originates from eastern Europe, which helps explain its foreign, even pretentious ring for British ears. It described a stratum in authoritarian societies which during the Enlightenment emerged through education from the common people between the dominant nobility and the great peasant majority, the traditional middle class being small, weak and mainly mercantile. Not fitting into the neo-feudal social structure and critical of it, the intelligentsia became the spear head of protest against absolutist rule. Its characteristic was its educated quality and predisposition to reform. The German Gymnasium or advanced secondary school was its model throughout the region. Its cause was liberalism and nationalism, which could develop into socialism, as in Tsarist Russia. In religious matters it was secular-minded, in reaction to the role the Church played alongside the state power in authoritarian societies. The background to the impressive educational attainments of Slovenes like Linhart, Kopitar, Čop and Prešeren is apparent here, though Catholic seminaries and colleges also played a role. In Slovenia's humble circumstances they were not so radical, but they had wider intellectual perspectives than Welsh leaders, which took in contemporary European culture as well as the classical heritage a man like Walter Davies, certainly an intellectual, possessed.

Thus, alongside its Titans, men of energy and intellect – Hiraethog for one – Welsh debate also showed much ill-informed mediocrity. This appeared in some of the responses to Brutus's attack in *Seren Gomer*. It helps explain how William Owen Pughe's misguided views and idiosyncratic orthography could exercise such a hold on many, not all, Welsh writers, to the Welsh language's lasting detriment at a sensitive time. Embraced as up-to-date 'best practice' by young enthusiasts, they put off ordinary Welsh readers, beginning a disjuncture between conversational and 'proper' Welsh which has made many Welsh speakers feel inadequate in their mother tongue. Their far-fetched scientific coinages contributed to the failure of this genre of writing.[55] Other small nations at this time also often engaged in purism, rejecting the adaptation of international words of classical origin, but by the time Welsh practice changed it was too late to re-engage readers' interest. Pride in Wales's long literary past and the 'copiousness' of the Welsh language lay behind much of this. Walter Davies illustrated the pride in Welsh cultural tradition less negatively in championing the complex patterns of *cynghanedd*, seen as suited to the 'genius' of the Welsh language, against advocates of blank verse.[56] The same conservatism meant that the first sonnet to be written in Welsh did not make its appearance till 1830, just four years before Prešeren's famous sonnet wreath.[57] In fact, the first half of the nineteenth century was more noted for quantity than quality in Welsh poetry as poets, Walter Davies among them, imitated Goronwy Owen's revival of *cynghanedd* without his skill.[58] The two who have retained a place in the Welsh pantheon, Ieuan Glan Geirionydd (Evan Evans) and John Blackwell (Alun), both Nonconformist peasant sons become literary parsons, wrote graceful lyrics in more modern style.

In broader terms, Welsh patriots lacked the strategic vision of Slovene intellectuals, a Čop or, earlier, a Zois. He and Prešeren saw the Slovene language in an international context and were aware of the need to make it culturally competitive so as to appeal to urban bilingual Slovenes. One can easily overestimate Slovene farsightedness and its success. Slovene was on the slide at this time in the Carinthian provincial capital Klagenfurt. But in Ljubljana some of the seeds sprouted in more fertile ground, while in Swansea, where Joseph Harris and his son may have had similar hopes, Welsh declined. That is not to say that 'language planning', a live question in contemporary Wales, can have much effect on social processes. But it is a reminder that language concerns were considered more deeply in Slovenia than in Wales and had a higher priority in educated circles. That priority belonged in Wales to religion, without which, as the *Traethodydd*'s writers and editors like Gomer and Gwilym Hiraethog made plain their view, the much-desired enlightening of an ignorant people could not succeed. This was all the truer, they thought, in a stormy time when that people was exposed to many pressures which could lead it astray and blight the promised better future. Religion, education and social upheaval came together to vie for Welsh patriots' attention in the 1840s and come onto the agenda here.

NONCONFORMITY AND SOCIAL UNREST: TO THE 'TREASON OF THE BLUE BOOKS'

In this period, particularly in the second quarter of the century, Nonconformity became the dominant form of worship in Wales. The British religious census of 1851 recorded 808 Calvinistic Methodist places of worship there, 700 Baptist, 659 Wesleyan, and 634 Independent against 1,180 Anglican. Three-quarters of those attending services on the census day were Nonconformists.[59] The story behind this is one of the most remarkable in Welsh history. It was at the least a striking organisational feat for a community with few resources to create so vast a network and equip it with some thousands of ministers, effectively overshadowing a religious establishment backed by the authority of the state and centuries of tradition. Yet the new structures did not emerge from some masterplan. They were the product of countless initiatives and interactions building from the base of society itself within the framework of four denominations which, while pursuing independent courses different in a maze of details, came to mirror each other in essentials.

The process which redrew the Welsh landscape, dotting its remotest corners with the white-washed boxes of the Nonconformist chapel, had several stimulants. Most obvious was the effect of the great preachers of the Methodist movement and of old Dissent which followed them, setting in train a succession of fervent 'revivals' at regional or local level, like those of 1807–9 in the south, 1815–20 in the north, 1828 in Carmarthenshire and 1839–49 in Gwent and Glamorgan. But there was also some planning, conscious campaigns of expansions like the Baptist push into north Wales of 1776 and, most significant, the drive of Wesleyanism to implant itself in Wales from the 1790s. Wesley himself after many visits had left Wales to Calvinistic Methodism but the later movement was spearheaded by Welsh-speakers of his persuasion who could overcome the language barrier. English-style Arminian Methodism thus became known as Wesleyanism in Wales. Besides rivalry between denominations, splits within them on personal or theological grounds inevitable in the charged atmosphere gave further impetus to chapel building. Nonconformity's freedom from inherited structures facilitated this process which, however chaotic it appeared from the outside, did not impede a movement carried forward in a momentum of growth. By contrast Anglicans bound by with their historic parochial system were unable to react at first to the shifts of population industrialisation brought in the south Wales valleys, where Welsh nonconformity won over 90 per cent of the new working classes. Nor were the doctrinal splits which Anglicans (and posterity) have mocked so deserving of their scorn. The tradition of freedom of conscience inherited from the old Dissent of Baptists and Congregationalists, and the taste for Scripture of the large literate population created by the Sunday Schools, disclosed genuine dilemmas of Christian doctrine which older Churches had resolved (or covered up) in creeds dogmatically imposed and passively accepted. Many intra-Baptist debates for example, involved problems of Trinitarianism – Morgan John Rhys for one had Unitarian tendencies – though orthodoxy regularly triumphed.

The most serious doctrinal dispute was that between Wesleyans and the rest (for Baptists and Congregationalists were also Calvinists) on the issue of predestination: did Christ's sacrifice make salvation open to all, or, as 'High Calvinists' argued, only to the elect. The debate led to multi-volume polemical exchanges between the two camps in the 1800s and 1810s which only died down when High Calvinism was tempered by more moderate voices. Some but not all of its fierceness was due to Welsh resentment at Wesleyan 'poaching': the Welsh-speaking Wesleyans succeeded in winning their native spurs but remained permanently a weaker fourth behind the roughly evenly matched other bodies. The arguments ring oddly today. High Calvinism was an extreme form of the Calvinist stress of the absolute sovereignty of God vis-à-vis sinful man. Its chief champion John Elias's attempt to reconcile it with his passionate desire to preach God's mercy to all who accepted Christ in their hearts seems logic-chopping to today's reader. The most famous preacher of his day, Elias (1774–1841), bears witness like several other leaders to protracted spiritual wrestlings before he felt worthy to apply for church membership and ministry. His memoirs written months before his death relate how as a child he was impressed by an 'excellent' young boy who swore freely, but the same words stuck in the pious Elias's throat.[60] His fellow Methodist preacher John Jones Talsarn (1796–1857), strikingly strong and handsome but bashful, once ignored his mother's pleas and went to a distant fair where his companions brought him a beer and a girl for company; he got up in disgust and walked the long way home without food or drink all day.[61] Not all Methodist stalwarts were so severe. John Jones's biographer, though the austere regimenter of Liverpool Welsh life in later years, had as a youth swum across the Menai straits and walked on his hands from one end of Holyhead to the other.[62] It is necessary to get rid of stereotypes and recognise the religious reformers of this period as flesh and blood figures, born into what by any later standards was harsh poverty and fired by the only ideas (Biblical) and respected role models (preachers) open to them to take up a course which offered intellectual clarity, disciplined self-respect and a prospect of service and esteem in their own communities. John Jones was the last person prominent in Welsh life to know no English. An earnest self-improver without schooling and feeling it too late and time-consuming to learn another language, he sent a list of topics of useful knowledge to all the Welsh publishers soliciting the relevant books available in Welsh. Lost guideless in London once, with only an address to offer, he scoured the streets for Welsh-looking compatriots and eventually made his way to his lodgings.[63] With the large body of Anglo-American Protestant theology translated into Welsh and friends who satisfied his avid curiosity about what was not, he played an important part in Welsh Methodism's turn away from High Calvinism.

This raises the question of the nature of the Nonconformist ministry. The first two generations of Methodist leaders had been conventionally educated Anglican clergymen, very much like their counterparts in contemporary Slovene life. The ministers of Old Dissent had a background of education in Nonconformist academies. The mass movement of the early nineteenth century brought a great social change. Much of the preaching till well into the century was still carried out by 'itinerants' who sprang up in the wake of the Methodist revival, without formal training and frequently unlicensed by the authorities. Many of them were 'quacks'. The bulk of those who sought a denominational ministry came from a purely rural background. Of some fifty biographies of ministers in the present writer's possession relevant to this period only five came from towns, the largest having two thousand inhabitants. Most were from isolated farmsteads and began life as shepherds, farmers or craftsmen with negligible education or none, though they learnt to read Welsh from relatives. Interest in reading and listening to sermons was what attracted attention and led to their being directed into schooling and increasingly to the denominational colleges. These sometimes went back to eighteenth-century Nonconformist 'academies' or were new foundations like those at Abergavenny (1807), Brecon (1835) and Bala (1837) for Baptists, Congregationalists and Calvinistic Methodists respectively. These and other colleges taught the classics, theology and some secular subjects, with the more ambitious like Carmarthen and Brecon aiming at a link with the University of London and its degrees. As much as anything, however, they taught English, the language of instruction, and their records are littered with references to the difficulties of this hurdle for unprepared students.[64] Discipline problems were also common, particularly with adult students; the attractions of Carmarthen's theatre and pubs drew due attention.[65] By the 1840s a handful only began to graduate through these means; the goal of a full-time ministry was far from achieved. John Jones Talsarn was a quarryman, then relied on his wife's shop for income. But the goal itself remained dubious to many Calvinistic Methodists in particular. The mystique of the untutored charisma of many founding fathers long retained power for the developing movement.

The progress of Nonconformity can seem almost haphazard in these circumstances. Yet gradually it took on very similar forms in all the denominations. All developed patterns of regional associations with monthly and quarterly meetings and annual regional conferences. Individual churches remained the central focus, however, commonly choosing their own ministers, but usually after these had preached convincingly at a monthly or quarterly meeting. The Calvinistic Methodists and Wesleyans were somewhat more centralised. The former as befitted a purely Welsh organisation had an annual all-Wales conference, and eventually developed an association for English-speaking causes. Baptists and Congregationalists formed an all-Wales body only after this period and their English-speaking chapels in Wales were generally affiliated to English associations. Inter-denominational meetings for matters of common concern, like mission work, anti-slavery and temperance were quite frequent, and fund collecting tours by individual ministers for such causes, and notoriously to clear debts incurred by chapel building, were also common practice. Denominations came to specialise in areas of foreign mission. The 'enthusiasm' of the Methodists which so alarmed their Anglican critics and the Morris circle came to infect the soberer style of the older Dissenting bodies, while Methodists owed much early on to their help till structures settled and rivalry rose. The basis was laid for the denominational loyalties of the future as each celebrated their great preachers, published their own hymn books, developed their own Sunday schools and expanded their press. Central to the whole was the figure of the great preacher, even as the pulpit took over from the open fields and the churchyards in which Rowlands and Harris had made their mark. Christmas Evans for the Baptists, Williams o'r Wern for the Congregationalists, John Jones Talsarn and John Elias for the Methodists were the giants of the preaching festivals to which adherents travelled long distances and which provided stimulus and excitement with messages of sin and salvation. The struggles of the providential Christian life for every individual soul were the stock-in-trade of sermons and of the memorials to leading ministers ('cofiannau'), which ironically for fervent Protestants mimicked some of the tropes of medieval saints' lives. That of the well-educated Thomas Jones, ordained as an Anglican, was typical in recording three all but miraculous brushes with death in childhood.[66]

Yet this phenomenon of a highly individualistic religion, wholly orientated to the world to come, was occurring at a time of unprecedentedly stressful change in Welsh society. Perhaps that explains its power. It is true that the religious census of 1851 showed only about half the total population attending church on the census day. It might be argued that this still left many people apparently out of the religious loop. In practice nineteenth-century observers were agreed in giving nonconformist values something near a hegemonic role in Welsh-speaking culture. A correspondent of *Seren Gomer* as early as 1831 claimed that no other nation had preachers less worldly than Wales, which bound them to the common people more than anywhere else.[67] Though in origin a wholly international movement, and very strong in nineteenth-century England too, Welsh nonconformity had developed its own aura. The very quality of simplicity implicit in the *Seren Gomer* view above distinguished it in native eyes from the sedate coolness of the English version. The only hint of national distinctions in Christmas Evans's biography appears in his tirade against English nonconformists' mockery of Welsh open-air preaching.[68] And there is prima facie plausibility in the appeal of a new, unworldly creed to people whose familiar society was being turned upside down.

The extent of the challenge of change to Welsh people in just these years must be appreciated. Between 1801 and 1841 industrialisation multiplied the population of Bedwellte parish, Monmouthshire thirty-six-fold, the same proportion as the increase of iron production on the south Wales coalfield, which amounted to nearly half the total for England and Wales. More than three-fifths of the population of Monmouthshire and Glamorgan were employed in industry. A contemporary recorded how the people of what was becoming 'the valleys' in modern parlance, looked on in wonder as their world vanished before their eyes. This new world reinforced still more strongly the sharp class and ethnic divide of the old. To the domination of a few great landed families, who had shared out parliamentary seats and lord lieutenancies for generations, indeed centuries, came a stream of English ironmasters monopolising the new industry without even the notional connection to Wales of the wholly anglicised Morgans of Tredegar Park's descent from the eleventh-century Cadifor Fawr; actually, the connection had died out in the male line, as in most old Welsh families. Upwardly mobile bourgeois industrialists forged links with great landlords which could be sealed in marriage as in the Morgans's case. If the two Glamorganshire men who founded the first blast furnace in Dowlais in 1759 had to turn to others because they could not raise the £4,000 required, how could local capital mobilise the £300,000 apiece needed for the Blaenavon and Merthyr Iron and Coal Companies in the 1830s?[69] South-east Wales was caught in the vice of incipient industrialisation as higher wages than elsewhere came with recurrent slumps, poor housing, sanitary neglect, child labour and all the other problems of exploitative, unregulated early capitalism. Only half the children of Merthyr Tydfil reached their fifth birthday in the early 1830s. There is something colonial in this situation of workers almost universally speaking a language not known to their social superiors, as one London newspaper reported the situation.[70] As a passage in the 1847 Report on Welsh education (the notorious 'Treason of the Blue Books') put it, South Walian society showed 'the phenomenon of a peculiar language isolating the mass from the upper portion of society ... Rude and primitive agriculturalists living poorly and thinly scattered' were constantly changing places with 'smelters and miners wantoning in plenty and congregated in the densest accumulations'. But they did not thereby change their social position. 'They are never masters ... [their] language [keeps them] under the hatches.'[71]

This statement, almost engaging for its brutal candour, needs qualifying to bring out the full complexity of the situation. Welsh workers were not wholly 'cut off' from the wider world about them by the 'brass wall' of language, as Lingen went on to say. In the mining districts of Monmouthshire and Merthyr, at least, a fair number will have picked up some English; there was awareness of political movements like that for parliamentary reform and Chartism, subsisting alongside much older Welsh tradition; by the 1830s there was an active press in both languages including a bilingual paper for workers in Merthyr. Educated Welsh speakers like Hugh Williams and Zephaniah Williams and people who had acquired Welsh like John Frost, mayor of Newport in 1839, were active in popular protest. Overall, it was quite likely a milieu closer to that of newly arrived migrants in modern Europe or of South African Soweto a generation ago than to the more fully bilingual Dowlais, say, of two generations later which may lie behind much historical evocation. But it is not so much Welsh ignorance of English as English ignorance of Welsh which is most indicative of and relevant to the issue of power at stake in the situation. In the absence of a regular police force, the deployment of troops was often a potentially hazardous necessity.

Discontent remained at a fairly high level throughout the period but went through a number of changes. The frequent food riots that had occurred in the 1790s, several needing intervention by troops or the militia, differed only in sharpness from traditional patterns. In certain areas 60 per cent of the rural poor's income went on corn for bread, so that price rises had immediate effect. Two thousand were involved in the Merthyr riots of 1800, when three men received death sentences. Protests against enclosures were also common, with motives varying from appeals to American republicans and John Locke, to traditional moral assumptions about just prices and the right to the *tai unnos* (see p. 31) by the

Welsh laws of Hywel Dda.[72] The mix of modern and traditional motifs began to make its appearance. Extensive troop deployment was required in 1816 to cover several trouble spots in south-east Wales at a time when depression, unemployment, rising food prices and wage issues led to shifting strike action accompanied by threats, damage to property and coordinated marching gangs of workers. The printing and circulation of Welsh translations from William Cobbett's *Political Register* was stopped at pain of imprisonment. The workers' tactics were later generalised in the movement of the *Tarw Scotch* (known in English as the Scotch Cattle, though literally Scotch Bull), active for most of the period 1820–34. This movement, as mysterious as its name, was effectively a secret society of colliers operating in north-west Monmouthshire and adjacent parts of Glamorgan. Night-time mountain meetings planned demands and if these went unheeded, intimidation of non-strikers and employers by noisier mountain meetings, threatening letters, 'midnight visits', destruction of mining company property and rapid deployment of forces between the various valleys followed. Its unapprehended leader spoke of his 'naw mil o blant ffyddlon' (nine thousand loyal children). In an environment where the bulk of mine owners were English and the great majority of workers Welsh-speaking Welsh – though English workers were already a not trivial minority in Monmouthshire – the Scotch Cattle had a distinctly ethnic profile. 'We, who are natives and real owners cannot stretch a foot without being trod on' ran one of their messages to 'these children of Hengist and Horsa' as they called the proprietors. These are the traditional names of the leaders of the Anglo-Saxon invasion of Britain in the fifth century.[73] The overwhelming majority of Scotch Cattle prosecuted bore Welsh names. One of them refused to give evidence in English though he was said to know it well.

Three outbursts best illustrate the social stress of the period. The Merthyr riots of 1831 show how underlying tensions could spark off major incidents almost by accident and misjudgement, without a single overriding issue; Merthyr's economic situation had been relatively favourable in the 1820s. But with twenty-two thousand people crowding the one parish, inadequate administrative structures and a thin band of shopkeepers and professionals alone between the industrialists and the overwhelming body of their workers, it had all the potential for unrest. It had, though, had a philosophical society, associated with Iolo Morganwg and his son Taliesin, and a strong radical tradition, which had been stirred by the struggle for

British parliamentary reform (1830–2). Some consensus in favour of this between workers, businesspeople and a liberal-minded industrialist foundered on a wide range of workers' grievances. Radical workers, with confidence drawn from the power of numbers and a successful demonstration, sought to impose their own version of reform. A debtor's court was destroyed and troops called in; distrust mounted, negotiations failed, shots were fired and several days of rioting followed in which over twenty died. The hanging of a possibly innocent young miner, Richard Lewis (Dic Penderyn), bequeathed Wales a working-class martyr who has loomed far larger in death than in an almost wholly anonymous life. One can say only that his letter to his sister from Cardiff jail the night before his execution shows surprising dignity in, for all we know, an ordinary young man in the circumstances:

> I beseech you to come as soon as possible to fetch my body since there is no likelihood of any other outcome at present. Go to Phillip Lewis and get him to bring the cart down with as many men as he can manage to bring with him. I believe the Lord has forgiven me my various sins and transgressions but of that for which I charged I am not guilty and for that I have cause to be thankful.[74]

The Newport rising also had a wider British backdrop, the Chartist movement which built on the incipient trade union movement to press for more radical parliamentary reform and manhood suffrage. But this time it appears, though secrecy obscures a totally clear picture, that in the operational area of the Scotch Cattle plans had been drawn up in advance and arms gathered for action in the event of the rejection of the Charter. Whether the 5,000 men who converged on the Westgate Hotel in Newport in November 1839 intended to gain their object by intimidating the small body of troops present or by force and how far-reaching that object was has been much debated – it is quite likely that the marchers themselves did not know; they fled when shot at, with many casualties – but it seems that the mayor of Newport, John Frost, did believe in the possibility of spurring an uprising of fellow Chartists elsewhere on the lines of France in July 1789. His own motivation was a hatred of government rigged in the interests of aristocrats and state pension holders at the people's expense. Yet one of the marchers was reported to have thought that the goal was to march on London and win a great kingdom – shades of ancient Welsh prophecy! Welsh Chartist meetings regularly began with prayer, though Zephaniah Williams was an unbeliever. The mix of motives and levels of feeling typifies the impact of rapid change imposed on disrupted communities.

The Rebecca Riots of 1838–9 and 1843 against new toll-gates highlighted the nonconformist factor. They took place in an area where population growth (up by 65 per cent in the three south-western counties) exacerbated problems caused by stagnant or falling real wages, declining rural industry and enclosure. It was also home to some of the most intense resentment of the state church, its tithes, church tax and power to impose the obligations of church wardenship on Nonconformists at a time of distress. Nonconformists replied by flooding church vestries and voting to prevent the levying of church rates, battles avidly followed by David Rees of the *Diwygiwr* in nearby Llanelli. Unpopular vicars were often objects of the *ceffyl pren*, a Welsh version of rough music closely linked to Rebecca. The movement's name was taken from the Rebekah in *Genesis* whose seed are enjoined to 'possess the gates of those which hate them'. Hugh Williams, the Carmarthen-based lawyer who lent his aid to the Chartists, did so also to Rebecca. It was through him that Carmarthen acquired the first branch of the Chartist Working Men's Association to be set up in Wales. At this time Carmarthen was still as large as Cardiff and the region was important in the migration of labour which supplied the mining valleys and was to do even more so thereafter. Another common link was the London press's fascination with Rebecca, the Scotch Cattle and Welsh Chartism, though the *Revue des deux Mondes* also found her the stuff of which legends are made.[75] The fact that many of the ringleaders of these episodes were never captured no doubt strengthened this aspect. Foundations were laid for the 'Welsh radical tradition' which has been such an important part of the Welsh self-image and thereby of Welsh nationality. They are all the more important for telling the overall story of paths to nationhood, which this study is attempting to do.

This chapter brings the story of these paths up to a turning point. It is of the nature of turning points that their presence somewhere ahead can often be sensed, but the exact point at which the turn will come cannot be predicted, still less the outcome. It seems fitting to give an account of the dénouement in a pendant chapter to this one and thus to reserve a full judgement on the whole period up to 1848 till the end of that chapter. Here some interim remarks may be made.

The period covered in this chapter was one of transition from traditional patterns of social authority and economic organisation to the more
dynamic, democratic possibilities implicit, but only theoretically, in the
eighteenth-century Enlightenment. In most of Europe and certainly the
still absolutist Habsburg Monarchy it was only very gradual, but in Britain
it was quite rapid, particularly in industrialising areas. However, a basic
divergence between Welsh and Slovene courses held in prospect in this
study had not yet taken place, nor was it easily foreseeable. Both countries
were linguistic communities playing inactive roles in larger empires. The
structures of political and social power had not altered, though industrialisation had brought change at the bottom of the social scale in parts
of south-east Wales. Language slippage on the margins was somewhat
greater in Wales than Slovenia but remained basically that – marginal.
Knowledge of English had certainly increased, no doubt faster than that
of German in Slovene lands. In 1840, the Revd Jones reported an estimate
that it had advanced twenty miles into Wales in twenty years but not to
the eclipse of Welsh.[76]

Still, significant shifts had occurred. Social continuity was maintained
more strongly in Slovenia than in Wales, where industrial Britain found
one of its most productive areas. Yet cultural continuity did not wholly
correspond. With less of a background tradition to follow, Slovene literary
'high culture' – at least in poetry for there was as yet little prose – struck
in Prešeren modern, European notes not found in Wales. This reflected
the 'intelligentsia' syndrome which has been described and can be taken
back to the origins of the Slovene revival in men like Linhart, Zois, even
Vodnik under Zois's influence. The overall effect was to make for more
cultural continuity in the small band of Slovene cultural reformers than
between the Morris circle and Welsh life two generations later. The lineal
descendants of the eighteenth-century Morris circle, fusing patriotic, linguistic and historical interests in their mould, were Anglican intellectuals
like Walter Davies. Yet these had become considerably less influential in
Welsh life because their religion aligned them with a minority elite out of
step with a changing society. This tended to reinforce in such people the
nostalgic attitude to things Welsh long characteristic of Welsh tradition.
Ieuan Glan Geirionydd's finely crafted poem 'Cyflafan Morfa Rhuddlan'
(The Massacre of Rhuddlan Marsh) invoking an ancient Welsh defeat at
Saxon hands is suffused with patriotic resignation.[77] Relating the growing
anger which wells in him on a quiet night as he recalls the high hopes of

the warriors, overcome only by numbers, he concludes by searching for their graves and taking respite in the hospitable home of the local vicar and his barking dog. The gulf opening up between Nonconformists and the state church sapped the unity of educated pro-Welsh opinion, making for a certain diffuseness of patriotic energy in what was otherwise an impressively diverse scene. People actively concerned with Welsh culture were still more numerous than such figures in Slovenia but lacked the focus provided to a language-driven intelligentsia, tiny as it was.

Nonconformists, who after overcoming theological wrangles had in the last generation become an overwhelming majority in rural and industrial regions, had scarcely had time to take the place of the old order. Men of powerful gifts had come forward in earlier generations – not to mention the celebrated hymn writer Ann Griffiths – and now figures Lewis Edwards and Hiraethog, but the person most fitting to represent the dawning industrial age is probably the Independent minister Evan Evans (Ieuan Gwynedd (1820–52). Born to a poor peasant family in Merionethshire whose mother had sought books for him in homes of the better off, first coming forward to preach as a tall, thin, piercing-eyed country youth in a coat of homespun cloth, striped trousers and big strong boots in which he had walked forty miles the previous day,[78] he moved to the mining town of Tredegar in Monmouthshire to become a passionate advocate of the miners, teetotalism and anti-slavery, multiple editor (including the first Welsh-language paper for women), critic of Welsh 'English worship', eisteddfodic poet and opponent of state control of education. Succumbing to TB preceded by his wife and child, he died three days after completing 'The Miner's Song', a powerful portrayal of coal workers' harsh, dangerous, ill-paid toil to ease the life of uncaring others.[79] The poem is not wholly modern. Ieuan Gwynedd does not formally indict the 'others' or the system which made for the miners' hardship. But the emotional drive casts vivid light on what was to become a central theme in Welsh national life.

A word is due, too, for the empires in which our peoples were shaping. Pre-March Austria – a common term for the pre-1848 years – was neither the home of stability and even-handedness for all, including its nationalities, as Metternich portrayed it, nor the censor-ridden police state of European liberal denigrators. The Civic Code of 1811 offered equal civil rights to all, but the semi-feudal land system belied its spirit. Austrian state servants needed to know German but were not obliged to become Germans. The dominance of German culture in the towns was both accepted and resented. Politics was basically taboo. What of the Great Britain of these years? It was not just an English state but paid much less attention to ethnic difference than Austria. Its vaunted claim was to be a constitutional polity, which guaranteed its subjects' liberties as individuals, leaving them free to pursue their own interests, economic or cultural (laissez-faire). Ireland remained the exception. It did not benefit from British prosperity, while its government-backed national school system (1831), its national police force and the frequent coercion acts applied to it breached laissez-faire principle in the interest of maintaining London's control. The British reputation for political skill hardly applied.

As to Wales, the treatment of those sentenced in the Newport and the Rebecca trials shows something of the British state's liberalism in individual matters. The three men sentenced to death in the former were pardoned and transported to Tasmania. John Frost was eventually licensed in 1857 to return to a hero's welcome in Newport and London. No Rebecca figures were executed. This certainly helped allay resentment; Welsh respect for British constitutional liberties contrasts with Habsburg subjects' sense of alienation on this score. But a consequence of Welsh social unrest was some tendency by the 1840s for officialdom to tar the Welsh with the Irish brush. A letter about Rebecca from home secretary Graham to prime minister Melbourne significantly linked Wales with Ireland, an association others made at this time. Graham blamed poverty and landlord misconduct for crime and discontent in both countries. To this humane insight he added, however: 'this is a truth none the less dangerous because it cannot openly be declared'.[80] In other words, the class basis of the state could not be cast in doubt. Strength is lent to John Frost's indictment of an aristocratic regime. Bound up with English attitudes to Ireland was a vein of racism reflected in simian-like caricatures in the English press; the contempt was transferable to Ireland's Celtic cousins, the Welsh. Rebecca occurred in the same decade as the Irish famine, a reminder of the limits of British competence.

Shortly, however, the terminal incompetence of the Austrian *ancien régime* would open up new perspectives and a whole new ball game.

NOTES

1   W. J. O'Daunt, *Personal Recollections of the late Daniel O'Connell* (London, 1849), p. 14.

2 Roy Jenkins, *Gladstone: A Biography* (New York, 1997), p. 279.
3 H. Rumpler, *Eine Chance für Österreich 1804–1918: Bürgerliche Emanzipation und Staatsverfall in der Habsburgermonarchie* (A Chance for Central Europe. Bourgeois Emancipation and State Collapse in the Habsburg Monarchy) (Vienna, 1997), pp. 208–9.
4 J. Hösler, *Von Krain zu Slowenien: Die Anfänge der nationalen Differenzierungsprozesse in Krain und der Untersteiermark von der Aufklärung bis zur Revolution 1768 bis 1848* (From Carniola to Slovenia. The Beginnings of the National Differentiation Process in Carniola and Lower Styria from Enlightenment to Revolution: 1768–1848) (Munich, 2006), pp. 235–6.
5 Hösler, *Krain zu Slowenien*, p. 142.
6 Hösler, *Krain zu Slowenien*, p. 145.
7 Calculated from figures given in ibid., p. 141.
8 For Čop's ideas see H. R. Cooper Jr, *France Prešeren* (Boston, 1980), 41–5.
9 Cooper, *Prešeren*, 59. Cooper's work is also helpful for Prešeren's life and an illuminating analysis of his poetry.
10 R. Lenček, 'Kopitar's Place in the Evolution of Slavonic Philology', in R. Lenček and H. R. Cooper (eds), *To Honor Jernej Kopitar (1780–1980)* (Ann Arbor, 1982), pp. 1–25, partic. 12–14.
11 J. Sommer, 'A Step away from Herder and the Question of National Language', *The Slavonic and East European Review*, 90 (2012), 1–32.
12 J. Pogačnik, *Kulturni pomen slomškovega dela* (The Cultural Significance of Slomšek's Work) (Maribor, 1971), p. 22.
13 Ivan Prijatelj, 'Več Prešerna!' (Let's have more of Prešeren!), *Ljubljanski zvon*, 20 (1900), 724–32 (732).
14 Prijatelj, 'Prešerna!', 727.
15 August Šenoa, *Karanfil s pjesnikova groba* (A Carnation from the Poet's Grave), ed. by Anka Nazečić (Sarajevo, 1965), pp. 49–119.
16 Hösler, *Krain zu Slowenien*, pp. 250–2.
17 *Novice*, 6 August 1843: 'Ilirske dezhele nekadaj in sada' (Illyrian lands then and now).
18 Hösler, *Krain zu Slowenien*, pp. 339–50.
19 Hösler, *Krain zu Slowenien*, pp. 204–5.
20 John Stuart Mill, *Utilitarianism, Liberty, Representative Government* (London, Toronto and New York, 1910), p. 364.
21 Hösler, *Krain zu Slowenien*, p. 228.
22 The present author's paraphrase of material from a sermon of 1814 by Matija Vertovec, published in the latter's *Shodni ogovori* (Ljubljana, 1850) and cited in P. Vodopivec, *O gospodarskih in socialnih nazorih na Slovenskem v 19. stoletnem* (Economic and Social Thought in Nineteenth-Century Slovenia) (Ljubljana, 2006). Vertovec was a leading clerical writer of such handbooks.
23 J. Prunk, *Slovenski narodni vzpon* (Slovenia's Rise to Nationhood) (Ljubljana, 1992), pp. 43–4.
24 Hösler, *Krain zu Slownien* (Ljubljana, 1992), pp. 241, 236.

25 Huw Walters, 'Y Gymraeg a'r Wasg Gylchgronol' (The Welsh Language and the Periodical Press), in Geraint H. Jenkins (ed.), *Gwnewch Bopeth yn Gymraeg: Yr Iaith Gymraeg a'i Pheuoedd* (Do Everything in Welsh) (Cardiff, 1999), pp. 327–52 (p. 348); Aled Jones, 'Yr Iaith Gymraeg a Newyddiaduraeth' (The Welsh Language in Journalism), in ibid., pp. 353–74 (p. 357).

26 *The English Works of the Rev. Walter Davies, MA*, ed. by the Revd D. Silvan Evans, B.D. (Carmarthen and London, 1868), p. 367.

27 Davies, *English Works*, p. 386.

28 Davies, *English Works*, pp. 355–6, 445.

29 Celyn Gurden-Williams, *Lady Llanover and the Creation of a Welsh Cultural Utopia* (PhD thesis, Cardiff University) (Pro-Quest Dissertations Publishing, 2009), p. 86.

30 Gurden-Williams, *Lady Llanover*, pp. 93–5.

31 Gurden-Williams, *Lady Llanover*, p. 80. Oddly, the common claim that Lady Llanover had little command of Welsh comes from a Welsh National Museum site that plainly has laudatory intent. It may owe something to the first Archbishop of Wales, no friend of Welsh, who commented sardonically that she had failed on their meeting to recognise the name for (Pharaoh's) butler given in the Welsh Bible: see The Archbishop of Wales (Alfred George Edwards), *Memories* (Cardiff, 1927), p. 89.

32 J. Davies, *Cardiff and the Marquisses of Bute* (Cardiff, 1981), pp. 28, 30, 100–2.

33 Gurden-Williams, *Lady Llanover*, p. 86.

34 Davies, *English Works*, p. 445.

35 Davies, *English Works*, pp. 387, 496.

36 *Gweithiau Gomer* (The Works of Gomer), ed. by D. ap Rhys Stephen (Llanelli, 1839), pp. xvi–xvii.

37 *Seren Gomer* (hereafter *SG*), 7 (1824), Brutus, Lleyn, 'Y Gymraeg' (The Welsh Language), pp. 80–4, 369–73.

38 *SG*, 9 (1826), pp. 114–15, 137–9, 237–42.

39 For example, *SG*, 7 (1824), 150–2 (rhetorical); 155, 172–5, 186 (education). On p. 114, Cyfaill y Cymro (The Welshman's Friend) argued against the alleged excellencies of Welsh as a language that nothing had worth in itself but only as it brought benefit to its possessor.

40 Ibid., (Gedeon = Harris), 'Nodiadau ar Ysgrif y digyffelyb Brutus' (Notes on the Article of the Ineffable Brutus), 403–9. This article is reproduced in *Gweithiau Gomer* (Gomer's Works), 343–53.

41 *SG*, 11 (1828), Rhagymadrodd (Foreword); *SG*, 14 (1831), Rhagymadrodd (Foreword).

42 *SG*, 13 (1830), 297–9 (Welsh-language college).

43 *SG*, 13 (1830) (Eiddil Ifor), 334–5.

44 R. Elwyn Hughes, 'Yr Iaith Gymraeg ym Myd Gwyddoniaeth a Thechnoleg' (The Welsh Language in the World of Science and Technology), in Geraint R. Jenkins (ed.), *Gwnewch Bopeth yn Gymraeg: Yr Iaith Gymraeg a'i Pheuoedd 1801–1911* (Do Everything in Welsh: The Welsh Language and its Domains 1801–1911) (Cardiff, 1999), pp. 375–98.

45 The Revd T. Roberts and D. Roberts, DD, *Cofiant y Parch: W. Rees, D.D. (Hiraethog)* (Life of the Revd W. D. Rees (Hiraethog)) (Dolgellau, 1893), p. 239.

46 See particularly 'Addysgiad y Genedl' (The Education of the Nation), *Y Traethodydd*, 3 (1847) and J. Hughes, 'Traethodau i'r Cymry' (Essays for the Welsh), *Y Traethodydd*, 2 (1846), from which the quotation is taken.

47 *Addysg Chambers i'r Bobl: Cyfieithiad o'r argraffiad Seisnig diweddaraf,* cyfrol 1 (Chambers's Education for the People: Translation of the most recent edition, vol. 1) (Pwllheli, 1851), Rhagdraeth (Preamble).

48 *SG*, 7 (1824), 1: 'At y darllenwyr' (To the Readers).

49 Iorwerth Jones, *David Rees, Y Cynhyrfwr* (David Rees, the Agitator) (Swansea, 1971), p. 270.

50 The Times circulation was only 7,353 in the year the Diwygiwr began. In 1850 the latter's was 2,400; Jones, *David Rees*, p. 88; Dot Jones (ed.), *Statistical information relating to the Welsh Language, 1801–1911* (Cardiff, 1998).

51 *SG*, 14 (1831), 129–31; 10 (1827), 204–6.

52 Mark Ellis Jones, '"Dryswch Babel": Yr Iaith Gymraeg, Llysoedd a Deddfwriaeth yn y Bedwaredd Ganrif ar Bymtheg' (The Confusion of Babel, Courts and Legislation in Wales in the Nineteenth Century), in G. Jenkins (ed.), *Gwnewch Bopeth yn Gymraeg*, pp. 553–80.

53 Elwyn Hughes, 'Yr Iaith Gymraeg ym Myd Gwyddoniaeth', in G. Jenkins (ed), *Gwnewch Bopeth yn Gymraeg*, pp. 375–94 (p. 387).

54 Leo Graf von Thun-Hohenstein, *Über den gegenständigen Stand der böhmischen Literatur* (The Present State of Bohemian Literature) (Prague, 1842), p. 5.

55 Elwyn Hughes, 'Yr Iaith Gymraeg ym Myd Gwyddoniaeth', p. 395.

56 *English Works of the Rev. Walter Davies*, pp. 392, 440–1.

57 H. Jones, *Y Soned Gymraeg hyd 1900* (The Welsh-language sonnet till 1900) (Llandysul, 1967), pp. 11–47.

58 To be fair, Gwallter Mechain did contribute one fine and anthologised englyn, given here for readers of Welsh: 'Y nos dywell yn distewi – caddug/Yn cuddio Eryri,/Yr haul yng gwely'r heli/A'r lloer yn ariannu'r lli.'

59 Dot Jones (ed.), *Statistical Evidence*, p. 425; R. Tudur Jones, *Hanes Annibynwyr Cymru* (A History of the Welsh Independents) (Swansea, 1966), p. 191.

60 *Hunangofiant John Elias* (The Autobiography of John Elias), ed. Goronwy P. Owen (Swansea, 1974), p. 51.

61 Owen Thomas, *Cofiant John Jones Talsarn* (The Life of John Jones Talsarn), pp. 51–5.

62 D. Ben Rees, *Pregethwr y Bobl: Bywyd a Gwaith Owen Thomas* (The People's Preacher. The Life and Work of Owen Thomas) (Liverpool, 1979), p. 11.

63 Thomas, *Cofiant John Jones*, p. 193.

64 For example, Geraint Dyfnallt Morgan, *Ysgolion a Cholegau yr Annibynwyr* (Schools and Colleges of the Independents) (Llandysul, 1939), pp. 71, 80, 99.

65 Morgan, *Ysgolion*, pp. 37, 60.

66 Y Parch. Jonathan Jones, *Cofiant Thomas Jones o Ddinbych* (The Life of Thomas Jones of Denbigh) (Denbigh, 1897), pp. 25–8.

67 *SG*, 14 (1831), 197–200.

68 See W. Morgan, *Cofiant, neu hanes bywyd y diweddar Barch: Christmas Evans* (The History of the Life and Work of the late Revd Christmas Evans) (Wrexham, 1883), pp. 68–74.

69 I. Wilks, *South Wales and the Rising of 1839: Class Struggle as Armed Struggle* (London, 1984), pp. 15, 38.

70 Wilks, *South Wales*, p. 26.

71 *Reports of the Commissioners of Inquiry into the State of Education in Wales...in three parts*, vol. I (London, 1848), pp. 3–4.

72 David Jones, *Before Rebecca. Popular Protests in Wales 1793–1835* (London, 1973), pp. 60–1. Jones's book is the basis of this paragraph.

73 Jones, *Before Rebecca*, p. 88.

74 Gwyn A. Williams, *The Merthyr Rising* (London, 1978), p. 208.

75 David Williams, *The Rebecca Riots: A Study in Agrarian Discontent* (Cardiff, 1955), p. vii.

76 Revd W. Jones, *A Prize Essay in English and Welsh on the Character of the Welsh as a Nation in the Present Age* (London, 1841), p. 24.

77 *The Oxford Book of Welsh Verse*, ed. Thomas Parry (Oxford, 1962), pp. 359–60.

78 *Cofiant, a gweithiau barddonol a rhyddieithol Ieuan Gwynedd* (The Life and Poetical and Prose Works of Ieuan Gwynedd) (Wrexham, c.1880), pp. 30–1.

79 *Cofiant Ieuan Gwynedd*, pp. 431–2.

80 Williams, *Rebecca Riots*, p. 18.

Chapter 4

THE PARTING OF THE WAYS, 1847–1848

In March 1848, just weeks after the Monarchy had been deposed in France, revolution broke out in Vienna and quickly spread. Everywhere it called for the end of absolutism and for constitutional liberties, freedoms of speech, assembly and the press, and popular share in government through elected bodies. Everywhere, the equality of individuals was linked with the equality of peoples, expressed through the free use of their languages in school, administration and law court, and the restoration of former rights, if under the Habsburg sceptre. Liberalism and nationalism went together. 'The rights of nations are the rights of nature' was the Czech leader Palacký's ringing phrase. Slovenes found themselves plunged into a political vortex scarcely imaginable in a British world empire at its most confident height. A rather smug view of the revolutionary events on the continent is reflected in Tennyson's famous ode on the death of the Duke of Wellington, the hero of Waterloo, in 1852, which depicts them as a matter of 'brainless mobs and lawless powers':

> O Europe, keep our noble England whole/And save the one true seed of freedom sown/Betwixt a people and their ancient throne/ That sober freedom out of which there springs/Our loyal passion for our temperate kings.

What happened was that though the revolutionaries shared the common mix of liberal and national values, the framework of their application was disputed. The stronger nations went as far as to demand independence. Austria was soon involved in war with Italian nationalists claiming her territories in Lombardy and Venetia for the united Italy they wished to create. By autumn a second war had broken out between Vienna and the Hungarians. Meanwhile, German-speaking Austrians rallied to the cause of a new united Germany whose constitution was to be worked out in a parliament in Frankfurt. Their radical wing led a rebellion in Vienna for fear of the dynasty's reneging on the concessions it had made to the revolution; they were crushed. The Czechs did not seek independence but full autonomy for their former kingdom, which its hitherto dominant German minority opposed. Confrontation was eventually brought to a close by a reassertion of Habsburg absolute power, with military intervention by Tsarist Russia and support from Habsburg Slavs who feared inclusion in the proposed new Germany. The whole episode demonstrated the potential fragility of the multinational empire and obliged its component parts to see their prospects in a wider perspective.

THE SLOVENE LANDS IN 1848

Slovenes reacted less dramatically than larger groups. Metternich's fall was greeted by an illuminated theatre performance in Ljubljana and some demonstration against the town authorities by dissatisfied townsfolk and youth. But the national consciousness that had been in the making found expression now that the authoritarian hand had been removed. 'Only one thought filled all of us', reported Bleiweis on a Carniolan deputation to Vienna nearly a month after the revolution, 'that we should strongly raise up and affirm our nationality', adding all were not agreed how.[1] But others broached the question of a Slovene entity, like Viennese Slovenes in an emotional call on their 'dear brothers' to believe the same 'ineffable desires' animated them as they did 'Carniolans, Styrians, Carinthians and Primorians' and join in begging the emperor to unite them in 'a concord of the whole Slovene nation': what was bound together by blood, heart and speech should not be severed by force.[2] Petitions and declarations from prominent individuals, students and other ad hoc groupings poured in, some responding to campaigns for more/petitions, increasingly combining the language and the wider Slovene national theme. Newly formed 'Slovenija' societies established in Vienna and Graz, claiming the name barely known a decade before, just part of a blizzard of such initiatives in the empire as a whole. A punch-drunk central government granted freedom of the press, promised a constitution to be drafted by a parliament to meet in Vienna in July, and in general acquiesced in a host of often contradictory demands. In Slovenia's case the call for an all-Slovene administrative unit ran up against the opposition of Styrian and Carinthian Germans to the breaking up of their illustrious provinces and of Slovenes themselves to accept the dominance of Carniola and Ljubljana. Calls for Habsburg Slavs to boycott elections to the pan-German parliament in Frankfurt assembly succeeded overwhelmingly among the Czechs but went largely unheard in Slovenia. Only four Slovenes attended a 'Panslav Congress' in Prague, which called for Austria to orientate itself towards its Slavic majority rather merge in the projected new German state. Most practically, the Slovene representatives in new Styrian and Carinthian provisional Diets did not oppose declarations of the German majority that these provinces were indivisible, issuing rather feeble protestations that they trusted their German colleagues and valued the ancient provincial ties. Ordinary people's loyalties to the traditional provinces still outweighed the aspirations of nationally committed Slovenes.

No doubt it was awareness of this that swayed Bleiweis's leadership in the Slovenes' strongest province, Carniola. His temperament also inclined him to gradualism: 'everything great matures slowly', as he once remarked.[3] Constant fulsome expressions of loyalty to dynasty and empire by Slovene spokesmen reflected realpolitik but also conviction. In Carniola at least, this strategy had some success. The indifference of which Prešeren complained in the 1830s appeared now to yield to support on all sides, in principle, for furthering Slovene's public use, including bodies with a fair number of German speakers. A political newspaper, 'Slovenija', appearing twice-weekly, was launched in July. The Ljubljana Slovene Society decided to change the language of its minutes from German to Slovene. The crowding of officials and lawyers into this society may have been partly opportunistic, motivated by people's desire to safeguard career prospects in the changed atmosphere, but this felt need in itself suggests changes in perception. The winning over of the urban middle classes which Čop had championed seemed suddenly to have come about in Ljubljana. Of course, there was general recognition that a complete fulfilment of language demands could not immediately come about. The introduction of Slovene into secondary schooling now sought was initially a very modest affair. Discussion in *Novice*'s pages reveals kindred issues which ring a bell to present Welsh ears. Patriots put down officials' reluctance to operate publicly in their mother tongue to unfamiliarity; critics of the movement for Slovene blamed the language's inadequacy. Other languages should be respected, it was urged, but the prime concern should be righting the wrongs to Slovene.[4]

Yet the more circumspect of Slovene patriots, knowing their weaknesses in numbers and development, saw the bigger picture beyond their local successes. They saw the need to guard against the powerful forces of German nationalism and looked to the dynasty for support. Following the Czechs, they trusted that court circles would recognise the Slav majority in the empire and implement their promises of national equality. This so-called Austro-Slav tendency strengthened when an imperial strong man crushed the autumn rising of German radicals in Vienna, with Slav support. Part of the strategy for some Slovene thinkers entailed the hope that Austria would turn away from concentration on Germanic central Europe and direct the Monarchy's focus towards the south-east and their brother Croats and Serbs: the Illyrian idea. This was geopolitical thinking on some scale, but it was whistling in the dark. In March 1849 a resurgent Vienna government dispersed the parliament granted during the revolution and vetoed the constitution it had drawn up. Later in the year the Kingdom of Illyria, long existing only on paper, was abolished. The Slovene societies and newspapers were closed down. *Novice* by 1850 was the only Slovene journal alongside a conservative Catholic organ still permitted to exist. Initial attempts during the revolution to use Slovene in the courts and public life foundered on the opposition of Slovene officials themselves, the so-called *nemškutarji*, a negative term directed at Slovenes who acted as Germans in things national. Habsburg Slav bitterness at betrayal deepened historic resentment at subaltern status. For the editor of *Slovenija*, siding with the Habsburgs had always been 'the lesser evil', a barrier against the worse evil of Germandom and denationalisation. 'Everything points to centralisation', he now wrote, 'but God willing that will not be built for all time'.[5] The minority of Slovenes who were 'nationally conscious' had experienced the dilemma of a small people in a multinational zone. While the multinationalism had been a stimulus for their own development, it made them liable to be crushed by more powerful beasts. Their situation led them to dream dreams but, twist and turn as they might, they lacked the means to realise them. In comparative context it showed the problem of an 'intelligentsia'-based style of development: the mixture of sophistication in intellectual leaders, exposed to manifold influences by their situation in the centrally placed, insecure Habsburg Monarchy, and on the other hand the weakness of its mass base in a poorly educated, semi-feudal peasantry. The interest of the peasant majority went almost wholly on removing the remains of feudalism on the land, particularly the hated *robota* or unpaid labour service for the landlord. Evidence of peasant engagement with Slovene national cultural preoccupations in this period is hard to find. Though Bleiweis paid great attention to the need for peasant education and improvements in agricultural practice, his outlook was conservative and centred like that of the clergy on a hierarchical, patriarchal view of the peasant household. *Novice* only alluded twice before 1848 to conditions on the land, and then to stress the importance of compensating the landlord in the event of change; the landlord–peasant relationship was based, Bleiweis thought, on legal contract. The land question did figure prominently in the first of the Slovene petitions in 1848 but lost this position in later ones. The Habsburg regime quickly took steps to end *robota*, which finally passed into law by a vote of the new parliament in September 1848, but on condition of payment of compensation, which peasants opposed. Here Bleiweis and the whole Slovene press intransigently upheld compensation and the rights of property. They were equally hostile to the artisanal and working-class movement in Vienna which culminated in the harshly suppressed October revolt. Events in 1848 showed that their movement had reached the second stage of Miroslav Hroch's helpful typology of nationalism, in which it broadens from a cultural, almost antiquarian base to become a keen concern of the educated classes with a programme of language renewal. But it was far from the third and final stage in which all sections of the population were engaged in the national cause.

Yet this would be too down-beat a verdict on the Slovene experience of 1848–9. The idea of a United Slovenia continued to percolate in following decades through steadily broadening reaches of the population to become eventually a national mantra. Meanwhile, the Austrian school reforms of the revolutionary years, with substantial Slav, including Slovene input, set pointers for the future. They widened access to the educational ladder, set the principle of mother tongue primary education, strengthened teacher training, inspection and syllabuses and in general increased popular influence on the schooling process, cutting back the hitherto dominant role of the Church. Not all this was lost in subsequent reaction, particularly the growth of teacher consciousness, strongest at Gymnasium level. Conservative Slovene opinion did not yet exploit possibilities the reforms offered the language in this quarter, while the Church establishment hit back against laicising tendencies. Here too, future patterns were foreshadowed, not least in the call for a Slovene university, first voiced in 1848.[6]

WALES AND 'THE TREASON OF THE BLUE BOOKS'

The 'Blue Books' controversy in Wales had nothing of the international dimension and drama of the revolutions of 1848. Yet in one sense it impacted in ways related to nationhood on wider circles at the time than the nascent national movement in Slovenia, touching intimately as it did on religious matters which had become so important to much of the population's sense of self. It developed in response to the 1847 reports of a parliamentary commission into education in Wales and particularly into 'the means afforded to the Labouring Classes of Acquiring a Knowledge of the English Language'. Parliamentary reports appeared in blue, hence the famous name. Originating with a Welsh MP who had made a fortune after leaving Carmarthenshire for London as a boy and wished the same for his compatriots, the idea of a commission sailed through an open door in governing circles. The state of unrest seemingly endemic in Wales had aroused much alarm in these, fuelled further by a host of disturbing official reports on working-class health, education and the operation of the new Poor Law, not only in Wales. Wales, however, could offer a chance to grapple with the pressing issue of the governmental role in education. Britain was well behind most European states in confronting this question because of its laissez-faire traditions and because it raised the hackles both of Anglicans and Nonconformists. Anglicans claimed that any national system should give priority to the established Church. Many Nonconformists therefore took the 'voluntary' position, that government should not provide for education at all, but leave it in the hands of parents and denominations. The secretary of the government's rudimentary educational administration, himself a Nonconformist, gave instructions that the Commission of Enquiry for Wales should be especially sensitive on religion. Yet on this very point of balance everything went wrong. The three commissioners, laymen not divisive religious figures as he advised, but Anglicans, were upper-middle class barristers with no knowledge of Wales or Welsh, and instinctively suspicious of the 'strange and abnormal features of [Evangelical] revival'. Seven of their ten Welsh-speaking assistants were Anglicans recommended by bishops, as were 232 of the

311 witnesses consulted, whose often violently worded denunciations of their rivals were cited in detail.

The reports were devastating. They recorded inadequacies in the day schools they inspected as to buildings, teaching materials, untrained and incompetent teachers (for some of whom they needed interpreters) and instruction vitiated by the language problem. Worse, a requirement to comment on the morals of the Welsh people had been added – it is not clear how – to their instructions, which induced repeated reference in the reports to 'moral degradation', 'moral depravity' (159, 108), 'revolting habit' (165), intemperance, dishonesty and female unchastity (183) which could be linked to living conditions so that the 'squalid huts' of Welsh peasants (87) and total inadequacy of educational provision became emblematic of 'the Welsh character' (84).⁷ The perceived contrast between the 'barbarism' of much of Welsh life and the standards of 'civilisation' from which the Welsh lower classes were isolated 'in an underworld of [their] own' (Commissioner Lingen's phrase) likewise infected the commissioners' judgements on the Welsh language. For Symons it was 'a disastrous barrier to all moral progress' whose 'evil effects' it was hard to exaggerate, as in the mockery it made of the operation of the law, encouraging perjury, fraud and disrespect for truth until the people learnt English. 'Little or nothing of such light [of civilisation] has as yet penetrated the dense darkness which, harboured by their language ... enshrouds the minds of the people' (187). Lingen, ablest of the Commissioners, wrote of 'the peculiar moral atmosphere' Welsh wove around the population. All of them agreed that Welsh literature had little worthy of the name and that the Welsh-language press, about which they relied on their witnesses, preferred denominational squabbles and theological speculation to practical secular matters. An undertone linked these inadequacies with the negative phenomena of Chartism and Rebecca.

The reports' comments were not all negative. There was praise of Welsh warmth of character, the mental acuteness of Welsh people, their greater command of their mother tongue than their English counterparts – and of the contribution of the Sunday schools. For Lingen these were

the most characteristic development of native intellect, and the efforts of the mass of the people, utterly unaided, to educate themselves upon their own model ... They gratify that gregarious sociability which animates the Welsh towards each other. They present the charms of office to those who, on all other occasions, are subject, and of distinction to those who have no other chance of distinguishing themselves.

Yet the obverse of liveliness and warmth, in the absence of proper education, was susceptibility to demagoguery and 'an utter want of method in [Welsh people's] thinking and acting' (184). This is a judgement common later in contacts of English administrators with colonial populations. There is no doubt that the Commissioners showed remarkable industry and were actuated by a strong commitment to the educational reform ideas of their age. Their view of the problems they saw was not really denied by concerned Welsh opinion, nor can their verdict that the Sunday schools offered no appropriate remedy be easily challenged. But their arrogance, their freedom in censure of a society foreign to them and in particular their generalised aspersions on Welsh morality and society had a lasting effect. David Williams, the leading Welsh historian of the early post-war decades, was to call the commission 'the main landmark in the nineteenth century, not only in the educational but in the social and political history of Wales'.[8]

The reports drew a remarkable range of commentary, both in scholarly refutation and press expostulation. As Ieuan Gwynedd Jones has noted, resentment was compounded by the fact that Welsh opinion was already beginning to hone in on the idea of Welsh religious exceptionalism.[9] The rapid expansion of Nonconformity, with constant lengthy press reports on the foundation of new chapels and Sunday schools and induction of new ministers, had given rise to pride. The great transformation in the last century, the 2,200 chapels which had arisen at a cost of a million pounds and an annual upkeep of £132,000, all from the people's purse, had made Nonconformist Wales the most moral and religious nation under the sun, exclaimed Ieuan Gwynedd, one of the commissioners' most vigorous critics.[10] The Welsh papers had been following closely and with some suspicion the unusual reportage from London on Welsh affairs.

> Englishmen, in the shape of Editors, Newspaper Correspondents, Government Commissioners and suchlike creatures, are crossing Offa's Dyke like flies, and these wily knaves, in the fullness of their official dignity, look us up and down, and take upon themselves to understand everything about our numbers, morals, religion and fashions, and then, knowing no more about us than moles about

the sun, they return whence they came concocting their stories and fashioning far-fetched, absurd and baseless fables about us.[11]

So commented David Rees's *Diwygiwr* on the phenomenon. But men like Ieuan Gwynedd, still more the opponent of the Chartists, Sir Thomas Phillips, Lewis Edwards, founder of *Y Traethodydd*, and the Baptist minister and future prominent MP Henry Richard, provided exhaustive evidence for the bias of the commissioners' witnesses. They exposed the fallacy of judging Welsh children's knowledge confronted by supercilious questioners and slipshod translation, and through documented comparisons with English and foreign situations they refuted charges of Welsh bastardy and immorality.

The political implications of all this were far-reaching. The divide was finally overcome between Calvinistic Methodism, with its Anglican roots and politically quietist leanings, and the radicalism of old Dissent. Henceforth Anglicans and Nonconformists confronted each other as hostile forces, like Catholics and Protestants in Ireland, where every aspect of life took on a confrontational aspect. The Methodists had begun to move away from John Elias's Toryism in the early 1830s. A split in the congregation in Jewin Church, London, brought in a younger current, prepared to side with Irish Catholics on grounds of political liberty, showing the continuing influence of the capital. Lewis Edwards had defied Elias in going to study for a degree in Edinburgh against his wishes, fulfilling his wider intellectual ambitions in a great Presbyterian centre, the first in the denomination to take this step. Edwards now ended his articles on the Reports in the *Traethodydd* with a hard-hitting attack on the state Church and a call for Welsh Nonconformists to enter the electoral fray. He rejoiced at Welsh protests against the wrong done them 'as a nation' by the reports, arguing for a concerted movement to register 'principled Nonconformists' in each Welsh county to end the Tory hold on Welsh politics: the Liverpool Welsh community had already bought a hundred such franchises.[12] Sociologically, the choice of Liverpool to lead was sound, though still premature. That it should come from a temperamental moderate showed how the Anglican–Nonconformist divide had become dominant in Welsh life and had taken on a quasi-national form. Sir Thomas Phillips, Tory Anglican mayor of Newport, whose criticism of the 1847 Reports was the most comprehensive to appear, greeted the 'overpower[ing]' of sectional interests in Wales 'when a spirit of nationality is aroused by injustice and contumely'. Yet he felt 'discomfort and anxiety' at 'a spirit of isolation from England' which the Reports had provoked.[13] This anxiety was justified in the event. The contribution of patriotic Anglicans like himself and others to the rejection of the Reports came to be all but forgotten in popular recollection. Already in the denunciation of the commissioners by the young radical – and later socialist pioneer – R. J. Derfel in his book-length verse play 'Brad y Llyfrau Gleision' (The Treason of the Blue Books, 1854) the Church featured alongside them as the alien enemy. The national wrong was immortalised in the name he gave it, playing on the ancient Welsh tale of Anglo-Saxon perfidy in 'The Treason of the Long Knives'.

To depict this cause célèbre as righteousness exposing injustice would be incomplete, however. Welsh Nonconformists were actually divided on the educational issue. Ieuan Gwynedd passionately appealed to readers not to deny 'the principles for which our forefathers suffered and bled', nor let 'our country sink once more into the dreadful barbarism in which it was found by the Welsh reformers'. He warned that the state church's interest was not in education but authority, the power 'to keep the people in ignorance of the nature of the oppression which is a shame on man and an insult to God ... which bound the world for long ages by brass fetters in the deepest, densest, most infamous ignorance'. But this eloquence was actually a plea not to accept state grants with which men like Kay-Shuttleworth hoped to build up a national system of education.[14] Ieuan Gwynedd believed fervently in the voluntarist principle that education should be left to the people, and that Welsh Nonconformists had shown in building up their own institutions unaided how it could be done. The 'principles' of which he spoke were those of uncompromising radical liberalism, with deep distrust of the inevitable power drive of government and faith in the importance of individual 'character'. These were universalist principles which owed something to the age. But in Ieuan Gwynedd they were indissolubly fused with the evocation of Welsh Nonconformist heroes, with the experiences of a poor Welsh peasant youth born into a community traditionally remote from government, keenly aware of the injustices of the local power structure of anglicised landowners and Church and energised by a transcendent sense of the relationship of the individual to God. Such a sense touched his whole generation. In this brilliant young man, brought up in rural Merioneth, spending his adult years ministering to miners in industrial Monmouthshire, tirelessly productive as editor and writer through a life of personal hardship and tragedy, it took on an emblematic quality which helps explain why a leading Welsh historian of this period should bear his name.

Yet most Welsh Nonconformist leaders had doubts about the voluntarist principle and by the time of Ieuan Gwynedd's death in 1852 it was already clear that its cause was doomed. In 1843 Hugh (later Sir Hugh) Owen in his 'Llythyr i'r Cymry' (Letter to the Welsh People) had called on them through the Welsh periodicals to accept the principle of state aid to schools, to be administered by the two main educational bodies, the National Society for Anglicans and the British Society for Nonconformists. Hugh Owen urged Welsh support for the latter and this became the pattern of future development, as the British Society overtook the early lead of its rivals in school building in Wales. Beyond this organisational matter the substance of the 1847 commissioners' case on the language issue was also de facto accepted. Instruction in the developing school system proved to be in English only despite the extent of calls for a bilingual approach from men like the Bishop of St David's, Connop Thirlwall, and Sir Thomas Phillips as well as traditional pro-Welsh elements like the Welsh societies. The 1847 Reports themselves had acknowledged that a 'not inconsiderable nor uninfluential' body of Welsh clergy, established and dissenting, advocated this. Yet study of the Blue Book protests shows that objections to the treatment of Welsh were cast in general terms or rhetorically, as when Ieuan Gwynedd asked how one could suppress a language spoken weekly from two thousand pulpits. Brutus's attack on the Welsh language in the 1820s had provoked a range of proposals for 'academies' teaching practical subjects through Welsh and with appropriate textbook provision. This was not repeated after the Blue Books. Some initiatives, like the translation of *Chamber's Encyclopædia*, were a direct response to the Commissioners' strictures but it seems that action at this more general level rather than actively educational was now the assumption. A partial exception was the foundation of Llandovery College as a kind of public school, partly funded by Sir Thomas Phillips and Lady Llanover, though it specified only Welsh as a subject rather than a medium of instruction, a pledge which came to be honoured in the breach more than the reality. It is striking that the strongest protest was directed to the Reports' charges on morality and religious ignorance and that here refutation often took the form of concrete statistics. Such material was not so readily available on language matters but had the motivation existed the Blue Books might have stirred some attempts to supply it.

Indeed, it is interesting that the controversy over the 1847 Reports did not serve to focus attention on other matters where Welsh values were engaged. The need for Welsh-speaking judges and bishops, the appointment of non-Welsh speaking clergy to parishes where Welsh was spoken: all these had been subject of considerable debate in preceding years. Lewis Edwards did take up the case of judges at the end of his first *Traethodydd* article. With his customary acuity he pointed out that it would be more logical to appoint judges who knew Welsh rather than make all the Welsh English. Indeed, he called for all cases in the courts to be conducted in Welsh and in the article's final clause urged persistent petitioning to parliament in the matter. Yet this almost throw-away style of broaching an issue of revolutionary constitutional dimensions for a resolutely monoglot state, which would have required an immense proportionate effort, hardly suggests serious thinking in a very thoughtful man. It shows perhaps how Edwards had been momentarily driven from his comfort zone by sheer exasperation at the Reports. His reference to Welsh in this context as 'yr hen Omeraeg' (the old language of Gomer), playing on a sentimental old trope, reinforces this suspicion.[15] In fact, as will be seen, Welsh responses went in the opposite direction, to build a school system which would teach English more effectively but under Nonconformist auspices. The mobilisation of Welsh public opinion in an outpouring of national protest yielded an equivocal result.

MID-POINT REFLECTIONS

The events recounted in this chapter mark a turning-point in the development of our two countries. In both, the rebuffs to national aspirations and self-image recounted here were at least partly made good in less than a generation. In the Monarchy the neo-absolutist regime of the 1850s presented itself as modernising and efficient, dismantling feudalism and systematising an upgraded, still subordinate role in education for national languages (including the now officially termed 'Slovene language'), in place of political freedom. This meant that when it fell in 1860, Slovenes found themselves on a common constitutional playing-field playing by the same rules as other Habsburg peoples, if the smallest on the park. In Wales the general British atmosphere was turning against landlordism and Anglican intolerance. By the time William Gladstone's Liberal government had disestablished the Anglican church in Catholic Ireland in 1869 a Welsh Nonconformist middle class was growing up which could assert itself against the church and Tory party under the same disestablishment banner. Yet this phrasing betrays a parting of the ways, at least in germination. It puts the emphasis on language in the national affirmation of the Slovenes and on religious Nonconformity as the defining political character of Welshness.

This binary opposition is too crude to reflect the situation fully, particularly on the Welsh side. Language continued to be a key factor in Welsh life and self-definition. But the opposition conveys an essential truth which was to disclose itself more fully over time. It is a matter of priorities. Few Slovenes denied the value of learning German, but they prioritised nurturing their own language. Few Welsh people denied the value of nurturing Welsh, but they prioritised religion and learning English. No formal demotion of language as the defining characteristic of Welsh nationhood is to be found. But pride in the achievements of Nonconformity which have been cited and the differential response to the Blue Books are straws in the wind for a new perspective. A note of exceptionalism can be sensed in Welsh regard for their engagement with the Scriptures. For the influential Congregationalist minister Thomas Rees in 1867, it was 'not possible' that the 'vast store' of Welsh religious literature, weighty biblical commentaries and dictionaries, the 120,000 copies of its weekly and monthly denominational papers and journals, could be matched by any other community of similar size, and consumed, moreover, mainly by the poorest section of the people.[16] Remarkable as they were, the means subserved the religious message. For Ieuan Gwynedd himself: 'Though the accents of our venerable old language have such charm for me, I would much rather see it perish than my country's religious privileges.'[17] The repeated emphasis on the age of Welsh indicates its association with the past which could take on a sentimental note. This was a time when the trope 'Oes y byd i'r iaith Gymraeg!' (May the Welsh language live as long as the world!) was in vogue, expressing as pious wish what it would not have occurred to members of more confident peoples to say about their languages. In practice Welsh language publication was flourishing compared with any previous period, as Lewis Edwards stated in 1852, concluding that there was not the slightest chance of Welsh dying 'soon'. But this word implied a dispassion about its long-term prospects which a Habsburg Slav language patriot was unlikely to have shown.[18]

Priorities won out as they have a habit of doing. When people set their mind to something they very often succeed. Things not ultimately prioritised remain important, yet what happens to them can be very different. By opting for English-language education Welsh leaders made irrelevant the sort of efforts Arfonwyson had put into conveying arithmetic and others modern agricultural methods in Welsh. The whole attempt to provide 'useful knowledge' of this kind which had been part of the programme of the Cymmrodorion Society, of the spurt in periodical production in the 1820s and 1830s, and of the *Diwygiwr*'s call of 1848 for a society to publish Welsh books on every branch of knowledge, was undermined by acquiescence in English-only public education. Effectively, the Welsh had taken the line Edwards criticised in the *Traethodydd* when he said judges should know Welsh rather than a whole nation learn English. For a whole nation now would learn English rather than acquire the relevant materials in their own tongue. If everything English offered was available untranslated, what spheres would be left to Welsh? Literary and cultural matters, yes, but only insofar as they related to Wales, since the range of world culture would also be available in English; there would be no need to translate Shakespeare – or Tolstoy. The sphere of Welsh would ineluctably decline as knowledge of English grew. And with this would logically develop the conviction that knowledge of English was not just a cultural good but an essential for life which would hobble the development of the mother tongue in after years. The idea that it could have been otherwise vacated the popular consciousness.

Slovenes, fellow Slavs and Balts followed another logic. In their model, work on agricultural, medical, veterinological, technical, mechanical, general knowledge publications, and the like which had begun in Welsh too, continued and with the aid of corresponding associational life, journals and book clubs proved sufficient for the great majority of citizens. Subsequent economic developments like cooperative societies and local 'peoples banks' likewise used the mother tongue. Big capital and most post-primary education operated till the First World War in the dominant language and its speakers in the larger towns. Those Slovenes who went on to secondary education (a fairly small minority as everywhere in Europe at that time) attended German-language schools while pressing for more Slovene. The pattern will be described in following chapters, as will be the pattern in Nonconformist Wales. Both had their own logic, and worked, though each are strange to, in fact unimagined by, the other.

The Welsh en masse learned English, though not without difficulty; the Slovenes acquired Hroch's 'cultural sovereignty' and functioned, though not without difficulty.

How one may summarise the deeper hinterland of this parting of the ways? The Slovene experience building up to it can be described by the German word *Konjunktur*, more expressive than its English equivalent. It conveys the idea of different factors coming together to create a new situation pregnant with possibilities. The breaking of the cake of custom for the ancient, authoritarian Monarchy, followed by the lagging of reform from above; the Herderian ideology which could energise vegetating ethnic groups into potential nations; the existence of a small body of intellectuals trained in German Gymnasien and Catholic colleges able to take advantage of this; the emergence of a peasantry from feudalism coincidentally with primary education and, in 1848, the awakening of organised political life; the association of all these impulses of change with simultaneous linguistic renewal: this was what laid the foundations of modern Slovenia. An important aspect was that liberal national ideas enjoyed a quasi-monopoly in the small group of the educated and that the native catholic clergy were largely onside. Josephinism, reform Catholicism and the roots of the parochial clergy in the people were instrumental here. So was the fact that cultural nationalism was actually an international movement, operating in an atmosphere of mutual emulation – but also mutual rivalry. The above passage should not disguise the discomforting, sometimes demoralising nature of the encounter with a wider, more powerful world, felt more keenly in 1848 than the sleepy Napoleonic years. However, the 'conjuncture' gave a certain unity to the Slovene cause; the language became the fulcrum around which public issues turned, from school textbooks, agricultural manuals and legal formulae to theatrical, musical and associational life in general as well as personal and collective dignity. It was part of a syndrome affecting the multi-ethnic Monarchy and the east-central European area as a whole.

This relatively sudden conjunction of factors was not so marked in the Welsh context. British state and society had been evolving towards modernity over a longer period and offered less chance for the insertion of novel demands. There were certainly aspects of it. The coinciding of industrialisation, religious fervour, Sunday school literacy and a burgeoning vernacular press, and the failure of a self-serving Anglican establishment to respond worked together to spur the advance of a more flexible Nonconformity to majority status in Wales in the crucial second quarter of the nineteenth century. But it was Nonconformity rather than language which benefited from this process. The sense of Welsh as message as well as medium of modernity, clearly present in *Seren Gomer*'s founding statements, yielded the high ground to the good news of religion. This was the ideological driving force. Welsh development lacked the Herderian-style belief in language as a universal force and its ongoing contribution to 'Humanity'. Welsh patriotism had traditionally been pride in its own past tradition and linguistic antiquity, reinvigorated but not fundamentally changed by the Morris circle. The timing and pace of change favoured Slovene but disadvantaged Welsh. For an overwhelmingly illiterate Slovene population, the beginnings of modernity came together with partially mother-tongue schooling in quite a short period. In contrast, the sheer rapidity of change threatened to overwhelm Welsh in the industrial south-east, allowing no time for adjustment of old attitudes to new circumstances. Welsh did not become the medium of the workshops Eiddil Ifor envisaged in industrialising Monmouthshire, where its retreat began precisely in this period. The teeming immigrants of the new townships, engaged in a harsh struggle for survival, naturally did not concern themselves with cultural matters, while the few people who did, like William Owen Pughe, often belonged to an inward-looking tradition of Welsh/Celtic exceptionalism.

The obverse of Welsh patriots' views of their ancient culture was the general conviction in the wider society of its outmodedness and 'uselessness'. The cumulative impact of such attitudes cannot but have impacted on cultural self-confidence. Scorn for Slovene and scepticism of its viability existed in Austria also. Familiarity with the presence of non-dominant speech was so much more widespread in the Monarchy, however, that it did not induce quite the sense of anomaly and intellectual outrage to be found in the English-speaking majority at the survival of Celtic speech in Britain. An extended essay on Welsh nationhood by the Anglesey rector William Jones in 1840 expresses some of the mixed feelings of affection, embarrassment and defensiveness the language could arouse in its educated speakers. After comparing the tales Welsh village worthies told about their ancient glories to an African chief who, when he ate, formally summoned the rulers of the world to attend the banquet, the writer goes on to say that nonetheless no good reason appears for English scorn for the Welsh language and the malicious ill-will displayed whenever it is mentioned.[19]

All the evidence adduced so far in this study shows how difficult thoughtful Welsh people found it to project a future vision of their language, so that the practical effort which was so effective in building up the new Nonconformist denominations never looked like going into securing a place for Welsh in matters of law or public administration.

It is this passivity on the Welsh language which has led scholars from east-central Europe to be dismissive of Welsh claims to nationhood. This scepticism is warranted from their own historical perspective. Slovenes, for example, with their diverse regional backgrounds and allegiances, could hardly have emerged as a nation when they did without the development of a unifying literary language in the period studied here. But the degree of stress on language is a generalisation from a particular regional conjuncture of forces. It illustrates this book's theme that comparison can illuminate blind spots that fall below the radar of a given society's assumptions. For nationhood can take different routes or combine a variety of factors. Over-emphasis on language leads Miroslav Hroch, a leading authority on nation-building, to miscue the Welsh case. Having in his first major work stated baldly that Wales is an example of a society that everyone agrees is not a nation, he has since, in 2015, gone into more detail. In south Wales 'the Celtic population was assimilated' but conversely 'prevailed' in the north; 'the national movement in Wales in the beginning of the 1840s was triggered by a parliamentary proposal for English to be the compulsory language of teaching'.[20] Presupposition leads Hroch to force the facts into an ethno-linguistic prism. Welsh historians are agreed that the moral-religious aspect of the Blue Books riled Welsh opinion more than the linguistic, resented as that was. Wales has had its own experience. Historically, the Welsh did have a form of medieval nationality, indeed of collective consciousness from the struggles with the Anglo-Saxons, which had been recorded and recalled through succeeding generations. These traditions posed problems of adaptation in the later modern period but they meant that the Welsh brought into the age of enlightenment a coherent identity which similar small ethnic groups in eastern Europe often lacked. They were already not just an 'ethnic group'. The language and its literature had already played their existential role in bringing that about. From this viewpoint, in hindsight, it is possible to see why Welsh leaders were less engaged with language than some struggling ethnicities elsewhere. After all, as Edwards said, it did not appear as a pressing problem; Welsh literature was thriving. That patriots in other situations could be relaxed on such matters was clear from Daniel O'Connell, who had stated that English was 'the medium of all modern communication'.[21] Nationhood is not just a matter of language; history, tradition and religion can also be involved.

Indeed, religion has played and continues to play a far greater role in issues of national identity than contemporary opinion is inclined to think. It is fundamental to that of Serbs, Croats and Bosniaks (Bosnian Muslims), of most Ulster Protestants and Irish Catholics, of Israelis, of most inhabitants of the Indian sub-continent and Sri Lanka and of most Orthodox peoples. In our own islands different types of Christianity mark a formative distinction between modern identities of all four nations. Religion traditionally carries a moral force as embodiment of values which language has had only recently. Wales's vigorous religious life and press help explains the wider penetration of ethnic self-consciousness among ordinary Welsh than ordinary Slovene speakers in the period we have so far covered, though a Slovene intellectual stratum was more alert to external ideas and circumstances than was the case in Wales. That religion should be a field for Welsh national self-assertion was therefore a common feature of the age, true of Polish Catholics' struggle with Orthodox Russia, Balkan Christians against Muslim Ottomans, not to speak of the Irish. Yet though Welsh Nonconformist religion helped demarcate a very specific cultural evolution for Wales within Britain, which will be discussed further below, it in no way paralleled the divides involved in the national-religious struggles above. Wales as a nation remained invisible to the outside world. At the international level a common Protestantism linked English, Scots and Welsh. The events of 1848 highlighted this reality. The Welsh figure who took most interest in them, Gwilym Hiraethog, did so almost wholly from a British standpoint through his paper *Yr Amserau*'s enthusiastic support for the Hungarian revolutionaries and their leader, Lajos Kossuth. He duly received Hungarian thanks for his effort. A Welsh aspect, shared with Britain, was that Kossuth was a Protestant who played on this in his dealings with Britain and the United States. However, the Hungarians or Magyars, though resentful of Viennese control, were a ruling nation in their own half of the Monarchy, bitterly opposed by the non-Magyar peasants they dominated, the true social equivalents of the Welsh. Indeed, Kossuth's leading emissary in Britain actually believed that the non-Magyars should follow the example of the Welsh who made no fuss about language rights and the like.[22]

That the Welsh fought harder for religious than linguistic rights was no doubt partly also because it was easier. To make headway on such an issue in multi-faith and religiously tolerant Britain was more plausible than on language, where the state was rigidly monoglot. For the Slovenes in multi-lingual Austria language was a less problematic route. This is one of many points where the differences between the two empires had an influence. The greater vulnerability of the Monarchy is another. It offered Slovenes a chance of broader experience, at least as onlookers on big events in the Napoleonic wars and 1848–9. Great Britain on the other hand was the greater power, in whose reflected glory Welsh people could bask. 'Welsh and Saxons together will conquer the world', as George Borrow reported barefoot 'brats' shouting in Llangollen on the (misreported) fall of Sebastopol in the Crimean War, adding in allusion to Welsh myth that the shared triumph 'for a time reconciled the descendants of the Ancient British to the seed of the coiling serpent'.[23]

A distinction between our two societies over most of the period studied has been between the two lines of evolution. The Slovene line took a relatively unilinear track along linguistic lines. Its evolution began with the Enlightenment, owing less to previous centuries than the Welsh and following a regional pattern of small nation development in the Monarchy. Initiating in a group of language patriots with a Gymnasium or Catholic college education, it expanded into a fledgling intelligentsia, which formulated plans for language reform and public use of a unified Slovene language. The crisis of the multinational Monarchy in 1848 spurred its more advanced wing into a political programme of administrative autonomy for the Slovene-speaking area. The Welsh pattern was more diffuse. Its initial strand was also linguistic with roots deeper-seated in past traditions. Soon it was flanked by a religious movement and by the end of the period by a social current sprung from industrialisation. Active cultural patriots were divided into several groups by religion and/ or region and cannot easily be spoken of as an intelligentsia, though in literary and journalistic terms their collective production continued to exceed that in Slovene lands. The nearest Wales saw to a programme were the calls of Nonconformists for reform of the state church. The religious and social strands had contacts with the broader British society, the literary strand less at the end than the beginning of the period. Both Wales and Slovenia were on the brink of developing embryo bourgeoisies which could exercise political influence, but faced multiple difficulties.

The Slovene intelligentsia-based movement was more cohesive, sophisticated and goal-orientated than would-be Welsh equivalents, but 1848 had shown their isolation from the masses, as well as problems from local German speakers and the pro-German *nemškutarji*. Welsh Nonconformist leaders were closer to the people but only beginning to enter the political arena.

In many ways the two societies were still closely akin, subaltern communities in their own homelands. At the grass roots level, the language/religion divide ventured as a generalisation here tends to break down. Parents in both showed a wish for their children to learn the dominant language. As stated above, many clergymen and ministers favoured Welsh being introduced in the day schools. No doubt many Slovene priests like Welsh clergy put their faith before their patriotism. Later in the century, a Catholic Church purged of national liberals entered the political fray. Parallels suggest that a wide field of research into Welsh language circumstances is open for historians, particularly in the towns and incipient middle class. Indeed, Welsh historians have been strangely indifferent to language matters, as if there is nothing to say about the fate of Welsh other than that it was doomed by modernity – a proposition obviously brought in question by the Slovene comparison here offered. The temptation for any national historiography is to assume things happened as they had to happen, even, in keeping with a natural human trait, that they happened for the best. Beyond speculation, the real story is of how both national stories progressed to the stage of respective local hegemonies, of Nonconformism liberalism and Slovene linguistic nationalism; then of how these two hegemonies grappled with dominant Anglo-Britons and Austro-Germans above, with emerging socialists below, and with integral Catholics and assorted anti-modernists in other sections of the population. It is a rich and absorbing story, as Welsh observers are all the more entitled to feel in view of the variety and complexity of the forces which shaped it in their case. To these further developments Part Two will now turn.

NOTES

1 Ivan Prijatelj, *Slovenska kulturnopolitična in slovenstvena zgodovina 1848–95 / Slovene Cultural and Political History 1848–95* (6 vols, Ljubljana, 1955–85), vol. 1, p. 47.
2 Prijatelj, *Kulturnopolitična zgodovina*, vol. 1, pp. 46–7.

3 J. Pogačnik, *Kulturni pomen slomškovega dela* / The Cultural Significance of the Work of Slomšek (Maribor, 1991), p. 23.

4 *Novice* 6 (1848), pp. 74, 107, 141, 145.

5 Prijatelj, *kulturnopolitična zgodovina*, vol. 1, p. 58.

6 Vlado Schmidt, 'Šolstvo na Slovenskem v buržoaznodemokratični revoluciji (1848–51)' (Schooling in Slovenia in the Bourgeois Democratic Revolution, 1848–51).

7 Page numbers given after quotes in this paragraph and the next are those of Gwyneth Tyson Roberts's book, *The Treason of the Blue Books* (Cardiff, 1998) from which they are taken.

8 D. Williams, *A History of Modern Wales* (London, 1969: first published 1950), p. 254.

9 Ieuan Gwynedd Jones, *Mid-Victorian Wales: The Observers and the Observed* (Cardiff, 1992), p. 131.

10 *Cofiant a Gweithiau Barddonol a Rhyddieithol Ieuan Gwynedd* (Life and Poetry and Prose of Ieuan Gwynedd) (Wrexham, n.d.), p. 330.

11 Jones, *Mid-Victorian Wales*, p. 103.

12 L. Edwards, 'Adroddiadau y Dirprwywyr' (Reports of the Commissioners), in *Traethodau Llenyddol* (Wrexham, 1867), pp. 406–21 (p. 421).

13 Frank Price Jones, *Radicaliaeth a'r werin Gymreig yn y bedwaredd ganrif a'r bymtheg* (Radicalism and the Welsh common people in the nineteenth century) (Cardiff, 1997), pp. 49, 62, quoting from Phillips's book, *Wales: the language, social condition, moral character and religious opinions of the people* (London, 1849).

14 *Cofiant Ieuan Gwynedd*, p. 330.

15 L. Edwards, 'Addysg yn Nghymru' (Education in Wales), in *Traethodau*, pp. 374–405. (For 'yr hen Omeraeg', p. 405).

16 T. Rees, *Miscellaneous Papers on Subjects Relating to Wales* (London, 1867), pp. 40–9.

17 *Cofiant, a Gweithiau Barddonol a Rhyddieithol Ieuan Gwynedd* (Wrexham, c.1880), p. 91.

18 Edwards, 'Barddoniaeth y Cymry' (Welsh Poetry), in *Traethodau*, 153–66 (p. 153).

19 Reverend W. Jones, *A Prize Essay in English and Welsh on the Character of the Welsh as a Nation in the Present Age* (London, 1841), p. 69.

20 M. Hroch, *Social preconditions of national revival in Europe: a comparative analysis of patriotic groups among the smaller European nations* (Cambridge, 1985), p. 4; M. Hroch, *European nations: explaining their formation* (New York, 2015), pp. 105, 213.

21 W. J. O'Daunt, *Personal Recollections of the late Daniel O'Connell* (London, 1849), p. 14.

22 For Hungarian thanks, see T. Rees and D. Roberts, *Cofiant y Parch: W. Rees, D.D. (Gwilym Hiraethog)* (Life of the Revd W. Rees, D.D. (Gwilym Hiraethog)) (Dolgellau, 1893), p. 285. For emissary Pulszky's view, see Marian H. Jones, 'Wales and Hungary', *Transactions of Hon. Society of Cymmrodorion* 1968, 1–27 (15, 25).

23 G. Borrow, *Wild Wales: Its People, Language and Scenery* (London, n.d.) (first published 1862), p. 300.

PART TWO

Chapter 5

THE PICTURE TAKES SHAPE, 1848-c.1880

Within two decades of the failed revolution of 1848–9 the setbacks of these years were overcome and social mobilisation resumed. The key change came with the abandonment of neo-absolutism in 1859. Much of the next decade was taken up with manoeuvrings between Emperor Franz Joseph and his peoples before a settlement was reached in 1867 which was to last till the Monarchy's fall. The Hungarians gained full internal home rule, turning Austria into Austria-Hungary, the 'dual Monarchy', both halves of which were to have parliamentary constitutions. Effectively, this meant that the Emperor ruled through the German liberals in Austria and the Magyars in Hungary while the Slavs were denied the federal status they claimed. True, the 1867 settlement in Austria revived the 1848 principles of national equality and people's right to public use of their language but the equality was essentially a formal declaration and the language rights were granted to individual citizens, rather than nations. The importance of nationality, defined by language, became a structural component of Austrian politics, which long revolved around two camps: the German national liberals who favoured state centralism and pro-federalist Slavs. In 1865, for example, the Ljubljana town council with its Slovene majority congratulated a new Austrian prime minister, a Pole, on his federalist principles, in a telegram written only in Slovene.[1] This was a symbolic gesture, but in psychological terms it reflected the sense of legitimacy that Slovenes could derive from the Slav cause of which they were a mere fraction, and it was plainly unreproducible in a British context. In 1867 the Slovene party was to win the provincial elections in Carniola.

The divergences in the two situations prefigured at the end of Part One now clarified. The Slovene movement was unambiguously national, while Welsh patriots worked through the British Liberal Party, more open to Nonconformist demands than the Tories, for centuries the party of Church and landlord. In the British general election of 1868 Liberals won twenty-three of the thirty-two Welsh seats. Only three of these were Nonconformists. However, they had only once before held a seat and the bulk of Whig-Liberal MPs were sympathetic to their grievances. This was the start of an evolving process.

Franz Joseph had been driven to constitutional concessions by defeat in wars with France and Prussia. By contrast, this was a time of mounting confidence in the British state and in English self-image. These basked in the glow of Thomas Macaulay's 'Whig interpretation' of England's history as a seamless process, whereby the 'Glorious Revolution' of 1688 had ensured that she alone was unshaken by the revolutions of 1848, nor yet faced any threat to her place as the 'workshop of the world'. Public opinion embraced notions of national exceptionalism with an 'Anglo-Saxon' racial tinge. Yet while Wales figured low in this scale of values, the Welsh economy benefited as an integral part of British dynamism. Thus Slovenia advanced politically, Wales economically in these years. Hopes of Slovene benefit from the new age of bourgeois capitalism and the Vienna-Trieste railway (1857) were largely dashed. Freer market conditions in general worked in favour of bigger interests than those of humble Slovene centres. Local business was undermined by more competitive imports, while rural life suffered from the ending of the carting trade, compensation payments for land emancipation and loss of traditional rights of pasture and forest use. Population growth in the Slovene lands slowed as emigration began which was eventually to reach high levels, mainly to the United States.[2]

MID-VICTORIAN WALES: A SOCIETY ON THE MOVE

Whereas change in the Slovenian lands came from political upheaval in the Habsburg Monarchy, in Wales it came from the drama of Britain's industrial revolution. Wales had already been involved in its early stages. The first trial of a steam locomotive in Britain, indeed the world, was at Penydarren near Merthyr in 1804 and there too were made the rails for the initial Liverpool to Manchester line. The 165 blast furnaces of south Wales provided one-sixth of Britain's pig-iron production in the

1850s and it was there that the Thomas-Gilchrist and Siemen processes to speed the manufacture of steel were developed. Welsh iron workers largely built up Middlesborough while Thomas Hughes founded the Russian iron industry in the town named after him Yuzhovka, now Donetsk. The south Wales iron industry drew heavily on connections it had with southern Spanish steel. The founder of the smelting of anthracite coal, David Thomas, became the father of the American anthracite industry, making Pennsylvania a centre of emigration for Welsh miners. The great dock in Cardiff built by the second Marquess of Bute in 1839 and the Merthyr to Cardiff railway of 1841 prepared the way for Cardiff's meteoric rise to be the world's largest coal-exporting port. Pits sunk in the Rhondda valleys from the 1850s opened up this remote sylvan setting to become in a couple of generations a *locus classicus* of British working class and Labour tradition. The eastern coalfield's high quality steam coal was that used by the East India Company, then the British Navy and chiefly responsible for the fact that south Wales provided one-third of British coal exports in 1913.

Economic success shaped demographic development. An impoverished countryside could not have supported its high birth-rate without the employment prospects offered by industry. Between 1851 and 1881 the population of Wales rose by nearly two-fifths. Cardiff swelled tenfold to over one hundred thousand in this period and Swansea fivefold to over ninety. The Swansea region showed perhaps the most varied industrial pattern, dominating British anthracite and tin-plate production, while the Swansea Metal Exchange in the mid-1870s was the centre of the world copper trade. The Great Western Railway, built by Isambard Brunel, had reached Swansea in 1850, the same year that the Britannia bridge complemented Telford's suspension structure over the Menai straits. The Welsh railway system was more or less in place by 1875. While improved communications brought competition which decimated the woollen mills of mid-Wales, as in Slovenia, slate in the north-west remained internationally important and coal and steel prospered in the north-east, if not on the southern scale. Wales was no longer an economic backwater. Rail links stimulated developments in social life too. A branch line from the 1848 Chester-Holyhead railway helped launch Llandudno into fame as a favoured seaside resort, largely built up in 1855–77 with a 700-metre pier and a host of fine hotels and attractions, while the Cambrian line to Aberystwyth arrived with the Royal Pier in 1869, whose opening drew 7,000 visitors. Rhyl and Colwyn Bay sprang to life in the same period.

Many features of modern Wales were coming into being, modifying the look of centuries.

That industrialisation and modernisation are solvents of ethnic groups, absorbing them into larger frameworks, is a sociological commonplace. Yet it does not sit easily with what happened in Wales. In the industrial townships and the thriving ports rose the hundreds, eventually thousands, of chapels of Welsh Nonconformity, little less in Cardiff than in the rural heartland. The iron industry had been pioneered and run very largely by incoming English entrepreneurs, but in the coal trade Welshmen played substantial roles. Key figures were the agent of the third Marquess of Bute, W. T. Lewis (1837–1914), who became a multiple colliery owner in his own right, and the poor farmer's son and railway contractor David Davies (1818–90) whose vast wealth came from the deep coal seams of the Rhondda which he was the first to exploit. Richard Davies, Anglesey's first Nonconformist JP and later MP, was a prominent shipowner MP, reminder of the vigorous life of Welsh coastal shipping in these years. The initial proposal for the development of Llandudno came from a Liverpool Welshman, Owen Williams. At lower levels the general business of the age was opening opportunities for a nascent middle class, poorer, to be sure, than its English counterparts. Only some 2 per cent each of people in Bridgend and Pontypool fell into the categories professional and commercial used in the 1861 British census; the average percentage for England and Wales was double that. But mid-nineteenth-century figures show steady growth in numbers of professionals, shopkeepers, agents and other tradespeople in Welsh towns, and Julie Light convincingly argues for a stratum of people socially active on health and school boards, gas and water concerns, mechanics' institutes, libraries and religious institutions.[3]

Nonconformity needs stressing because it was closely associated with the energy of Victorian Wales and its diaspora. Uncertain statistics suggest sixty or more thousand emigrants to the United States between 1850 and 1870, by which time there were already 384 chapels and (1870) five Welsh-language newspapers, which vigorously supported slave emancipation in the American civil war.[4] A similar vigour on a smaller scale was to be found in Australia. Spurred by the discovery of gold in Victoria, Welsh settlement there had swelled from 2,326 to 6,055 in the seven years from 1854. By the mid-1860s this community had founded over twenty chapels across the state and in 1867 launched *Yr Australydd*, the first of a number of Welsh-language newspapers.[5] Meanwhile, a Welsh colony had established itself in Patagonia in 1865, which soon acquired nineteen chapels in all, in the most distinctive and longest-lasting episode in Welsh migration.[6]

The chapels displayed the vitality of the culture which the emigrants took with them, as they did to other parts of Britain, most notably Merseyside. It was the Nonconformist culture which had become numerically dominant in Wales in the previous half century and was to flex its muscles to assume a quasi-national role in the next. It is highly significant that Welsh self-organisation outside Wales overwhelmingly had a Nonconformist stamp. Except for a couple of border towns and London, where the established church had long made provision for Welsh speakers, such provision was neither made nor sought. Thus, the role that language played in Slovene self-identification was mediated for the Welsh through religion. That the great majority of Nonconformists worshipped in Welsh had of course an emotional resonance, but the organisational struggle in these years was not carried out in contestation of languages but of churches. Here Welsh Nonconformists showed all the tenacity of Slovene linguistic nationalists. For all their previous growth they had been dismissed as a detrimental sect by English opinion at the time of the Blue Books controversy, and even the Anglican critic of the notorious reports, Sir Thomas Phillips, felt able to recommend a system of schooling which placed all control in the hands of the state church. By the 1880s, however, they dominated school boards and other features of cultural life through Wales. On Gwilym Hiraethog's death in 1883 the Liberal prime minister William Gladstone could write offering his condolences to a Welsh MP known for his patriotic sympathies.[7] How did a movement sprung from a poor peripheral rural community fare so well in the condition of dynamic industrial change often seen as corrosive of minority ethnicities? Till well into the twentieth century the relations between these two powerful forces, religious and industrial, were to frame the history of modern Wales.

Nonconformity replaced the structures and liturgies of more traditional religion with a strongly protestant reliance on the conscience of the individual. The will to internalise the values of the gospels could be best honed in the family and by social pressure, making for a serious approach to life, dignifying individual effort for one's own and other people's betterment. Revivalism continued to be a feature of the Welsh experience – that of 1859 was the greatest of the nineteenth century, adding some 37,000 to Calvinistic Methodist communicants and first sparked by Welsh migrants to America.[8] Nonconformity's role in nineteenth-century British life, not only in Wales, strengthened the earnest activity associated with 'Victorian values' in an age of development and belief in progress. The leading Welsh figures of the period felt this progress in their own lives, which had often begun in the poverty and low status described in previous chapters. Men like Gwilym Hiraethog, the poet and early literary critic Robert Ellis (Cynnddelw) and the historian and editor Thomas Rees had had no or a few months' day school teaching. They escaped lives as shepherds, farm servants, artisans or small shop-keepers by attracting attention through their desire for knowledge or sometimes what was perceived as their oddity. The Biblical expression 'what will this child be?' recurred in reference to them; fathers who could might send them to school because of their unfitness for anything else. Thomas Rees was one of those who benefitted from a neighbour's kindness in paying for three months' schooling for him. The little boy turned up with a spelling book and, asked to read the first page, said he had not got that far, then read out the title on the front, *Vyse Spelling Book for Teaching the Rudiments of the English Language, by Charles Vyse*. Rees soaked up everything he encountered; he had become interested in English when he first heard it spoken by a couple of gypsies. Usually, such children had learnt to read Welsh from relatives or a Sunday school, then sought out any Welsh book or almanac they could find, eventually coming across a local who had some literary interest, like a copy of *Seren Gomer*. What was different from the first stage of evangelisation was that almost all these youngsters did eventually attend a Nonconformist institution of some kind, though often as grown men. Similarly, the basic structures of denominational organisation did not differ much from what has already been described but showed some tendency to greater centralisation. Thus Welsh Baptists founded a Union in 1866 and the Independents followed six years later. As 'Nonconformists' many were unwilling to see these as more than organisers of annual conferences and means of sociability, but supervising the affairs of denominational training colleges and press organs gave them a practical role to which other functions could accrete.

Their press illustrates the business of Nonconformist leaders' lives. They were prodigious preachers and travellers. Roger Edwards gave 2,935 sermons between 1830 and 1841.[9] Where Pantycelyn rode and John Jones Talsarn trudged, trains now whisked ministers across Wales. When not preaching and travelling, they were scribbling and editing.

Roger Edwards was editor of the first Welsh political newspaper, *Cronicl yr Oes* in the 1830s, joint editor of the famous *Traethodydd*, from 1845 to 1863 and editor/joint editor of the oldest Calvinistic Methodist journal *Y Drysorfa* for nearly forty years till his death, contributing several serialised novels on teetotal themes to the last-named. Thomas Rees translated the multi-volume theology of the American Edward Baine, which sold a million copies in the original, co-founded an ambitious quarterly intended as the Independents' answer to the *Traethodydd*, wrote (in English) an archivally researched *History of Protestant Nonconformity in Wales*, and the four-volume *Y Beibl Teuluaidd* (The Family Bible), while contributing plentifully to Independent periodicals and being constantly engaged with public issues – temperance was his chief but not only cause.[10] His main work was a Welsh-language chronicle of every Independent church in Wales in four fat volumes (1871–5), combining oral testimony with other sources for a remarkable record. At a crude estimate, upwards of fifteen thousand participants in founding and running these are mentioned by name. Weighty tomes were a feature of Welsh-language publishing in the age, which together with large-framed pictures of Biblical scenes could attract the commercial interest of firms in London and Edinburgh. The 1867 large format edition of Pantycelyn's works was published by William Mackenzie in London, Liverpool, Bristol and Swansea.

In addition to preaching and press, chapels had an array of prayer meetings, Bible discussion groups, literary societies, penny readings and the lecture with tea to keep their members' attention. Temperance, first broached in Wales in the 1830s, had joined mission work as a major concern, with total abstinence winning out over moderate drinking as the goal. There were 450 Good Templar branches in Wales in 1873 with forty thousand members, while the Band of Hope preached the same message to children. Choral societies blossomed. *Y Cerddor Cymreig* (The Welsh Musician), launched in 1861, popularised the system of Tonic Sol-Fa, and from 1874 the Gymanfa Ganu or annual singing festival with hymns at its core became a staple of Welsh chapel life. Indeed, music outranked literature in public popularity in the movement to establish an annual national eisteddfod in the 1860s, during which *Hen Wlad fy Nhadau* (Land of My Fathers), composed by two Baptist weavers in 1856, quickly established itself as the de facto Welsh national anthem. Nonconformists' effective take-over of the eisteddfodic tradition in these years, previously largely the preserve of the Anglican gentry, indicates their rise to national leadership.

By 1882 membership of the four main Nonconformist denomina-tions stood at 352,249, but this was exceeded by the number of 'listeners' (*gwrandawyr*) who attended services but had not taken on the commit-ments of membership. Commenting on the great crowds which had attended the funeral of the Revd Henry Rees in 1869, H. T. Edwards, the Dean of Bangor, told William Gladstone that Rees had all the gifts of a true prince of the Church. But regrettably, because of the state church's neglect of the Welsh language, these gifts, he added, had been bestowed on a sect which rejected the very principle of episcopacy.[11] A movement whose members evoked such loyalty in its followers and respect in its opponents could not remain in the shadows of public life. Gladstone appointed the first native Welsh-speaking bishop for one hundred and sixty years but it was too late. Nonconformists' campaign for non-denominational British Schools against the National Schools of the Church, stimulated by anger at the Blue Books, was carried to success through their domination of the elected school boards set up by the Education Act of 1870. Local health boards instituted from 1848 had begun the erosion of landlord power. The protests against the expulsion of tenant farmers for voting against their landlords' wishes grew in the 1860s into an anti-Tory movement and had the greater symbolic impact, in victories for three Welsh-speaking Nonconformist candidates. Lloyd George was to say that 1868 was the start of a new epoch in Welsh politics.[12] The parallel with the Slovene electoral breakthrough in Carniola the year before is striking. Indeed, the expulsion of peasants from their holdings for voting against elite landlords figured prominently in native journalism (*Novice* and *Baner ac Amserau Cymru*) in each case. The immediate aftermath, though, proved something of a damp squib, with Tory come-back in the election of 1874 and the loss of the Carniolan Diet was to a German liberal revival in Carniola.

However, the setbacks did not endure. Indeed, Welsh life in the 1860s showed many signs of vigorous expansion. Dizzying demographic growth in the industrialising areas created a host of new communities lining the narrow mining valleys of south-east Wales with a topography as distinct-ive as the 'valleys' culture they developed: a blend of people flocking from rural Wales and increasingly England and Ireland into a teaming world of pubs, chapels and churches, choirs, dog racing and pugilism, in a febrile cli-mate of economic spurt and recession, accompanied by bouts of industrial strife. Life was hard and dangerous; some seventy-four fatal coal mine acci-dents occurred in these years, with upwards of two thousand deaths, and strikes were frequent.[13] But work was better paid and society more varied than in the countryside. The north-east Wales coalfield employing fifteen thousand men, and the slate quarries of the north-west, largest in the world, with sixteen thousand workers at their maximum, exemplified this vibrant world on a smaller scale. And it was an identifiably Welsh world. The accident of 1877 at Cymmer in the Rhondda valley when thirteen miners cut off in a flooded pit without food for eight days sustained their spirits with renditions of the hymn 'Yn y dyfroedd mawr a'r tonnau' (In the waves and mighty waters) first implanted in the British public the image of the singing, chapel-going Welsh miner. The strike of Flintshire miners in 1869 was against an unpopular English manager. It was industrial workers who flocked to Henry Richard's electoral speeches in Merthyr in 1868, just as earlier sailors had anchored their ships at Mostyn on Sundays to hear Hiraethog preaching. Workers were numerous among buyers of the lyrics of John Ceiriog Hughes (Ceiriog), whose 'Oriau'r Hwyr' (Evening Hours) sold 30,000 copies between 1860 and 1872.[14] This was in many ways the heroic age of modern industrial Wales, when things were still in flux and legends were being born.

SLOVENE RECOVERY FROM THE 1848–9 DEBACLE

Neo-absolutism did not set in immediately in Slovenia. For a short period some of the attitudes of the revolutionary episode remained, making disillusionment at the unrelenting rolling back of one-time hopes the more galling for patriots. All hope of political or cultural progress went with the emasculation of an official Slovene journal, the discontinuing of early cases of recording court witness statements in Slovene as well as German, and the abolition of two posts set up for lecturing in Slovene on alleged minimal student take-up. The arch-conservative Catholic organ *Zgodnja Danica*, which Bleiweis forbore to criticise too openly, proclaimed that religion, not language, was the root of nationality. Interestingly, its editor had earlier helped Bleiweis improve his written command of his mother tongue.[15] *Novice* became again the one Slovene patriotic journal, diligently recording the occasional inclusion of a Slovene song in concerts, as a Slovene national presence all but disappeared from public life.

In keeping with this changed atmosphere, the handful of literary periodicals which had appeared before full reaction also withered. They showed the limitations of the still-undeveloped native medium. The first, edited by a young man noted for pioneering the use of the literary language in everyday speech, was essentially didactic. It offered, for example, a model poem for would-be writers to learn from and lists of Slovene substitutes for common Germanisms. Its successor was more orientated towards strictly literary themes, urging study of native and other Slav folklore and showing how this could be turned to national ends: thus, the water supply expropriated by a neighbour could stand for a threatened national heritage. The short story was particularly advocated, but the reliance on translated material was heavy. The longest lasting such publication, *Slovenska bčela* had just 179 subscribers the year before it closed in 1853.[16] Yet limited sophistication was part compensated for by young acolytes' energies still charged by the revolutionary eruption of 1848. The publicity for *Slovenska bčela*'s launch in April 1850 announced its purpose as being 'to awaken the Slovene spirit and love for the mother tongue and its embellishment, acquainting Slovenes with native literature and that of our Slav brothers. All in the native tongue'. Evoking a Czech national revivalist, the paper hailed 'the poetry of the common man' as 'the history of the inner life and consciousness ... the key to the temple of nationality'.[17] There was room for ambiguity as to what constituted this native tongue. Practicality supported the line that one might hope for a movement towards fuller linguistic union, a Serbo-Croat imbued with Slovene elements perhaps, but should work meanwhile to secure the Slovene vernacular. This subtly balanced language drive would become a *Leitmotiv* for action when the dead weight of absolutism was removed.

The intensity of the romantic idealism felt by young patriots must be stressed. History should be the repository of self-cultivating humanity, wrote the law student Lovro Toman to his future wife in 1851, but German, Italian and Hungarian nationalists had shown no feeling for the Slavs, who deserved to enjoy the happiness of freedom's day. 'German centralisation is our death ... I expect only ill fortune for our nation in the future'.[18] His fiancée, at his urging, was one of Slovenia's first female writers. In her words to an editor: if Mother Slava's sons were hastening to bring their gifts to their country as proof of worthiness, why should not her daughters?[19] The role women could play was the theme of Ieuan Gwynedd's *Y Gymraes* at just this time, but the patriotism was different. This couple illustrate another aspect of the Slovene situation which has been touched on before. Though the bulk of Slovene activists were of quite humble stock, as befitted the national self-image, more of them arguably had some contact with elite society than was the case in Wales. Toman himself was born into a wealthy entrepreneurial family; his young wife's father was of noble stock. She was educated privately and was instilled with Slavic ideas by a priest who had imbibed them when living in Croatia. Personal influence of this kind had a role in spreading national ideas. Young patriots earning a living tutoring upper-class children could enthuse them for things Slovene, leading in a number of cases to their pupils later producing translations of Prešeren which helped introduce him to the German public. Tutoring was also important in the lives of talented young Welshmen but elite families' prior acquaintance of a kind with the language of the people seems to have been more common in Slovenia than Wales.

However produced, pent-up patriotic emotions could speak out more strongly with the abandonment of neo-absolutism. Yet Habsburg constitutionalism was a different animal from British. The Emperor continued to exercise effective control of foreign policy and the army. The operation of civil rights was heavily influenced by traditions of top-down government. New societies and journals still had to register with the authorities, no automatic process; press proprietors and journalists could find themselves prosecuted, if now through trial by jury. Government influence largely ensured that elections returned bodies reflecting official wishes. This had been the practice in eighteenth-century Britain but not nineteenth. Lack of parliamentary traditions made it all the more likely that the political parties of parliamentary government would emerge on ethnic lines. After all, the equality of nations and languages had been the clearest of the promises made by government.

This swayed the agenda of nationally conscious Slovenes. Patriots realised that participation in the new dispensation depended on the claim to nationhood and that in turn depended on the existence of a modernised Slovene language. They were aware that both common nationhood and literary language were very recent things, and essentially works in progress. Hence, while the Slovene autonomy programme of 1848 was reiterated from 1859 on, the concrete concern of Slovene politics was to establish the place of Slovene in public life. It was no mistake that *Novice's* commentary on the government's key constitutional declarations of 1859 concentrated on its promise of language equality, particularly in secondary schools. Actually, the 1859 promise was conditional on 'practicality' and was intended for Czechs and Poles; the Viennese press ruled it out for Slovenes.[20]

Early Slovene steps in the constitutional process were halting indeed. Groupings for the first Carniolan elections for the Diet and the Vienna parliament in 1861 were loosely associated with Slovene and German labels, yet the great majority of those elected had declared themselves for both these camps, in the spirit of traditional *Landespatriotismus* or provincial identity. In a system of voting based on 'curias' representing separately large landowners, the towns, and rural peasants, Slovenes won a majority only from Carniolan peasants and hardly any seats elsewhere. Most of those elected in Slovene areas were Germans or *nemškutarji*, Slovenes who spoke Slovene at home but saw German as the vehicle for higher culture and public life. At this time *nemškutarji* were the large majority of urban and in general educated Slovenes. The first political leader of the Slovenes and mayor of Ljubljana, Heinrich Costa, knew no more than twenty words of Slovene according to the prominent *nemškutar* Karl Deschmann.[21] As the decade advanced, the Slovene party encroached on the *nemškutarji* until in 1867 it gained enough non-rural seats to gain a majority in Carniola overall. It was helped by the emperor's temporary replacement of German centralists in government by pro-federalist conservatives, resentment of absolutism and neo-absolutism, and by strengthening Slovene consciousness. By the end of the 1860s a series of mass public gatherings (*tabori*) protesting against the centralist 1867 Austrian constitution, one with thirty thousand in attendance, attested to a new popular consciousness. This was a high point and unavailing. More consistent was the growth of cultural associations. The first *čitalnica* or Slovene reading society was opened in Trieste in 1861; by the end of the decade there were fifty-seven. These foundations were patriotic, often demonstrative affairs, involving speeches, songs and recitations and attended by sympathetic local notables and members of other Slovene and sometimes other Slav societies. In many ways they recall the Cymreigyddol societies earlier in the century and, like *Seren Gomer, Novice* was a zealous reporter of their doings. They had advantages, however, which gave them greater staying power than their Welsh counterparts. Inspiration from similar reading clubs in the wider Habsburg Slav world was a stronger spur than Celticism offered Wales. The Czech example, as in so many spheres, was particularly important; the energetic head of the Ljubljana choral society, for example, was a Czech. Bleiweis's tireless work provided the movement organisational backbone. It was in these years that he acquired the reputation of father of the Slovene nation. Besides the reading associations, Slovene gymnastic societies from 1862 and the Slovenska matica, from 1864, reinforced the growing network of cultural nationalism. The gymnastic movement was a direct borrowing, in structure, title – *Sokol* (Falcon) – and even in kit from the Czechs. The Matica institution had long existed among Habsburg Serbs (1826), Czechs (1831) and the Croats (1840) as cultural foundations for serious literary and scholarly publication. Its delay in Slovenia reflected lack of numbers and wealthy patrons – Bleiweis had thought it too ambitious – so its seven hundred members, the 24,000 florins (£2,000) in its funds and the one hundred and thirty present at its founding meeting, representing all Slovene lands and language opinions, were undoubted marks of progress.

Yet this is a somewhat rosy view overall. The reading societies' celebrations were infrequent and repetitive. There was much reliance on translated Slav and German material because of the paucity of Slovene which particularly held back amateur dramatics initially, otherwise ideally suited to such societies. The first full-length play performed by the Ljubljana society, in 1863, was a well-known German classic. Throughout the decade some speeches in the Ljubljana society continued to be held in German for the sake of members whose Slovene was uncertain. Its president resigned at criticism of his participation in a German cultural function, effectively leaving the Slovene camp. The atmosphere could be hostile. A reading society was formed by the Slovene minority in Maribor, Germanised centre of Slovene Styria, in reaction to a scornful gibe that Slovene material was fit only for the toilet. Bleiweis felt called to protest that pressure on officials not to join Slovene societies would be against official government policy. The fact is that Slovene national ideas evoked little interest in the mass of the population before the *tabori* gatherings. Accounts of reading societies thought it worthy of special mention if they contained peasant members. The distinction between Slovene language and Carniolan speech ('sprach' borrowed from German 'Sprache' for the latter term) continued to be a staple in Bleiweis's didactic armoury.

However, the sluggishness of the language movement charged one response not seen in Wales: a critique spear-headed by academic youth. This was a European phenomenon, traceable to the difference between the Gymnasium and the English public school, neither of them native to Wales. Many of the small Slovene intelligentsia were educated in Ljubljana Gymnasium and Vienna University and their student life was not experienced in Wales till the secondary schools and the Welsh university colleges came in the late nineteenth century, or really till the inter-war years. Mostly it followed the characteristic pattern of student activity: spurts of engagement interspersed with periods of socialising in beer houses. In 1861 more than ninety students in Vienna issued a letter of congratulation to Bleiweis and the leader of the first little group of Slovene MPs; in 1862 they helped form a Slav singing society in the capital. Smallness was again a factor; Slovenes were the only Slavs in Vienna without their own organised student society, lamented one activist in 1867, the year such a society, dedicated to literature and 'entertainment', finally formed. This soon merged with the Croatian society but debate on Slovene adoption of Croat as their language of high culture ended in the societies splitting up again. Meanwhile the first Slovene student congress, involving final year Gymnasium students also, was held in Ljubljana in summer 1868.

But not all was small beer. The Vienna intake of 1865 included the founder of Slovene literary criticism, Josip Stritar, and the 'Slovene Walter Scott', Josip Jurčič, both deeply influenced by the engagé journalist Fran Levstik – names which will recur in this narrative. We have an evocative record of life in the 'Stritar circle' as members baked potatoes and drank beer in Stritar's lodging while he played the piano, then read aloud from Levstik, the Russian writer Lermontov and the Azerbaijani Persian poet Mirza Shafi Vazeh, a Russian subject.[22] What these figures did was provide a critical edge to Slovene discourse, stifled, as they saw it, by the patriarchal and anti-intellectual style of Bleiweis's role in Slovene life. They rightly saw Bleiweis's hesitancy on a Slovene political paper and the Matica (our people are still too backward for such things) as reflecting opposition to a possible rival for his *Novice*. In particular they resented his preference for the patriotic bombast of a second-rate poet Koseski against the genuine article Prešeren, whose work they republished. From 1864 a gap in Slovene journalism opened up between 'Young Slovenes' and the 'Old Slovenes' of the Bleiweis school, labels taken over from the Czechs. Welsh readers may think of Emrys ap Iwan's challenge to the dominant figure in Welsh Calvinistic Methodism, Lewis Edwards, in the 1880s. That challenge was twenty years later, however, and Emrys ap Iwan was an isolated figure.

The most persistent of Bleiweis's critics, Fran Levstik, represented a willingness to question their leaders widely shared among educated youth. 'Let those who wish well for Slovenes cry: a blessing on criticism', he had said already in 1857.[23] Levstik's many-sided activity centred around twin commitments. 'Nationality is a lofty, fruitful, life-affirming thought', he wrote, like freedom and religion. Central to it was the importance of mother tongue schooling. 'The world knows that no nation can be educated on the basis of a foreign tongue'.[24] These standpoints were not new but Levstik advocated them with a novel vigour and boldness. He upbraided Slovenes in the Carniolan diet, who still preponderantly debated in German, German doctors who belittled their Slovene peasant patients and Germans who lived for decades amongst Slovene communities without troubling to learn their language. He called for all the Diet minutes to be available in Slovene, Slovene students in Vienna to have instruction in their own language and literature and for a Slovene style reflecting the natural speech of the people without German impress. He led the campaign against Bleiweis's 'shameful' decision to found a German-language organ to advocate the Slovene cause politically rather than one in Slovene: Bleiweis wanted to appeal to the *nemškutarji*. It was Levstik's rejection of gradualism and his stress of the harsh fate of Slovenes before 1848 which made him an inspirational figure for youth.

Language concern was not confined to students and youth. *Učiteljski tovariš* (The Teacher's Comrade), founded in 1861, stressed repeatedly that only mother tongue instruction was really effective for heart, mind and truth. While other languages might be taught, it was the teacher's 'holy duty' to see that this did not harm the child's mastery of his own language first. These were hortatory maxims not greatly observed in practice outside Carniola. There was much discussion in *Učiteljski tovariš* about the stage in rural primary schools when German should be introduced. Contributors noted how town school pupils flattered themselves they could do anything with some knowledge of German and cited popular doubts about the point of teaching Slovene in school when it was not used in administration. Significant, too, was the journal's strong association of nationality and religion, seen as the only things left Slovenes from centuries of repression. Education was 'all for the glory of God and the happiness of our nation' stated the opening number. Reading opened the way to 'the great book of God's boundless nature'.[25] Such sentiments show the strength of the conservative patriotism on which Bleiweis's position rested and explain why, though not particularly religious himself, he allied himself closely with the Church, whose parish priests were the Slovene movement's main rural support base. Young Slovenes recognised the role of the Church but were critical of it as partner of neo-absolutism. Events were to show the weakness of their position.

Indeed, the uncertainties of this early Slovene nationalism need reiterating. Slogans were fine but what could they mean in practice? A united Slovenia, trumpeted by a handful of patriots in 1848 would entail breaking up the ancient provinces of Styria and Carinthia against the outraged will of their German majorities. No wonder Bleiweis concentrated on language concessions. The natural right to use one's own language did not trample on historic traditions; but in practice it did raise daily more concrete questions of custom, implementation and ingrained socio-psychological relations. Questions as to historic rights or natural rights as a basis of social organisation which 1848 had raised came to dominate Habsburg debate as public consciousness spread. Czech-led Slav rejection of the 1867 Dualist settlement which perpetuated German domination reached little Slovenia in the form of the *tabori*) in which the idea of a united Slovenia first took popular root. But the impotence of Slovene liberal MPs in Vienna, indeed, their support of the government for the sake of minor concessions, arguably including personal favours, eroded enthusiasm. Controlism remained intact.

A FALTERING LANGUAGE IN WALES?

In this very period, uncertainties in Welsh attitudes to their national language came to the fore. Advances in Welsh social life and consciousness brought no corresponding change in the status of Welsh in the public sphere. Education, justice and administration, the key areas singled out in the Austrian nationality law of 1867, remained out of bounds. Only in recent decades have scholars, often not historians, begun to address this, comparatively speaking, striking fact. The richly researched study of the Eisteddfodic movement in the 1860s by Hywel Teifi Edwards, a professor of Welsh, throws a flood of light on the mentalities of the time.

Edwards depicts a strenuous effort by the no longer insignificant cohorts of Welsh patriotic sentiment to make the Eisteddfod a kind of governing body for intellectual and cultural life. A sense of the need to catch the train which was driving 'the tide of civilization higher and higher', for a 'fulcrum on which the lever of popular elevation might play with telling effect upon the mass of society in Wales's animated discussion'.[26] There is much here which recalls the Matica movements in the Habsburg Monarchy. But the parallel is not quite exact. The Eisteddfod was an institution of ancient pedigree which, through intermittent local practice and then the more serious revivals since the 1790s, had developed powerful traditions. It was not so easily refashionable to suit new purposes. Initial plans of 1858 and 1860 introduced features which have remained, like provision for annual national gatherings alternately in north and south. Yet whereas these gave a special place to linguistic preservation and to poets, another programme of 1866 spoke more generally of promoting Welsh literary culture and stressed moral and social improvement. It was also in English. Behind these nuances lay a different valuation of the bardic literary heritage. Traditionalists thought it was being undervalued, while one modernist could attack classical Welsh *cynghanedd* as an alliterative throwback to a primitive past, abandoned by modern prosody. This approach came from a school of thought deeply swayed by English utilitarianism and the power and prestige of the British Empire. Hugh Owen (1804–81), a London-based civil servant and pious Nonconformist, was foremost among those who argued for the modernisation of Welsh life on these lines. He had made his mark first by his *Llythyr i'r Cymry* (Letter to the Welsh people) (1843), urging his fellow-countrymen to accept government money to build up British Schools which would counter Anglican control of education. He now made proposals to bring the Eisteddfod 'into accord with the spirit of progress ... the world moves on continually, and we must move with it or we will be trodden in the dirt'.[27] Owen advocated adapting the Eisteddfod to the norms of the Association for the Promotion of Social Science founded in 1857. It should be reorganised into several sections dealing with different aspects of life, one of which, the Social Science Section, would hold its meetings in English. In the event, he succeeded in getting the last day of the Caernarfon Eisteddfod of 1862 devoted to lectures, all but one in English, on scientific and improving topics. Audiences had no stomach for such fare. The linked scientific exhibitions were certainly innovatory. Observers convinced that Wales's claims to moral excellence had been undermined in English eyes by the 1847 educational reports thought her wealth of mineral and geological resources could be used to counter the negative image.

The concern, if not obsession, with English opinion testified to national pride wounded by the Blue Books, the sense of being subject to a scornful gaze. English self-assurance could take racist overtones. Welsh 'natural indolence and want of perseverance' contrasted with 'that indomitable energy and spirit of improvement which has raised the Anglo-Saxon race'. 'No people can thrive on faded myths and extinct traditions, encumbered with a language which isolates them from general civilization'. Language was a recurring point of attack. Abandonment of their 'determination' to maintain it was the sine qua non in these views for the Welsh to be taken seriously in the modern world. It was 'the curse of Wales', ran *The Times*'s comments on the 1866 Eisteddfod: 'their anti-quated and semibarbarous language shrouds them in darkness ... For all practical purposes Welsh is a dead language.' The famous historian Froude aroused some English criticism for being too generous to the Welsh when he praised them for accepting their fate and submitting loyally to rule 'by those who are nobler and wiser than themselves'.[28]

Obviously, there was some Welsh reaction to this refrain but it lacked the vigour of the rebuttals of Brutus forty years before. Welsh people were themselves embarrassed by their poor English. Dr Thomas Nicholas, a leading advocate of eisteddfod reform, worried about the figure cut by middle-class Welsh jurymen and their like in other public positions. He was impressed by the much better command of the state language produced by middle-class education in Brittany. This helps explain why periodic grumbling about the exclusive sway of English in the courts got nowhere at a time when this issue was gaining attention in Slovenia. The problem was not helped by the mixed views of educated Welsh themselves on their vaunted literary heritage. The balance between the traditional metres and freer forms remained an uneasy one, but the prestige associ-ated with the former did not yield the acknowledged Welsh epic that was craved. Llew Llwyfo, a prominent literature and musician, laboured to produce half a dozen of these for eisteddfodic glory in the 1860s. In fact, he was more successful on the musical front which gained the upper hand in popularity in this decade. Zealous folk tune collectors, gifted soloists, dedicated choir masters, the prolific composer of the first Welsh language opera Joseph Parry and shrewd organisers like Brinley Richards, professor at the Royal Music Academy, London, together gained an enthusiastic audience in English cities. The *Illustrated London News* wrote of 'an extra-ordinary sensation', the *Daily Telegraph* of the uniqueness of such singers, 'entirely raised from the ranks of hard toil'. The first prize at the Crystal Palace in 1872 and 1873 was carried off by a Welsh male voice choir to ecstatic acclaim. This did not mean the full vindication of their culture that Welsh people would have wished, however. The *Athanaeum* implied a familiar criticism, in that these beauties were 'jealously' shut off in a language 'which must become obsolete at no very distant period'.[29]

Hence it did not enter official minds to take cognisance of the Welsh language in the 1870 Act which made education compulsory in Britain. Nor did the Welsh at the time call for it. Many Welsh teachers active in Welsh language culture implemented the practice of the 'Welsh Not', whereby pupils caught speaking Welsh were punished unless they managed to pass on the incriminating stick bearing these words to another child. The gradual shift in priorities between learning German and mother tongue education among Habsburg Slavs did not occur in Wales. The rhetorical view of the common people as the collective repository of national values and language was common to both situations but one corollary was not. By the Victorian era the *Cymro uniaith* (monoglot Welshman) was seen as an uneducated person behind the times; Pantycelyn and others' aim of instructing such people through Welsh was replaced by a bilingual goal. John Jones Talsarn was criticised for his monoglottism. Famous Nonconformist ministers tended to write to their children in English or a mixture of the two languages. Piquantly, Henry Rees, Hiraethog's equally prestigious brother, practised this with his children but only English in published letters to his grandchildren. He and Lewis Edwards recommended transferring their respective training colleges from Bala to a less Welsh environment for the sake of learning English and greater prestige. Ceiriog gave voice to the bilingual idea in a well-known poem 'Speak them both', where he refused to express a preference; he also suggested that the great Welsh epic poem craved for might be written in English. In terms of east European small nation patriotism by this time such an idea amounted to a contradiction in terms.

It is an aspect of such thinking that the movement for a Welsh university, one of the most cherished in Welsh annals, and which came to hard-won fruition in these years, did not envisage a University teaching through the medium of Welsh. The call for a Slovene University, first voiced in 1848, recurred occasionally in these years, but the statist mentality of central Europe assumed governmental commitment, which was never on the cards. The ambition of the Welsh project becomes apparent. The university college which opened in Aberystwyth in 1872 with a mere twenty-six students was funded and sustained in part by popular contributions, the regular Sunday offerings of Nonconformist chapels, 70,000 of them on one designated occasion in 1875, though without the large sums from the industrialist David Davies it is doubtful if it could have survived these crisis-torn early years. The period discussed in this chapter shows a curious disjuncture: between Welsh leaders plainly conscious of new times and new Welsh energies but as diffident as ever in the assertion of the mother tongue in the face of English disregard.

This disjuncture has been impressively demonstrated in a path-breaking comparison of European language movements by the literary critic Simon Brooks. Tellingly, Brooks notes how surprised German scholars were at the absence in Wales of any attempt at linguistic asser-tion. Rudolph von Raumer, commenting on the Welsh situation in 1861, outlined a practicable approach to the problem of different languages in the same state, reconciling the principle of political equality and the fact of different strength of language communities concerned.[30] Brooks explains the phenomenon that puzzled Raumer by Welsh Nonconformists' total acceptance of English liberalism's view of liberty. This emphasised exclu-sively the civic rights of individuals, so that the claim of communities to collective rights could be seen as a threat to the universalism which liberal-ism stood for. Liberals could and did support national/ethnic movements when they opposed authoritarian rule, to the applause of Hiraethog in 1848, or slavery, as the Welsh and Welsh American press did in the case of the United States. But Welsh observers saw no analogy with situations where civic freedoms already existed, as in liberal Britain; here concern for national rights was divisive nationalism. Moreover, Calvinist thinking with its providentialist background made it easier to accept social Darwinist categories as God's will, suffering of which could be seen as a pious humil-ity. In this way the Welsh themselves prepared the way for the erosion of their language and their steady assimilation into a British Protestant world empire, which identified its values with universal ones.

Brooks makes a masterly case. Elements of fatalism in the face of English power can be seen before the triumph of Nonconformity, of course, in the exaggerated sense of the spread of English which has been noted above and the relative ineffectuality of the Morris brothers. Brooks cites Heinrich Rolph who in the 1860s broached psychological roots for 'certain peculiarities of the Welsh mind', resulting from loss of independence and the 'incessant attack' to which the Welsh language was subjected.[31] Indeed, it is hard to overestimate the weight of millennial Welsh isolation compared to the position of the numerous Slavs in the Habsburg Monarchy, or the difficult position of the Monarchy relative to Anglo-British triumphalism. Brooks stresses the shift of the important minister and editor Samuel Roberts from militant defence of Welsh in the

1820s to belief in its inevitable eclipse by the English 'general language' in the 1860s.[32] This can be paralleled by R. J. Derfel's shift from language patriotism to (in his case) socialism in later life. Prudence, not mere passivity, and, as Brooks rightly underlines, genuine universalist ideals, helped shape Welsh attitudes. Not all English people were unsympathetic to Welsh otherness. George Borrow, the idiosyncratic polyglot traveller, wrote his 'Wild Wales' with its praise of Welsh literature, and Welsh common people's knowledge of it, in these years. A sturdy Anglican, he records vividly the hold of Welsh methodism on the people, down to persecution of the rector's poor, unloved 'Church cat' by the Nonconformists of Llangollen.[33] The whole book vividly depicts a people on the cusp of change, showing how important a link Protestantism was to both Welsh and English but how its internal inflections, as in much else of 'Britishness', marked the Welsh off from their neighbours.

SIX SKETCHES

This chapter plays a central role in the present study, for it covers the period when Welsh and Slovene divergence became quite clear and irrevocable trajectories were set for the future. A number of illustrative case studies may reinforce the message. The six people selected, three on each side, do not cover all relevant trends but the most distinctive in each nation. Thus, crucial figures like the Slovene 'father of the nation', Janez Bleiweis, need no further underlining, having had frequent mention already. Anton Slomšek, bishop of Lavant (1846–60) deserves more than the previous mentions for his work nationalising Styrian Slovenes, but the emphasis goes on three Slovenes whose focus was Slovene cultural development. There is a twist in the tale, however. One of the Slovenes moved from champion of the Slovene cause in 1848 to become the most prominent of the *nemškutarji*. For Wales, two choices are Welsh Nonconformist ministers whose deepest concern was religious, but the importance of the Welsh economy is acknowledged in the third, an industrialist, at the cost of another religious figure, the London-based secretary of the pathbreaking anti-war Peace Society, Henry Richard (1812–88), significant as a Welsh patriot of international horizons. As MP for Merthyr, centre of industrial Wales, he was, barring one Unitarian, the first Welsh 'dissenter' elected to parliament and major spokesman for Wales to the English. He will be allowed here a speech he gave during the campaign which spelt out the concept of Wales as a Nonconformist nation, which summed up his patriotism:

> What of the people who speak this language, read this literature, claim this history, inherit these traditions, respect these names and have created and maintained these wonders [the Nonconformist institutions] – people who together form three quarters of the population of Wales, do they not have the right to assert: We are the Welsh nation?[34]

Not material interests only should be represented in Parliament but 'the soul of a nation, its character and conscience'.[35] Ken Morgan, Wales's leading modern historian, has positively summed up this somewhat forgotten figure under the headings: Welshman, Nonconformist, democrat and internationalist.[36]

Let us begin with, for the Slovenes, Fran Levstik, whose basic views have been outlined above. Here the need is to convey the context which produced them. Levstik was the son of a poor Carniolan peasant, holder of only an eighth of the full plot of the old feudal order. His education, like that of many talented peasant youths, took him from a couple of years in a local school to a higher grade 'normal' school followed by Gymnasium in Ljubljana, where he already wrote a play in the fourth form and had five hundred copies of his poetry published. But this was the time of neo-absolutism and he was forced to leave because of his democratic views. His radical reputation followed him to college in the present Czech republic, which he also had to give up. On the way back home, he spent time in Vienna, meeting the leading Slav philologists of the day and broadening his horizons through study of the great German enlightenment thinker, Gotthold Lessing. It was in the time he spent in different places in the Slovenian countryside as tutor to a noble youth in 1857–8, that he received the inspiration which shaped his life: the way of life of the common Slovene people and the language that they spoke, unadulterated by Germanisms of vocabulary and grammar. Only through literature could the powerless Slovene people be saved and only in a purified popular speech could this be written. Yet the peasant had been left physically enfeebled and morally degraded by the system which had endured for centuries till the 1848 revolution. These were the impressions which underlay an outburst of publication: the first widely acclaimed Slovene short story in the form of a folk tale, a travelogue through the Slovene countryside combined with reflections on language, and an attack (*Mistakes in writing Slovene*) on current inflated and Germanised style. Not till Emrys ap Iwan and Sir John Morris-Jones later in the century did similar linguistic awareness dawn in Wales.

Levstik's life in the 1860s shows the many fronts on which Slovene reformers felt called to fight. Working for a Slovene reading club in Trieste, co-editing a Slovene paper in Klagenfurt till it closed under official pressure, writing for the Slovene Dramatic Society which he chaired, editing the forerunner Vodnik's work, compiling a new Slovene dictionary, pursuing his linguistic researches into Old Slav, briefly secretary of Slovenska matica, main contributor to a Slovene paper in Styria, all the while active politically, Levstik's overriding cause became the Young Slovene's fight against Bleiweis's leadership. But in the embattled state of Slovene politics, he made enemies and lost some direction. This and a disastrous relationship with a girl to whom he was briefly engaged, ruined by his jealousy, led to his withdrawal from the public stage to his now rather obsessive linguistic concerns, though he remained active journalistically. The last three years of his life were a struggle with illness, when he turned increasingly to a kind of religious mania till his death in 1887. His place in Slovene literature, however, is assured. The route taken in his 1858 countryside walk is now followed annually at the appropriate time by up to twenty thousand admirers.

Josip Stritar (1836–1923) has also appeared above, presiding over his literary circle in Viennese exile. Born in the same area as Levstik, Stritar likewise went from a village school to Ljubljana Gymnasium and early showed a talent for poetry. Once he went to study classical language in Vienna, however, he returned only four times in his life to Slovenia, though as tutor to nobility he made several journeys to other places, notably Paris in 1861. Finally taking his degree in 1874 – he had not sat the necessary exams under the absolutist regime – he became a Gymnasium teacher of classical languages, German and French in Vienna and married a Viennese woman. His two sons spoke no Slovene. This and lifetime exile is not so unusual among small nation intellectuals. The most famous of Habsburg Panslavs, the Slovak Jan Kollár, also did not pass on his language to his children. Stritar was not an activist in Levstik's sense, though he was always a patriot with panslav sympathies; one of his first poems had celebrated Montenegrin resistance to the Turks. His primary preoccupations were literary: European culture and the development of the Slovene language within its framework. His reputation as founder of modern Slovene literary criticism was established by his essay on Prešeren in 1866, linked with an edition of his works which laid out criteria for assessing national literatures and used Prešeren to show Slovene's claim to be one of these. In one play he had him set alongside Homer, Petrarch and Goethe in the pantheon.

Stritar contributed to almost every literary genre: novels, short stories, plays, essays, criticism and translations, together with poetry written in a wide variety of metres. His chief contribution, however, was as literary critic and mentor, and editor of a landmark literary review, *Zvon* (The Bell), in 1870 and resumed in 1876–80. His influences were from German literature (Goethe and Schiller), but also Victor Hugo and Rousseau, while his private library contained the leading works of Italian literature in the original. Curiously, for British readers, another major influence was Oliver Goldsmith's *The Vicar of Wakefield*, which had also inspired Levstik. The background here was the translation of this work into Slovene, showing the way a still infant but omnivorous literature built on what was to hand. Sir Walter Scott and Byron were more predictable British influences. Goldsmith's book fitted into Stritar's aesthetic framework in which idealism and striving for the beautiful were shot through with elements of Schopenhauerian pessimism and a sense of the incompatibility of the ideal and actuality. One of his two chief novels was about a wealth-seeking peasant who introduced industry into his village and opposed his son's marriage to a poor man's daughter, bringing disaster on the village and himself. Goldsmith's vicar hero in the other Stritar novel represented the opposite pole: goodness and balance and the possibility of overcoming life's difficulties. He is seen as the first Slovene writer to explore social themes, both urban and rural, based on his youthful and his later experiences. His many stage plays served to encourage the nascent, still amateur Slovene theatre. He was most productive in the period of this chapter, later interests being in Biblical translations and works for youth in aid of the St Hermagoras book club. Levstik, a great admirer of his Prešeren studies, had criticised the periodical *Zvon* for being too far from the simple tastes of Slovene readers. It is indicative of the speed of Slovene intellectual development that Stritar, who had been taught in secondary school by Metelko, one of the early pioneers of a would-be standard Slovene in the 1820s, should have spent his last months in Yugoslavia, invited back by a grateful government.

The remarkable nature of the change is confirmed, as the exception that proves the rule, by the career of the last of this Slovene trio, Dragotin Dežman (1821–89). Born son of a judge in a small Carniolan town, Dežman was brought up by his uncle in Ljubljana, a strong Slovene patriot. His education followed familiar lines of Gymnasium and Vienna University where he studied natural sciences, developing an interest also in archaeology. It was as Dežman, not his official birth name of Deschmann, that he returned to Ljubljana during the 1848 revolution, which he greeted enthusiastically in the interests of freedom and Slavdom. 'Glory to the Slavs', he hailed the new year 1849, editing *Slovenija*, the first Slovene political newspaper and for a time *Novice*, in Bleiweis's place. In the 1850s his archaeological discoveries as custodian of the Carniolan provincial museum kept him in the public eye. He lent Levstik a hundred florins in one of the latter's several periods without income, and it was natural that to this brilliant man Slovene academic youth turned in 1861 as someone who could edit the political newspaper they desired. Dežman, however, declined. In a speech of that year as elected member of the Vienna parliament he dissociated himself from the Slovene cause, saying he could not agree with any position which denied the civilisational benefits Slavs had received and still required from German culture.

There was a background to this. In private notes he expressed his disgust at the unscholarly historical claims made by Slovene romantic patriots like Trstenjak. It was not things German which were holding Slovenes back, he wrote to a student but 'our laziness, our pharasaical hypocrisy and meekness, our suppression of all healthy and rightful criticism ... our apathy towards public matters, ... our empty bragging, ... our crudity'. To Bleiweis he expressed his fears that the Slavs had not learnt the lessons of 1848, when they had sided with the reactionary dynasty against the revolution.[37] Much of Dežman's criticism of Slovene backwardness was made by other Slovenes but the key to his attitude was his passionate commitment to liberal freedoms and his lofty notion of German civilisation, which resembled Welsh leaders' endorsement of British universalist claims. The logic of his position was that Dragotin Dežman had to become again Karl Deschmann in public life. He had not repudiated all his Slovene loyalties. The political allies in Carniola he now joined called themselves the 'constitutionalist', not the German party, maintaining the stance that they stood for universal values, not narrow nationalism. Dežman tried to hold them to this, arguing for more propaganda material in Slovene to broaden its support. As the friction between Old and Young Slovenes grew, he saw an opportunity to win the latter over, as liberals. Levstik rebuffed him, taunting that he had no real friends for the actual Germans still suspected him of Slovene sympathies, while Young Slovenes would never do a deal which would renounce a united Slovenia, the sine qua non of Slovene patriotism, for paltry language concessions.[38] Indeed, Dežman did reject the principle of full equality between the languages beyond the primary school level. He opposed the cutting back of German language teaching urged by Slovenes in the Carniolan Diet because in his view at least eighteen hours a week of German was necessary for a Slovene child to acquire a thorough knowledge of the language. The bare bones of the language problem we have seen in Wales were thus exposed. A huge commitment was required for Dežman's professed bilingual goal of ensuring mastery of a world language (German) while giving what he called fairness to the mother tongue.

Despite the tensions, Dežman appeared quite successful as a politician in the 1870s, becoming leader of the Carniolan Constitutional Party and for a time mayor of Ljubljana. In practice, he tried as far as possible to fight on issues of provincial economic interest, avoiding national questions. The imbalance whereby a weighted franchise enabled the richer German 10 per cent of the population to hold power he justified in terms of the representation of valid interests. This was not a comfortable position for a professed liberal to be in, but there was no way back. Outside politics, Dežman was a very active worker for social bodies, both German and intercommunal. As custodian of the provincial museum from 1853 till his death, he arranged for its rebuilding as what is now the Slovenian National Museum, making a speech at its opening in what a later historian has praised as beautiful Slovene. In Dežman's life and choices there are many aspects which ring bells for a Welsh commentator, but perhaps for others too who like to ponder the diversity of life and the twists of fate.[39]

None of our Welsh trio was a literary figure. Ceiriog was a prolific and popular poet from the same Denbighshire borderland as the seventeenth-century Huw Morys, whose grave George Borrow visited. He had a genuine lyrical touch and an easy patriotism, writing on the Madog legend, mothers' concerns for their sons in godless England and the great mountains as symbols of Welsh survival. Nostalgia was his predominant mood and his life, ending as a rural station master, was a far cry from that of embattled Slovene poets who shared his humble origin. Islwyn (William Thomas) was the other most admired poet of the age, a

Calvinistic Methodist minister from industrial Monmouthshire, famous particularly for a near book length poem in blank verse ('The Storm'), inspired as a very young man by the death of his fiancée. There he rose far above the lugubrious religiosity of much of his later eisteddfodic muse. But the formative shapers of that age made their mark in the religious, perhaps better the politico-religious sphere. Two of many will be taken here.

Lewis Edwards has already figured in this story as the co-founder of the *Traethodydd* (1845), the leading periodical of nineteenth-century Wales. When he died in 1887 he received encomiums as Wales's most powerful thinker and he had already had in life a testimonial gift of £2,600 for his services, a vast sum for that time. His reputation has see-sawed somewhat since but he was undoubtedly a man of impressive intellect and his career is revealing of the ambiguities of Victorian Wales. The son of reasonably well-off Cardiganshire peasants, he knew from an early age that he was special. When his father, seeing his disinclination for farming, proposed an apprenticeship, the boy replied that he had 'spoilt his plans' and indeed he succeeded by hook or by crook in getting a grounding in the classics from a number of local schoolmasters before becoming one himself as well as starting to preach. 'For the present, here, I am nearly starved to death for want of mental food but if once I enter College I warrant not a book will be left unransacked. I'll ravage them like a hungry lion – or, rather, like a boa-constrictor ... one at a meal', he wrote in English to a friend.[40] Overcoming considerable opposition from Methodist elders he got six months at what became London University college before funds ran out, then a place in Edinburgh University (1833–6) where he carried off several prizes, the famous Scottish divine Thomas Chalmers teaching him his course for free. Edwards now founded a Calvinistic Methodist training college in the tiny north Wales town of Bala which he headed till his death. His emotional commitment to his denomination, 'the poor Methodists', was bound up with what he called his 'devoutest aspiration ... to see my beloved Wales restored to her proper place among the nations of the earth as the land of intellect and virtue'.[41] He insisted on high standards to shake Wales from its mental lethargy; the *Traethodydd* should be unlike any other Welsh periodical in depth and seriousness, adopting the strengths and avoiding the weaknesses he saw in the English-language journals he followed so avidly. His own contributions ranged widely in theology, philosophy ancient and modern, education, current affairs and literature. It was natural to his thoroughness to begin an essay on J. S. Mill and William Hamilton's treatment of innate ideas with passages on Hindu and Greek philosophy.

In practice, Edwards encountered many difficulties as educator, wrestling with financial limitations and the problem of dunning the knowledge of English he deemed necessary into the heads of Welsh peasant youths. But he contributed greatly to establishing the idea of a regular rather than peripatetic ministry, sound funding and a Presbyterian-style system of organisation so as to turn what he once called 'a small contemptible sect in the mountains of Wales', into a respected and powerful body in Welsh life. His goal was not just to make Christians but 'Christian gentlemen' and his means diverged widely from those of Habsburg small nation patriots. Welsh was not taught at Bala. Edwards's correspondence with his closest *Traethodydd* collaborators, as with his children, was almost wholly English. His respect for English culture could lead him to tell a colleague, as guidance, that he had learnt that 'in the highest circles Englishmen generally hesitate in speaking'.[42] Though he had written earlier that there was no chance of Welsh dying out soon, he plainly became influenced by the rapid advance of English. In 1867 he commented that this was no reason to yield to the English 'inroad' but to adapt and take advantage of it for 'our' purposes, as the Jews had used Greek. Edwards was a big supporter of what critics mocked as the 'inglis côs' (English cause). Towards the end of his career he responded to criticism of it by saying that it was a question of going with the tide or harming the Methodist connection.[43] This may seem surprising in view of Edwards's patriotic profession quoted above, but then it was Wales's 'virtue' that he had wished to promote. As to Welsh 'intellect', virtually all his considerable output was published in Welsh, an irony he noted in advising his son to minister to an English congregation in Liverpool, not one of the numerous Welsh chapels there. His best-known book, on the doctrine of the atonement, was translated into English. It reflected the triumph of moderate over 'high' Calvinism, a further contribution to the stabilisation of Welsh nonconformity on its way to national dominance. It was judicious rather than original and in its balanced consideration of the Church fathers and also Aquinas and medieval theology, reflected Edwards's scholarship and breadth of view. His identification of Wales with its religious heritage proved unperceptive, however. The very power of the structures which he with others was creating dazzled them, so that he could defuse the language issue for himself by saying Welsh could live on for five centuries for the sake of Welsh religion.[44]

Thomas Gee (1815–98) was a man of equally imposing appearance and talent but different type. Born of a Welsh mother and an English father become Calvinistic Methodist, who had moved to Denbigh to print Welsh religious books, he was ordained and preached all his life but did not take up a regular ministry. His professional life was as printer and publisher, notable for two landmark undertakings, a massive Welsh-language ency-clopedia, *Y Gwyddoniadur*, and the most influential Welsh newspaper of Victorian Wales. *Y Gwyddoniadur*, in ten volumes, each containing some 800,00 words, came out monthly from 1854 to 1879 at a cost of £20,000. A second edition (1896–1902) added 1,800 articles, making ten thou-sand in all. Coverage was comprehensive with fine maps and illustration, though religious and biblical themes featured much more prominently than in the (in part) already translated *Chamber's Encyclopædia*. The news-paper was *Baner ac Amserau Cymru*, incorporating Hiraethog's *Amserau* in 1859. Gee intended something more than its rivals, which would offer readers, as well as Welsh materials, a digest of everything important in the English press. Divided into three sections, with separate editors for politics, religion and literature, *Y Faner*, as it was known for short, quickly expanded from twelve to sixteen pages and came out twice weekly. Higher figures have been given for its circulation but its upper range seems to have been about fifteen thousand.[45]

Unlike Edwards, Gee was a whirlwind of public activity. Besides local and national aspects of Victorian reformers' customary concerns like water supply, sanitation, temperance and railways, he played a leading role in the most sensitive questions: education, religious life, the land question and parliamentary politics. In all these he was a diligent researcher himself into complex past and current backgrounds, circularising *enquêtes* and organising and usually chairing countless public meetings in Denbigh and throughout north Wales, less often in the south except Aberystwyth, geographically suited for all-Wales gatherings. As a believer that Wales must be shaken into public life, he became well-known to many English politicians, and the *Faner* something of a bogey for English Conservatives. For Gee was a man with a grievance, a passionate Nonconformist who aimed to break the hold of landlord and Church power over, as he saw it, a Nonconformist people. He stood for full religious equality through disestablishment of the Anglican Church in Wales and removal of injus-tices in matters of church tax and tithe and burial law; the application to Wales of Irish land reforms with security of tenants and compensation for improvements for tenants; and free non-denominational education under local control. All this clashed with the interests of landlords and clergy who used economic power to refuse land for non-denominational schools and Nonconformist chapels, dismissed or increased the rent of tenants who voted against their landlords' wishes, and exploited ancient or assumed rights to maintain privileges of a small minority. Abuses were not universal; landlords often claimed they did not know what their land agents were doing. But in circumstances of popular arousal, conservative obstruction of reform even in minor matters was patent and resented. For example, a simple measure restricting rectors' power to impose terms on Nonconformists' burial took twelve years to get parliamentary sanction. Gee's activity was probably most important on the issue of tenants' expulsion for voting Liberal. His denunciation on this score at the 1868 electoral hustings of Sir Watkin Williams Wynn, head of a dynasty which had controlled Denbighshire politics for two centuries, electrified the huge crowd. But *Y Faner*'s reportage on the anti-tithe riots in the Vale of Clwyd in the 1880s, which involved many police and soldiers and drew French and German press attention, runs it close.

Gee was accused by his opponents of stirring up violence by demagogic journalism. This was unfair. He was scrupulous to keep within the law and strongly loyal to constitution and kingdom. He fits well Kenneth Morgan's definition of the Welsh movement as desiring equality, in no way separation. This raises the question of language. No more than Edwards did Gee voice the key Slovene issue of equality in this sphere. His public speeches, like the electoral attack on Sir Watkin Williams Wynn, were often in English. Probably considerably more Welsh people by this time understood some English than Slovenes German but in north Wales that was less marked. Monoglots were less likely to be present, however, and the many who were learnt from others what Gee was saying and were enthused, from contemporary accounts, by their champion's mastery of the dominant tongue on their behalf. The situation may have been not dissimilar to that in contemporary South Africa. Gee was a typical emotional Welshman in this regard. He felt cool to upper-middle-class Whiggish Liberals who spoke little or no Welsh and worked to displace them among Welsh MPs, as happened increasingly in this period. *Y Faner* protested against the appointment of a monoglot Englishman as professor of agriculture at Bangor University College: when told he had two Welsh-speaking assistants, it asked rhetorically if the Welsh were to play second-fiddle in their own country.[46] Yet Gee did not campaign on this issue, as he did not against the 'English cause', though he disapproved of it. His growing inclination to Welsh 'Home Rule' will be touched on in the next chapter. But it is as the champion of the 'Nonconformist nation' and the grievances of the common man, whom he sought to enlighten, that he merits a special place in this account.

The work of David Davies (1818–90) lay in a different sphere from Gee's, though they had a rigorous Calvinistic Methodism in common. The son of a poor Montgomeryshire farmer at Llandinam in the Severn valley, he left school aged eleven. The 'Top Sawyer' in his locality, a title he bestowed on himself which stuck life-long, this vigorous and tirelessly active man – he was reputed to work eighteen hours a day – was soon a successful farmer, acquiring new properties, before undertaking bridge-building and railway-contracting projects all over mid-Wales, which included the then deepest cutting in the world on the Newtown–Machynlleth line in 1862. From this he turned his attention to the south-Wales coalfield and invested all his income in land leased in the Rhondda valley, risking bankruptcy before striking coal at Cwmparc, Treorchy. His men had agreed to go on working without pay at this point. Through the sixties he sank many more pits in the Rhondda and adjacent valleys, building up capital which enabled him to construct a dock at Barry (1889) and a railway to it from Rhondda. This success, which entailed a hard battle for parliamentary sanction, allowed him to avoid the expense of conveying coal to Cardiff by means under Bute control and helped make him the first Welsh millionaire, employing 5,583 men in his Ocean Coal Company as of 1890. By the new century Barry was exporting more coal than Cardiff, thirteen million tons of it in 1913.

Not surprisingly, a man of Davies's energy did not neglect the political field. He stood for parliament as a Liberal for the Montgomery county seat in 1865, narrowly losing to a Whig member of the traditional elite, before becoming an MP in 1874. He lost his seat in 1886, after breaking with Gladstone over Irish home rule and joining the Liberal Unionists. Gee also had some doubts on Gladstone's Irish policy, showing the vein of feeling for empire unity in Welsh attitudes in the nineteenth century. The large majority of Welsh voters stuck by Gladstone, however. One should remember that Lewis Edwards and the bulk of Welsh Nonconformists had opposed the conservative John Elias on Catholic emancipation earlier in the century and belief in liberty on the whole overrode hostility to

Catholicism in this period. Davies's political career is a minor part of his legacy, which gets respectful mention overall rather than enthusiasm in the pantheon of Welsh heroes. His role as captain of industry, albeit one who always identified himself as a working man, has no doubt played a part in this in a left-wing country. Davies certainly exemplified Victorian values and the self-made man who, in Disraeli's jibe at him, worshipped his maker.[47] His combination of methodical calculation and willingness for bold action was awesome. He once bought up a whole year's produce of sheep's wool in Cardiganshire to support a railway track's foundations across a notorious bog. Welsh patriots look askance at his remark on his mother tongue that much as he admired it and opposed its detractors, English was the better language for making money and Welsh people should learn it thoroughly, unless they wanted to eat brown bread all their lives.[48] Yet this is what many Welsh people thought and thought common sense. Davies himself combined it with Calvinist piety. A teetotaller who avowed never to open letters on a Sunday, he provided houses for miners at his pits above the jerry-building standards of the time and was a generous benefactor of chapels and by far the biggest contributor to the University college at Aberystwyth, which he served as treasurer. Davies's descendants suggest a philanthropic inheritance. His grandson of the same name, likewise a Liberal MP and made a baron for public service in 1932, was prominent in international peace movements and inspiration behind the Welsh 'Temple of Peace' in Cardiff's Civic Centre; his granddaughters turned a Montgomeryshire country house into an arts and crafts centre for Wales, and left their fine collection of French impressionist paintings to the Welsh National Museum. They preserved the family tradition of teetotalism and Sunday observance. All in all, the Davies family testify to the variety of directions Welsh life took from humble beginnings in the remarkable nineteenth century.

COMMENTARY

In both our countries a far stronger national profile had been created by 1880 than existed in 1850. To greater external impact came growing internal self-awareness as the nexus of communication through which a mature culture is transmitted in larger nations began to spread its filiations in Slovenia and Wales. The public opinion that John Stuart Mill rightly thought to be a precondition of meaningful nationality but denied to

Wales and its like was emerging. What *Seren Gomer* and a generation later *Novice* had started had by 1880 diversified into an expanding market of regular publications of different genres: satirical journals in both countries, including a Welsh *Punch*.

Language for a self-respecting culture implies literature. Their literature had traditionally been a matter of pride to the Welsh.[49] In Slovenia a non-traditional literary culture was being energetically created, which paid homage to its progenitors going back beyond Prešeren to Vodnik. Just as Vodnik had been urged to note foreign models by Zois, then Prešeren likewise by Čop, so Levstik and Stritar directed aspiring writers to seek inspiration abroad. The creation of such chains of influence is central to the development of a national culture. Goronwy Owen had studied the classical Welsh literary tradition through Dafydd ap Gwilym and writers well into the nineteenth century continued to look to Goronwy, though English influences played on them as well, as they had on Goronwy. There could be much mediocrity in minor hands. Most nineteenth-century Eisteddfodic poetry has had short shrift from modern literary critics. Slovene beginnings lack sophistication, both the first popular short story by Levstik (1858) and the first novel by the nineteen-year-old Josip Jurčič, a lively tale of daring do, exhibiting anachronistically patriotic Slovene peasants in the Turkish period (1864). However, from a later start Slovenes had made the bigger strides towards public recognition of their language. This is the force of Simon Brooks's case for this period as one of disastrous abdication by the Welsh, laming the chance of full development as a nation – 'Why Wales never was'. His challenge goes to the crux of the matter.

At bottom, two different models for the role of language were in question in our two countries. Welsh leaders assumed that in this time of unprecedented great change the major instrument for modernisation had to be English; Slovene, in common with other Habsburg Slavs, that the majority could only be mobilised through their mother tongue. In each case the underlying issue was how awakening societies could progress. Mass education was essential, but in which language? The irony is that either perspective was workable, though both sides took their own position for granted. Slovenes showed that a folk language can assume all the functions of a high culture; the Welsh showed that a folk can acquire en masse the language of the elite.

Why did the Welsh take one route, the Slovenes the other? The basic reason lay in context: the different character of the states of which they were part. The Habsburg Monarchy was a multinational empire lacking a truly dominant nationality. With the growth of democracy this made for the instability shown in 1848, allayed by shared Austro-German and Magyar dominance which only increased Slav discontent.

Constitutional Austria had to recognise a variety of nations and languages and language-based nationality became, alongside the Emperor, the organising principle of the state, whose international prestige steadily declined. By contrast, Great Britain was an economically very successful state flanked by a global empire, where the English language was totally dominant. Pressure from the majority community on Welsh as an outmoded language facing only extinction was indeed extreme. The sense of 'scandal that a Celtic language should be used in this way' was directed as much against the medium of the Welsh Nonconformist press as its radical message.[50] Given these circumstances, the Welsh option for English as their main public language had a persuasive rationale. But reason sees only so far into the future. Mid-Victorian Wales could not know how effective the Slovene and wider east European wager on the mother tongue was to be or how quickly, in historical time, the glories of the pax Britannica would pass. Rightly realising that Wales had to break out of its historic isolation, its leaders bought into the English self-image at its most hubristic. The consequences, though, were serious. Welsh publications on matters of practical concern like agriculture, domestic chemistry, family medicine and technology, which had risen from fifty-one to one hundred and thirty volumes between the years 1800–29 and 1830–59, spiralled downwards to one hundred and six and forty-three in the following periods.[51] Welsh journalism remained strong, but while the first Slovene daily paper followed only fifteen years after Lestvik's path-breaking tale, a daily newspaper never appeared in Welsh. The drive of Slovene political nationalism was now making itself felt. The effect was cultural too. The first full translation of a Shakespeare play appeared in Welsh and Slovene in 1864 but many more Slovene translations were to follow and only a handful in Welsh.

The key point is that as the liberal principle of free public association gained ground it expressed itself more and more in the Habsburg monarchy in non-dominant languages, but not in Britain. Habsburg Austria saw a process whereby nationally mixed societies which had conducted their affairs in German, as before 1848 in the Ljubljana Casino or the Philharmonic Society, separated out on language lines, producing alongside continuing German organs bodies like the Slovene matica, the

Slovene music society and the gymnastic *sokols*. In Wales the Cambrian Archaeological Society had patriotic aims but the question of separate organisations did not arise. Such splits can be regretted, though in placid Slovenia they were not necessarily antagonistic and people could belong to both groups. A comparison might be with the existence of Merched y Wawr and the Women's Institute in contemporary Wales. Certainly, however, the default public use of English in an age of an expanding public sphere told against Welsh in the longer term.

Of course, the chapels were in the public sphere as a powerful instrument of multiple association in themselves. Their widespread press engaged with the issues of the day in Welsh and they justifiably saw themselves as expressing an awoken public opinion. But this meant that Welsh opinion was bound by chapel parameters, aloof from the emulative instincts of the small Slovene intelligentsia. A small case study suggests the difference: attitudes towards tourism at a time when picturesque landscapes in our two countries were drawing attention from richer outsiders, prone to see in the sublimity of mountains a substitute for waning traditional faith. The English were pioneers of European mountaineering. They were behind the first alpine hut built in Slovenia in 1863, quickly followed by Swiss, Italian and Germans. The Austrian German Alpine Club took a particularly nationalist line in the exclusive use of German in the several huts and paths it established: the founding of the Deschmann hut in 1887 was accompanied by invocations to Mount Triglav to stretch out its arms 'over our German earth'. A Slovene mountaineering society was not founded in Ljubljana till 1893 and forbore initially to challenge German control of Triglav's upper slopes. However, a local parish priest alienated by German arrogance bought a patch of land on the summit and established a small tower there in 1895 which survived German legal bids for its demolition to become an icon of Slovene pride.[52] There was no equivalent Welsh response to English monopoly of Snowdonia. From Christmas and Easter meets in Pen-y-Pass and Pen-y-Gwryd young Englishmen sallied forth in summer to the Alps. Though there were indeed skilled Welsh climbers they were Liverpool or London Welsh or Anglican and never aroused a significant response in Welsh opinion. Merfyn Jones has commented: 'that formidable ideological construct, Welsh nonconformist culture, could neither contain them nor fully identify with them in their triumphs and tragedies'.[53] A mountaineering literature in Welsh did not appear till the 1960s.

Comparison is complicated. Most of Wales at this time was a buoyant place, more so no doubt than economically challenged Slovenia. Thomas Gee said he wanted the *Faner* to have a railway and steam character and predicted his Vale of Clwyd rail line could raise Denbigh's population tenfold as had happened to Llandudno.[54] Emerging industrial Wales was also still a predominantly Welsh-speaking area to which incoming workers from the countryside brought their Nonconformist culture with them. This culture gave Welsh people a sense of pride in its creation and its dupli-cation in the densely built-up industrial valleys of south Wales lent it an additional energy and vibrancy. Many people were not yet swayed by the arguments of the utilitarians for English. The Social Science section of the national Eisteddfod was a failure. The very achievement of Nonconformity as a social phenomenon made it seem a great rock to its adherents all but beyond analysis, which might be chipped away in places but stood immune as a symbol of Wales itself, like the steadfast puritanism of its creed.

This is strange because in another sense Nonconformity as the name implied arose in protest against the conservative structures of Anglicanism. Revival gave it birth and the rhythm of revival punctuated its growth thereafter. In between revivals its great preachers had often laboured under an oppressive sense of the weakening of faith and lukewarmness of the flock. A tension in feeling between states of grace and the withholding of grace was common to devout believers, producing an insecurity that could be both spur and burden. A certain Anglican revival, expressed through a more positive attitude to the Welsh language and an energetic church building programme by bishops still Englishmen (Thirlwall and Ollivant) but also energetic native Welsh speakers (John Griffith, rector in industrial Aberdare, the 'unmitred bishop', and David Howell, Dean of St Davids), played an increasing role. They challenged the notion of the 'Nonconformist nation'. The effect was limited, however.

Insecurity of a different kind existed, of course, as it did everywhere prior to the twentieth century. The brilliant but tubercular son of the Revd Meirydd ap Rhys, Golyddan (John Robert Pryse), a prize-winning student at Edinburgh University with high hopes of fame as a poet – he sent off no less than eight compositions to the Denbigh Eisteddfod in 1860 – succumbed to his illness at the age of twenty-two. He informed his father on his last morning that he would be leaving him that day and hoped his father would take the news as calmly as it was given. 'About what time, my son', his father answered, struggling to respond in kind; 'about eight in the evening or eleven, perhaps' was the reply. 'Right, my son', said his father, adding that Golyddan seemed quite ready for the journey. 'Oh yes', said Golyddan, 'and I can say unhesitatingly in the words of the Apostle Paul, I have a yearning to depart and be with Christ, for that is much better'.[55] He died that night at eleven. Hiraethog lost a favourite son at twenty-one who he believed had the makings of a major poet. Lewis Edwards apparently never fully recovered from the death of two young daughters in close succession. There was a moral intensity in the lives of many Nonconformist leaders which invites respect and which indeed made them heroes to a people who had been largely abandoned by their upper classes and left to their own devices by a supercilious authority. The nineteenth-century Welsh national myth suffered from lack of confidence in the face of a supremely confident English neighbour, did not subject over-praised leaders to the searching criticism offered by a number of Slovene radicals, and suffered from not being part of a wider movement like Herderian cultural nationalism which offered Slovenes a clear trajectory. But it was a creation *sui generis* which did enable the pride and self-belief that increasingly characterised Victorian Wales.

NOTES

1 Dragan Matić, *Nemci v Ljubljani 1861–1918* (Germans in Ljubljana) (Ljubljana, 2002), 40. For the constitutional reorganisation of the Monarchy, see Robin Okey, *The Habsburg Monarchy c. 1765–1918* Basingstoke, 2001), pp. 76–90.

2 Peter Stih, Vasko Simoniti and Peter Vodopivec, *Slowenische Geschichte: Gesellschaft-Politik-Kultur* (Graz, 2008), pp. 273–8.

3 Julie Light, 'The Middle Classes as Urban Elites in Nineteenth-Century South Wales', *Welsh History Review*, 24/3 (2009), 29–55.

4 John Davies, *Hanes Cymru* (London, 1990), pp. 397, 398; Jerry Hunter, *Llwch Cenhedloedd. Y Cymry a Rhyfel Cartref America* (The Dust of Nations. The Welsh and the American Civil War) (Llanrwst, 2004).

5 See *https://origins.museumsvictoria.com.au/countries/wales*.

6 For the explicitly patriotic motives behind the Patagonian venture, see in a large bibliography E. Wyn James and Bill Jones (eds), *Michael D. Jones a'i wladfa Gymreig* (Llanrwst, 2009).

7 Y Parch. T. Roberts, D.D., *Cofiant y Parch. W. Rees D.D. (Hiraethog)* (Dolgellau, 1893), p. 499.

8 The permanent gain seems to have dropped by ten thousand from this level. See J. J. Morgan, *Hanes Dafydd Morgan Ysbyty a Diwygiad 1859* (The story of Dafydd Morgan Ysbyty and the 1859 Revival) (Mold, 1906), pp. 606–8.

9 T. M. Jones (Gwenallt), *Cofiant Roger Edwards* (Colwyn Bay, 1908), p. 171.

10 John Thomas, *Cofiant y Parchedig T. Rees, D.D. Abertawy* (Dolgellau, 1888).

11 H. T. Edwards, *The Church of the Cymry: A Letter to the Right Hon. W. E. Gladstone* (Aberdare, 1869), p. 44.

12 Prys Morgan, 'The Emergence of Empire 1750–1898', in Prys Morgan (ed.), *The Tempus History of Wales 25000 BC–AD 2000* (Stroud, 2001), p. 200.

13 *https://www.Welshcoalmines.co.uk.*

14 Davies, *Hanes Cymru*, p. 401 (Ceiriog).

15 Ivan Prijatelj, *Slovenska kulturnopolitična in slovenstvena zgodovina 1848–95* (6 vols, Ljubljana,1955–85), vol. 1, p. 191; pp. 243–4 (Bleiweis).

16 Prijatelj, *Kulturnopolitična zgodovina*, vol. 1, p. 228.

17 Prijatelj, *Kulturnopolitična zgodovina*, vol. 1, pp. 219, 223.

18 F. Kublar, 'Toman, Lovro (1827–1880)', *Slovenska biografija*, ZRC SAZU, 2013, *http://www.Slovenska-biografija.si.*

19 K. N. Poniž, 'The Representations of Slavic nations in the writings of Josipina Turnograjski', in Amelia Sanz et al., *Women Telling Nations* (Amsterdam and New York, 2014), pp. 169–90 (p. 175).

20 Prijatelj, *Kulturnopolitična zgodovina*, vol. 2, pp. 33–8.

21 Matić, *Nemci v Ljubljani*, p. 36.

22 Prijatelj, *Kulturnopolitična zgodovina*, vol. 4, p. 36.

23 A. Slodnjak, 'Fran Levstik (1831–87): the first representative of radicalism in Slovene literature', *Slavonic and East European Review*, 15 (1956–7), 24–39 (31).

24 Prijatelj, *Kulturnopolitična zgodovina*, vol. 2, p. 394.

25 *Učiteljski tovariš* (The Teacher's Comrade), 1 (1861), 138 (repression); 2, 58 (God).

26 Hywel Teifi Edwards, *Gŵyl Gwalia: Yr Eisteddfod Genedlaethol yn Oes Aur Victoria 1858/1868* (The National Eisteddfod in the Victorian Golden Age 1858/1868) (Llandysul, 1980), p. 62, 66.

27 Edwards, *Gŵyl Gwalia*, p. 65.

28 Edwards, *Gŵyl Gwalia*, p. 314 (*Blackwood Magazine*: race); p. 326 (*Morning Post*: myths); pp. 327–8 (*The Times*); pp. 313–14 (Froude).

29 Edwards, *Gŵyl Gwalia*, pp. 247–8, 281 (obsolete language).

30 S. Brooks, *Why Wales Never Was: The Failure of Welsh Nationalism* (Cardiff, 2017), pp. 32–3, 90–1. For Raumer, p. 33.

31 Brooks, *Why Wales*, p. 33.

32 Brooks, *Why Wales*, pp. 66–72.

33 George Borrow, *Wild Wales: Its People, Language and Scenery* (London, n.d.), pp. 33–4, 35. (First published 1862.)

34 I. G. Jones, 'Henry Richard ac Iaith y Gwleidydd yn y Bedwaredd Ganrif ar Bymtheg' (Henry Richard and the Language of the Politician in the Nineteenth Century), in Geraint H. Jenkins (ed.), *Cof Cenedl*, 3 (1988), 117–49 (131).

35 Gwyn Griffiths, *Henry Richard: Heddychwr a Gwladgarwr* (Henry Richard: Pacifist and Patriot) (Cardiff, 2001), p. 118.

36 'The Realist: Henry Richard', in Kenneth O. Morgan, *Revolution to Devolution: Reflections on Welsh Democracy* (Cardiff, 2014), pp. 75–100.

37 Prijatelj, *Kulturnopolitična zgodovina*, vol. 2, pp. 72–5.

38 Matić, *Nemci v Ljubljani*. pp, 102–3.

39 For a modern Slovene view of Dežman, see P. Vodopivec, 'Die sozialen und wirtschaftlichen Ansichten des deutschen Bürgertums in Krain vom Ende der 60-er bis Anfang der 80-er Jahre des neunzehnten Jahrhunderts' / Economic and Social Views of the German Bourgeoisie in Carniola from the end of the End of the 1860s to the Beginning of the 1880s, in H. Rumpler and A. Suppan (eds), *Geschichte der Deutschen im Bereich des heutigen Slovenien, 1848–1941* / A History of Germans in the Area of Present-Day Slovenia (Munich, 1988), pp. 91–3.

40 Trebor Lloyd Evans, *Lewis Edwards: Ei fywyd a'i waith* (Lewis Edwards: Life and Work) (Swansea, 1967), p. 35.

41 D. Densil Morgan, *Lewis Edwards* (Cardiff, 2009), p. 101.

42 T. C. Edwards, *Bywyd a Llythyrau y diweddar Lewis Edwards* (Life and Letters of the late Lewis Edwards) (Liverpool, 1901), p. 496.

43 Morgan, *Lewis Edwards*, pp. 217, 219.

44 Morgan, *Lewis Edwards*, p. 219.

45 T. Gwyn Jones, *Cofiant Thomas Gee* (Life of Thomas Gee) (Denbigh, 1913), pp. 161–8. For some circulation figures, see Dot Jones (ed.), *Statistical Evidence relating to the Welsh Language 1801–1911* (Cardiff, 1998), p. 513.

46 Gwyn Jones, *Cofiant Thomas Gee*, p. 585.

47 Ivor Bulmer-Thomas, *Top Sawyer, A Biography of David Davies, Llandinam* (London, 1938), p. 211.

48 Bulmer-Thomas, *Top Sawyer*, p. 316.

49 Borrow, *Wild Wales*, p. 52.

50 Quoted from Aled Jones, *Press, Politics and Society: A History of Journalism in Wales* (Cardiff, 1993), p. 180.

51 R. Elwyn Hughes, 'Yr Iaith Gymraeg ym Myd Gwyddoniaeth a Thechnoleg' (The Welsh Language in the World of Science and Technology), in Geraint R. Jenkins (ed.), *Gwnewch Bopeth yn Gymraeg: Yr Iaith Gymraeg a'i Pheuoedd 1801–1911* (Cardiff, 1999), pp. 375–98 (p. 387).

52 Peter Mikša, '"Da je Trigav ostal v slovenskih rukach je največ moja zasluga". Jakub Aljaž in njegovo planinsko delovanje v Triglavskem pogorju' ('That Trigav remained in Slovene hands was largely thanks to me.' Jakub Aljaž and his mountaineering activity in the Triglav Highlands), *Zgodovinski časopis*, 69/1–2 (2015), 112–23 (quote, 115).

53 R. Merfyn Jones, 'The Mountaineering of Wales 1880–1825', *Welsh History Review*, 19/1–2 (1999), 43–67 (quote, 67).

54 Gwyn Jones, *Cofiant Thomas Gee*, 161, 138.

55 Enid P. Roberts, *Detholiad o Hunangofiant Gweirydd ap Rhys* (Selection from Gweirydd ap Rhys's Autobiography) (Llandysul, 1949), pp. 188–9.

Chapter 6

THE NATIONAL MOVEMENTS MATURE: SUCCESS AND SHORTFALL

The decades after *c*.1880 were the classic age of incipient democracy in Europe, bound up with middle-class elements who self-identified with the march of 'progress' and were only beginning to be challenged by socialism in their turn. The national movements we have been following made substantial progress, the more so because their fledgeling leaderships had themselves newly risen from the ranks of 'the people'. But elements of frustration can be seen because these remained subaltern societies whose middle class was thinly spread and unable to advance goals like an autonomous Slovenia or a kind of 'home rule' associated with the Welsh movement 'Cymru Fydd' in the 1890s. State politics became more complex as the German liberals lost power to an amalgam of Slavs and German clericals in Austria and Irish nationalism grew into a major force in Britain, but Welsh and Slovenes needed allies to make their mark and were too weak to win them. National rivalries meant that the Emperor retained ultimate power in the Monarchy, which sapped its democratic credentials. In Britain, however, the idea of the Empire acquired popular force in an imperial age and figured also in Welsh consciousness. Arguably, Welshness and Britishness strengthened together. To be seen as gallant junior partners in the gigantic imperial enterprise, as in the spread of Protestant faith in its far-flung lands, was an attraction for many: a record of Welsh missionary activity published in 1897 lists 153 who had served or were serving in this field.[1]

This subject matter will be treated in three interlinked chapters which can each cover material from the whole period. This chapter sets out the basic structures, socio-economic, demographic and linguistic, in which the Welsh and Slovene leaderships emerged and the politics that resulted. The second takes up cultural themes which offer a wider view of the role of nationhood in collective consciousness. In the Welsh case it is the Welsh-language culture which is considered, as befits the ongoing comparison with Slovenia. It also reflects the fact that though monoglot English speakers had become a majority by 1914 they did not represent a united social group and relatively few played a major part in public life. Yet the rapid transition to a bilingual and English-speaking Wales is too momentous a development not to have a substantial section to itself. This will be in the third chapter of the trio, which will also consider the impact of socialism on our two societies and the development of the south Slav problem which came to involve the Slovenes and indeed all of Europe in the First World War.

ECONOMICS AND SOCIETY

The story of the Welsh economy continued to be one of rapid growth. Population rose by 50 per cent, half of the advance coming in the decade 1901–11 to approach two-and-a-half million. By this time immigration from England and Ireland exceeded that from rural Wales, shifting language patterns. Coal was the key to this dramatic shift. In 1913 the south Wales coalfield produced 56 million tons of it, the bulk of which was exported, making Cardiff the greatest coal port in the world. Meanwhile, a wholly new dock town of 27,000 people had mushroomed on its doorstep to share the load. Four railways linked the produce of the Rhondda valley to these outlets, as four lines linked Swansea to its hinterland, where an anthracite coalfield had sprung up in the western section of the field to join the steam coal of the east and bituminous coal of the centre. The quarter of a million Welsh coal miners in 1914 must be set against the 10,738 engaged in all mining and metallurgy in Carniola and lower Styria, the bulk of the Slovene lands. Only against this background can the coalfield of north-east Wales, with 16,000 workers by 1914, and the slate quarries of the north-west, including the largest in the world, with nineteen thousand workers at maximum in 1898, be considered minor concerns. The Welsh iron industry now increasingly took a back seat. The sheer scale of south Wales industry enabled it to overcome periods of difficulty, as the tin trade survived American tariffs in the 1890s and Gwynedd's slate industry the fall in overall demand for its product. Like coalmining, slate quarrying was hard and dangerous, and worker–employer relations were often conflicted. The lockout on the Penrhyn estate lasted three years for three thousand quarrymen (1900–3), then the longest dispute in British industrial history, before ending in their total defeat.

The general population rise veiled a substantial fall in rural Wales. Between 1851 and 1911, nearly four hundred thousand people emigrated from rural districts to other parts of Britain, many to the south Wales coalfield. Only 10 per cent of land was owner-occupied compared to 16 per cent in England: four hundred estates exceeded a thousand hectares (2,400 acres). The figure for family farms, however, was the same at the end of this period as the beginning, about thirty-five thousand units. It was family dependants and the hard-worked and low-paid farm labourers who registered their discontent by emigration. The exhaustive report of the Royal Commission of 1894–6 on Welsh agriculture took much of the heat out of the farmers' grievances which had provoked it, though its chief proposals were actually shelved by an incoming Conservative government. Current historiography tends to the view that the anti-landlord campaign on the land question (*pwnc y tir*), which figured prominently in the programme of Welsh radicals like Thomas Gee, was an expression of mobilised Nonconformity as much as of economic distress. The overall problem of lack of land cannot be denied, however, or the financial difficulties behind Welsh tenants' reluctance to innovate.[2]

The Slovene economy continued to be a more muted affair. Slovene population growth was among the slowest in the Monarchy, despite a routinely high birth rate. Lavro Toman was one of nine children, the poet Simon Gregorčič of eight; Slovenia's richest entrepreneur, Josip Gorup (1834–1912) had fourteen children from two marriages, yet net emigration to other parts of the Monarchy, Europe and the United States totalled 310,000 between mid-century and 1914.[3] At the start of the twentieth century, 36 per cent of agricultural holdings were less than two hectares (five acres); 10,000 farmers had to sell up in Carniola between 1867 and 1892, whose emotive power can be appreciated bearing in mind the distress caused by loss of homesteads in rural Wales.[4] The substantial industrialisation necessary to provide an outlet did not occur, numbers employed in industry and mining rising merely from 7 to 10 per cent; indeed, the share of artisans increased. What capital there was remained heavily with local German firms before passing under Viennese or French control. Coal production grew to half a million tons on the eve of war, a fraction of that in south Wales. Trieste, not Ljubljana, was the strongest regional force in Slovene industry and contained more Slovenes but these were overwhelmingly a dependent work force. Attempts to raise local capital, both by Germans and Slovenes, largely failed. Slovene entrepreneurs were especially thin on the ground though they seem to have been more patriotic than their larger Welsh counterparts. Fidelis Terpinc, owner of a paper-making factory who had to sell out to a German concern, was a member of the Slovenska matica. Josip Gorup, of the fourteen children, with shipping, building and tax farming concerns, funded the leading poet Gregorčič and gave large sums to Ljubljana town council for Slovene student scholarships.[5] From the 1880s, emigration produced a substantial Slovene community in the United States, proportionately larger than in the Welsh case. The 1910 American census recorded some one hundred and eighty-three thousand residents with Slovene mother tongue, so that Cleveland, Ohio acquired the third largest concentration of Slovene speakers in the world. Typically for émigré life, choirs, benefit societies, insurance companies, newspapers and the like reproduced the patterns of the homeland, being organised on Catholic or liberal/anti-clerical bases.[6]

Two aspects brighten the negative domestic picture. The impressive developments of credit cooperatives, first on the initiative of the brother of a leading Young Slovene politician, then of Catholic organisations, allowed peasants access to loans on far better terms than banks or moneylenders. Taken together, by 1910 every ninth Slovene was a member of one of the many hundred cooperatives that had arisen, whose combined savings came to exceed the deposits of the German-dominated traditional banks.[7] This achievement far overshadowed the dozen or so agricultural cooperative societies founded by a Cardiganshire landowner, W. A. Brigstocke, on the lines of Sir Horace Plunkett's major movement in Ireland. Plunkett's movement's purpose, too, was for socio-economic uplift only, intended originally as a counter to the Irish nationalist movement, and so lacking the patriotic motive which went with the economic in Slovenia.[8] The second significant Slovene economic advance was the creation after earlier failures of a bank in Slovene hands, the Ljubljana Credit Bank, destined to become the most successful bank of communist Yugoslavia. It was mediated through the Vienna branch of the pride of Czech economic progress, the Živnostenska Banka. Though Slovenes stood in the top leadership most staff initially were Czechs, another case of the ubiquitous big brother relationship. But even Czechs were no real match for German economic power. Germans, just one-third of the population of Bohemia, paid two-thirds of Bohemian taxes because of their greater wealth. The cooperative movement, for all the virtues praised by Toussaint Hočevar, could not provide the capital for the industrialisation needed to prevent peasant emigration. By 1914, only one-ninth of industrial, mining and bank capital in the Slovene lands had a Slovene basis, as against one-third in 1873.[9]

Thus, while Wales and the Slovene lands had started off alike as overwhelmingly peasant societies, by the early twentieth century two-thirds of Slovenes still lived on the land while only one-seventh of the Welsh depended on it for their livelihood. Industrial workers had become as hegemonic in Wales as peasants in Slovenia. Yet over half of Wales in area was almost as rural, and a high proportion of influential figures in Welsh life continued to come from the countryside. As elsewhere in Europe at this time, most workers lived poor and hard lives. Socio-economic and political change and rise of peasant consciousness with primary schooling (85 per cent of Slovenes were literate in 1911) had, however, contributed to eroding the traditional order. Wales's two biggest landowners lost their seats in the 1885 general election and Liberals won every county but one when local power passed to newly created county councils three years later. Offended at being passed over for the role of Cardiganshire Council chairman, which went to a Nonconformist minister, the Tory leader, Lord Lisburne of the historic Crosswood (Trawsgoed) estate, resigned his seat and withdrew into private life. Later, he began selling off parts of his holdings, in which he was joined by many other landowners whose families had dominated Wales for centuries.[10] Ironically, the recommendations of the 1896 Land Commission report, which amounted to legislation for a transition to peasant proprietorship like that taking place in Ireland, was substantially effected within a generation through the acts of landlords themselves.

This mirrored the retreat of the Slovene upper classes in this period. A glimpse into the process is provided by the ownership of opera boxes at the Estate Theatre in Ljubljana, a long-standing indication of social status. In the 1810s, thirty-four boxes had been held by members of the landed elite and only ten by commoners, the ramified Auersperg family clan alone holding six. By the later 1880s, the boxes were awash with merchants and representatives of the 'nationally conscious' Slovene literati and public men, the Auerspergs now having two. The landed nobility was increasingly seen in Slovene media as an alien, indeed hostile presence. Count Anton von Auersperg, praised by a Slovene historian in 1885 as 'the greatest son of Carniola', for anti-regime poems famed in the German-speaking world, had no part in the Slovene canon by 1914.[11] This Auersperg showed, incidentally, the greater connection with the 'native' culture retained by some in elite circles than in Wales. He remained a life-long friend of Prešeren after their student acquaintanceship in Vienna and published a noted translation of 'Carniolan Folk-Songs' in 1850. That does not mean he sympathised with the Slovene political movement. He opposed the extension of teaching in Slovene, once entering the Carniolan Diet with a small package of books in his hand to demonstrate the paucity of the relevant literature.[12] This was the spirit which kept the large landowners' curia in the Carniolan Diet a German stronghold, though there could be exceptions that proved the rule. Such a case was Barbo von Waxenstein (1825–79), or to convey the full flavour of central European aristocracy, Count Joseph Emmanuel Maria Dismas Otto Vincenz Barbo von Waxenstein, a member of Slovenska matica and of the Slovene group in the Vienna parliament in the 1870s. His son Joseph Anton, however, moved in a German direction. His grandson, last of the ancient male line, translated Prešeren. Much deference survived among the general public to the old upper classes in both countries. The National Eisteddfod was frequently addressed, after fawning introductions, by members of old families like the Watkin Wynns, whose names headed the list of subscribers. Nonetheless, by the end of the era the titles of industrial magnates like Lords Merthyr, Rhondda, Aberdare and Swansea were evocative of a new order.

Industrialism has a mixed image for some Welsh patriots. The dynamism of south-east Wales cannot be overlooked in any assessment of Welsh social consciousness and confidence, but its role in weakening the Welsh language is regretted. A distinguished Welsh economic historian, Brinley Thomas, has argued that industrialisation performed a great service for the language too. At a time of poverty and high birth rates in the countryside it ensured that a great surplus rural population could remain in Wales rather than emigrate, thereby aiding its survival; the contrast is with Ireland. Yet the linguistic aspect of his argument is hardly borne out in the longer term. In Blaenafon, Monmouthshire, the 1911 census showed 31 per cent of the population as speaking Welsh, but already only one in five hundred and thirty-five children aged between three and five.[13] Monmouthshire was an

extreme case of Anglicisation at this time. Glamorgan still offered some
support for the Thomas language thesis.

LANGUAGE PATTERNS IN TURN OF
THE CENTURY WALES AND SLOVENIA

Language has had a prominent part in this study. Decennial state language
censuses help us to grasp the situation. The first such Austrian census of
1869 followed the promise of language equality in the constitutional era
and reflected its sensitivity. To prevent the census from causing national
disputation, it formally did not register citizens' nationality or mother
tongue, but their 'language of daily communication'. In practice this did
not stop controversy. Slavs took it as a bid to lessen their numbers by having Slav workers returned as German speakers by their German employers.
Britain's Irish language censuses from 1851 similarly showed Ireland's political importance. Its addition for Wales in 1891 was actually suggested by
Scottish MPs whose census already had a Gaelic clause. That the British
language forms, unlike the Austrian, allowed respondents to state whether
they were monolingual or bilingual was probably due to British assumptions about the gradual assimilation of Celtic speakers and a desire to trace
this process. The assumption is clear from discussion of E. G. Ravenstein's
paper on the topic presented to the Statistical Society in 1879. The chairman of the meeting opined that it was 'a hopeless task' to try to preserve
these 'ancient languages' as spoken vernaculars, a statement of the unpro-
pitious climate in which the Welsh language functioned throughout the
nineteenth century.[14] In fact, some voices in the Welsh language press
called on readers to return themselves as speaking Welsh only and though
these voices probably had little influence there is difficulty in interpreting
the 1891 census result.[15] This recorded 898,000 or 54.4 per cent of the
population (excluding infants) as speaking Welsh, over half of these being
monoglots. A quarter declared themselves bilingual and 46 per cent as
speaking English only. Welsh speakers were well below Ravenstein's own
estimate of 71 per cent; possibly because he overstated Welsh speakers in
the expanding large towns.[16] By 1911, their number had risen to 977,000
but the percentage had fallen to forty-three. The substantial numbers of
Welsh speakers in England were not recorded.

A detailed study of the 1891 Welsh census shows changes in process which accelerated thereafter. Along the border, Monmouthshire and

Radnorshire were now overwhelmingly English-speaking, as was the east of Breconshire and Montgomeryshire. The sixfold rise of English mono-glots between the oldest and the youngest generation in Llanidloes showed the further advance of English down the Severn valley into mid-Wales. In industrial Glamorgan the decline of Welsh was still well behind that in the adjoining Monmouthshire valleys. A majority in all of them could speak Welsh: 90 per cent of young adults in Pontardawe in the Swansea valley, for example.[17] Where two monoglot Welsh speakers married the children were overwhelmingly reported as monoglot themselves but there was some seepage to English among children of bilinguals, which became very large where only one parent spoke Welsh. Striking was the lack of assimilation of the children of immigrant English monoglots, which suggests the language of children among themselves was often English. Jack Jones (1884–1970), the later novelist of valley life (in English), brought up on a street where Irish, English and Scottish outnumbered the Welsh, relates how his miner father was annoyed when he started answering him in English. His mother said, in Welsh: 'Oh, let him alone. What's the odds, anyway?' 'Plenty of odds', his father said, but he was rarely around.[18] In 1911, the population born outside Wales had risen to 19.4 per cent and with it came a greater shift to English among younger people in the Glamorganshire valleys. Privately, officials in the Welsh Department of the Board of Education conceded 'it must be largely a matter of opinion in the case of some dis-tricts in Wales if one would consider them as Welsh-speaking districts or not'.[19] Here so-called 'mixed areas' like much of the south Wales coalfield were meant.

Yet in 1891, and for some time afterwards, the country was more Welsh speaking than the figures might suggest. The English-speaking population was largely recent and concentrated among coalminers in the south-east and the swelling coastal towns of Cardiff, Newport and Swansea. In great swathes of rural west, north and mid-Wales the census reveals very few monoglot English speakers outside a number of towns like Aberystwyth and Holyhead, and not many bilinguals. This latter group was to grow rapidly, though increase in basic familiarity with English in rural areas barely influenced the language of daily life. The victorious Labour candidate for Caernarfon in the 1922 general election was to address eighty-nine meetings, all but one of them in Welsh.[20]

The Slovene lands showed a much more uniform language situ-ation. In 1910, the Austrian census recorded 1,325,000 Slovene speakers, without indicating how many of these could also speak German. In their strongest territories Slovenes held their own (Gorizia) or increased their majority, as in Carniola. In Styria there was a slight fall to just under one-third of the population, with some assimilation of Slovene industrial workers, while immigration swelled Slovene numbers to one-quarter of the whole in Trieste. Overall, historians estimate that Slovene speakers had fallen from 89 per cent to 77 per cent of the population in their traditional territory since the mid-nineteenth century, much of the drop being accounted for by one area, Carinthia, an interesting case comparatively. A Carinthian Slovene historian once told the present writer that what he understood of Wales recalled the Carinthian experience. The province had traditionally been a leading player on the Slovene stage. Its capital Klagenfurt (Celovec) was the seat of the Saint Hermagoras society, chief publisher of Slovene books, and a Slovene reading association was founded there before Ljubljana's. The Carinthian Slovene leader, Andrej Einspieler, published and edited the sole Slovene political newspaper of the middle of the 1860s. Carinthia's economic position declined in the Dualist era, however. The Slovene-speaking area lacked an urban centre, Klagenfurt, just inside it, being already heavily Germanised. Einspieler advocated national and language equality between Germans and Slovenes in Carinthia rather than a united Slovenia which would split his province. His unbending adherence to the historical principle at a time Slovene opinion was turning to 'natural right' approaches owed much to a fear of radical change in this, in many ways, quite liberal Catholic priest and narrowed Slovene options.[21] Faced with a choice between him and the German liberals, liberal-minded Slovene speakers, including crucially teachers, increasingly took the Dežman option, to be politically German. German liberals offered concessions to Slovene feeling when convenient but themselves veered to nationalist positions, condemning Slovene calls for recognition as panslavism. The provincial Diet legislated for bilingual schools in Slovene areas, weighted in practice towards German. By the new century, urban and rural Slovenes began turning to the German-led Social Democrats whose gestures to national equality were no doubt more sincere than those of German liberals had been, though basically also rhetorical.[22] In 1920, in a referendum area with 75 per cent Slovene speaking, 60 per cent voted to stay in Austria rather than join the new Yugoslavia.

The Carinthian case shows a pattern apt to arise when a historically dominant group meets a subordinate one beginning to assert its identity.

The one group feels challenged and the other aggrieved. Experience suggests that the appeal to universal values is a doubtful guide in such matters. All too often the dominant side will claim to represent these values and deadlock results. The solution lies in intelligence and goodwill, not ideological claims. German responses to Slavs till 1945 continued to demonise them as backward ethnic nationalists, tropes which cloud western democracy's stance to the non-western world today. Carinthia's dilemma lay in an ineffective assertion of Slovene identity which nonetheless fuelled a negative German reaction. The Slovene people's more confident development as a whole made ultimately for a healthier relation with its Austro-German neighbours. Einspieler's appeals came to provoke the response of the bully. Contemporary Austrian neo-Nazism is centred in Carinthia.

TOWARDS DOMESTIC NATIONAL 'HEGEMONY' IN WALES AND THE SLOVENE LANDS?

The growing success of the respective national awakenings of the late nineteenth century helps explain why, in the Welsh case, language decline did not shake Nonconformist Liberal leaders' self-confidence. The decline was relative, not absolute, occurring among the young, not the socially active, and perceptible mainly in hindsight. Dominant in the School Boards set up by the 1870 Education Act, the county councils established in 1888, the periodical press and the new Welsh university colleges, Liberal Nonconformists and a few Lib-Lab candidates swept away all Conservative MPs in the 1906 general election. The Slovene situation showed a similar strengthening of national revivalists. They were dominant in the Carniolan Diet from 1883, and nearly half the members in that of Gorizia. In Styrian Slovenia primary schooling in the mother tongue had become as widespread as in these two provinces. The Slovene musical Glasbena matica had surpassed the traditional German-orientated Ljubljana philharmonic society. By the twentieth century there were four Slovene daily papers, three in Ljubljana. The replacement of the Liberal government in Vienna by a Slav-German clerical coalition in 1879 was reflected in increased rights to use Slovene with the authorities.

This collective rise of native sons in public life signalled the breakthrough which subaltern peoples need in the transition from traditional to modern life. Established nations had long had their elites, centred around their monarchies and aristocracies. Mid-eighteenth-century

Finland counted some 420,000 inhabitants, 95 per cent rural, where the tiny urban population were either native Swedish speakers or lived under total Swedish cultural domination. In these circumstances it was impossible to speak of a Finnish middle class or intelligentsia, consequently of a Finnish nation in any modern sense. Wales and Slovenia, like Finland subsequently, fitted the pattern of the emergence of educated strata which is now being re-enacted in developing nation societies globally: hence the idealisation of the *gwerin* or common people in modern Wales and his people's characterisation as a 'proletarian nation' by Ivan Cankar, the outstanding Slovene writer of the pre-war period. Smaller nations can be suspicious of the mutation of some of their forefathers into a 'bourgeois elite', a loaded term, though some kind of educated leadership is a necessary stage in emancipation from under-class status. The rise of disregarded peoples arouses different reactions, whether admiration for plucky underdogs made good, conservative disdain for *infra-dig parvenus* or would-be universalist exasperation at the whole phenomenon of nationhood. The sociologist Ernest Gellner has shed light on it in a well-known thesis explaining modern national movements in the context of modernisation.[23] Peasant members of subaltern societies starting to move into the towns, he argues, find themselves thwarted by existing inhabitants of different, dominant ethnicity, who use their monopoly of 'high culture' to block their rise. They must either accept continued under-class status or upgrade their own homely 'low culture' to compete. The concept is flexible because the resented 'high culture' against which struggle proceeds can take various forms, like an official language, say, as in Slovenia, or official religion, as in Wales. Its weakness is that it does not in itself explain why struggle is sparked by different issues in particular cases. That can best be explained by admitting cultural, psychological and political factors and the overriding role of regional context stressed in this work.

Gellner was born in Prague and the Czech case is a classic example of how a national intelligentsia forms in an underdog nation. Sons of better-off peasants who moved into the towns and artisans, urban or rural, married daughters of Germanised families and with them launched Czech lineages. From these came professional people, lawyers, doctors, teachers and journalists but also civil servants, surveyors, architects and businessmen. In later generations, university professors, major entrepreneurs, publishers and politicians were possible. In smaller or less developed societies, merchants and parish priests were key players for their contacts. A large majority of figures in Slovenian public life in this period were born in the countryside but lived or studied at some time in Ljubljana; most were of peasant origin, with some of artisanal background and a few, like Ivan Toman and Ivan Hribar, with fathers in business. Study at a Gymnasium, usually in Ljubljana, and often thereafter at Vienna university, was their route to a wider world. All six leading speakers at the largest *tabor* meeting against the Dualist constitution in 1869 held doctorates in law.[24] By 1914 Ljubljana had become a Slovene city with a German minority, a turn-around mirrored by the fate of once-dominant Germans in Prague, Swedish speakers in Helsinki and Protestants in Dublin.

Given Wales's long neglected secondary education, the emergence of a public legal path came later but by the 1890s it was in full swing. As Lloyd George rose towards power, he drew with him fellow lawyer-politician patriots like Sir Ellis Jones Ellis-Griffith, Bart (for the day of the double-barrelled Welshman was at hand!), President of the Union at Cambridge and Under-Secretary at the Home Office; Sir John Herbert Lewis, Lord of the Treasury 1905–8, Under-Secretary for local government, then education, and Sir Samuel T. Evans, Solicitor General and President of a division of the High Court. All of these were Liberal MPs active in the new Welsh educational and cultural institutions, while being also British Privy Councillors and GCBs (Knight Grand Cross holders of the British Empire). Other paths were more directly cultural, like the lineages formed by peasant sons Lewis Edwards (whom we know) and Owen Morgan Edwards, writer, editor and historian who was knighted at the end of his life. The former's son became the first president of Aberystwyth University College; the latter's son the founder of the patriotic youth movement Urdd Gobaith Cymru (The League of the Hope of Wales) and father in turn of the first executive director of the Welsh-language television channel, S4C. Among entrepreneurs were David Davies Llandinam, Viscount Rhondda (David Thomas), founder of the Cambrian Collieries and Baron Merthyr (William Lewis), head of the South Wales and Monmouthshire Coalowners' Association, both of 'valleys' stock. The lower ranks of the new Welsh leadership were the thousands of Nonconformist ministers and chapel elders.

With social ascension came a distinctive lifestyle and values, whereby propriety, culture and a sense of importance as role models figured in both our countries. 'The Well-Bred Slovenian' was the title of an early Slovene book on the topic in 1869, based on German forerunners. Welsh ministers aspired to the same qualities, for in Wales and Slovenia the man of the cloth was considered to best embody them; Catholic priests wrote several of the relevant Slovene texts. The nobility or gentry tended to be looked down on as degenerate but cautiously so in Slovenia because urban petit bourgeois still admired them. Slovene litterateurs of the Enlightenment period had written about peasants and nobles; the bourgeois writers only later came to make their own class their subject.[25] Notable in Wales were the new styles of chapel building (Gothic spires, neo-Renaissance elements) by more prosperous congregations alongside the simple square boxes of the countryside and the valleys townships. The wealthier members of the middle class now inhabited the elegant streets which sprang up in Cardiff and Swansea. Cardiff's two great department stores, Howell's and Morgan's, which survived into the twenty-first century, were both founded by former drapers' assistants from rural Wales. Howell's employed 500 staff in 1905. Under the firmly nationalist mayor Ivan Hribar Ljubljana also acquired its first department store. The growth of press advertisements for fashionable products in Slovene show people's growing aspirations and an attitude to the once humble native tongue which was not taken in Wales. In smaller centres like Bangor or Aberystwyth the new middle class which aped bourgeois norms was predominantly Welsh speaking, but in Cardiff and Swansea such a class lived as a minority, if quite influential, in a population which largely shared their Nonconformist religion.

As aspirations grew so did interest in secondary and tertiary education in both our countries. The effect of the 1848 Austrian school reforms in easing access for previously excluded groups continued in the constitutional era. From 1880 to 1913 the number of Slovene university-level students rose from 336 in 1880 to 936. As well as Vienna and to a lesser degree Graz they now also went in increasing numbers to the new Czech-language university of Prague (1882). The relative liberalism of Austrian academia aided the proliferation of student clubs and journals, in keeping with the development of associational life which was characteristic of the age. In Slovenia itself the Slovene reading societies had mutated into a variety of literary, musical/choral, sporting/gymnastic and amateur dramatic societies, Slovene students largely remained liberal in outlook, with rival clerical organisations or more radical groups not emerging till the 1890s or later. A small Slovene intelligentsia began to form on characteristic central European lines, with the German model of the classical Gymnasium at its core. However, students made up only half the Slovene population proportionately compared to Austrians as a whole, and their largest cohort for most of the period were peasants studying theology, the cheapest choice and often made on a parish priest's recommendation. A factor making for frustration was that calls for a Slovene language university, first voiced in 1848 and then taken up at times of national tension like the *tabori* movement and the turn of the century. By the latter point the government was prepared to fund talented students to train as potential university teachers, some of whom did in fact help staff the Slovene university set up in 1919. But hardline German voices could still affirm that a century ahead such a university would remain a pipe dream.[26]

Differences of tradition and structure between Britain and Austria hinder direct comparison of our two countries' educational experience. However, the desire to use it as a means of emancipation both personal and national, of raising the profile of a subaltern society, was common to both and had a particular charge at this time. Moreover, the British state, which only introduced compulsory education in 1870, was now prepared to overhaul its ramshackle laissez-faire approach to schooling. A Welsh organiser of great energy, whom we have already encountered, took advantage. The goal of Hugh Owen, founder of Bangor Normal College for teacher training (1858), was quite explicitly to build up a Welsh middle class which could compete with their English, Scottish and Irish peers. Possessed by the dream of a ladder of progression up to university level, he was the driving force behind the Aberdare Committee of 1880 whose key recommendations were for university colleges in south and north Wales, and a new kind of secondary school linking the primary and tertiary levels. The first recommendation was duly approved and the colleges set up in Cardiff and Bangor in 1883, with annual government grants of £4,000 apiece. Only the energetic advocacy of Henry Richard and other Welsh MPs, and the money of David Davies saved the grant for Aberystwyth University College which would otherwise have been abolished. Plans for a federation of all three colleges in a national 'University of Wales' were then successfully promoted against the predictable opposition of Anglican lobbies which disliked its Nonconformist aura. The university goal had historical roots in Glyndŵr's Pennal Letter of 1406, seventeenth- and eighteenth-century ideas of a college for Wales and the mid-nineteenth-century schemes of the Association of Welsh Clergy in the West Riding of Yorkshire.[27] The first Vice-Chancellor, John Viriamu Jones, a brilliant young scientist and highly effective organiser as Cardiff University

College Principal (appointed at the age of twenty-seven), belonged to a band of talented brothers, one destined to become a knight, another ennobled for public service. It was an interesting portent that none of these, Radnorshire-born and brought up in London and semi-anglicised Swansea, mastered Welsh. But all chose to devote themselves to Wales. Three things combined to make Viriamu Jones's plainly inspirational personality: deep religious faith inherited from his Nonconformist minister father; a belief in 'the Welsh genius' and its intellectual capacity; and a passionate conviction 'in a democratic age' of the importance of education to foster 'the equality of rights for all men'. 'A national life is not so much to be talked about as to be lived' summed up his engagement.[28] Overwork undermined his health at the age of forty-five.

The second of the Aberdare Committee's recommendations was realised in the Intermediate Education Act of 1889. It provided for a system of Welsh secondary schools to be run by county councils jointly with the Department of Education, which actually preceded state-funded secondary schooling in England. These were greeted with great public enthusiasm, leading by 1914 to the opening of some hundred intermediate or county schools, a network that was particularly dense in previously educationally deprived rural areas. The path was open for the 'lad of parts' to escape from obscurity and poverty into Cymru Fydd, 'the Wales that is to be', in the famous rallying call of the time. It was reported in 1911 that 15 per cent of the 2000 pupils leaving the Intermediate schools every year went on to further education, yielding a figure of 300, substantially lower than in the Slovene case.[29] But this omits several categories of new secondary schools not founded under the 1889 Intermediate Schools Act, notably in the populous industrial areas. In Wales, too, theology students for the several thousand chapels and churches were largely trained in denominational colleges. The secondary school movement, building on memories of the 'pennies of the poor' contributed by chapel congregations for Aberystwyth University College, helped shape the sense of a common people's thirst for betterment. The spirit it engendered can be felt from the report of a committee of the Board of Education's Welsh Department in 1919. In proposing a National Council of Education for Wales it recommended that this should have 'something of the character, and be clothed with something of the authority, of the State... to help in bringing the educational system into line with Welsh ideals of culture and civilisation'.[30] A powerful myth was being born.

In fact, the story was more complex. The evolution of the intermediate schools was enmeshed in a web of difficult compromises, between denominational tensions, Welsh desires for a Welsh tailored education system and the British framework in which it operated, the Central Welsh Board created by the 1889 Act and the Welsh Department of the Board of Education set up in 1907, between rural areas and industrial, the latter being less well provided for by the Act, resulting in separate provision for municipal secondary schools in larger towns of the south-east: above all, in retrospect, in the investing of national sentiment in a system run in the English language. Though the Aberdare Committee envisaged more attention to practical, technical skills, as did O. M. Edwards, chief inspector of the Welsh Department of the Board of Education, the intermediate schools' curricula were thoroughly literary-humanistic with many reflections of English public-school practice. The majority of early headmasters were Englishmen. A preference for humanistic education is actually quite common in small nation contexts and contemporary developing societies. Slovenes, like many Habsburg Slavs, were initially slow to take to the *Realschule* whose claims were increasingly being pressed by German educationalists rather than the prestigious classical Gymnasium. The Welsh went much further, however, in favouring the elite language itself. While Welsh was taught as a subject in the great majority of the new schools by 1917, only 42.6% of pupils actually chose to study it.[31] In Wales the truth of the county schools for many of those it educated was that they provided, not an escape into an idealised 'Wales that is to be', but to England, depriving rural Wales in particular of successive generations of its ablest children.

German remained the predominant language of secondary education in Slovenia till 1918, of course. The key difference for Wales was the far longer neglect of Welsh at primary level. Individually, mother tongue teaching did not solve the practical problems which drove Slovene emigration, though collectively it strengthened Slovene solidarity. Yet the Welsh pattern meant that English speakers like Viriamu Jones could be emotionally committed to play a vital role in an important Welsh cause. Welsh and Slovene experience involved different developmental pros and cons whose implications are still being worked out. Overall, for all the reservations noted above, the Welsh educational movement counted itself a great success and a national achievement, which stimulated upward mobility and self-confidence.

Ironically, the Welsh-speaking middle class of Hugh Owen's plans took most substantial form in these years outside Wales itself, in the Welsh community in Liverpool, which bears striking comparison with that of Slovenes in Trieste. Both cities were key ports in their respective states which had accelerated rapidly from the eighteenth century. Trieste had 224,000 inhabitants in 1911 and Liverpool 772,000. Including the dozen surrounding villages Slovenes made up one-quarter of this population, while 120,000 Welsh people migrated to Liverpool between 1851 and 1911, making the respective cities the largest aggregations of Welsh and Slovene speakers anywhere. Trieste was the seat of the first Slovene reading society in 1861 and active in sokol and musical activities, with its own branch of the Glasbena matica. The paper *Edinost*, founded in 1876 and a daily from 1898, nurtured national feeling. About ninety Welsh chapels were built to serve the needs of swelling congregations in Liverpool and surrounding townships, whose most ambitious building, known locally as the Welsh Cathedral, arose in French Gothic splendour and elegantly betowered in Princes Road, Toxteth, with seating for 1,250 people. It was in Liverpool that Gwilym Hiraethog edited the *Amserau* and received the thanks of Kossuth's emissaries and that the *Cymro* and the *Brython*, two of the most influential of Welsh weeklies, acquired a national readership. The first Welsh total abstinence society was founded there in the 1830s; missionary bodies and eisteddfodau flourished, including visits of the National Eisteddfod in 1884 and 1900 and twice to adjacent Birkenhead. Chapel building and the whole area of housing still called the 'Welsh streets' helped launch self-financing Welsh building companies, while medicine and shipping also brought Welshmen into prominence. Sir Alfred Lewis Jones, President of the Liverpool Chamber of Commerce and a favourite of Lloyd George and Winston Churchill, was knighted for his work in dominating West African commerce through the African Steamship Company. The active Calvinistic Methodist William Thelwall Thomas, Liverpool's most famous surgeon and professor in its University, was one of many successful Welsh doctors in the city. The founder of modern Welsh historiography, Sir John Edward Lloyd, the long-standing administrator of the Welsh Department of the Board of Education, Sir Alfred T. Davies and the leading Celticist J. Glyn Davies were all also scions of the city.[32]

The bourgeois pretensions of the Liverpool Welsh have drawn mixed feelings from left-leaning Welsh historians. The long-standing minister of Princes Road, Owen Thomas (1812–91), embodied Nonconformity's organisational success and intellectual energy. A celebrated preacher, biblical exegetist and voluminous religious historian, he took the 'cofiant' into new territory with his massive work on John Jones Talsarn, which Lloyd George pronounced the best biography he had ever read.[33] One of three brothers who rose high in their denominations, like the siblings Henry Rees and Gwilym Hiraethog and the three Robertses of Llanbrynmair, Thomas illustrated a tendency to family clustering in nineteenth-century Welsh religious life, marked also by intermarriage. His comment 'our people are mostly of the working classes – but Providence was never kinder to me'[34] hints at the self-satisfaction such a rise from humble circumstances doubtless engendered. Chapel leaders made modest attempts to aid their poorer compatriots (burial payments, free meals, for example) but such acts were peripheral to their main concerns which, while they presented a cooperative Welsh face to the world, were denominational rather than national, as in nineteenth-century Wales as a whole. The issue of language preservation naturally faced them more sharply in exile. Four 'English causes' were set up in response to anglicising tendencies in mid-century but, as Owen Thomas noted in 1883, people were reluctant to sever their ties with Welsh chapels even when they barely understood the preacher. The recollections of J. Saunders Lewis (1893–1985), leading Welsh language writer of the twentieth century and nationalist icon, show both sides of the picture. Brought up in the home of a Wesleyan minister, Saunders had the typical education of a middle-class English boy and studied English at Liverpool University before being alerted to his Welsh roots in the First World War. There is irony in his claim to have been brought up amid 100,000 Welsh speakers in an atmosphere as Welsh as any in Wales: the bourgeois Welsh-speaking background of his youth had no parallel in Wales itself.

Similar social aspects, immigration from rural poverty and the eventual development of a middle class, characterised Slovene life in Trieste but were given an extra twist by the city's place in one of the Monarchy's most embattled zones.[35] Slovenes faced majority Italian speakers, traditionally dominant and resentful of Slovenes as Vienna's tool against their aspirations to join the new Italian state. Slovenes lived both in the city itself and the surrounding rural communities incorporated into it. But their six members in the fifty-two-member city council were invariably outvoted when they called for implementation of the nationalities law entitling them to mother tongue education in the city itself. The Italian liberal major-ity, like German liberals in Carinthia, argued as proponents of progress against a priest-ridden population of peasant stock. The stereotyping was relentless. 'Nationally conscious' Slovenes also feared pan-German nation-alist ambitions on Trieste as an outlet for Germandom on the Adriatic. Ordinary people were more concerned with the struggles of daily life. This is reflected in the economic issues reiterated in the Vienna Parliament by the Slovene Ivan Nabergoj, one of Trieste's four MPs between 1873 and 1897. The other Slovene prop was the Habsburgophile Catholic Church, alienated by Italian liberals' ideology and low Mass attendance. The result was that Catholic priests in Trieste were disproportionately Slovene, while Vienna and the Vatican, jointly responsible for episcopal appoint-ments, preferred to nominate Slav bishops or even a neutral German.[36] Helped by their priests, Trieste Slovenes mobilised the full resources of national associational life with considerable success, so that Italianisation eventually ceased to be a significant factor. *Edinost* was itself inspired by liberals but, in the spirit of its title (Unity), community collaboration was maintained. As Slovene self-affirmation progressed, Nabergoj's speeches included repeated calls for language rights and national equality. Political progress was harder, however. The sense of second-class citizenship in a neglectful Monarchy is echoed in meetings with his voters of 1893 and 1894. Despite Vienna's promises his people were still being 'pushed to the wall' by officials who repeated 'non capisco sciavo' or 'Ich versteh' nicht windisch' (Italian and German for 'I don't understand Slav').[37] This is a key difference between our two peoples, born of their different state situations. Slovenes resented the absence of rights the Welsh had barely imagined claiming, nor been spurred to claim by the existence of a great body of kinsfolk, like the Austrian Slavs, who were gradually becoming aware they were a majority in a new age when majorities began to count. Nabergoj's reports to his constituents express a frustrated sense of power-lessness in the face of injustice. His answer to constituents' complaints that Slovene MPs should withdraw their support for the conservative Catholic party in Vienna, as Czechs had done, was that the Czechs had far greater resources than Slovenes, who could only continue appealing to the govern-ment, while harbouring no illusions. In the second of these consultations Nabergoj hardened his stance to the government.[38]

The most spectacular mark of Slovene self-organisation in Trieste was the building of the Narodni Dom (National Hall) in the city, completed in 1904 as demonstration of their credentials as a nation of culture. Containing theatre, gym, bank, hotel and offices for *Edinost* and the city's various Slovene societies, the Narodni Dom was one of the most impressive of such cultural centres established in the South Slav world around this time. It was burnt down by Italian fascists in 1920. Later restored as a hotel, the premises have been recently formally transferred to the Trieste Slovene community. Princes Road Chapel, closed in the 1980s and standing mostly derelict thereafter, is to be restored as a community hub through National Lottery funding, not quite the same thing.

Liverpool and Trieste are testimony of the energy of forces arising in Wales and Slovenia itself. The contrasting outcomes just mentioned can provide ironic comment on the fate of the two movements thereafter. In purely electoral terms but also psychologically, however, Liberal Nonconformity's reach was wider before 1914 than Slovene nationalism. It certainly spoke a confident language.

> The Lord has shone his face on Wales through what has been called till now and doubtless will be till the world's end the Methodist Awakening ... It has cast the salt of sanctity into the fountain of our national life ... Possibly there is no example in the whole history of the world of a nation which has changed so much for the better in so short a time as Wales since 1735 [the start of the Methodist revival]

So declaimed the poet-preacher J. J. Roberts (Iolo Caernarfon) in 1901,[39] claiming the credit for his own denomination. But it was an Anglican clergyman, J. Vyrnwy Morgan, who wrote that 'The Victorian era is canonised because it is the era in which the glory of modern Welsh Nationality began to shine', freely acknowledging the Nonconformist leading role,[40] the more easily since many Anglicans hoped that their own efforts at emulation would help them regain ground over time. Welsh publications and speechmaking were awash with such self-congratulatory references to the spirit of resurgent Welsh nationality. Slovenes would be perplexed at this rhetoric in a country were the native language was largely invisible in official life. We must go back to the fact that the Welsh awakening was primarily religious, not linguistic, but also that Welsh perspectives psychologically were those of an old nation. Whether or not that lies behind Iolo Caernarfon's somewhat curious reference to the time since 1735 as 'so short', it is certainly the case that the religious revival then launched fitted mentally for the Welsh into a long span of time going back to conflict with the English, the recollections of medieval princes and poets, and the post-Tudor settlement of landlords and state Church bundled by Methodists into the time of darkness from which they had been liberated. Religious revival had been historicised until for late-nineteenth-century patriots it appeared as ineluctably preparing the way for the successive social, educational and now political awakening of the common people, the *gwerin*. Welsh nationhood had therefore a lengthier, more diffuse genesis than Slovene, which had been forged in the crisis of the 1848 revolution, so that Slovene patriots had a political consciousness from the start. Be that as it may, both peoples' development had reached a point by the later nineteenth century where their new leaderships had to play a more permanent part on a wider stage.

POLITICS: SLOVENIA

Politics is a difficult, frustrating process, the more so for small peoples obliged to ally with larger forces not necessarily acting in their interest. Before the twentieth century there were few sovereign states. The natural desire to control one's interests as far as possible had to be satisfied by grades of autonomy, either territorial or institutional. Hungary had won complete internal autonomy in 1867 and this home rule was the objective of most national movements, like the Czech, the Irish and the Indian. It was also the Slovene objective, beyond what has been called here cultural sovereignty. But their prospects were negligible, short of revolutionary change. Rather, they felt mainly on the defensive against German and Italian nationalists, who saw Slovenes as a barrier to their Adriatic ambitions. This naturally increased Slovene support for the anti-nationalist Habsburg Monarchy. The alternative was to play the Slav nationalist card and throw in their lot with stronger Croats and Serbs. Yet that would put them in the dynasty's bad books and yoke them to peoples who had mainly different interests and did not take them very seriously. The result was that Slovenes mostly acted out the part of empire loyalists quite as effusively as the Victorian Welsh. Their MPs sat with the coalition of German conservatives and Slavs which succeeded the German liberals in 1879, the government we have seen Nabergoj complaining about, quite realistically.

The Welsh situation was more similar to the Slovene than at first appears. Britain was itself a disguised multinational state and the disguise was wearing thinner with the assertion of the Irish national movement, holding under Charles Stuart Parnell over eighty seats in the House of Commons. That was half as many again as the Scots, who had their own Celtic-speaking Highland crofters who formed their own party and won a couple of Westminster seats in the 1880s. Welsh patriots could emphasise their loyalty as opposed to the rebellious Irish or take a leaf from the Celtic book. Parliamentary arithmetic could potentially play into their hands, giving them some bargaining power between the major parties, as it could for the Slovenes. But it was a slim chance, for Gladstone's Liberals would always put Irish home rule before the Welsh desire for disestablishment and disendowment of the Anglican Church in Wales. As for traditionalist Tories, they saw the state Church as central to the constitution and its disendowment as daylight robbery on a par with Irish Fenianism. Nonetheless, Welsh and Slovenes were to have a sniff of influence, and at roughly the same time, in the mid-1890s.

It was on a detail of secondary education that Slovenia became for several weeks the focus of Austrian politics in 1895. The Slovene political outlook had changed for the better when Austro-German dominance in Vienna in 1879 yielded to a coalition of Slavs and German clericals, which Slovenes joined. In return for power in the Carniolan diet and the right to communicate with the authorities in Slovene, even Slovene liberals tacitly dropped talk of Slovenian autonomy, a so-called 'elastic' policy which cost them support. Disillusioned by limited progress some Slovene MPs in Vienna switched their support to the Croats. To check such defections the government agreed in 1895 to parallel classes in Slovene in the four-year lower Gymnasium in Celje, Styria, a mainly German town in a Slovenian countryside. But German nationalism was on the rise. A German backlash developed in the form of Austria-wide demonstrations against this concession to Slavs, in favour of Celje Germans who already felt threatened. The Government fell, though the Slovene classes went ahead.[41] Austrian politics had yielded the Slovenes a crumb, but they remained incidental to other forces.

Fault lines were changing. Liberalism with its urban, professional, intelligentsia base was losing out, not yet to socialism but to nationalism and in Catholic Europe to a Church beginning to flex its muscles. In Austria Catholic activists rejected current compromises with the state and a society based for them on capitalist materialism or godless socialism. Their vision was a social order inspired by the Gospel, as interpreted by Catholic teaching: this could bespeak a sense of Catholic entitlement which others found unsettling. In Slovenia the call of the theologian Anton Mahnič (1830–1920) for a 'parting of the ways' between truth and error signalled an open Catholic entry into Slovene politics which strained the cooperation of Old and Young Slovenes to breaking point. From the early 1890s this alliance was superseded by explicitly Catholic and liberal parties, eventually to become the People's Party and the National Progressive Party respectively, with the latter on the defensive.[42] Indeed, its fears of absorption led to an unlikely collaboration of Slovene liberals and the German landholders' party in the Carniolan Diet between 1895 and 1908 to hold the People's Party at bay. One reason for the Catholics' strength was the natural advantage of a party of peasants and parish priests in a pious, heavily rural society. But it also owed much to the success of their social policy. Here the decisive figure was a less ideological priest than the conservative Mahnič, the social activist and skilled organiser of the Catholic cooperative movement, Janez Evangelist Krek (1865–1917).

Krek is a deeply impressive figure. He combined the energy Slovenes attribute to his mountainous Upper Carniolan region, organisational ability, high intellectual gifts – he was an outstanding linguist – and an optimistic nature devoted to the idea of service. This had led him to the Church whose formidable educational ladder he climbed. Raised in humble circumstances – his teacher father died young, leaving six children – he was spotted for a scholarship by the Prince Bishop of Ljubljana, Jakub Missia, and after lengthy theological training in Vienna and Rome was able to begin his life's work. He had already spoken at his first mass as priest of a socialism based on Christianity. In 1894, Krek founded a Slovene workers' movement, with attention also to women workers. He engaged too with the cooperative movement described above but founded his own version based on Raiffeisen principles, which were intended for peasants only and did not involve members holding shares: all profit was reinvested. This led to a rapid growth and an extension of activity into producer and then consumer cooperatives. After successive reorganisations the Carniolan Cooperative Union was founded in 1903, though its work went further than Carniola. In 1908, a cooperative training school followed, the first in Europe. Krek also launched societies to build workers' homes and for young workers. A tireless publicist, he was credited after his death with three thousand speeches and six thousand articles, his major publications being a 'Black Book' on peasant circumstances in Europe and the Americas and a history of socialism, based on pastoral work with Slovene workers in the Rhineland and America. Like many Slovene activists he also wrote short stories and translations, with a fondness for English.[43]

Krek was a long-serving member of the Vienna parliament and Carniolan diet, expressing himself boldly on the need for universal suffrage, democratisation of life at all levels, and full self-expression for all the Monarchy's peoples. Truth-telling was important to him. He is reported as saying that no one who had contributed importantly to the life of the Church had not at some time been suspected of heresy. The truth he had to tell was that 'the only basis for progress is to materially strengthen the Slovene farmer. Where there is hunger there is room neither for ideas nor morals'.[44] But he also said: 'Only the cooperative movement of the Slovene peasants can stop the Germanization and Italianization of our territory', through possession of their own loan institutions.[45] The connection of the social and the national runs through the Slovene experience as with the other small nations of east-central Europe. Krek was a resolute believer in the idea of Yugoslav or south Slav unity, though he always meant unity within the framework of the Habsburg Monarchy. His charge of disrespect against the Carniolan governor for addressing the Diet largely in German took place shortly before the Governor's fall in 1905.

This episode reminds us of the uncertain state of the Slovene national movement in the early twentieth century. Even in their strongest province, Carniola, Slovenes were still far from control in 1905. Their first full Gymnasium was yet to open the next year and then as a private, Catholic foundation. That it was founded in a village on Ljubljana's outskirts, not the liberal-voting city itself, showed the seriousness of the liberal–Catholic divide and that the Slovene nation's emergence into modernity was not unproblematic. They had negotiated the linguistic aspect of transition better than the Welsh, but the clash of religious and secular values proved more difficult. The energetic Liberal mayor of Ljubljana from 1895 to 1910, Ivan Hribar, sponsor of important public works, was so hostile to the Catholic movement that he tried to get the government to ban some of its institutions, and he opposed broadening the provincial franchise to stop 'obscurantists' coming to power.[46] Slovene liberalism was driven to this illiberal position by its narrow social base and fear of the deep-rooted Catholic Church. A leading Slovene historian has raised the question as to whether it may be called liberalism at all.[47] Besides the above factors, national divisions in the Monarchy enabled the emperor and bureaucracy to retain much power, impeding a drive for fuller democratisation. Hribar's reelection as Mayor in 1910 was rejected by Franz Joseph, something which would not have happened in Britain. Liberalism survived longer and stronger there because of its link with the powerful British state and economy and the different religious landscape. In Austria, a 'chicken and egg' relationship between dynastic conservatism and popular nationalism developed, but not the social liberalism associated with Lloyd George.

Hribar was linked to the 'neo-Slav' movement, whose conferences, talking shops really, concentrated on relations between Habsburg Slavs and near Balkan neighbours rather than the headier dreams of Panslav unity. Not that Hribar, a convinced Yugoslav, was suspicious of the Russian bear. When his train crossed the Russian frontier, he was so elated at hearing the Russian language that it seemed to him angels were speaking. In the liberal Hribar we see a weakening of traditional Slovene Habsburg loyalty. He recorded later that he first doubted the Monarchy's viability in 1903.[48] As frustration deepened, so the south Slav option gained ground.

Slovene MPs made various combinations with Croats from the mid-1890s, accepting to be part of a 'trialist' unit in Austria-Hungary based on Croat 'historic right'. But Croats were weak themselves. Supporters of the trialist idea in Austrian circles did not include Slovenia in it but saw it as a means of weakening Hungary in favour of a 'Great Austria'. The Croats who favoured alignment with Slovenes belonged to the right; more liberal Croats were keener on an alliance with (Orthodox) Serbs. This did not sit easily with Catholic, Habsburgophile Slovene opinion. Krek's sturdy Yugoslavism, which included the Serbs, was therefore in a clear minority position in Slovenia, but not much to the liking of Orthodox Serbs either: Krek was actually a believer in the unification of the Catholic and Orthodox Churches under the Papal sceptre. These complications explain why most Slovenes had little interest in alternatives to their becalmed little political barque. The conclusion to be drawn fits the paradigm of small peoples' lot outlined at the start of this section: twisting and turning between limited options. The leader of the Slovene People's Party was a conservative Habsburgophile lawyer, Ivan Šušteršič, whose brother, a rear-admiral in the Austro-Hungarian navy, styled himself Alois Schusterschitz. The tradition of the *nemškutarji* was not dead.

POLITICS: WALES

It is time to cross-cut to another tale of blocked horizons, the fate of Cymru Fydd, chief effort at self-assertion in nineteenth-century Wales. What gave Wales a potential influence was a generation of remarkable progress. Between 1868 and 1892 the number of Nonconformists elected in just over thirty Welsh seats had risen from three to twenty-two, largely Welsh-speaking, six with only primary education, while fourteen lawyers and the same number in industry or commerce had all but displaced Tory landowners. Welsh disestablishment ranked second after Irish Home Rule in the Liberal Party's 'Newcastle Programme' of 1891, and Gladstone's parliamentary statement that the Nonconformists of Wales were the people of Wales was a big advance on his earlier cagey response to Thomas Gee's pressure on the issue, no doubt bearing in mind that the Welsh MPs were close to having the balance of power.[49] Moreover, two of the recently elected MPs were David Lloyd George, the most significant politician Wales has produced, and the man Lloyd George looked up to at this time as his leader, Tom Ellis.

In his biography of Ellis, Neville Masterman (son of a Liberal MP who was Ellis's contemporary) calls him a forerunner, one of those figures in the onset of national movements who preserve a liberal opening to other influences before the movement hardens. He is presented as the light as opposed to Lloyd George's fire.[50] Ellis (1859–99) is indeed a fascinating figure. His life exemplified the dawning democracy. His peasant father, dedicated Methodist elder, pillar of the local community, keen reader in his only tongue with a single term's schooling but successful enough to pay for Tom's education at Aberystwyth and Oxford, fits all the stops of the cultivated Welsh *gwerinwr* of legend. Thomas himself was an endlessly curious, diligent youngster, his earnestness alleviated by an innate good nature which charmed contemporaries of all classes throughout his life. It is illuminated by his correspondence from young boyhood with his friend D. R. Daniel. Begun in Welsh but continued from grammar school days in steadily improving English, it shows the two boys setting themselves and mutually correcting examination tests – 'I'll write this answer in Welsh (excuse me)', says Tom, confronted with a question on a ship's compass.[51]

Ellis responded avidly to all stimuli, which then informed a developing patriotism. He was particularly alert to Irish affairs and Celtic motifs at a time when Charles Stuart Parnell was holding together a mass political party and combative Land League. After speaking in Dublin during the trial of a militant Irish nationalist he was hailed as 'the Parnell of Wales'. He introduced the Land League campaigner William O'Brien to his Merionethshire constituents and coupled the grievances of Irish and Welsh farmers in the House of Commons, resorting to what English critics called parliamentary 'obstruction' – the notorious Irish and Habsburg nationalist tactic – on the 'tithe war' issue in north-east Wales. But his attention ranged more widely than this. In a lecture on the need for memorials to Welsh history and life he could refer to funerals he had witnessed in the Tyrol, Zurich, Pisa, Naples, Egypt, South Africa and Paris, though he concluded that they lacked 'the passionate searching and ... genuine impressiveness' of extempore prayer at a graveside in a Welsh glen.[53] In seeking benefactions from Welsh businessmen for Cymru Fydd he was aware of the role of émigré merchants' contribution to the Greek national movement in the Ottoman Empire. He saw the international significance of the early socialist Robert Owen whose atheism denied him recognition in his native country. As a devotee of Ruskin, he called for Welsh schools of art and architecture and for the technical and vocational training of the craft school tradition strong also in central Europe. He had European awakeners' alertness to the need for 'accessible' literature in Welsh and for literary criticism in a balanced journalism, 'conversant with the master minds of the ages'.[54] He advocated a hall and library in every village, a Welsh statistical service and for the University of Wales' Guild of Graduates to take over the archiving of Welsh records. More central to his omnivorous concerns was his pressure for a Land Court as fulcrum in the regeneration of Welsh agriculture and, on the disestablishment issue, the diversion of funds from a disendowed Church to Welsh cultural purposes. Above all, in notes on Cymru Fydd written in 1888, he urged 'the one dominant element which nationalises the programme ... For self-government is at once the inspirer and the goal of nationhood ... Without a national assembly [Wales'] position as a nation can not be assured, and her work as a nation can not be done.'[55] From Cairo in 1890 he told Daniel, this time in Welsh, that even with a free church and free schools in the people's hands this would be freedom without unity and vowed as his life's goal 'to win unity for Wales in the fullest sense of the word ... EDUCATION – FREEDOM – UNITY'.[56]

Ellis's position was not the most radical in this period. Two Nonconformist ministers who took a more sceptical stance to the British establishment deserve mention. A generation separated Michael D. Jones (1822–98) from Emrys ap Iwan (Robert Ambrose Jones 1848–1906). The former was orientated towards the United States, where he had been pastor in Cincinnati, the latter studied and travelled in Europe, knew French and German and had literary interests lacking in Jones. Both were motivated in their views on nationality by strong religious faith. For Michael D. Jones the 'Great Babylon' of the Bible was the mother of harlots with which the kings of the earth had prostituted themselves. For Emrys ap Iwan, 'Let it be remembered that the God who made men ordained nations also; and to exterminate a nation is next in seriousness to exterminating humanity.'[57] Both were stern in denunciation of English/British imperialism. 'If the history of the English be studied ... it is impossible to evade the conclusion that they must be called a thieving and murderous nation ... unceasingly afflicted with the itch to covet the possessions of weaker nations than itself.' So Michael D. Jones.[58] Emrys ap Iwan for his part adjured the Welsh:

> Be not ashamed of the things that distinguish you from other nations; and if you wish to imitate that nation which is your neighbour, imitate it in those things in which it has the better of you, and not in its pride, its arrogance, its ostentation, its warmongering, its levity, its intellectual narrowness and its lack of sympathy with other nations.[59]

Both these writers identified language as the indispensable core of nationhood and the English bid for denationalisation, while criticising Nonconformist leaders for an individualistic liberalism betraying national and Christian values. A piece by Ap Iwan, entitled 'Bully, Taffy a Paddy' in which Taffy is mocked for the sycophancy induced by long subjection, conveys the general message.[60] Michael D. Jones did act, working for the colony in Patagonia where the Welsh could enjoy the self-government he claimed for them in Wales itself. He laboured in his organ 'Y Celt' for this and various radical causes, moving close to socialism, but in decentralised form. He had more influence in his own life-time, for example on the young Lloyd George, than did Emrys ap Iwan whose approval for the ministry was initially blocked after an excoriating attack on the Methodist patriarch Lewis Edwards over the notorious 'English cause'.

There were thus several varieties of Welsh feeling. Ellis was right to stress the theme of unity. Cymru Fydd had begun as a cultural, literary movement with its first branches in London and Liverpool (1886–7), but then developing in north more than south Wales before a wider expansion in 1892, coinciding with the potentially powerful position of the Welsh parliamentary party vis-à-vis the Liberal government. This body had formalised itself with its own whips and an agreement to concert action on Welsh matters for each parliamentary session. Ellis himself, however, had accepted the post of deputy, then chief governmental whip in 1892. The outcome fell short of the goal. Welsh parliamentary party threats to organise independently on Irish lines if the Government delayed with the bill for Welsh disestablishment ended in only four members resigning the Liberal whip when it did so – the abortive 'Welsh revolt' of 1894. In fact, the government did subsequently twice introduce the bill which passed the Commons but was defeated in the House of Lords, as with Irish Home Rule. The issue was squarely presented by Home Secretary Asquith in national terms, as wholly legitimised by the wishes of the Welsh people. The controversial aspect was no longer this principle, except for Tory die-hards, but disendowment, the fate of tithe, charities and other funds which had historically accrued to the Church or been appropriated by it. Controversy on an amendment for a Welsh national council to administer the tithe fund, proposed by Lloyd George, led to the government's fall. As he wrote to Thomas Gee in September 1895: 'I maintain strongly that all our demands for reform, whether in Church, Land, Education, Temperance or otherwise, ought to be concentrated in one great agitation for national self-government.'[61] Throughout 1895 Cymru Fydd had become the vehicle for such sentiments, moving to amalgamate its branches into a national League, to which the North Wales Liberal Federation adhered in April. Lloyd George set out to south Wales, ostensibly to lecture on Llywelyn the Great, most successful of medieval Welsh princes, in fact aiming to win the south Wales Federation for the same step. At a rowdy meeting in Newport in January 1896 packed, he claimed, with local Englishmen, he was shouted down when the leader of Cardiff Liberals, Robert Bird, a Bristol-born Cardiff businessman, denounced the 'dominance of Welsh ideas'. It was a demoralising blow and the effective end of Cymru Fydd.

Disunity in various forms is the main reason given for this damp squib of Welsh national politics in the 1890s. Cymru Fydd attracted a wide range of talented people over whom neither Ellis nor Lloyd George had overall control. The disunity exposed at Newport between the two Liberal

Federations, personalised in the split between Lloyd George and the Welsh coal owner David Thomas, had arguably a deeper structural base: the widening gap between a Welsh-speaking north and the dynamic south-east zone, with a further distinction possible between the industrial valleys and the Anglo-Welsh commercial economy of the great coastal ports. Yet the north–south divide was not set in stone. It was the South Wales Liberal Federation which had pushed for unification against north Walian opposition in immediately preceding years. David Thomas (1856–1918), had been one of the strongest supporters of Cymru Fydd and one of the four MPs, with Lloyd George, who had renounced the Liberal whip in the 'Welsh revolt'. Whatever his apparent indifference to cultural nationalism, he had a quite concrete reason for resentment of the North Wales Liberal Federation over its refusal to recognise Glamorgan and Monmouthshire's numerical preponderance in dividing up the proceeds of church disendowment. It seems the sort of dispute capable of compromise if handled skilfully. Kenneth Morgan very plausibly argues for differences in outlook as a key underlying factor in the fissure, though 'highly likely' might be safer than inevitable. David Thomas is an intriguing figure. Born the fifteenth of seventeen children to a Baptist coal-owner in the Cynon valley, he was sent for his education to Clifton, near Bristol where his uncle was a minister. The family moved from their Welsh chapel to an English one when he was three, a sign of parental ambition. Failing to get the high Liberal office he sought, he founded the Cambrian Combine company with a capital of £2 million and plans for industrial cooperation in Britain, America and Canada. Plainly, with his capitalist career and indifference to mother tongue and to religion – he became an Anglican on marriage to his Radnorshire wife – he does not fit the conventional patriotic Welsh image. The handful of Slovene entrepreneurs matched their national patriotic story much more closely, though the scale is different. That the period produced an economic and a political titan in him and Lloyd George testifies to a vitality in Welsh life not to be lost sight of because they played their biggest roles on a wider stage. As British prime minister in the First World War, Lloyd George called on Thomas to be President of the Board of Trade with responsibility for food supplies. Elevated to the peerage as Lord, then Viscount Rhondda, he had conspicuous success. One cannot ignore his years of participation in Cymru Fydd. He is part of the rise of a new element of the Welsh story, that of industrial Wales, lived, though still not universally, through the English language.

Kenneth Morgan's remarks on 'an unreality about Cymru Fydd' and Welsh opinion's concern all along for disestablishment rather than not home rule is undeniable.[62] But from a European perspective it overlooks the strange absence of any significant language demands in the movement's programme. This weakens Morgan's argument that the Welsh sought equality in the state, not separatism like the Irish.[63] Welsh people had had equality before the law from the 1536 Act of Union. It was their language which, as Commissioner Lingen wrote in 1847, kept them 'under the hatches'. Three hundred thousand Welsh monoglots were recorded in the 1891 census, leaving aside the right to recognition of the language raised by German commentators. It seems that Cymru Fydd tacitly accepted the official assumption that the language issue would be resolved when the whole population learnt English. The confusion on the question noted by the Newcastle Commission of 1861 remained. Nothing in the British framework prompted the detailed thinking that went into the matter in east-central Europe. Morgan's finding it 'scarcely conceivable' that an ambitious Lloyd George, contemptuous of chapel parochialism, 'would cut himself off from the sources of central power' suggests little understanding of the springs of small nation nationalism, however pertinent to Lloyd George.[64] Many small nation leaders of great ambition and abilities have sought to exercise these to relieve their people of their defects. Much of Ellis's expression may have been 'ethereal' to his audience in Morgan's terms, but he had a good grasp of concrete aspects of a national cultural programme. One conclusion on the paradoxes of Cymru Fydd might be that Welsh people's long but isolated experience lent them quite a strong national consciousness but little comparative insight into their situation.

The Cymru Fydd episode is a suitable point at which to pause this chapter's political narration. It nudges readers to feel something of the political frustration present in our two societies early in the new century. In Slovenia the main tendency remained a strengthening of the Catholic camp at the expense of the liberal, aided by the introduction of universal suffrage in Austria (1907). The move to a Yugoslav orientation also continued. In Wales political devolution remained off the agenda but Cymru Fydd had a significant cultural-political aftermath. The Conservatives' 1902 Education Act aroused Nonconformist fury by extending public funding from the non-denominational Board schools of 1870 to schools effectively Church run. Lloyd George was the heart of an all-Wales campaign for non-implementation of the Act, which proved a more successful 'Welsh Revolt' than in 1894. Nearly all Welsh local authorities followed his call to refuse cooperation, even when the Government introduced a Default Act threatening to take over non-cooperating schools. The cause inspired some of Lloyd George's most high-flown rhetoric:

> Wales exhibits a true spectacle of a well-ordered and highly disciplined community where intense political and religious convictions produce ... a patriotism at once as ardent and as broad as that which inspires any nation in the world...a patriotism which was almost purely literary before it became religious, and which was religious fully a century before it annexed politics to the national life.[65]

With courage and restraint 'this great struggle' would see Wales emerge 'with a national position surpassing the dreams of the line of prophets who foretold great things for *Gwalia Wen*, ere they passed to their rest in the shadow of its hills'. Welsh defiance made the Default Act largely a dead-letter until the return of the Liberals to power in 1906 though, since the House of Lords vetoed the Liberal alternative, public funding of voluntary schools actually remained, if their number declined. The stage was set for a show-down with the House of Lords over its absolute right of veto. After two more Liberal election victories in 1910, this was curtailed when it tried to block the landlord-bashing 'People's Budget' of Lloyd George, become Chancellor of the Exchequer. Welsh disestablishment and Irish Home Rule could now be passed by the House of Commons in 1912, to become law automatically after an interval. It was fortunate for Nonconformists that Wales's last and greatest Revival had re-energised flagging religious zeal some years before. An irony of the present study is that as religion increased its public profile in Slovenia, so its omnipresence in Wales was waning.

CONCLUSION

This chapter has tried to show something of the shape of activity in two small peoples, as history moved into a period the elderly can still visualise through grandparents' memories. Patterns of transport, education, economy, political organisation and mentality can speak across the generations. It has tried to do justice to achievements – of Welsh industry and education, of the Slovene cooperative movement and national integration – as well as indicating aspects of shortfall and frustration to which all national societies are no doubt prey, but certainly small ones. Welsh opinion seems to have been more buoyant than Slovene in 1914; the historian Pleterski has written of a 'gloomy' view of national prospects at that time.[66] This should surprise only in hindsight. The vastly greater economic dynamism of pre-1914 Wales, the large part played in this by Welsh-born entrepreneurs, British prestige and the power of the self-image of successful revival projected by Welsh Nonconformity provide one explanation. The Welsh could take themselves seriously and briefly were so taken. This was a time when the Methodist minister and prominent editor Thomas Levi argued in the *Traethodydd* that as a nation which had won influence among the four British nations Welsh opinion in a democratic age should play a role in the foreign policy of the empire, on classic liberal free trade lines.[67] But another explanation is that the Slovene project of achieving autonomy and cultural sovereignty was inherently more difficult than the Welsh, which did not aim so high and could draw on the English language and British identity when convenient. The largest Welsh entrepreneurs were Welsh by birth and in certain traits but the British Empire was the stage within which they acted and more central to their lives than a language and sometimes a religion they had left behind in childhood. Of course, as has been argued above, the British context made issues of language less salient than the Habsburg. Yet language and culture must always have some role in identity and to these the next chapter will turn.

NOTES

1 M. Wynn Thomas, *In the Shadow of the Pulpit: Literature and Nonconformist Wales* (Cardiff, 2010), p. 5. Slovenes also had a history of missionary activity. Its most famous figure is Bishop Baraga (1797–1868), who earned a European reputation for his ministry to native Indians in the United States.

2 David W. Howell, *Land and People in Nineteenth-Century Wales* (London, 1977), pp. 149, 154.

3 Marina Lukšič Hacin et al., *Socialna, gospodarska in kulturna zgodovina slovenskega izseljenstva, 1870–1945* (Social, economic and cultural history of Slovene emigration) (Ljubljana, 2018), p. 51. This is a completed research project of *ZRC SAZU* (The Research Center of the Slovene Academy of Arts and Sciences) and is available online.

4 *Slowenische Geschichte*, p. 274.

5 For Terpinc and Gorup, see J. Šorn and F. Adamič, 'Terpinc, Fidelis' (1799–1875), *http//www.slovenska-biografija.si* and Josip Gorup, wikipedija, prosta enciklopedija respectively.

6 Hacin et al., *Zgodovina slovenskega izseljenstva*.

7 Toussaint Hočevar, *The Structure of the Slovene Economy, 1848–1963* (New York, 1965), pp. 64–73.

8 H. James-Davies, 'The History of the Agricultural Movement in Carmarthenshire', *The Carmarthenshire Antiquary*, 1 (1942), part 2.

9 J. Pleterski, *Die Slowenen, Die Habsburgermonarchie 1848–1918*, vol. 3, part 2, pp. 801–38.

10 R. J. Colyer, 'The Gentry and the County in Nineteenth-Century Cardiganshire', *Welsh History Review*, 10 (1980), 498–535 (517–18).

11 V. Konik, *Small Places, Operatic Issues: Opera and its Peripheral Worlds* (Newcastle upon Tyne, 2019), pp. 55, 77–8.

12 V. Melik, *Slovenci, 1848–1918* (Slovenes, 1848–1918) (Maribor, 2002), p. 135.

13 R. Brinley Thomas, 'Pair Dadeni: Y Boblogaeth a'r Iaith Gymraeg yn y Bedwaredd Ganrif ar Bymtheg' (Cauldron of Rebirth: Demography and the Welsh Language in the Nineteenth Century), in Geraint H. Jenkins (ed.), *Gwnewch Bopeth yn Gymraeg: Yr Iaith Gymraeg a'i Pheuoedd 1801–1911* (Cardiff, 1999), pp. 79–98.

14 E. G. Ravenstein, 'The Celtic Languages in the British Isles', *Journal of the Royal Statistical Society*, (1879), 547–643; discussion, 636–43; chairman's quotes, 643. Ravenstein himself had said that Welsh 'clung to with such affection' might survive for centuries, 'if not for ever', 622 (emphasis added; a unique statement to my knowledge).

15 For the background, Geraint H. Jenkins, 'Na wadwch eich iaith: y cefndir hanesyddol i gyfrifiad 1891' (Don't deny your language the historical background to the 1891 census), in Gwenfair Parry and Mari A. Williams (eds), *Miliwn o Gymry Cymraeg! Yr Iaith Gymraeg a Chyfrifiad 1891* (A Million Welsh speakers!) (Cardiff, 1999), pp. 1–30.

16 Ravenstein put Welsh speakers at 74 per cent for Swansea, for example.

17 Parry and Williams, *Miliwn*, p. 314 (Llanidloes), p. 200 (Pontardawe).

18 Jack Jones, *Unfinished Journey* (London, 1937), p. 22.

19 The National Archives, ED, 91/13, W/911, T. G. Roberts to O. M. Edwards, 19 January 1911.

20 Neil Evans and Kate Sullivan, 'Yn Llawn o Dân Cymreig: Yr Iaith Gymraeg a Gwleidyddiaeth yng Nghymru 1880–1914' (Full of Welsh Fire: The Welsh Language and Politics in Wales 1880–1914), in Jenkins (ed.), *Gwnewch bopeth*, pp. 527–52 (p. 530).

21 I follow here J. Pleterski, *Narodna in politična zavest na Koroškem* (National and Political Consciousness in Carinthia) (Ljubljana, 1965), pp. 141–9.

22 Pleterski, *Narodna zavest*, pp. 337–9.

23 See Ernest Gellner, *Nations and Nationalism* (Oxford, 1983).

24 J. Prunk, *Slovenski narodni vzpon* (The Rise of the Slovene Nation) (Ljubljana, 1993), p. 86.

25 For the Slovene experience: J Dežman et al. (eds), *Slovensko meščanstvo od vzpona nacije do nacionalizacije (1848–1948)* (The Slovenian bourgeoisie from the rise of the nation to full nationhood) (Klagenfurt, 2008), partic. J. Hudalec, 'Olikan meščanin – olikan Slovenec' (A cultured citizen – a cultured Slovene), pp. 99–112.

26 V. Melik and P. Vodopivec, 'Slovenski izobraženci in austrijske više šole 1848–1918' (Slovene students and Austrian university-level institutions), in *Zgodovinski časopis*, 40 (1986), pp. 269–82.

27 J. Gwynn Williams, *The University Movement in Wales* (Cardiff, 1993), pp. 1–9.

28 Katharine Viriamu Jones, *Life of John Viriamu Jones* (London, 1915), pp. 385, 374, quoting from his speeches.

29 Gareth Elwyn Jones, *Controls and Conflicts in Welsh Secondary Education 1889–1944* (Cardiff, 1982), p. 29.

30 T. I. Ellis, *The Development of Modern Welsh Secondary Education* (London, 1934), p. 34.

31 Jones, *Controls*, p. 52.

32 Most of this material is drawn from D. Ben Rees, *Hanes Rhyfeddol Cymry Lerpwl* (Talybont, 2019).

33 I am indebted to Dr D. Ben Rees for this anecdote in extension of his biography of Owen Thomas, *Pregethwr y Bobl*, p. 126: 'ever written' should be 'he had ever read'.

34 Rees, *Hanes Rhyfeddol*, p. 112.

35 M. Cattaruzza, 'Slovenes and Italians in Trieste, 1850–1914', in M. Engman (ed.), *Ethnic Identity in Urban Europe, 1850–1914* (New York, c. 1992).

36 E. Saurer, *Die politischen Aspekte der österreichischen Bischofsernennungen 1867–1903* (Vienna, 1968), pp. 95–9. The German Franz Xaver Nagl very reluctantly accepted to be bishop of Trieste in 1902.

37 Peter Rustja (ed.), *Med Trstom in Dunajem: Ivan Nabergoj v avstrijskem državnem zboru (1873–1897)* (Trieste, 1999), pp. 29–44 (quotation p. 42).

38 Rustja (ed.), *Med Trstom in Dunajem*, pp. 40–4.

39 Address to the General Assembly of the Calvinistic Methodists, cited in T. R. Jones, *Cofiant Iolo Caernarfon*, n.d.), pp. 202–4.

40 J. Vyrnwy Morgan, *Welsh Political and Educational Leaders in the Victorian Era* (London, 1908), p. 11.

41 Helmut Rumpler, *Österreichische Geschichte 1804–1914: Eine Chance für Mitteleuropa* (Vienna, 1997), pp. 508–9.

42 For this process, F. Erjavec, *Zgodovina katoliškega gibanja na Slovenskem* (The History of the Catholic Movement in Slovenia) (Ljubljana, 1928).

43 I. Dolenec, 'Krek, Janez Evangelist (1865–1917)', *Slovenska Biografija*, ZRC SAZU, 2013.

44 B. Černik, 'The Role of Dr Janez Evangelist Krek in the Slovene Cooperative Movement', *Slovene Studies*, 11 (1989), pp. 75–81 (here pp. 76–7).

45 Černik, 'Role', 78.

46 C. Rogel, *The Slovenes and Yugoslavism 1890–1914* (Boulder, Colorado, 1977), p. 42.

47 P. Vodopivec, *O gospodarskih in socialnih nazorih na Slovenskem v 19. stoletju* (Economic and Social Thought in Nineteenth-Century Slovenia (Ljubljana), 2020), p. 17.

48 C. Rogel, *The Slovenes and Yugoslavism, 1890–1914* (Boulder, CO, 1977).

49 T. Gwynn Jones, *Cofiant Gee* (Denbigh, 1913), pp. 552–7.

50 N. Masterman, *The Forerunner: The Dilemmas of Tom Ellis 1859–1899* (Llandybie, 1972), pp. 15–16.

51 T. I. Ellis, *Thomas Edward Ellis, Cofiant. Cyfrol 1: 1859–1886* (The Life of Thomas Edward Ellis. Vol. 1: 1859–1886)

52 (Liverpool, 1944), p. 41. Ellis deduces that the answer probably came from the translation of *Chambers Encyclopædia* in the family library, which was well stocked with Welsh books.

53 T. E. Ellis, 'The Memory of the Kymric Dead', in *Speeches and Addresses by the late Thomas E. Ellis, M.P.* (Wrexham, 1912), p. 4.

54 Masterman, *The Forerunner*, p. 58.

55 Ellis, *Speeches and Addresses*: 'Notes for Cymru Fydd', pp. 187–93 (p. 189).

56 Masterman, *The Forerunner*, p. 129.

57 R. Tudur Jones, *The Desire of Nations* (Llandybie, 1978), p. 185.

58 Tudur Jones, *Desire of Nations*, p. 183.

59 Tudur Jones, *Desire of Nations*, pp. 181–2.

60 *Detholiad o Erthyglau a Llythyrau Emrys ap Iwan* (Selected Articles and Letters of Emrys ap Iwan), vol. 1 (Denbigh, 1937), pp. 1–13.

61 K. O. Morgan, *Wales in British Politics 1868–1922* (Cardiff, 1970), p. 162.

62 Quotations from Kenneth Morgan in this paragraph come from his *Rebirth of a Nation* (Oxford, 1981), pp. 114–20.

63 Morgan, *Rebirth*, p. 114.

64 Morgan, *Rebirth*, p. 120.

65 J. Hugh Edwards, MP, *The Life of David Lloyd George with a Short History of the Welsh People* (4 vols, London, 1916), vol. 4, p. 20. Gwalia Wen means 'Fair Wales'.

66 Pleterski, *Slowenen*, p. 817.

67 T. Levi, 'Lle Cymru fel rhan o ymerodraeth Prydain' (The Place of Wales as Part of the British Empire), *Y Traethodydd* (1901), 460–71.

Chapter 7

CULTURE, CONSCIOUSNESS AND CHALLENGE, 1880–1914

N ow that the new Welsh and Slovene leaderships had established some presence on a public stage, albeit constricted, what did they have to say for themselves in the less fettered field of cultural self-expression? The desire to disprove the charges of cultural backwardness levelled in the 'Blue Books' or in Viennese editorials had after all been a major stimulus for patriots. The field is potentially vast: from the 'high culture', through which in Gellner's argument aspiring peoples sought validation, to the concerns of ordinary members of still subaltern societies. What is offered here are only tentative soundings, taking up major issues already touched on like press, literature and religion and noting newer ones like popular drama and historiography.

THE PERIODICAL PRESS: A CULTURAL BAROMETER?

A prime sounding board for cultural consciousness is the periodical press. While it offers insights most helpfully into those who wrote and read it, it is a constantly suggestive source, posing difficulties in its very bulk. Educated contemporaries viewed it with pride and wonder as a sign of the progress they had made. Reviewing a popular journal without intellectual pretensions, launched in the early days of the national movement, *Dom in svet* in 1888, its opening year, contrasted the 'slim morsels' available to Slovene readers in the 1840s with the 'fine, thick portions' of today.[1] A *Traethodydd* reviewer of Welsh periodicals in 1902 claimed to find some of its productions quite the match for their English counterparts.[2]

These two periodicals are among four which will be highlighted in this survey. To the *Traethodydd* as a would-be heavy weight journal may be linked *Ljubljanski zvon* (The Ljubljana Bell, 1881–1941), of Slovene liberal persuasion. *Dom in svet* (Home and the World, 1888–1944), more popular and Catholic in approach, may be coupled with *Y Geninen* (The Leek, 1883–1928) whose shorter articles and sub-title 'My Language, My Country, My Nation' likewise signalled this intent. About two hundred and fifty periodicals in Welsh were published over the second half of the nineteenth century, mostly short-lived, and some one hundred and twenty in Slovene in the 1907–12 period alone. This last figure indicates that Slovene production now exceeded Welsh, as the Welsh-speaking population increased more slowly and a turn to English outlets grew.

The fit in journal type in my exemplars is not exact. *Ljubljanski zvon* and *Dom in svet* were typical central European literary monthlies, which alongside essays, reviews and poetry serialised short stories and novels. The Welsh duo dealt less with original prose and while increasingly open to short stories left novel serialisation to weeklies and monthlies like *Y Celt* or *Y Drysorfa*. They were originally quarterlies, in practice mainly bi-monthlies, larger than in the two Slovene cases so that the flagship volume was initially not too different but decreased relatively over the period. The different flavour of the four featured above may be tapped most quickly from their opening year, taking 1881 for the already established *Traethodydd*. Between them the two Slovene journals in the very first issue began four serialised novels, launched article series on knotty language points (historical change in Slovene vowels; the relation of spelling to pronunciation) and discussed new Bulgarian literature, Balkan folk poetry; German views of the Slovene national poet Prešeren and the role of the Russian language in the Balkan, besides bringing articles or reports on shortsightedness, new chemical elements and Graham Bell's concept of the photophone. Their Welsh counterparts discussed the New English Bible translation, the Bronte sisters, Tennyson, a Carlyle biography, education, the Irish question, Gladstone and also Russian history, earthquakes and money. The typical emphases of each side were clearly on show, as well as the stronger influence of the dominant culture in the Welsh case.

Though the journals discussed here remained broadly faithful to their aim of providing a general historical, literary, folkloric, scientific and contemporary coverage their preoccupations remained. *Ljubljanski zvon* in 1910 and 1911 printed article series on Slovene verbal aspects and broken spelling rules, debated the correct Slovene forms of Greek and Latin names and of historical names formerly written in German, reviewed works on Slovene stenography and on rules for the stress of Slovene words, and took to task a regional writer for literary solecisms. Astonishingly, half the contributors to the 1913 numbers of *Y Traethodydd* and two-fifths to the *Geninen* were ministers of religion, a higher proportion than in 1883, though the number of religion-related articles had slightly fallen, showing how far the ministry had infiltrated the field of culture in general. Thus matters of philosophy and newer issues like psychology, anthropology and archaeology were commonly discussed in relation to religion. Scientific topics, somewhat less frequent than in the Slovene journals, were rarely without possible religious referents either, as in astronomy and geology. On religious matters there was some division of Welsh labour, with religious history and denominational issues common, but the *Geninen* specialising on ministers' obituaries and the *Traethodydd* on theology; recent German Protestant work featured increasingly as the number of Welsh ministers doing doctoral studies in Germany rose. For its part, *Ljubljanski zvon* eschewed religious matters – less than one per cent of an overall index is taken up by them[3] – and *Dom in svet* expressed its Catholicism mainly through frequent pictures of churches, bishops and religious art, reports of papal activity and the tone of its poems and stories.

All our journals, however, devoted much space to literature. There was perhaps no place on earth where the common people took as much pleasure in some kind of literature as Wales, was one comment to the *Geninen*.[4] The very number of authors offering views on the nature of poetry and surveys of Welsh literary history, particularly in the less austere *Geninen*, testified to the self-image. Yet many articles were just compilations, focusing on traditional Welsh debates like free verse versus *cynghanedd* rather than categories of European literary criticism and operating in a narrow frame of reference where Tennyson, Browning and Wordsworth were the main non-Welsh authors adduced and an article on the German poet Heinrich Heine was a rarity. An exception were T. Gwynn Jones's frequent, knowledgeable, if largely descriptive essays on European writers to *Y Traethodydd*. Treatment of prose fiction appears fresher to a modern reader. Amid much ingrown mediocrity the voluminous literary material could throw up thoughtful and incisive contributions, like the sharp appraisal of Edward Foulkes in 1884, noting the changes in European society brought about since Rousseau and the French revolution: Wales's great literary heritage had lost its vigour and fallen behind other nations through political subjection, isolation and too exclusive a 'Judaic' concern with the religious and the moral.[5] All in all, both Welsh journals reflect a society deeply interested in its own history and traditions, an earnest society with an individualist orientation seen in the frequent articles on education and the advice to youth on public speaking and coming on in the world. It is a society of philosophical-religious rather than scientific bent. The myriad shifts of Calvinist religion's engagement with Darwin and the 'New Theology', often intellectually taxing, mixed with the problems of miners, agriculturalists and quarrymen in a shifting landscape which involved also early socialism and feminism to shape a potential Welsh outbreak from what Matthew Arnold called the philistinism of British nonconformity – though, lacking the English bourgeois commercial streak, it meant that Welsh youth's outlet would lie in teaching and radical politics.

What somewhat redeems the element of Welsh cultural narrowness is the sheer number of different article contributors, relating to the size and demotic traditions of the Nonconformist pastorate, domiciled in countless rural localities. This intense localism and grass roots engagement as a subaltern community found a voice was matched in the activity of the network of Slovene social and cultural associations. The Slovene case had a more centralising, urban structure, though, in the role of Ljubljana as fulcrum of a young intelligentsia and overarching bodies like the Slovene matica. This was the role intended for the Eisteddfod by its promoters in the 1860s and partially achieved thereafter but its peripatetic existence pointed to the absence of a natural centre. The constant shifting of place of publication of Welsh journals told a similar tale. The strongest institutionalisation in Wales was provided by the religious denominations. Slovene cultural life was not totally centralised of course: the St Hermagoras Society was based in Klagenfurt and the Young Slovene organ was founded in Styria, but its move to Ljubljana where it became the first Slovene daily paper indicates a line of movement. Slovene journals used a smaller range of contributors with more formal education than Welsh ones till the intermediate schools and the University of Wales evened the situation. Operating in the emulative framework of cultural nationalism, they gave a large place, besides the musical themes they shared with Wales, to theatre and the arts. The goal was to be the taste of Germanic central Europe's cultured middle class, shaped in the age of Goethe and Schiller, which would show them to be a *salonsfähig* people, fit for (good) society, instead of the peasants they were taken for. A Slovene professional company offered regular plays and opera alongside its German counterpart in a rebuilt Provincial Theatre from 1892. Its thousandth performance was announced in *Dom in svet* in 1900. They were exhaustively reviewed, with seventy-three operatic reports in *Ljubljanski zvon* alone, to which one of the contributors had also submitted forty-seven theatre reviews by 1909.[6] The programme was international, with the occasional Slovene play. Art started more slowly. The first exhibition of the newly formed Slovene artists' society was held in Ljubljana in 1900, with a speech by the mayor expressive of the Slovene self-image. It was of 'modest dimensions' for Slovenes lacked the resources of others, but with their energy and enthusiasm they would show they could handle the paint brush and chisel and hopefully progress to better things and a happier people.[7]

This 'little man' tone was characteristic. Whereas cultural isolation could lead to the hubristic and self-satisfied note struck occasionally in Wales, Slovenes lived in a multicultural environment where many smaller nations were striving to catch up with the norms of 'civilised countries'. Reminders were frequent of the important topics 'greatly neglected' by them and of their undeveloped public taste. *Dom in Svet* introduced a 'training' column for readers' poems in which the most frequent errors would be selected for comment; while aspirants should not be discouraged, those lacking skill should be clearly told to serve their language and nation in other ways.[8] The emulative climate made for the extensive reviewing of other periodicals' productions, in the first place Slovene but then Croat and Czech, less often Russian and Polish, more sporadically French, English and Italian. (*Y Traethodydd* reviewed extensively too: individual books rather than collective surveys.) The sophistication of criticism or readers should not be exaggerated. Discussion of Emile Zola in *Ljubljanski zvon* in the 1880s was mainly by university students, often relying on literary critics rather than the actual French texts. In 1913 *Dom in svet* was still writing that ballads were what the people liked best and commending appropriate choices that instilled moral-pedagogical principles.[9] But there was considerable improvement in this respect. *Ljubljanski zvon*'s discussants of Croatian, Czech, Russian and Polish literature were clearly in command of their subject and made demands of their readers. Thus Paul Bourget, whose latest play was reviewed at length in 1911, was 'the well-known literary critic, philosopher, novelist and dramatist'. Some pieces were a tour de force, like the art historian Vojislav Mole's sweeping contribution on art and nature ranging through all the great names of European art with addition of Slavic figures.[10] Still, an article on modern Czech authors noted how a friend of literature could find the human spirit everywhere in Prague's exhibitions and bookshops, only to return to Ljubljana and see nothing changed after two months.[11] Guest performances by Czech stars of Vienna opera were seen as a means to advance local 'taste'.[12]

Since the competition was with the German language and its unwelcome domination, Slovene efforts went to build up other models, particularly Slav. German literary culture was not regularly reviewed, though German was the default reference base for their knowledge of the wider world and German quotations were never translated. Also involved was a negative attitude to the German-speaking 'other' fostered by the language struggle, detectable in occasional allusions to German prejudice and pedantry. It was a scandal that there were monuments to the poetic German Jewish genius Heinrich Heine in Paris and New York but not in Germany, said the leading poet and critic Anton Aškerc, but 'we Slavs' need not bother about German opinions.[13] German opinions were taken up mainly in connection with the national poet France Prešeren, all foreign references to whom were avidly recorded by the Slovene press, particularly in the much celebrated centenary of his birth, when *Ljubljanski zvon* printed foreign languages translations of his work amid much commentary. Actually, the international fame of Prešeren owed much initially to German translations and the admirable tradition of world coverage and translation in leading German literary journals, not matched in the English-speaking world. Slovenes could comment tartly, though, that Austro-German neighbours in Vienna and Graz were less appreciative of Prešeren than Reich Germans.[14] The fact that the Austro-Germans were only a minor part of the German nation as a whole and that Britain was still culturally so dominant in the anglophone world, even over America, is a small detail in the higher degree of Slovene psychological independence from the historic masters, as compared with Welsh attitudes to the English.

This was a sensitive issue. Both peoples saw themselves as historical underdogs. In the Slovene case the intrusion of the dominant language into all dealings with authority had been diminished by the growing use of Slovene by officials. The first instalment of *Dom in svet*'s opening novel, set somewhat in the past, made the point that the Germanised postman character would now have had to know Slovene.[15] On the other hand, the awareness of the social advantage of knowing German, the cachet thereby attained or assumed comes out as a constant feature in Ivan Cankar's fiction, as a sign of Slovenes' second-class status and lack of national pride. The one view that found universal expression in Wales was that they had been oppressed. This was usually not stated with particular heat, but simply as a fact. That the English were an imperial people, arrogant in their dealings with others was a corollary, but it was often accompanied by respect for their practicality, independent-mindedness and persistence, qualities which the Welsh rarely claimed, especially the last named. They had gradually become 'accustomed to the yoke' so that deference to the Englishman had become 'second nature', explaining the paucity of Welsh people in positions of authority in Wales, wrote Morgan Lloyd, himself a high-ranking lawyer, in 1886 in the *Geninen*.[16] The Boer War brought out Welsh radical hackles in criticisms of British bullying but also passionate defence of the imperial cause.[17] A basic problem, thought the novelist, translator and editor E. Morgan Humphreys, was that the English, through ignorance of the language, knew nothing of the inner life of Wales whereas the Welsh on the whole understood the English. In particular, he objected to English views of Welsh mysticism and melancholy.[18] Worse than that others did not understand them was Peter Williams's fear that their very existence had slipped from the consciousness of Europe. Of humble stock, former policeman become Baptist minister, popular poet and eisteddfodwr, Peter Williams (Pedr Hir) was typical of the Welsh-language press's demotic intelligentsia, one of many with some acumen but unknown to posterity.[19] Fears like his account for the constant reference in Welsh periodicals to the alleged fame of the Mabinogi and to the handful of French and German Celticists.

Our small peoples wanted reassurance from others' view of them. But what did they think of themselves? Journals show more Welsh introspection than Slovene, partly perhaps because Slovenes were self-consciously Slavs among several Slav peoples in a similar situation which meant they could lean on common patterns of struggle and sentiment. Resentment of dominant nations and a determination to develop their own culture on Herderian lines characterised this underdog mentality. Surrounded by 'overbearing nations' (Germans, Italians and Magyars), Slovenes, the second conference of Slovene Catholics were told in 1900, were a suffering but 'very tenacious' member of the smaller Slav peoples. *Dom in svet*'s opening number had linked this tenacity with the development of Slovene literature whose story it promised to tell and what the future held for it.[20] That literature was the measure of every nation's vitality and embodiment of the national spirit was a view echoed in the liberal *Ljubljanski zvon*.[21] The denationalising impact of long German influence should provoke not just complaint, but active engagement with the language of Serbs and Croats which Slovenes knew too little. The age of the national revival and its cultural epigones were greatly to the forefront. A typical example would be the tribute to the musicologist and romantic composer, Benjamin Ipavec (1829–1908): after a wholly German education in German-dominated Styria he had been 'awoken' to his nationality in 1848 to inspire the rebirth of the 'Slovene song', now at the 'excellent level of perfection on which we find ourselves today'.[22]

Welsh journals' introspection owed something to the relative weakness of an underlying driving narrative of cultural and linguistic revival. In a country where a mild Celticism was no equivalent to evocative Slavdom the failure to concert a coherent line on the Welsh language in the 1860s and earlier now took its toll. Unfocused national feeling produced a variegated and individualist discussion, ranging from idealised pictures of Welsh nature simple, pure and eloquent in the native cottage and conventional invocations of the language 'as alive as ever', to sweeping generalisations about national character, heredity and environment, and Welsh racial stock surviving in foreign cities to disprove the English positivist thinker Buckle. Characterisations of unworldly simplicity were given an interesting twist by William Jones, MP for Anglesey, in his claim nonetheless that the Welsh came closest of the Celts to showing some ability to accommodate to reality, echoing the view of the Breton-born French writer Ernest Renan that Welsh organising power made them the Celtic Prussians. Racial purity was denied in O. M. Edwards's stress of mixed Welsh origins, yet Welsh tenacity in maintaining their identity basically unchanged over hostile centuries was a belief that brought common pride and consolation. Among contributions which focused most analytically on criteria of nationhood, Pedr Hir's public lecture of 1894 remains particularly impressive for its systematic coverage of the concept in medieval and in modern Wales, but his cry that loss of language presaged loss of literature and nationality was empty without a concerted strategy.[23] Most writers were content just to cite language and literature to assert Wales's claim.

The driving narrative in nineteenth-century Wales had come from the effort to give institutional body to the inheritance from the religious revival. As that proceeded and a sense of discrimination slackened a pervasive but vague preoccupation with the identity which had developed can be felt in articles asking if Welsh literature was advancing or declining, whether the Eisteddfod was help or hindrance to Welsh culture, what the changing balance sensed between the Welsh and English language signified. This was undercut in the period leading up to Cymru Fydd by optimism of a new Welsh dawn, followed by a fall off, then some revival of Welsh identity themes. The intermittent discourse lacked wider intellectual underpinning but largely agreed in positing a distinctive spiritual inheritance almost as an ethnic trait in the racialising terminology of the times. It is not impressive, though scholarly study of nationality Europe-wide was still surprisingly undeveloped in an age of rising national consciousness. It is bizarre, in view of its subtitle, that *Y Geninen*'s opening number should include an article by the Wesleyan minister Kilsby Jones, arguing that the death of Welsh would be an advantage to Wales. The laws of Providence determined its fate and their drift was plain from the changes in general lifestyle brought about by the 'revolutionary influence of the Englishman' and his railways; the monoglot Welshman faced a choice between continued poverty and the lucrative careers through business and the pen achieved by Welshmen whom Kilsby exampled. Echoing Vraz's warning to Prešeren, he contrasted the one million Welsh with the seventy million English speakers.[24] The appeal to materialism, in glaring contrast to vaunted Welsh spirituality, was repeated less blatantly by another leading Wesleyan minister. Lauding the gems of Welsh poetry, Herber Evans stated that the tide was coming in and the cosy isolation in which such things had flourished was no more. How could the most brilliant work in Welsh win the fame and rewards of fellow Welshman Sir Lewis Morris's English epic 'Hades'? The Welsh should build chapels for English incomers; Cymru Fydd could save Britain from sin, dart boards and playhouses.[25] The Messianic role accorded the Welsh in Britain's story was to become a familiar trope, echoed later by socialist leaders.

The language issue remained one of the *Geninen*'s major preoccupations. Arguments changed little, but pro-Welsh pieces, stressing the language's national role, gained the upper hand. The shift of attention from the monoglot Welsh to alleged employment advantages of bilingual Welshmen implicitly acknowledged part of Kilsby's argument.

Correspondents reflected their own circumstances in a highly diverse linguistic landscape, with little sense of an overall perspective. A *Traethodydd* correspondent, noting that some said many Welsh people were losing the language, nonchalantly recommended them, 'if there be any such', a patriotic English-language journal, 'Young Wales'.[26] The only sign of a general view of the matter was the assumption that Welsh would benefit from being taught in the schools. Yet while the pedagogical case for mother-tongue primary education was increasingly made,[27] the extensive discussion of secondary education in the 1900s, in *Y Traethodydd* particularly, said little on language in this sphere. In a 1907 article setting out a would-be patriotic Welsh syllabus it merited just one sentence.[28] Articles by two outsiders, Englishmen acquainted with and sympathetic to Welsh, came closest to objective overview. Southall judged that Welsh in existing circumstances had no long-term prospects; Darlington that monolingualism was the natural course for a society. Yet the latter stressed the powerful force of national consciousness on Welsh's side and Southall called for fair play.[29] A thoughtful Welshman, the writer Watcyn Wyn, faced with prophecies of language death, or revival, said in 1893 he could not tell. He was willing for Welsh to go, but before its time, anticipating Southall, would be 'unfair'.[30] Years down to 1914 only made plainer that Welsh's fate depended not on automatic renewal through the generations but mental factors, Darlington's national consciousness, and willed structural adjustments, as in education. Occasional recognition that Wales now had two languages marked a significant shift in perceptions.[31]

It is telling that in the discussions of nationhood in *Y Traethodydd* and *Y Geninen* Welsh religion is rarely invoked as the primary, formative factor, though its role as a source of national values is ubiquitous. This is important. It meant that in a scale of values religion consciously ranked higher than language or nationality for most nineteenth-century Welsh people. This could occur in Slovenia too for certain religious figures. But for most Slovene Catholics such a distinction or ranking between faith and language was an issue below the radar. The two went together. The fact that, as posited above, neither language nor religion could stand for the full force of national identity in Wales is a key weakness for that identity in this study. The problem with language has been shown; now religion comes on the agenda. Since it affected Slovenian identity too, in the Liberal-Catholic split, the religious theme deserves a section to itself. For if modernity posed a language issue for minor cultures, an issue the

Slovenes had faced head on, it also posed a problem of religion for all cultures: how were entrenched religious belief systems to accommodate with post-Enlightenment values and their inherent sceptical potential?

RELIGION AND IDENTITY IN WALES AND SLOVENIA PRE-1914

Religion, particularly Nonconformist religion, served as a surrogate nationality for many in Victorian and Edwardian Wales. At the gateway to the twentieth century, the lyric poet Eliseus Williams (Eifion Wyn) urged his people to respond to its Poet and its Teacher in song and the community of nations. But above all he urged it to respond to its Prophet: 'Cling, my country, like a dear disciple, another century to the Cross.'[32] Indeed, Wales seemed fertile ground for the religious-minded. In 1905, in addition to regular services in 6,072 church buildings served by 6,038 clergy and a host of ancillary society meetings during the week, some 40 per cent of its population attended Sunday schools, studying books of the Bible with the aid of 70,000 Sunday school teachers and course manuals published each year by the separate denominations.[33] Popular religiosity was shared by the educated laity. The evident puzzlement of a *Traethodydd* writer at the immunity of the astronomer Isaac Roberts DSc from this trait, indeed mere indifference, is telling.[34] A magisterial study of the huge denominational publication output by Professor R. Tudur Jones has seen in this period, however, signs of spiritual decay to come. The ambitious, over-academic Sunday school study programmes, the element of centralisation, the fact that the chapels had to make good the absence of Welsh cultural themes in public institutions: all this risked diverting what had been a demotic religious movement of the common people towards wider cultural ends, increasing the gap between ministers and elders and their flock. This is to leave aside the disquiet that the 'Higher Criticism' of Biblical texts now imparted to a wider audience could arouse in learners set in their ways. It is possible to see analogies with Carl Schorske's famous analysis of the German Social Democratic movement at the same time, when the weakness of German liberalism in the Kaiser's only half-democratic Reich willy-nilly turned working-class institutions into instruments for inculcating notions of civil society, doing the democrats' work for them, and losing sight of their outwardly massive movement's socialist goals.[35] In Wales, popular reaction to these trends was part of the background to the great outpouring of the greatest and last of the Welsh religious revivals in 1904–5 when for eighteen months congregations were successively drawn into nightly emotional services of sermons, hymn singing and extempore prayer, which aroused international attention, like Henri Bois's French monograph on the subject. The young leader, a former miner and a candidate for the ministry, was a man of unusual religious sensibility who had had visions which he believed to be a direct answer to his prayers for revival; he died forty-six years after his extraordinary experience without ever accommodating himself to it or to normal life. Some eighty thousand members were added to the three main denominations during the revival, or 18 per cent, but many were not retained, only one-quarter in Glamorgan and Monmouthshire in the weakest case. This produced some deflation. Nonetheless, overall membership in 1912 was 10 per cent higher than in 1903.[36]

A widely shared interpretation is that it was a protest of ordinary workers, particularly but not exclusively Welsh speaking, alienated in a time of rapid social and cultural change. Tudur Jones adds his own judgement that the shift involved the abandonment of the Calvinist doctrine of the Methodist revival for an accommodation with contemporary trends like evolutionism and liberal progress theories. He singles out particularly the Methodist theologian David Adams who blurred the distinction between the natural and supernatural by seeing both nature and man as developing towards perfection, on the pattern of Christ himself. What Jones shows is the extent to which Welsh theologians were reacting against the Calvinism of their predecessors. He himself, a sharp critic of their liberal approach, acknowledges the efforts that were made to shape a theology that could help alleviate the felt problem of declining fervour behind the impressive edifice. The non-specialist is struck by the number of scholars who wrote weightily in Welsh in this field. There is room only for some mentions here. One, John Gwili Jenkins (Gwili), who studied in Bangor and Oxford, wrote most of his major theological works after the First World War and is probably best remembered as a representative of the genre of poet-preacher in the Welsh-speaking world. But he testifies to the optimism which underlay the attempts to loosen up Welsh religion and culture in the spirit of Cymru Fydd, about the 'dawn of the unprecedented awakening which is stirring all circles of Welsh life at the start of the twentieth century', about opening Welsh eyes to 'the poetry of the world', about the hope for a Welsh 'poet of the Awakening'. 'The world is coming to Wales; the point is, is Wales going to the World?'[37] Gwili's journalism attacked hypocrisy and limited vision in the chapels, and neglect of recent Bible studies.[38] One of his early articles was entitled. 'Where has Hell gone?' His own reviews were mainly of English books. Thomas Rees (1869–1926) is another interesting figure. Of Pembrokeshire peasant background, he worked eleven years as farm labourer, then miner – a reminder that most ministers still lived hard lives – before study in Cardiff, London and Oxford. Rees's conviction was that Protestantism had not wholly freed itself from the, for him, baleful influence of a Catholic divinity based on Greek philosophical abstractions, distancing the priest from the common believer.[39] He was part, therefore, of the powerful movement emphasising the manhood of Christ (the God-Man). There is a pathos in his story. A long-term TB sufferer, he persisted in overworking to complete the comprehensive Welsh-language Biblical Dictionary he edited, a massive undertaking entailing 1,400 letters from him to the multiple contributors. The sub-editors returned the final set of corrected proofs to the press on the day of his death.[40] The irony is that by that time the vogue for such work was passing.

This was a significant shift for a country which had prided itself, somewhat vaingloriously, on its religious tradition. Had not Owen Thomas, the leader of Liverpool Methodism, boasted that the sustained standing and intellectual influence of the Welsh pulpit for its people exceeded anything known in the history of the Christian Church?[41] A desire of the pre-war years was for a systematic theology which would not be derivative but distinctively Welsh. D. Miall Edwards was just beginning his life's work on behalf of a self-consciously modern theology with his *Crefydd a Bywyd* (Religion and Life, 1915), influenced by Henri Bergson's philosophy and taking up issues of nationality and the social question. Its theological liberalism has incurred the censure of R. Tudur Jones's Barthian rigour and is now judged to be as dated as Cynddylan Jones's multi-volume *Cysondeb y Ffydd* (The Consistency of the Faith, 1905–11), a lucid presentation of traditional Calvinism. Balancing divine love with divine justice, so that atonement for man's sin retained its central role, Cynddylan Jones's work reflected a self-confidence no longer solid even when it was published. The twentieth century was only to deepen problems of presenting the Christian faith. The memoirs of an unremarkable Congregational minister, W. Glasnant Jones (Glasnant, 1879–1951) give a helpful picture of how things appeared at the grass roots below the level of the academic theologian or the eminent preacher.[42] Glasnant was one of eleven children of an Aman valley family who went down the pit at eleven years of age, earning 1/6d a week. Following four moves due to pit closures, he attended the popular post primary school of the poet-preacher Watkyn Wynn and after briefly considering becoming a policeman accepted a call from a local chapel, one of six pastorates in his career, all of which paid him a pittance. Glasnant steered clear of theological controversy in his ministry but took a role in local issues for the public good. His life experience – as a miner he had once seen a hundred dead bodies on a pit head after an accident – made him fairly radical politically, but he opposed compulsory trade union membership. He was on the side of the Zulus, then the Boers in their conflicts with the British Empire, and regretted that Lloyd George and Tom Ellis, the hero of his youth, had been as he saw it seduced by imperialism. In all the places he served in he noted the language situation carefully but though a 'red-blooded Welshman' took one English-language cause, in Monmouthshire, and after encountering bilingualism in Maesteg foresaw this as the way of the future.[43] His impression was of a decline in religious commitment year by year before the 1905 revival and a return to the pubs afterwards, though chapel attendance remained good on the whole. Glasnant's recollections are from an old man in a different age, but it can safely be said that they fit a picture of a movement as much doubtful as dynamic by 1914.

This is an impression gained from the two Welsh periodicals given emphasis here too. Others with fresher perspectives will be mentioned below but general circulation figures for Welsh periodicals where available show gentle decline: for example: *Y Faner* from sales of 15–16,000 in the late 1870s to 13,000 in 1914, *Cymru'r Plant* (The Children's Wales) from 11,250 to 9,850 (1898–1910), and the penny *Almanac y Miloedd* from 60,000 (1886) to 33,000 (1905).[44] *Y Traethodydd* shrank from a regular 500 pages to 400 pages annually by 1913, where *Ljubljanski zvon* often exceeded 700. If *Y Traethodydd* in that year contained an ecstatic hymn to Mazzini and his inspiration for a Wales whose blood was stirring more than ever before,[45] *Y Geninen* brought pieces in different vein. Prewar titles like 'Signs of the Times', 'Lack of National Unity' and 'Where Stands Wales?' bespoke anxieties. Were all those educated in the new secondary schools and colleges sound on religion? Did not loss of language bring loss of nationality and literature? Welsh consciousness, which had narrowed its span by limiting the range of its language, was further limited by the religious framework which now inhibited its response to a changing world.

The tension between religion and modern trends showed up in the Slovene situation too. The background of assertive political Catholicism has already been touched on. Here more of the intellectual dimension may be sketched in. In 1896 the Leon Society was founded in Ljubljana. Named after the long-lived Pope Leo XXIII (1878–1903) it echoed his wish to engage with modern trends condemned in his predecessor Pius IX's notorious Syllabus of Errors. Its periodicals *Katoliški Obzornik* (The Catholic Observer, 1897–1905), succeeded by the programmatically named *Čas* (Time, 1906–40) lacked Leo's emollience, however. The engagement was to be a comprehensive confutation of 'free thought' over the whole range of intellectual enquiry, the natural science which was its 'fortress', the revisionist history which spoke of myth and legend, the literature and art preoccupied with the morbid and perverse rather than the beautiful, the philosophy of nihilism rather than the positive and rational.[46] The key to this was the 'neo-Thomist' creed of the Catholic revival, the reaffirmation of the philosophy of St Thomas Aquinas (1225–74) and its famous reconciliation of reason (Aristotle) and revelation (the Bible). For the leading figure behind the Leon Society, the theology professor Ales Ušeničnik, there could be no culture war of science versus religion, such as he saw being pushed by 'free thought', because contradiction between the two was impossible: all truth emanated from God. Ušeničnik was primarily a philosopher but an omnivorous and well-read intellectual whose long career was inspired by this one conviction tirelessly reiterated in his writing and teaching: 'If the glorious doctrine (dogmatika) of Catholic Christianity is not true I deny all truth', as he once wrote.[47]

Ušeničnik was therefore a dogmatist in the most literal meaning of the word. His assurance is reminiscent of Cynddylan Jones's but more embattled. The context is different. Ušeničnik worked in the framework of the international Catholic Church, whose wide-ranging institutions he constantly refers to but which felt itself under heavy attack from dominant intellectual currents of the age, even in little Slovenia. This was not a matter of the vague unease of Nonconformist Wales but of overt confrontation where the 'satanic' influences on university youth were explicitly called out in *Katoliški Obzornik*'s opening number. The sense of the danger to the faith was greater than in Wales where it could still bask, if complacently, in a glow of public esteem beyond the merely popular level. But the historic strength of the Catholic Church made its relative downgrading in the eyes of the educated harder to bear. *Katoliški Obzornik* asserted itself on the social question, placing itself between the twin errors of socialism and capitalism in line with Leo XIII's innovative position; its opening number carried a detailed article on problems of housing. Catholicism thus had an authoritative stance on social issues which Welsh Nonconformity lacked. Its range was wider than the theological matters debated by Cynddylan Jones; sociology was a frequent term in its literature, as also the national question, issues which awaited the work of Dr Miall Edwards for systematic treatment in Wales. We have seen this in the life of Evangelist Krek who remains a more attractive figure to outsiders than Ušeničnik. Krek shared the latter's critique of liberalism and socialism but his approach had a more human touch. In his policies designed to thwart socialist 'materialism' he advocated as watchword not the 'dogmatika' so beloved of Ušeničnik but 'Jesus Christ'.[48] This has echoes across the Catholic–Protestant divide of Welsh theologians' concern in this period to draw out the God-Man aspect of the Trinity.

Ušeničnik's programmatic introduction to *Čas* in 1906 moderated his tone somewhat, stressing the material benefits brought by modernity, while identifying it as a time of chaos and transition, which he said aroused doubts even in liberal and Protestant circles.[49] It should be remembered how radically tastes evolved in the *fin de siècle*, with the popularity of Nietzschean nihilism and the sexuality of Egon Schiele and Aubrey Beardsley. Ušeničnik could exploit too the limitations of scientific knowledge of the time: decrying those who held the dating of the world to 4004 BC against the Church (it was never official doctrine) he cited scientists' differing estimates, perceiving a tendency to reduce it, to a mere 15,000 years in one case, not so far from the much-impugned date – a case of having his scientific/religious cake and eating it![50] Another piquant aspect of the debate on values is that Evgen Lampe's attack on *fin de siècle* literature concentrated on liberals' indulgence of the dangerously subversive poetry of the Italian socialist Anna Negri, splendidly translated by T. Gwynn Jones. Lampe, editor of *Dom in svet*, plainly thought she should have stuck to her more appropriate female role as schoolteacher.[51] A weightier object of Lampe's ire was that on the tercentenary of the burning at the stake for heresy of the famous philosopher Giordano Bruno, the editor of the liberal *Ljubljanski zvon* had praised him as a martyr for freedom of thought. Lampe denounced Bruno as flawed thinker, hypocrite and libertine; what was needed was not free thinking but right thinking, unbound except by the eternal law of God. Where in the free-thinking Lampe denounced was the greatest of all freedoms, that of small nations to exist and flourish?[52]

Religion and language were the two biggest issues for small nineteenth-century ethnicities in negotiating their way towards modern nationhood. Both Wales and Slovenia developed a lively cultural and literary discourse in the mother tongue in a way that some other small peoples, like the Bretons, did not. Unlike the Slovenes, however, the Welsh did not really try to assert the equality of their language in the public sphere. This placed a weight on religion as an identity-bearing marker which was put under potential strain when religious commitment began to weaken. It should not be exaggerated at this time, however. The real crisis of faith in Wales did not come till later, after the Second World War. The liberal-Catholic split was more serious for Slovene political unity before 1914 than the Nonconformist-Anglican division in Wales. The very decline of traditional Calvinism as implicitly liberal theology developed, noted by R. Tudur Jones, made an accommodation with modern notions easier and more widespread, enabling Welsh leaders to retain a sense of achievement. There was no intransigent Ušeničnik, who lived long enough to be divested of his university chair by the communists. Important to note, of course, is that the Slovene split was political; both sides were committed to the Slovene national idea and the national language. Welsh nationhood, because of the equivocation on language, was less firmly rooted. The development of the language divergence has been a central theme of this book and the present chapter has continued to underscore it. By 1914, the Welsh periodicals which have been highlighted were to this writer clearly less impressive as reflections of the full range of modern discourse than their Slovene equivalents. But this is not the last word of what should be said. The Welsh scene was changing in the generation before 1914 in ways which disrupt the narrative as it has so far been shaped. Wales was in one important respect becoming more similar to the Slovene lands and in another, still more fundamental one, increasingly different. The similarity is that Welsh language culture was beginning to move closer to the Habsburg small nation model represented by Slovenia. The difference is that an English-speaking Wales was emerging in the populous industrial and commercial areas which would eventually marginalise Welsh-speaking Wales altogether.

LANGUAGE AND LITERATURE

For a Welsh historian of the Habsburg Monarchy somewhere in the 1880s developments in Wales became more conducive to the kind of cultural nationalism which had arisen in central-eastern Europe. Something of the intellectual infrastructure which had fed the national 'turn' in the Habsburg Monarchy half a century earlier was in process of creation in the educational movement and the influence of a 'neo-Hegelian' idealism associated in Britain with the philosopher T. H. Green. The Hegelian reference deserves a gloss. Hegel's idealism, the notion of an 'absolute spirit' moving through history to a final consummation, differed from both the conventional religion and the fact-based 'positivism' of the mid-Victorian age, opening a way for evolutionary theories of progress and a vaguer, less dogmatic spiritual climate. The Oxford graduates Tom Ellis and O. M. Edwards and the celebrated Glasgow philosophy professor Henry Jones reflect this tendency and much of the intellectual background to Cymru Fydd. In this period concern for the Welsh language, its purification and literary renewal, recall earlier trends elsewhere.

We have seen this process in operation in the Slovene lands, in the role of the major linguist Jernej Kopitar, a scholar integrated into the cultural German world which led language studies in nineteenth-century Europe. A second Slovene giant in this field was Franc (Franz) Miklošič (1813–91), a Styrian village boy, who after doctorates in Graz and Vienna followed Kopitar as court librarian and censor for non-German languages in the empire and occupied its first chair of Slavic studies from 1849 till 1886. Miklošič pursued studies in many languages great and small, including Albanian and Romani, giving them equal status as research fields, and maintaining a clear Slovene identity while publishing in German. He had chaired the 1848 society which drafted the first programme for a united Slovenia but thereafter confined himself to academia, becoming rector of Vienna University in 1854–5 and ennobled member of the Austrian Parliament's upper house. The expansion of vocabulary required to justify and then implement the public use of Slovene produced a figure like Matej Cigale (1819–89), of village birth, educated in Graz and Vienna universities and employed in the Ministry of Justice on Bleiweis's recommendation, where he remained till his death responsible for the creation of Slovene legal terminology and by extension Slovene technical terminology in general. It was Cigale who completed the first major printed German-Slovene dictionary for publication in 1860, together with a supplement on Slovene scientific vocabulary for secondary school use. The work had been in gestation for fifty years, with financial support from the bishop of Ljubljana. Cigale later produced a landmark German-Slovene terminological dictionary (1880) which devised vocabulary for twenty-four branches of public and scholarly enquiry. The fact that a monument was erected to him in his native place shortly after his death, not dissimilar to that in Cilmeri to Llywelyn ap Gruffydd nearly seven centuries after his, testifies to the importance of linguistic matters in the Slovene national movement: the memorial carries a statement by Cigale that nationality is as important to a people as air to a living creature. In all, one-third of modern Slovene vocabulary has been constructed on the basis of sister Slavic tongues.[53]

By the end of the century language concern was operating in Wales too on several fronts, the place of Welsh in the schools, overhaul of the language itself and literary renewal. The first sign was the foundation of the Society for Utilising the Welsh Language in 1885. Comparatively, however, we should stress its extreme timidity. Its founder denied any intention to perpetuate the Welsh language, emphasising the use of Welsh in schools as a more effective way of teaching English as a means for worldly advancement. Welsh should be the second language in Welsh schools. Yet his references to the 'heavy anglicising yoke we have put about our neck' and the 'violence and oppression' Welsh people 'had ignored, or suffered, to our shame' suggested an emotional drive. It seems that the evidence for a ready acquisition of Welsh by English miners which he adduced had changed D. I. Davies's previous negative attitude to his mother tongue, leading him to hope that the greater employment of bilingual officials and modicum of school Welsh he called for would suffice to create a stable diglossia in industrial Wales and the 'three million bilingual Welshmen' of his dreams.[54] The report of the Cross Commission on Education in 1888, after his early death, granted his modest demands. The precedent was set for Welsh patriots' pressure for bilingualism, different from the pattern of predominantly unilingual Slovene primary education which had emerged first in Carniola. In the Cross Commission Henry Jones argued explicitly for bilingualism, while stating that 80 per cent of rural Welsh people did not need English in their daily lives, surprising the chairman whose questions implied a Slovene model.[55]

Next came the championship of language reform associated with John Morris Jones and the Dafydd ap Gwilym Society of Welsh students at

Oxford founded in 1886, where Nonconformists had only achieved fully equal rights fifteen years before. A mathematics student, Jones switched to Celtic studies under the inspiration of John Rhys, first holder of the recently established Celtic chair of Celtic there and Cardiganshire farm worker's son who had attracted patronage. Rhys became Wales's greatest modern philologist and a knight but retained his peasant persona; as master of Jesus College he is reputed to have told students who complained at the lack of baths, 'but gentlemen, the term only lasts eight weeks'. However, his philological interests, honed in Germany and France, did not change his scepticism about his mother tongue's future. He used his knowledge of its history, though, to propose improvements in its spelling, which was Morris Jones's first concern before he widened his interest to a general cleansing of Welsh from the influence of English and Owen Pughe's eccentricities. Welsh writers should return to the classics of Welsh prose and verse to rescue the natural music of the language; the 'new poetry' of the latter nineteenth century with its vogue for philosophising abstraction should yield to the grace of the lyric. Morris Jones's unsparing combativeness in this pursuit of higher standards, in writing and criticism, engaged him in frequent journalistic controversy. The tension between the new and the old in Welsh cultural life recurred in the enmity of eisteddfodic traditionalists towards the new academic spokesmen and orthographical changes, though Morris-Jones's own frequent adjudications for the chair competition of the National Eisteddfod contributed to his growing reputation as 'Teacher of the Nation'. The founding of *Y Beirniad* (The Critic, 1911–20) under University of Wales auspices gave him as its editor an additional platform; like Slovene literary journals, it aimed to publish the best new work from the leading writers. His *Welsh Grammar* (1913), *Cerdd Dafod* (on Welsh prosody, 1925) and the definitive Welsh orthography (1928) are his main memorials.

A more emollient figure, Owen Morgan Edwards (1858–1922), became the most universally popular representative of the new cultural affirmation. From a Merionethshire village, Aberystwyth, Glasgow and Oxford educated, he exemplified its values in the graceful style of his travelogues in Europe and throughout Wales where he depicted the homes of famous Welsh people, tracing the lineage of the *gwerin* as the cultured common people he wished to see it. As an Oxford history don – he had won all three main history prizes there as a student – he founded and edited a stream of periodicals and publications free from the fustiness of much Nonconformist journalism, including a long series of cheap editions of Welsh classics, before becoming chief inspector in the new Welsh department of the Board of Education (1907). There he had considerable freedom to implement a child-centred curriculum, rooting pupils in their own environment and, in Welsh-speaking areas, their language. Welsh was also to be taught, as far as practicable, in English-speaking areas and Welsh history and geography everywhere. The English historian and one-time minister of education Herbert Fisher described Edwards as a man of genius who displayed the innate melancholy of an aggrieved people.[56] No doubt he did not achieve all he might have hoped. His authority was limited by the Welsh Joint Education Committee set up under the 1889 Intermediate Education Act, which did not share his imagination and stood for an exam-orientated curriculum, anglicising in its effect, of which he disapproved. Not interested in politics, he accepted to follow Tom Ellis as Liberal MP for Merioneth on the latter's death but resigned within a year. His romantic view of his people is less in tune with modern taste than in his own lifetime but fits in well with what we have seen of 'cultural workers' in the Slovenian Habsburg context. The present writer encountered the image he still has for many Welsh speakers in the anecdote of a conference in a Cardiff meeting in the 1960s: asking as a small child in school one day why his teacher was crying, he had never forgotten her answer: 'The greatest friend of the children of Wales is dead'. O. M. Edwards also launched an English-language journal *Wales*, to correspond with his very successful *Cymru*. He recognised that nation and language were no longer coterminous but defined Wales as a land of mountains and through its history, drawing strength through admixture. *Wales* did not meet up to his hopes.

Making a country's language more flexible and expressive is an essential step in shaping a 'literary language'. The link between literature and national consciousness is a universal story. The Old Testament is the literature of the Jewish people with the psalms of David at its heart; the Homerian epics were central in the education of ancient Greeks, and Virgil's Aeneid was essentially an attempt to provide a similar pedigree for imperial Rome. Prešeren's role at a crucial time in Slovene national development is plain, and we have seen that the Welsh too rated their literature highly. As the Wesleyan minister T. J. Pritchard put it in 1901, its literature was 'the mirror image of a nation's character ... the diary of its self-conscious life as a nation'.[57] To look at what Slovene and Welsh writers were producing in the pre-1914 period should be more, therefore, than a conventional nod to a few names.

Preconditions for small nations' literary development go beyond an effective literary language. A literate public sufficient for a market at sustainable prices, adequate publishing outlets and a body of competent editors and critics are also hard to meet requirements, above all an ability to strike a balance between the needs of small readerships at different levels of taste and sophistication. Small nation publishing is always a minor miracle. If it is objected that too much may be made of a published 'literature' in humble societies where the great majority's lives were orientated to basic needs, it should be remembered that a fundamental impulse behind the national 'revivals' of groups like the Slovenes and Welsh was a wish to give a voice to the previously voiceless, from whose ranks most of their leaders came. Combining horizons expanded by education with the popular culture and sense of self all communities inherit was to seek to fuse notions of high and low culture which Gellner has usefully but too schematically separated. The collection of 'folklore' was at the heart of the romantic movement which along with Enlightenment rationalism shaped the modern mind in peoples small and large. Under a host of labels like English 'by-gones', Welsh 'hynafiaethau' (records of things past) and Slavic 'starine' the columns of the new weeklies and monthlies were filled with 'lore' alongside original poems and tales and snippets of information from the classics, politics and scientific discoveries. It is this wider context which gives overblown abstractions like Pritchard's words above their genuine content.

Much was achieved for our two literatures in tackling the difficulties listed above, creating an ample framework for writers to debate and an audience to respond. But it is also clear that developments went further in the Slovene lands, aided by examples from the polyglot Habsburg realm and the cultural climate of emulative Slav nationalism. Wales had older literary traditions, in some ways a two-edged sword, and an environment politically more benign but culturally less so. The Welsh educational movement helped create a generation closer in spirit to the young patriots of central and eastern Europe, however, if still open to a narrower range of European influences. This was the result of the mid-century utilitarianism which went with the emphasis on the learning of English, but also owed something to Welsh religious predilections and lack of a cultural centre. Translation was a particular sphere where Slovenes were to the fore. *Uncle*

Tom's Cabin was twice translated into both languages. Thereafter, translation remained a more common feature of Slovene literary life, in various genres: thus, Edgar Allan Poe (1905), Arthur Conan Doyle (1906), Jonathan Swift (1884: only Lilliput), Robert Louis Stevenson, Marryot, Brett Hart, Fennimore Cooper all appeared before 1914, together with the leading writer of adventure stories in German, Karl May.[58] The Slovenska matica and the Saint Hermagoras Society both published several books a year for general readerships and their large membership enabled publication at affordable cost, with up to 50,000 copies of some titles being printed. The latter society had distributed fifteen million copies of its books.[59] The subscribers to the Saint Hermagoras society rose from rose from 1,116 in about 1860 to 78,103 in 1900, one-quarter of whom were peasants and one-quarter artisans, showing the characteristically high role of this social group in nineteenth-century patriotic movements. All told, some 60 per cent of book club reading available was of native and 30 per cent of foreign origin, with the largest number of readers being between twenty and thirty years of age.[60] The extensive provision for translation of popular fiction marks a significant difference from Wales. With the growth of bilingualism it seems likely that Welsh youth in particular explored this realm in English but Welsh publishers were keenly aware commercially of the popularity of religious material. W. J. Gruffydd, a good example of the emerging Nonconformist intelligentsia, tells of his monoglot grandfather's love of theological reading, not merely pietistic, and his lifelong ambitions, to learn English and to put his religious knowledge to the test. He never achieved the first but, on his retirement, indulged himself with a preaching tour round his native county. Acknowledging that his efforts in no way matched his preacher heroes and roused no stir, he returned home nonetheless a happy and contented man.[61]

However, Welsh publishing achieved a striking success early in this period in the novels of the Flintshire tailor Daniel Owen (1836–95). This pious Methodist bachelor and lay preacher with only primary education, voluminous writer for the press in both languages, lifelong enthusiast for the books he read with his tailor associates in his border town, produced work emblematic of the distinctive Welsh Nonconformist society to which he belonged. Serialised in a denominational journal, it achieved instant fame for the variety and faithfulness of its characters and the subtlety of the author's delineation as that most interesting of observers, the critic from the inside. Owen's style lacked the new sensitivity to language which was about to be born; he was aloof from Cymru Rydd enthusiasms and his plots suffered from the looseness of serialisation, but his historical sense of his society, sly humour and breadth of coverage of a small milieu made him still the most successful of Welsh language novelists. The three leading books depict in turn the clash of old and new values in the Mold strike of 1869 (Owen's father and two brothers were miners who died in an accident, like the idealistic Bob who disconcerts his monoglot mother with his radical 'English books'); a consummate case of hypocrisy of a chapel elder; and the ending of the patriarchal age of squire and parson with the appearance of a charismatic yet unsettling young Methodist preacher. Two of them also touch on emigration to America. They continued to sell widely generations after Owen's death. A fair number of novels were produced in Welsh from the first attempt in 1830, often reprinted in book form after journal serialisation. Like Owen, if less skilfully, much of this engaged earnestly with issues discussed, of religion, teetotalism and the social and personal relations involved in the clash of a declining state Church and its Nonconformist challengers. In this period the patriotic aspirations of Cymru Fydd also featured, perhaps even more in women's writing than men's. O. M. Edwards noted the ascent of women authors, several of whom published in his periodicals but also in those of the formidable Cranogwen (Sarah Jane Rees, 1839–1916). Cranogwen, prize-winning poet, preacher, lecturer and teacher, particularly of seamanship which she had learnt from her sailor father, edited two journals in which men contributed as little as women had in Ieuan Gwynedd's pioneer *Y Gymraes* ('The Welshwoman') in 1850. In her deep piety and teetotalism she was more conventional. The novels of Gwyneth Vaughan, the Patagonian Eluned Morgan (born on the ship to the colony) and Moelona (Elizabeth Mary Jones) among others show patriotic and feminist traits. Women's participation in patriotic movements is a wider phenomenon, to be seen also in Slovenia and the Habsburg Monarchy as a whole. Because of the Welsh Intermediate Education Act the proportion of girls in secondary schools rose from just over one-third to equality between 1881 and the end of the century, and there were proportionally more professional women in Wales than in England instead of one-half, as fifty years before.[62]

Stage presentation of Owen's first novel, Rhys Lewis, played a role, too, in the sudden expansion of a Welsh drama movement in the 1880s and 1890s, though it went back decades earlier. Several score amateur societies sprang up in small places all over Wales, in slate-quarrying and coal-mining townships and rural villages. First featuring Welsh historical plays in Shakespearian vein, it moved steadily towards the contemporary social scene – partly by the expense of the costumes, scenery and many characters involved! – but found it difficult to advance beyond stock types of bullying Scottish land agents lusting after Welsh peasant daughters. This was another field where Welsh organisation lagged behind Slovene. Improvement in acting standards was a problem for both, solving which was part of the brief of the Ljubljana Dramatic Society founded in 1879 and a preoccupation of Beriah Gwynfe Evans, an early Welsh pioneer. Instability of the local societies was frequent. Ioan Williams sees the movement's motivation as primarily a grass roots' desire for self-expression stemming from the atmosphere of Cymru Fydd and a population whose language and culture were ignored in official life. The position of the chapels was equivocal. Many Nonconformists were sympathetic but the drama movement bore in it secularist frames of reference which hollowed out traditional Calvinism. Williams thus has some understanding for the notorious Baptist condemnation of the theatre movement occasioned by a Rhys Lewis adaptation in 1887.[63] The adaptation in fact omitted the confrontation of Bob and his mother's positions, which was at the heart of the novel and concentrated on the humorous characters. The new Welsh drama went well beyond this, however. Notable is the opening of Welsh minds to wider influences, and the positive role 'an open and unmolested stage' could play, 'to become as it should become, a part of the nation's life', in the words of the influential Cardiff city librarian, Ifano Jones in 1906; 'molestation' referred to puritanical opposition.[64] The realist challenge to portray life and the questions it posed even if they could not be answered was the journalist E. Morgan Humphreys's call, citing Ibsen, Strindberg, Shaw and Galsworthy. Ibsen was the chief inspiration here, though the Dublin's Abbey Theatre in the contemporary Irish literary and national renaissance also had its part. The leading young dramatists were all graduates of the Welsh university colleges, another sign of convergence with continental patterns of intelligentsia formation. The confrontation of their generation with chapel elders' hypocrisy was the thrust of W. J. Gruffydd's landmark play 'Beddau'r Proffwydi' (The Graves of the Prophets) in 1913. It roused great enthusiasm. 'The native dramatist must realise himself and in so doing reveal the soul and heart of Wales', wrote the Cymru Fydd lawyer-author Elphin (Robert Arthur Griffith), evoking a parallel with Norway, a small country 'dominated by ...

parochial primness, yet animated by an intense national consciousness which had never found full utterance' – before Ibsen. Might one hope for a similar 'miracle' in Wales?[65] The modernisation of Welsh-language culture that college-educated contemporaries thought had been achieved continued to be snagged by a line of fracture with conservative religious values, however.[66] Fracture, both religious and social, existed in the development of Slovene drama too, as witness many reviews in *Dom in svet* and *Ljubljanski zvon*,[67] but the deeper roots of a patriotic intelligentsia in a provincial capital (Ljubljana) made progress easier. Yet this picture of the Welsh scene is incomplete. The Welsh drama movement involved writers in Welsh but in English too, bound by common nationality, as will be explored in the final chapter.

No early Slovene novels achieved the widespread popularity of Daniel Owen. Their themes related to the experiences of their writers, a youthful educated stratum as they made their way in the big city Vienna or as teachers of the children of higher-class families. Characteristically, Slovenes were more influenced by European trends, though the earnest pursuit of international examples meant that criticism of the early realist Slovene novel (Fran Govekar's *In the Blood*, 1896) concentrated on its failure to reproduce the posited model of such a category rather than its success as a novel. Slovene literary criticism has retained a concern for genre assignment and quantification: thus we are told that, by 1945, 235 texts of peasant tales had been produced by 86 authors amounting to 7.7 billion words in all or an average length of 33,600 words a tale, which is sixty per cent of the average length of historical narratives. The preference for these types of subject and for the novella form rather than the longer novel reflected the tastes of readers. Whereas half of male authors of fiction were of peasant background, women writers, who are only now gaining full recognition, came from bourgeois milieux. This class aspect applied less to Welsh writers, with the difference that some middle-class Welsh women novelists wrote in English, though often patriotically.

One Slovene writer needs special attention. Ivan Cankar (1876–1918) was a prodigiously productive figure in all genres and styles as poet, dramatist, critic, journalist, essayist and political commentator but above all as writer of novels and short stories. All his thirty-three books date from the second half of his brief life following his departure to study in Vienna, his main base thereafter. The son of a poor village tailor, he responded with passionate sensitivity to the fate of the powerless and the injustice done them everywhere, which led him from disillusionment with conventional Slovene politics to socialism. His work abounds in lacerating descriptions of men driven by poverty into the army for a pittance, being marched off surrounded by crowds of imploring wives and sobbing children; of emigrants forced to take leave of their native land; of the mistreatment and abuse of orphan children in heartless institutions; of the cynicism of lickspittle petty officials; of the crushing of hopes for love and beauty and the narrowness of village and small town life, interspersed with brilliant depictions of the Slovenian countryside and tantalising glimpses of a heaven, frequently invoked but as frequently fleeting. Cankar's socialism went with a deep patriotism, a sense of outrage at his small people's reduction to servility and acceptance of their own inferiority through German overlordship and a system where 'everything you aren't ordered to do is prohibited'.[68] The words are those of an idealistic young teacher in one of his best-known books, his heart aflame to better the life of his charges and their community through education, but who is ground down by the cynicism of colleagues and superiors and the suspicion and distrust of boorish villagers. He was always a controversial writer, attacked for his bleakness, his socialism, even the alleged 'pornography' of his treatment of sexual abuse. As an influential figure in the Yugoslav Social Democratic Party, he advocated a republic of the south Slav nations, while hotly defending the integrity of Slovene language and culture against those who sought to revive 'Illyrian' ideas about cultural fusion. Above all, he argued for Slovene pride, for the end of a situation where creative, path-breaking Slovene artists – he had painting and sculpture particularly in mind – were least appreciated by the public at home. One of his stories features a young Slovene writer visiting a representative of this philistine tendency, generally considered one of the 'pillars of society', who tells him candidly that there are two kinds of truth: the public truth when the great man exudes, sincerely, on the progress of Slovene culture and the private truth that the Slovene people are primitive and have not the slightest interest in the productions of young dreamers. Cankar speaks for the struggles of all small cultures that fight for recognition in an unequal world.

Cankar was a product of the distinctive central European situation. The Welsh writer who comes closest to him in talent, productivity and, to an extent, cast of mind is perhaps T. Gwynn Jones (1871–1949). Son of a Methodist tenant farmer of literary interests (the cultured *gwerinwr* of O. M. Edwards's heart), Gwynn Jones was born too early to tread the educational ladder talented Welsh youth increasingly followed after 1889. An earlier pattern of encouragement from perceptive observers in his native Vale of Clwyd, who helped him with Latin and French with a view to Oxford, was frustrated by illness and he spent nearly twenty years, frequently marred by depression, as journalist on successive Welsh-language papers in north Wales and Liverpool before getting a post in the new National Library of Wales at Aberystwyth. This opened the way for this immensely hard-working semi-autodidact to become professor of Welsh there till his death. Much of his vast output of novels, plays, essays, translations and, above all, poems had already appeared before 1914, however, including the chair-winning 'Departure of Arthur' for the 1902 Eisteddfod which first brought him to fame. W. J. Gruffydd recounted later his fit of astonishment when T. Gwynn Jones shyly produced some pieces of paper from his pocket and read from the first draft. Gruffydd could not take his eyes off a man whose 'unbelievable treasure of inspiration' had been hidden to him for so long. Jones, however, had to be persuaded to submit his work and on the day of the chairing ceremony was attending a funeral elsewhere, to be greeted by five thousand cheering townsfolk on his return.[69] The cycle of poems the prize awdl opened on the ancient Welsh and Celtic past have contributed to the author's reputation as a romantic. The variety, range, experimentation and openness to other literatures of his work reveal modernist aspects, however. T. Gwynn Jones, like Cankar, was a strong socialist, nationalist and internationalist. His first published poem as a fourteen-year-old was on popular resistance to church tithes in his native region and he recalled that as a small boy he organised hundreds of imaginary armies to restore his country's independence, exploring every cave in his vicinity as a possible resting-place for Arthur.[70] Perhaps his most interesting trait comparatively is in showing the Welsh mind's escape from Victorian insularity in his generation. Like leading authors in small countries elsewhere he translated extensively from other literatures, like German, Italian and Irish. His masterly translation of Goethe's *Faust* (1922), reproduced seemingly effortlessly the different metrical patterns of the original. W. J. Gruffydd and Robert Silyn Roberts, authors of the influential *Telynegion* (Lyrics, 1898) also translated, under the influence of Heine, like the linguist John Morris Jones, no mean poet, who made a stab at learning Persian for his version of the *Rubaiyat of Omar Khayyam*. Thomas Parry-Williams studied in Freiburg and Paris, from 1911 to 1913, the latter experience figuring in his prizewinning chair poem of 1915,

'The City', considered the first major modernist poem in Welsh. He and his elder cousin Robert Williams Parry moved Welsh poetry further from the philosophising religious vein of the Victorian age but also from the lyricism which succeeded it towards more probing, reflective styles. Interesting in view of Welsh tradition is that both of them, like T. Gwynn Jones, were essentially religious agnostics.

There is some link here with the Slovene experience. A country's most significant art rarely reproduces its people's majority beliefs in conventional form, though it may be coloured by them. Two of Slovenia's three leading poets in this period were Catholic priests but both had difficulties in their calling. Simon Gregorčič (1844–1906) and Anton Aškerc (1856–1912) were both peasant sons with a long education at Gymnasium and seminary, at Gorica and Maribor respectively, before the liberal-clerical split had become definitive. Both felt love for a woman in early manhood but persisted in their vocations. Both, as liberals, were contributors to *Ljubljanski zvon*, which Aškerc actually edited from 1900 to 1901. By this time, however, he had fallen out with his bishop and decided for premature retirement, taking a post as archivist for the Ljubljana municipality till his death. Gregorčič had requested release from parochial duties in 1887, remaining, with a brief resumption of pastorship, a priest without charge. In each case they were accused of heretical tendencies. The second of Gregorčič's four volumes of poetry was denounced harshly by Mahnič in a lengthy diatribe. Aškerc became an enthusiast for evolution, seeing Christ as the highest degree of intelligence, with echoes of David Adam's ideas. Neither abandoned Christianity. As a poet of love and patriotism, Gregorčič had enthused the young Cankar with his first volume but thereafter Cankar saw only 'sorry decline', linking him with Aškerc in a similar trajectory in showing the shortfall of Slovene liberalism from its original emancipatory values.[71] Their reputations have survived into the modern period, however. Aškerc is known for his melodiousness and his ballads, which touch on almost all fields of Slovene history. Gregorčič's birthplace in Gorizia his poetry defended from Italianisation is now an ethnographic museum, where his most famous poem, to the River Soča, written in 1879, is displayed. After describing the peaceful beauty of the upper Soča (Italian Isonzo) river valley, as lively and graceful as its highland girls, as vigorous as the chants of its highland youth, its tone becomes darker as the Soča passes 'the graves of Slovene homelands' and enters the warm plains to the south from where 'the wrath of raging storms' threatens.

'Rains of blood and storms of tears' will follow when 'bitter steel' will bring much blood, 'our blood' to nourish, 'the enemy's' to muddy the river, which Gregorčič exhorts to rise over its defences and 'drown the foreigners ravenous for land'. A decade after the poet's death the mountainous Soča region indeed became the centre of probably the most horrific campaign of the First World War, when hundreds of thousands of Italian and Habsburg troops fought and died through three Alpine winters. With the Monarchy's collapse the area, and over 300,000 Slovenes, fell under Italian rule where the fascist regime banned the public use of their language. After 1945 it became part of Yugoslavia and now independent Slovenia. Still, the poem, though written defensively in the face of perceived Italian denationalisation pressures, shocks modern sensibilities and shows how questions of language and nationality had a brutal actuality for some in nineteenth-century Slovenia compared to T. Gwynne Jones's evocations of a distant age.

Oton Župančič (1878–1949) represented a different, more cosmopolitan strain in Slovene literature, moving in various directions and experimenting with several genres. Born into a mercantile family he was first under Catholic influence, then turned towards liberalism and modernism. After studies in Vienna which he did not complete, he spent years abroad in Paris and as tutor to an aristocratic German family. A playwright, essayist, poet, translator and friend of Cankar, he became responsible in 1912 for the drama programme of the Provincial Theatre, now in Slovene hands after the Germans had moved elsewhere. A well-known poem in 1908 set out the beauties of the Slovene countryside and traditional folk ways against the poverty and disorientation of many of its people as emigration seemed an unwelcome but increasingly persuasive escape route. It is significant that this urban sophisticate shared in his imagery the association other writers made of their country with green meadows, steep-roofed peasant houses and village churches. It showed how tenaciously societies reproduce the characteristic images of their national stories.

HISTORIOGRAPHY

Indeed, history has been a powerful tool for national representation in Europe. Shadowy evidence and earlier susceptibility to myth and legend long dogged systematic enquiry, until social development widened the range of potential subjects beyond noble and clerical elites. With dawning democracy 'the people' began finally to attract attention and the liberal national era opened a golden age for historians. It is no accident that the founders of national history in many European countries were also leading politicians, from France to Poland, Lithuania and the Balkans.[72] Not surprisingly, non-state societies like Wales and Slovenia followed well behind larger countries. The annual German and English historical reviews were founded in 1859 and 1886 respectively, but the Slovene and Welsh not till 1947 and 1960. However, modern-style periodicals began to appear at the start of the 1890s, and two important works of synthesis emerged almost simultaneously somewhat later, another instance of parallel development. However, the paths to them had been quite different.

Proto-Slovene near anonymity amid jostling Avars, Bavarians, Longobards, Franks, Byzantines or Hungarians and then under German-controlled Duchies long hampered the emergence of a coherent Slovene story. Two works in German outstripped these limitations: Valvasor's great comprehensive study of Carniola and Linhart's history of that province and the surrounding Slavs who spoke its language have already been mentioned; and as the Slovene identity strengthened, which Linhart saw but could not yet give a name, so its adherents made voicing its history a part of their cultural mission. Hence the pressure in the Carniolan Historical Association for a national history in Slovene, which appeared in 1866. Yet tension between Slovene enthusiasts and those who thought their romantic approach falsified reality was a prime cause of Dežman's dramatic national defection. This mid-century period saw archaeological societies in Carniola and in Wales, the Cambrian Archaeological Association contributing to the withering away of Welsh myths of origin stemming from Geoffrey of Monmouth. The Association operated in English whereas linguistic nationalism already divided similar bodies in Slovenia. The academic history which made its appearance at the century in both countries towards the end of the nineteenth century followed, among Slovenes, the three-stage pattern typical of non-dominant peoples of the regions. A period of simple but sterling lifestyle of peasant communities under their own leaders was succeeded by a long period of subjection to alien rulers and landlords and finally by the national revival. Linhart's pioneer sketch had been filled in.

By contrast with Slovenia, Wales's identity had long been well established. The stark outline of the Welsh story, starting from the Anglo-Saxon invasions, is part reason for the early emergence of a Welsh ethnonational narrative. These events, the asymmetric relationship between two peoples they produced and the wealth of myth and legend to which they gave rise, have stamped Welsh history for a millennium and a half. They dominated the Latin texts of the sixth-century Gildas, who saw them as the punishment for British sins, and of the ninth-century Nennius, who added a hint that they might yet be reversed; they provided the climax of Geoffrey of Monmouth's remarkable *Historia Regum Britanniae* (*c.*1136) with its bravura presentation of treachery, wizardry and the figures of Arthur and Merlin; from them flowed the prophetic poetry of the fifteenth century and its influence on the Welsh response to the Tudor dynasty. Twists in Welsh fortunes thereafter were also seen in the providential light which Gildas had first shone on his people's fate. Some sixty medieval Welsh manuscript translations of Geoffrey's work have survived; David Powel produced the first printed version of the story as *Historye of Cambria* in 1584. Dafydd Glyn Jones mentions fourteen histories of Wales published in the two languages between 1800 and 1830, testifying to the continuing popularity of Welsh history, as did the massive Welsh works of Carnhuanawc (1842) and Gweirydd ap Rhys (1872–4), among others.

The two authors of works of recognisably modern synthesis mentioned above were men of different traditions but similar patriotic goals, trained in the Rankean mould. Josip Gruden (1869–1922) was a Catholic priest, John Edward Lloyd a Congregational lay preacher who had thought of entering the ministry. The former was backed by the St Hermagoras Society; the latter was a product of the Welsh educational movement and became the History professor at Bangor. Both were medievalists with, however, a wide command of the whole span of their country's history. Gruden's great work was his multi-volume *History of the Slovene Nations*, Lloyd's his study of Wales till the loss of independence in 1282.[73] Gruden's preface reminded Slovenes of the classical injunction 'Know Thyself' in order to find strength in the 'harsh struggle for existence'. In his preface Lloyd wrote affirmingly that it was 'for a far distant generation to see that the last prince had not lived in vain but by his life-work had helped to build solidly the enduring fabric of Welsh nationality'.[74] Though Lloyd continued to contribute articles on Welsh history to Welsh-language periodicals and was an enthusiastic supporter of the Welsh Language Society, he chose to publish this book, as also his later study of the fifteenth-century national hero, Owain Glyndŵr, in English, with the aim of drawing attention to

Welsh history. In this he succeeded, winning high praise from English medievalists for producing a standard work. The measured, dignified style, itself part of the self-confidence of a developing discipline, lent weight to his purpose, which remained grounded in the Cymru Fydd inspiration of his youth. Already in 1882 he had written: 'no Welshman has the right to consider the study of his national history and literature a barren and aimless pursuit'.[75] In a later survey, *A History of Wales* (1930), his emphases were those of his own liberal national era, the Methodist revival, the educational movement from the late nineteenth century and the growth of Welsh industry.

Welsh historiography thus had a longer genesis than Slovene. It rested on the ongoing relationship with the eastern neighbour which underwent successive phases of successful resistance, prophetic denial and accommodation but always with a sense of providentialism, alternately wary or buoyant. Lloyd's period was one of optimism about Wales's place in the British Empire. His work was the academic face of O. M. Edwards's popular presentation of a land of 'incessant activity', characterised by unity in diversity and the democratic spirit. Its people, 'rude and ignorant at first, retaining the servile traits of centuries of subjection', was gradually becoming 'self-reliant, prosperous and thoughtful', with a 'certain pride' not so much in what had been but what was going to be achieved.[76]

Modern historiography is not quite so upbeat. Dafydd Glyn Jones has detected an element of moral exceptionalism in O. M. Edwards's patriotism, which in a comparative context can compensate for lack of political power.[77] More insidious is that the vaunted spiritual aspect of Welshness could impose standards the Welsh could not live up to. One may see this in the sceptical stance taken up to Cymru Fydd by the neo-Hegelian professor of moral philosophy at Glasgow, Henry Jones. Wales had all the characteristics of nationhood, said Jones, but that was not sufficient. A moral binding of the entire people was required, strong enough for them to hold together on a principle against the whole world. Would the Welsh farmer be prepared for that, to be baptised into the Kingdom of Man, or would the revival be revealed as superficial? The stakes were loaded when set in these daunting terms, the more so when Jones called England the greatest polity the world had seen and adjured the Welsh gnomically that he would prefer them to be struck dumb rather than to commit any 'oppressive' act (probably a warning against an Irish course).[78] In his autobiography Jones gave a moving account of his chapel-centred village upbringing and the Welsh struggle for education exemplified in his own career, when 'the common people of Wales proved so much above the common'.[79] But he had also argued that the interests of the 20 per cent of the rural population who would benefit from English language education should be put before those of the 80 per cent who did not need it. Henry Jones believed he had retained 'the essentials of the faith' of the community of his youth but the ease with which its concrete beliefs 'became obsolete' to him as he entered the world of learning showed how the emotional attraction of childhood could lead to an association of Welshness with simple piety, not intellect. His mental formation, unlike that of Tom Ellis, O. M. Edwards or T. Gwynn Jones, included no formative contact with Welsh literary culture. It was in Glasgow that he first came to value 'one of the greatest of our national treasures namely our literature' and it was English literature he meant. But his fondness for high-minded rhetoric tapped into a vein of Welsh religiosity which made him a fabled figure to his countrymen. Welsh history as the record of the ascent of democracy and the common man was the dominant trend of this period but, as with all hegemonies, it could come in a variety of forms pointing in different directions.

Similarly, the varied matter of this chapter is not easily reduced to a neat conclusion. By 1914 it is clear that the Slovene language had assumed a wider role than Welsh in national life. Complete internal sovereignty could not be said to have been won in that most secondary education continued to be in German, a good knowledge of which was still almost as necessary to cultivated Slovenes as was English to the Welsh. Far more ordinary Slovenes could live effectively through their own language, however. A modern urban lifestyle could by enjoyed and advertised with access to financial services and a daily press in a substantial centre, Ljubljana. Yet much of this was on a limited scale. Slovene print circulations were no higher than for Welsh ones, except in the provision of popular reading for the masses, which most Welsh people could now access in English. Increased Welsh bilingualism reflected a long-standing Welsh alignment with the British state, generally felt as a source of benefit economically and internalised in widespread pride in citizenship of a prestigious state. A sense of resentment of English attitudes was also widely felt, but probably surpassed by that of ordinary Slovenes in a German-dominated state. But new issues were arising alongside long-standing legacies of the respective national 'awakening'. In Wales, the industrial dynamism was seen as positive but it also brought cumulative social shifts, not least of language; in Slovenia, the Yugoslav question intruded itself. These twists in the tale combined to feed into wider tensions in domestic and international affairs in the pre-war years. The outcome – 1914 – was to exceed the fears.

NOTES

1 DS, 1 (1888), 159–61 (review of the periodical 'Drobtince').
2 *Y Traethodydd*, 57 (1902), 68–80 (78): Nodiadau llenyddol a diwinyddol.
3 *Bibliografsko kazalo Ljubljanskega Zvona*, compiled by J. Munda and N. Rupel (Ljubljana, 1962).
4 Pwyll, 'Y Beirdd a Beirniadaeth', *Y Geninen* (1907), 11–14 (11).
5 E. F. Foulkes, 'Diwylliant llenyddol yng Nghymru', *Y Geninen*, 3 (1885), 271–6.
6 Calculated from *Bibliografsko kazalo*.
7 LZ, 20/12 (1900), 649 (modest dimensions).
8 DS, 2 (1889), 34 ('Vadnica').
9 DS, 26 (1913), 36 (ballads).
10 LZ, 30 (1910), 27–34: Molé, 'Umetnost in narava'; LZ, 31 (1911), 279 (Bourget).
11 LZ, 31 (1911), 259,
12 LZ, 20 (1900), 61–2 (taste).
13 20 (1900), 66–7 (Heine).
14 LZ, 1 (1881), 55.
15 DS I, no. 1, p. 5.
16 Morgan Lloyd, QC, 'Dyfodol y Cymry', *Y Geninen*, 4 (1886), 91–2.
17 See, for example, Edward Foulkes's attack and the Anglican E. Eilir Rees's counter in *Y Geninen*, 28 (1900), 76–81, 155–62.
18 E. Morgan Humphreys, 'Y Ddau Gymro', *Y Traethodydd*, 62 (1907), 13–20.
19 Peter Williams (Pedr Hir), 'Y Cymry yn Genedl' (The Welsh as a Nation), *Y Geninen*, 11 (1893), 76–9, 154–8.
20 DS, 1 (1888), 14; ibid., 13 (1900), 480 (Drugi slovenski katolički shod).
21 LZ, 1 (1881), 57–9.
22 DS, 13 (1900), 276–9 (Ipavec).
23 See note 19.
24 J. R. Kilsby Jones, 'Pa un ai mantais neu anfantais i Gymru fyddai tranc yr iaith Gymraeg' (Would the death of the Welsh language be an advantage or disadvantages to Wales?), *Y Geninen*, 1 (1883), 18–23.
25 Herber Evans, 'Cymru Fydd', *Y Geninen*, 11 (1893), 56, 261. The irony is that Morris's poem, which sold 50,000 copies, is now considered a very second-rate appeal to Victorian bourgeois sentiment. Morris was a great grandson of Lewis Morris of the eighteenth-century Morris Circle.
26 *Y Traethodydd*, 57 (1902), 78.
27 For example, Hettie Williams, 'Yr Iaith Gymraeg yn yr Ysgolion', *Y Geninen*, 23 (1905), 120–3.
28 Caleb Rees, 'Addysg a'r Genedl', *Y Traethodydd*, 62 (1907), 241–9.

29 T. Darlington, 'Iaith Cymru Fydd', *Y Geninen*, 11 (1893), 224–31; J. E. Southall, 'A ydyw y Gymraeg yn marw?' *Y Geninen*, 16 (1898), 242–5.

30 Watcyn Wyn, 'Cymru ar ddiwedd y bedwaredd ganrif ar bymtheg', *Y Geninen*, 11 (1893), 182–7.

31 For example, by J. E. Lloyd, *Y Geninen*, 22 (1904), 217 and Charles Davies, *Y Geninen*, 17 (1899), 224.

32 Eifion Wyn, *Telynegion Maes a Mor* (n.pl., n.d.), p. 107.

33 Precise figures available vary somewhat. See, for example, Dot Jones (ed.), *Statistical evidence relating to the Welsh Language 1891–1914* (Cardiff, 1998), pp. 393, 442; and Russell Davies, *Sex, Sects and Society. 'Pain and Pleasure': A Social History of Wales and the Welsh, 1870–1914* (Cardiff, 2018), pp. 227–8.

34 Eleazer Roberts, 'Isaac Roberts DSc, FRAS', *Y Geninen*, 22 (1904), 276–82. Ironically, E. Roberts was himself one of the *Traethodydd*'s writers most engaged with secular matters.

35 Carl Schorske, *German Social Democracy, 1905–1914* (Cambridge, MA, 1955).

36 R. Tudur Jones, *Ffydd ac Argyfwng Cenedl: Hanes Crefydd yng Nghymru 1890–1914* (Faith and Crisis of a Nation: The History of Religion in Wales 1890–1914) (Swansea, 1982), vol. 2, pp. 215–17.

37 R. Cefni Jones, *Gwili: Cofiant a Phregethau* (Llandysul, 1937), pp. 77–8.

38 Jones, *Gwili*, p. 64.

39 T. Rees, 'Diwinyddiaeth yr Eglwysi Rhyddion', *Y Traethodydd*, 62 (1907), 300–7.

40 T. Eirug Davies (ed.), *Y Prifathro Thomas Rees: Ei Fywyd a'i Waith* (Llandysul, 1939), pp. 154–5.

41 Tudur Jones, *Ffydd*, vol. 1, p. 155.

42 W. Glasnant Jones, *Cyn Cof Gennyf a Wedyn* (Swansea, 1949).

43 Jones, *Cyn Cof Gennyf*, p. 73.

44 Dot Jones, *Statistical Evidence relating to the Welsh Language, 1801–1911* (Cardiff, 1998), pp. 513–15.

45 Pierce Owen, 'Cenadwri o'r Eidal', *Y Traethodydd* (1913), 107–20.

46 Ales Ušeničnik, '"Leonovo Društvo": Boj véde zoper vero', *Katoliški Obzornik*, 1 (1896), 1–9.

47 A. Ušeničnik, 'Ideali slovenske mladine' (The Ideals of Youth), *Katoliški Obzornik*, 5 (1901), 126–38 (133).

48 J. E. Krek, 'Materialistično modroslovje' (Materialist Philosophy), *Katoliški Obzornik*, 1, (1897), pp. 37–50, 137–56 (Jesus Christ, p. 156).

49 A. Ušeničnik, '*Naš čas*' (Our Epoch), *Čas*, 1 (1907), 1–4.

50 A Ušeničnik, 'Starost človeskega roda', *Katoliški Obzornik*, 5 (1901), 145–8.

51 E. Lampe, 'Leposlovje fin de siècle' (The literature of the fin de siècle), *Katoliški Obzornik*, 1 (1897), 63–72; T. Gwynn Jones, *Manion* (Cardiff, 1931), pp. 143–5.

52 Lampe, *Dom in svet*, 13 (1900), 188–91, 220–3. On the freedom of small nations (222), Lampe associated Slovene liberals with the hated German liberal enemy, with whom they were currently in alliance in Carniola.

53 R. L. Lenček, *The Structure and History of the Slovene Language* (Columbia, OH, 1982). For Cigale, see Rudolf Kolarič, 'Cigale, Matej 1819–89'. *Slovenska biografija*,

ZANU ZRC SAZU, 2013: http://www.slovenska biografija.si. (8.11.20); for the comparison of nationhood to air: *Primorski biografski leksikon*.

54 J. Elwyn Hughes, *Arloeswr Dwyieithedd. Dan Isaac Davies 1839–87* (Pioneer of Bilingualism) (Cardiff, 1984), p. 126.

55 J. E. Southall, *Bilingual Teaching in Welsh Elementary Schools, or minutes of evidence of Welsh witnesses before the Royal Commission on Education in 1886–7* (Newport, 1888), pp. 97–8.

56 H. A. L. Fisher, *An Unfinished Autobiography* (Oxford, 1940), p. 100.

57 Quoted from the 'Eurgrawn Wesleyaidd', in H. Teifi Edwards, *Codi'r Hen Wlad yn ei Hôl 1850–1914* (Llandysul, 1989), p. 1.

58 For popular fiction publishing in Slovene, see M. Hladnik, *Trivialna literatura* (Ljubljana, 1983).

59 J. Pleterski, 'Die Slowenen', in A. Wandruszka and P. Urbanitsch (eds) *Die Habsburgermonarchie 1848–1918*, III/2, (Vienna, 1975), pp. 801–38 (p. 819).

60 Hladnik, *Trivialna*, pp. 93–4.

61 W. J. Gruffydd, *Hen Atgofion* (Old Memories) (Llandysul, 1964), pp. 20–2. (First published 1936.)

62 Jane Aaron, *Nineteenth-Century Women's Writing in Wales: Nation, Gender and Identity* (Cardiff, 2010), pp. 63, 165. For this whole theme, see also Katie Gramich, *Twentieth-Century Women's Writing in Wales: Land, Gender, Belonging* (Cardiff, 2007).

63 Ioan Williams, *Y Mudiad Drama yng Nghymru 1880–1940* (The Drama Movement in Wales 1880–1940) (Cardiff, 2006), pp. 6–7, 26.

64 Edwards, *Codi'r Hen Wlad*, p. 287.

65 Ibid., p. 290.

66 Ioan Williams, *Y Mudiad Drama yng Nghymru 1880–1940* (Cardiff, 2006), pp. 3, 21–33, 57–65. O. Llew Owain lists some 930 plays published in Welsh up to 1943 in his *Hanes y Ddrama yng Nghymru 1850–1943* (Liverpool, 1948), pp. 267–308.

67 Thus a review of Engelbert Gangl's play 'The Son' which criticised the author's failure to combine naturalistic depiction of common life with clear endorsement of 'idealist' values: *Dom in svet*, 13/4 (1900), 124–5.

68 I. Cankar, *Martin Kačur, The Biography of an Idealist* (Budapest and New York, 2009), p. 23. (First published 1907.)

69 David Jenkins, *Thomas Gwynn Jones: Cofiant* (Denbigh, 1973), pp. 124–7.

70 Ibid., p. 35.

71 Ivan Cankar, *Materalien und Texte, zusammengestellt von Erwin Köstler* (Klagenfurt/Celovec,1999), pp. 57–8.

72 See in particular Monica Baár, *Historians and Nationalism in East-Central Europe in the Nineteenth Century* (Oxford, 2010), for five distinguished cases.

73 J. J. Gruden, *Zgodovina slovenskega naroda* (Celovec, 1912); Preface; J. E. Lloyd, *A History of Wales: From The Earliest Times to the Edwardian Conquest* (2 vols, London, 1911).

74 J. E. Lloyd, *History*, vol. 2, p. 623.

75 Huw Pryce, *J. E. Lloyd and the Creation of Welsh History: Renewing a Nation's Past* (Cardiff, 2011), p. 90.

76 O. M. Edwards, *A Short History of Wales* (London, 1906), pp. 127–8, 97.

77 Dafydd Glyn Jones, *Agoriad yr Oes: Erthyglau ar lên, hanes a gwleidyddiaeth Cymru* (Talybont, 2001), p. 39.

78 Henry Jones, 'Anghenion Cymru' (The Needs of Wales), *Y Geninen*, 8 (1890), 209–14. Probably Jones had the Irish in mind.

79 Sir Henry Jones CH, *Old Memories*, ed. by Thomas Jones, MA, LLD (London, [1923]), p. 14.

Chapter 8

NEW DIRECTIONS AND DÉNOUEMENT

A theme of this book has been that the fate of small peoples like the Slovenes and the Welsh is heavily dependent on factors outside their control. Little in the political and cultural narratives of the previous two chapters portended the bolt from the blue which was to come with the First World War and its aftermath. The early twentieth century was a time of stirring in Europe and globally when the nexus of nationhood, faith and class was particularly close. The earthquake of 1914 shuts off today the significance thoughtful contemporaries saw in tremors like the revolutions in Russia (1905), Persia (1906), the Ottoman Empire (1908) and China (1911), reminders that the period resembled our own in its one-world awareness, if non-European lands were viewed through the mirror of imperialism. In Britain the Irish question and the labour and suffragette movements ruffled the surface of Edwardian calm, while in the Habsburg Monarchy national tensions worsened. Rivalries between the European great powers which dominated world politics were reflected in a series of diplomatic crises. Yet hardly anyone anticipated in 1914 that in a few years the Habsburg Empire would be swept away and its Slovene subjects absorbed into a new 'Kingdom of Serbs, Croats and Slovenes', as Yugoslavia was officially termed in its first decade.

In these final years it is harder to discuss the experience of our two peoples as parallel processes. One significant pre-war theme, the advance of socialism, was still common to both. Two others defy direct comparison, though even here structural similarities are in evidence. Both countries were facing issues which potentially raised questions of identity. In Wales, the question was the rapid growth of a monoglot

English-speaking population. In Slovenia it was the increasing prominence of the Yugoslav question. What was Slovenes' stance to be to the mounting agitation among Croats and Serbs for closer union and common nation-hood among south Slavs as a whole, which could take an anti-Habsburg, indeed terrorist turn? Notoriously, the spark for the First World War was given by the assassination of the heir to the Habsburg throne in Sarajevo, Bosnia in June 1914. This problem did not arise from Slovenes' popular demand; in 1914 Slovene opinion strongly favoured remaining under the Habsburg sceptre. But it was imposed on them by the war, which resulted in the collapse of the Habsburg Monarchy and the end of the glory days of the British Empire, economically at least. Before addressing the issues outlined above, socialism, anglicisation and Yugoslavism, this last chapter will begin by recalling the role of the framing empires for our two peoples.

In 1932 the German-language writer Joseph Roth published a famous novel, *The Radetzky March*, which has ever since been viewed as a nostalgic evocation of the old multi-ethnic Monarchy. Roth was Jewish, member of the most Habsburgophile people of the Empire, because it served as their protectors in a strongly anti-Semitic environment. His novel centres round the descendants of an Austrian common soldier of Slovene peas-ant origin ennobled for saving emperor Franz Joseph's life in the battle of Solferino (1859). The soldier's son, now a District Commissioner, is portrayed as emblematic of the Austrian higher bureaucracy, rather stiff and unimaginative but fundamentally honourable, devoted to duty and the dynasty. His only son, an army Lieutenant, also basically decent but weak and confused, becomes involved in a scandal which can only lead to humiliating disgrace. His shocked father resolves on a personal appeal to the emperor for clemency for the grandson of 'the hero of Solferino'. In one of the novel's splendid set pieces the elderly Commissioner and the octogenarian Franz Joseph meet and recognise each other as kindred spirits, united in service to a venerable Monarchy both sense is doomed. Indeed, the feeling that the Monarchy's time is past and that the future belongs to its many nations increasingly pervades the novel. Its elegiac mood runs counter to much current revisionist historiography which seeks to retrieve the Monarchy's reputation from 'declinists' who overlook its strengths. Their defiant optimism is as much tarred by hindsight as Roth's pessimism, however. The psychological balance between an embattled centre and upstart non-dominant peoples was shifting towards the lat-ter already before 1914: to Roth's paranoid District Commissioner 'the whole world consisted of [recalcitrant] Czechs ... the originators of the concept "nation".[1] Roth chooses the Slovenes, smallest of the Monarchy's peoples, to represent the traditional loyalty imperial systems look for in their subjects.

The British Empire was better placed in this respect. It was at the height of its global power and influence. For all many Welsh people's resentment of historic subordination and English arrogance, Welsh patriotism usually went with British. Great Britain was not immune from the anxieties of the age. At issue was the poor performance of British troops in the Boer war of 1899–1902; Irish, trade union and suffragette agitation; fear of economic challenge from America and Germany; and awareness of the empire's relatively small island base. Geopoliticians like Arthur Milner, High Commissioner for Southern Africa at the time of Cecil Rhodes, sought ways to strengthen links between the mother country and the far-flung white colonies by embedding the idea of empire in centre and periphery, while Tory politicians argued for imperial tariff protection. The investiture of the future Edward VIII as Prince of Wales in an invented ceremony in 1910 was symbolically related to this strain of thinking. The fact it was proposed by Lloyd George showed how fully the Welsh shared the view of their loyal place in the imperial state. The English preponderance this reflected was reinforced by the swelling numbers of English immigrants into industrial Wales.

ENGLISH IMMIGRATION AND WELSH SOCIETY: A CASE OF DUAL ASSIMILATION?

How had the large English-speaking population swelled so rapidly? There had long been medieval English-speaking colonies and an anglicised elite. This was quite analogous to Slovene circumstances. The twelfth-century settlement in Pembrokeshire had a parallel in imported German speakers in the next century who formed the Kočevje (Gottschee) enclave in southern Carniola. 'Little England beyond Wales' with its four score parishes south of a stable border, the Landsker, against the three score in Welsh Pembrokeshire, was more populous than the fifteen to twenty thousand Kočevje Germans who, moreover, had begun to decline through rural poverty and emigration from the 1880s. They had, however, their own Gymnasium and returned the only German representation in the peasant curia of the Carniolan Diet. As to the anglicised landed elite scattered throughout the country, these were probably less significant than their Slovene counterparts. Apart from individuals like the Cardiff-based Marquesses of Bute and the Mostyn and Douglas Pennant families in north Wales they were inactive economically. O. M. Edwards wrote dismissively of them: 'They have never been hated or despised, *they are simply ignored*.'[2] A wholly different matter was the influx of the modern era, with industrialisation and the growth of large commercial coastal towns. Much was fortuitous, the contiguity of coal, iron and likely ports with an island's global access. Welsh entrepreneurs played a big role, with men like David Davies Llandinam and David Thomas leading players. Most of the earlier population growth came, too, from Welsh-speaking rural Wales. But the scale of development could not have occurred without the inflow of expertise from outside for the vast range of ancillary skills and industries which sprang up, for example, in Cardiff, in ship-building and repair, navigation and pilotage, insurance and brokerage, civil and electrical engineering, foundries and brick works, transport and the carrying trade, timber products, milling, fulling and brewing, all with their own specialisations and constantly upgraded innovations.[3] The associated names were mainly English. Famous examples are the unrelated Cory families, both starting in coastal trade before settling in Cardiff and branching into wider concerns. Devonshire-born John Cory (1828–1910) of Cory and Bros. Ltd was a ship and coal mine owner who founded a network of coal depots around the globe; John Cory from Padstow, Cornwall, of John Cory and Sons Ltd, owned twenty-one steamers with three more building when he died in 1891. His two sons directed some thirty-five companies. From the 1890s, and particularly the turn of the century, the English immigrants began to outnumber the Welsh, with marked effect on the language of youth in a society without a tradition of linguistic nationalism.

In this dynamic atmosphere a corresponding world of entertainment and culture sprang up.[4] The English music hall proliferated through all the complexities of frequent fires and rebuilding, changes of location and mergers. While the leading Cardiff department stores, Howell's and Morgan's, were Welsh foundations, the impresarios of music hall and theatre were all Englishmen. These were large establishments. The Grand Theatre, offering variety in Westgate Street, Cardiff (1887), seated nearly three thousand, the Empire Palace, Newport (1899) two-and-a-half thousand. Theatres intended for plays included the New Theatre, Cardiff, seating 1,570, which opened with *Twelfth Night* in 1904; Anna

Pavlova performed there in 1912 and 1913. Its first amateur production was Gilbert and Sullivan's *The Yeomen of the Guard*. Theatre prospectuses offered a host of facilities and novelties, a far cry from Nonconformist puritanism. This was reproduced on a smaller but still opulent scale in the theatres of the developing North Wales coastal resorts, like the Grand Theatre in Llandudno, only the largest, which opened in 1901 with accommodation for 1,100 in a town of 7,000 inhabitants. The North Wales Advertiser Board spent £3–4,000 a year to attract visitors from populous Lancashire, served by rail and regular steamship schedules. In Llandudno, just a few miles from the Snowdonian heartland, nearly one-third of the population was English born in 1891, of whom only 7 per cent spoke Welsh, while the Welsh population was becoming bilingual. In the last quarter of the century 97 per cent of holiday visitors came from outside Wales, including Disraeli, Gladstone and the Queen of Romania.[5] Rather different was the development of Barry Island as a tourist attraction. Already known as a watering place in the 1790s, with quite an upper-class Georgian clientele, it had become a favourite of the Cardiff middle classes by mid-Victorian times, with twelve thousand visitors in 1876. Its startling growth from the 1890s was, however, working class, drawn from the mining valleys as well as Cardiff and benefiting from the extension of the Rhondda Barry railway to the island in 1896. As the twentieth century advanced it was to become the third largest seaside destination in the British Isles, but unlike the north Wales resorts retaining a strongly Welsh demographic. This was a milieu in which the teeming mixed population of the south east, though mainly Welsh in origin, was moving rapidly towards the English language. In a ferment of socio-economic upheaval and lifestyle change the outlines of the predominantly English-speaking Wales of today were being prefigured.

This phrasing may mislead. At stake was not the birth of modern, south-east-centred industrial Wales. That had already occurred much earlier in the nineteenth century. Incipient language shift took place within a pre-existing society and people. What was happening was expansion and regularisation of the processes which had first drawn the eyes of British officialdom to Wales in the 1840s. By the new century the industrial area had spread out from north-west Monmouthshire, Merthyr, Swansea and environs to include the whole coalfield, as the emphasis moved from iron to coal. The religious life characteristic of this zone had reached its maximum point of institutionalisation, with the trebling of the two thousand

Welsh pulpits Ieuan Gwynedd had hailed within more centralised denominations. The rumbustious life of mining communities had continued, but
within increasingly organised sporting parameters, just as choral singing
and eisteddfodic activity had taken more formal shape. Industrial discontent was channelled into political consciousness and debate. This was a
very distinctive society which was to stir the imagination and pride of
Welsh people till our own day and fix an image of the country for others
too, if in cliché-ish form. It is worth elaboration. The argument here will be
that a variety of factors inclined this society towards a Welsh orientation,
though this was perfectly compatible with loyalty to the British Empire.

First comes the hegemony of Nonconformity, which for the majority
of Welsh opinion formers had come to be all but identified with national
values and the sense of Welsh awakening linked to religious revival from
the eighteenth century. True, one should not be too seduced by what
a commnunity's *bien pensants* maintain are its values. The number of
Nonconformist adherents was well short of the total population, even
when formal chapel membership was supplemented by the numerous
'listeners' who attended chapel services without it. Yet the omnipresence
of the Bethesdas, Bethlehems, Ebenezers, Moriahs et al. which thronged
Welsh streets, which stood at every urban corner and every lonely country cross road, the Welsh hymns spectators sang at sporting contests, the
sabbatarianism sanctioned by Act of parliament (1881) which closed
Welsh pubs on the holy day, the constant invocations to the earnest standards the Welsh were told made them an example to the nations: all these
were undeniable facts recognised by all, Welsh and newcomers alike.

It is the nature of hegemonies that they have a powerful influence on
minorities. The Welsh Anglican revival of the later nineteenth century
took on several features of Nonconformist practice, throwing up notably
energetic clergymen who made more provision for the Welsh language
and Welsh sentiment. To the single parish serving the Rhondda in 1869,
with its two churches and two mission rooms, had come nine new parishes and some thirty churches and school rooms by 1921. Yet this was
little compared to the one hundred and twelve Nonconformist chapels
of the Rhondda 1892, thirty-nine of them English.[6] It was a similar story
in the Cynon valley (Aberdare) where Anglican churches had leapt from
two to twenty (1837–97) and chapels from nine to some eighty over this
time, the great majority Welsh speaking.[7] Only in the rural backwater of
border Radnorshire did Anglicans approach Nonconformist numbers.

What Anglican efforts showed was the religiosity of the society as a whole. So did the establishment of a Catholic presence through Irish immigration in the south east; 10 per cent of Cardiff's population was Catholic in 1880. Irish identity still more than Welsh had a social and religious rather than linguistic focus. The successful struggle for the right to hold religious processions in Cardiff in the long run aided a course of accommodation with a Welsh identity which was more complex than in the case of English workers.[8] Many of these already had Nonconformist roots; nearly half the Rhondda English chapels of 1892 were Wesleyan or Primitive Methodist, the latter being an exclusively English working-class denomination perhaps closer in spirit to Welsh methodism. For the interesting thing about English chapels in Wales is that they seem to have developed on wholly Welsh lines, without the coolness of temperament which Welsh Nonconformists had traditionally felt in their English co-religionists' style of worship. Celtic peoples in Wales, Ireland, Brittany and Gaelic Scotland have all been noted for strong religious sentiment, whether Catholic or Protestant. The more latitudinarian English made the analogy in their own tradition, Methodist 'enthusiasm', a term of disparagement. The combined power of social context and historic heritage probably underlies this religious strain more than purported racial traits. In any event, the effect is shown in the substantial absorption of a mixed population into the emotional phenomenon of Welsh Nonconformity. There is an intriguing parallel in north and west Walian newcomers' adoption of the distinctive Welsh dialect of the industrial valleys' small pre-existing population.

But Nonconformity's absorptive capacity was not just a matter of the valleys, where the Welsh-language chapel tradition remained strong. It was almost as successful numerically in English-speaking south Pembrokeshire and cosmopolitan Cardiff, where some sixty Nonconformist churches and Gospel Halls were founded by the First World War. The Cardiff-centred Forward Movement, founded under Calvinistic Methodist auspices to evangelise new population growth points, tells us something of the form Welsh Nonconformity could take in an anglicised, 'mixed' milieu. A eulogy of one of its founders, John Pugh, on his funeral in 1897 depicted him as a man who saw Wales, 'his beloved country', in danger of being flooded and paganised by 'ungodly, ignorant people' of impure speech and corrupt conduct. The only solution was the Scriptures, for whose message he was credited with setting up forty-six Gospel Halls and a monthly newspaper.[9] At least the movement presented its old message

in novel ways. A huge poster featured a list of evangelists and their topics, each speaker identified by a soubriquet, for example: 'The Christian
Gentleman', 'The Muscular Christian', 'The little ball of fire'. Another
leader, Seth Joshua, presented his sermons as bouts with Beelzebub, who
duly 'went over the ropes'.[10] It is interesting that Pugh and Joshua had
strong links with Monmouthshire where Joshua was born, a county where
the Welsh language was in steep decline; Pugh came from a similar area of
Montgomeryshire, and then south Pembrokeshire. They indicate something of the outlook of the English-speaking Welshman in gestation, an
outlook both firmly Welsh and culturally narrow. Arthur Herbert Jones,
growing up in Monmouthshire at the start of the twentieth century, speaks
interestingly of the narrowness but also the power of the chapel and what
he calls 'the indigenous Welsh culture in which I was reared' with 'its all-
encompassing aura' for followers and non-followers alike.[11]

But there was another kind of camaraderie than religion. An old quip
holds that the Rhondda had more temples to God and to the devil than
any other mining district in Britain and there was certainly a dialectic
between teetotalism and heavy drinking. The hard life of the miner had
long found outlets in foot and whippet racing, bare fist fighting and wrestling on valley hillsides, pigeon-keeping, occasional circus visits and the
like. In the last quarter of the nineteenth century clubs for organised sport
developed, from which quite quickly national unions emerged, a process
in which the British Isles took the lead. The Football Association of Wales
(1876) was the third such union in the world and a founder member with
the other 'home nations' of the IFAB (International Football Association
Board), still recognised by the later developing FIFA as the body responsible for the rules of the game. Until a 1958 reorganisation each home
nation and FIFA held two of the ten places on the Board, whose annual
meetings are still held frequently by rotation in Wales. Rugby followed a
similar process, the Welsh Rugby Union (1881), having as a main function
the organising of a national team for annual competition in the Home
Nation Championship. It was an aspect of Britain's social modernity that
football became a mass sport there a generation earlier than elsewhere. The
first soccer clubs on modern Slovenian territory were actually founded by
Germans in Ljubljana and Celje and Hungarians in border town Lendava,
then in Dualist Hungary. Slovenia acquired international sporting status
only in the 1990s, though a football friendly with France was played in
1921. Typically, however, the first Slovene club Ilirija in Ljubljana, took

an ethnic name, while Welsh clubs titled themselves officially in English. Team mottos, like institutional mottos in general, were very largely Welsh. Newport rugby club in Monmouthshire affiliated to both the English and Welsh rugby unions; the Monmouthshire county motto adopted in 1948 was tactfully in Latin (Utrique Fideles, faithful to both). But overwhelmingly Monmouthshire-born sportspeople have opted to play for Wales, an interesting example of the tenacity of social tradition. Had not the famous poet Islwyn, a native, written that the county remained Welsh for all the change of designation: Gwyllt Walia ydwyt, Fynwy gu/Dy enw'n unig a newidiaist ti. (Wild Wales you are, fair Monmouth/, only your name have you changed.)? Pride in representing their country on the field of sport has been an inestimable force in Welsh national identity and in the absorption of newcomers. Welsh rugby success led to its coronation as the Welsh national game, though it was largely confined to the coalfield and the south-west. Wales won two of the first three football matches with England in the early 1880s but from then to 1914 managed only six draws and not a single victory. By contrast, after losing the first rugby encounter with England 92–0 by modern scoring, she won the Triple Crown eight times in the same period by beating the three other home nations, a symbolically piquant achievement because rugby became increasingly the prestige sport in the upper-class English 'public schools'. The 1891 game between Blackheath and Swansea, reputed the best rugby clubs in England and Wales respectively, was hailed by the Swansea press as the championship of Great Britain, and increasing Welsh success was attributed to 'Celtic genius' and the distinctive nature of Welsh three quarter play.[12] The most famous victory, however, was against the all-conquering New Zealand visitors of 1905, watched by forty-five thousand in Cardiff. Almost as emblematic in popular culture were the Welsh boxers of South Wales, the valley boys, Jimmy Wilde, European and world flyweight champion and Freddy Welsh, world lightweight champion, and the Cardiffian Jim Driscoll, of Irish origin and British Lonsdale belt holder. The tough working-class communities from which they came helped consolidate an identity already distinctive.

In short, the Welshness of twentieth-century Wales's developing English-speaking culture was over-determined. The peak of immigration came in a short pre-1914 period when patterns of working-class life had already been established. The diverse migrants lacked any institutional cohesion – except for the Catholic Church for the Irish; the

Welsh were predisposed to accept English as a lingua franca. The way was clear for intermarriage and a developing community open to Welsh sentiment and the English language, a path smoothed by the continued existence of Welsh speakers in the coalfield for an indefinite period – with some way still to go in the Swansea and Llanelli hinterland. Meanwhile, the implementation of a cultural form of Cymru Fydd continued. The National Library and National Museum whose charters were issued together in 1907 were projects long mooted and which drew on existing bases: the life labours of Queen Victoria's bibliophilic personal physician and accreted medieval Welsh manuscript collections in the one case, the museal department of Cardiff City Library in the other. The National Museum, first mooted in the 1879s and ardently promoted by Welsh Liberals in Parliament from 1892, was explicitly designed to win recognition of Welsh nationhood by the imperial state, against arguments that the British Museum represented all parts of the kingdom. The Scots and Irish, already in receipt of cultural funding from London, helped the Welsh through their own battles, while Welsh industrial muscle and the wealthy patrons it provided too played a part.[13] The Cardiff Civic Centre begun in 1905 also climaxed decades of negotiation to buy a suitable large park outside the city's borders from the Marquess of Bute, reflecting Cardiff's new status as a city and aspiration to the role of capital, not officially recognised for another half century. The statues commissioned for the new city hall, including St David, Llywelyn ap Gruffydd and Owain Glyndŵr, made a clear pitch for national representativeness. But only the Museum had gone to Cardiff because, it seems, a cosmopolitan seat of commerce where only one-tenth of the population now spoke Welsh was deemed not national enough. However, with its University College and other amenities Cardiff was now evidently the imposing urban centre Wales had lacked and it was overtaking places like Aberystwyth as a default conference centre for all-Welsh issues. City leaders saw advantage in such a role. This was an age of celebratory spectacle – think the golden and diamond jubilees of Franz Josef and Queen Victoria, the forbidding Teutonism of the 1913 centenary monument to Napoleon's defeat at Leipzig and the contemporary vogue for historical 'pageants' in the United Kingdom. Cardiff's elders were seduced by proposals for one such in Cardiff, in which Wales's oldest families, the Lord Mayor, a leading clergyman and other dignitaries agreed to play figures from Welsh history before cheering citizens. 'No race is more alive to the demands of patriotism', the Cardiff press trumpeted. 'When Wales is named the Welshman thrills with pride'.[14]

The 1909 pageant was scripted by a remarkable figure, Owen Rhoscomyl (Arthur Owen Vaughan), born of a Welsh mother and English father but brought up after their early death by his north Wales grandmother, who claimed descent from the brother of Llewelyn ap Gruffydd. Rhoscomyl was a passionate nationalist from childhood, and a fearless adventurer who left for America at fifteen where he was a cowboy and mining prospector, entered the Dragoons, won military medals in the Boer and First World Wars and wrote copiously on heroes of Welsh history. It is easy to underestimate Rhoscomyl, with his martial values and imperialist streak, as an unwelsh poseur but he lived in an imperial age and the British Empire for him was a conglomerate of peoples in which the Welsh had the chance to show their mettle as a 'special country' within it.[15] This was not a passive acceptance of subordination to the English. It is hard to recall how much the empire rather than Britain was the framework for many. The rounded side of Rhoscomyl's concerns is shown in his work for the Welsh theatre movement, in which his influence with Lord Howard de Walden, its wealthy benefactor, was critical. The climax was a week-long festival of its plays in Cardiff's premier theatre, three in Welsh and three in English, performed in June 1914 in Cardiff's premier theatre by a 'Welsh National Theatre Company' funded by Howard de Walden. The Lord Mayor and the Marquess of Bute attended the opening night and Lloyd George, Chancellor of the Exchequer, two subsequently. George Bernard Shaw wrote in the *South Wales Daily Post* with characteristic pungency: 'Just as the preachers of Wales spend much of their time telling the people of Wales that they are going to hell, so the Welsh writers of comedy will have to console many of them by demonstrating that they are not worth wasting good coal on.'[16] This was apposite. The opening play, *Change*, which had already been successfully performed in London and New York, depicted the clash between a dogmatic old minister and his three sons, one of whom had become a militant labour leader. The writer, J. O. Francis, was a college friend of the Welsh-language playwright D. T. Davies and from the same valleys' background but brought up speaking English, an interesting sign of what was beginning to happen. Their affinity shows how they belonged to the same emotional world, as a generation felt a tension between themselves and the inherited Nonconformist codes. Enthusiasts hailed a new theatre speaking for a buoyant Welsh public, putting Wales on the map.

It is possible to feel at this juncture how contemporaries might have felt of a Wales coming together, a prosperous, booming Wales, of course, but one also where civic life was working in favour of a Welsh identity, with National Museum and Library, an element of educational autonomy in the Welsh department of the Board of Education (Welsh history textbook proposals were rife in this period), a de facto capital where international sporting encounters took place and an easy relationship of people of Welsh or English mother tongue for common purposes. Obviously, the language of such contacts had to be English, just as Welsh history schoolbooks could contain chunks of untranslated Welsh, on assumption of widespread bilingualism. The language of local government was English but cities like Cardiff had active Welsh-speaking societies where many of their leading functionaries were members. There appears anyway to have been quite widespread assumption that whatever the injustices of the past Welsh would now get its due, whatever that was. While Cardiff was a milieu where the Welsh language was increasingly less spoken, aspirations to be seen as the 'metropolis of Wales' reinforced its symbolic importance to the city. A vigorous campaign for its teaching in all the city's schools, led by the Cardiff Cymmrodorion Society with its 1,250 members, secured two plebiscites early in the new century's first decade which only narrowly failed to endorse this idea.[17] The city authorities nonetheless were encouraged to continue expanding provision towards this aim till the lack of teachers, their reluctance and a 'British League of Cardiff' succeeded in making Welsh optional, not compulsory in 1907, though the League remained unhappy. The metropolis of Wales claim anticipated what Neil Evans has called 'one of the most prominent themes of twentieth-century Wales, the development of a sense of Welsh identity of a largely anglophone and often "foreign" population'.[18]

If this is how pro-Welsh elements felt it was a rather rosy view. Unity was not so marked. The north Walian press ignored the Cardiff pageant. The Central Welsh Board and the Welsh Education Department were at loggerheads, which scuppered frequent calls for full Welsh educational autonomy from the start; rural counties resented Glamorgan's dominance. Moreover, the ongoing vitality of the theatre movement, which for some spurred patriotic hopes, is open to question. Ioan Williams suggests a lack of unity in its goals. The main fissure, he argues, was not so much between its opponents and supporters: the puritannical deacons attacked in W. J. Gruffydd's *Beddau'r Proffwydi* were no longer typical of younger ministers.

It was among the supporters themselves, between educated 'college boys' and ordinary believers.[19] The line between the criticism and undermining of Nonconformist religion was a delicate one. Francis was to say in 1922 that insofar as the pre-war plays questioned anything in Welsh religion it was 'the sovereignty of an organisation, not the basis of a faith'.[20] The reaction of J. Tywi Jones, Baptist minister and editor from 1914 of *Tarian y Gweithiwr* (The Worker's Shield), the long-standing Welsh-language Lib-Lab weekly of Aberdare and east Glamorgan, is symptomatic of the problem. A playwright himself, he expressed unease at the possible impact of *Beddau'r Proffwydi* and *Change*. His backing of the drama was as a support of community involvement, the Welsh language and Welsh religious values, rather than of the Welsh professional theatre Howard de Walden aimed at. The tension between amateur and professional theatre sprang from the sudden acceleration of the Welsh drama movement and the limited role it had previously had for Welsh cultural patriots. In the Slovene revival the theatre had an important place from the start and the development towards professionalisation took place over a much longer period. Tywi Jones's position is also to be understood from a regional standpoint. Aberdare was still a centre of Welsh language culture in the industrial valleys, with eighteen presses as of 1900, but exposed to anglicisation in a way W. J. Gruffydd's Snowdonia was not; the morale of his flock in the face of multiple impinging pressures was clearly on his mind.

Here language did play a role and its salience was increased by a chance conjunction. In 1915, Caradoc Evans (1878–1945) published the first major work of Anglo-Welsh literature. Previous Welsh expression in English has a pedigree resembling Slovene in German in terms of topological work (Valvasor!) and family histories of members of the elite. In the modern era journals like the *Cambrian Register* (London, four numbers, 1795–1818) and the Swansea-based *Cambrian Visitor* (1813) aimed at presenting Welsh history and culture to others rather than soliciting original literary work, and in this differed from literary reviews like Carniola (1838–44) where Prešeren himself published German poems. Thus, *The Red Dragon* (1882), strictly a miscellany rather than a literary review, was really the first forum for Welsh writing in English, a version of the English regional periodical catering for a developing middle-class readership. Though there were a fair number of novels in English on Welsh topics, they were usually orientated to familiar themes of church and chapel and sought to present their own side of that story to English readers.[21] Caradoc Evans's short stories took this course too, but in skill and bite were devastatingly original. Provocatively entitled *My People*, they excoriated Nonconformist ministers and deacons for bigotry, hypocrisy, lechery, cupidity and other sins, representing the speech of Welsh peasants in a grotesque jargon suggestive of crude superstition and mental vacuity. In his most notorious tale, 'Be This Her Memorial', a poverty-stricken old woman sacrifices everything she has to buy an ornate Bible for the pompous Respected Rev. Josiah Bryn-Bevan she worships, and is found lying starved to death with a roasted rat in her hands. Evans, brought up Welsh-speaking in Cardiganshire, wished to shock Welsh Nonconformists out of smug self-satisfaction, but the hostility he aroused caused a rift between writers in Welsh and English not healed for many years. Most of the latter object to the convenient term 'Anglo-Welsh literature', claiming there is nothing English about them except their medium. M. Wynn Thomas argues that the strength of anti-nonconformist animus driving early Welsh writing in English reflects the power their youthful experience of it had in the writers' own formation: it is the revolt of the sons against the fathers. His case is uncontestable. Family quarrels are often the most contentious. He has also said that the case might have been different if Welsh writing in English had first made its mark with J. O. Francis rather than Caradoc Evans.

The language issue cannot, therefore, be elided. The north Walian W. J. Gruffydd, one of a group of Welsh-speaking university academics prominent in the Rhiwbina garden village project on the city's outskirts, wrote in his memoirs of his sense of exile, mentioning the death of the last Welshman in the neighbourhood, a farmer surnamed George. The present writer remembers the death of a farmer surnamed George in Rhiwbina in the 1950s, presumably this man's son, making his father not the last Welshman, therefore, but the last Welsh speaker. Gruffydd, as an intellectual acquainted with his country's literary heritage, was entitled to be puzzled at the idea of a Welshman who did not speak Welsh. The link between language and nationality is a natural assumption. But nature comes in many forms. The case made here for the Anglophone variety of the species is for a popular state of mind, emotionally rooted and heavily dependent on traditions shaped by Welsh-speaking ancestors. What is to be noted is how fully the mixed population of the south Wales valleys, less so that of the great ports, acquired a common mentality and national loyalty. This was helped by intermarriage and by the fact that the Welsh element was overall in a substantial majority and had the advantage of original occupation. What is also to be noted about this state of mind is the weakening of the intellectual underpinning which knowledge of Welsh could bring to its native speakers' patriotism. Loyalty was not exclusive but shared for most with another, to a Britain still more empire than nation, hence lacking something of the intimacy of nationhood. In all this, though, differences between Welsh and English speakers were matters of degree rather than kind. But Great Britain if not Ireland had achieved the supranational idea for which Habsburg loyalists like von Trotta yearned.

SOCIALISM

All that granted, a powerful force shaped the emerging profile of industrial Wales, one which did mark a new direction in Welsh life, though it drew from Welsh as well as British radicalism. Just as liberalism had taken over from the European *anciens régimes* in the nineteenth century, so socialism was to eclipse it in the first half of the twentieth. The Habsburg Monarchy was no less affected than Great Britain, offering the chance to bring our Slovene subject belatedly into this chapter, as also themes from European socialism little treated in British discussion.

At first sight it might seem odd that socialism should have been significant in the heavily agricultural Habsburg Monarchy. The Monarchy did have important industrial zones, with large-scale mining and factory production, however, particularly in Bohemia. Elsewhere, as mainly in Slovenia, the workforce potentially open to socialist ideas was more artisanal than large-scale industrial. But we should remember the role of such elements in early British labour history, and also the psychological drive of less developed economies to emulate radical movements in more advanced ones, which made socialism a force in late Tsarist Russia and then China. Above all, the Habsburg Monarchy was bound up with the cultural zone of central Europe, dominated by a dynamic Germany and its powerful socialist movement, the largest in Europe in 1914. There Marxism prevailed, the most elaborate school of socialist thought, while a well-known claim has it that British labour 'owed more to Methodism than to Marx'. Austria returned more socialists in the first election under universal suffrage in 1907 than more industrialised Britain the year before. Moreover, Austria's ethnic composition assured more attention than in Britain to the relations of class and nationality which are relevant to this study. In fact, much of the most sophisticated thinking on this matter came from Austrian socialists under the Monarchy.

At the broadest level, historians of the Habsburg Monarchy see three stages in the interaction with ethnicity which industrialisation brings about. Initially, the contact with foreign workers or new technology evoked a hostile ethnocentric reaction, followed by workers' realisation that employers could exploit ethnic differences and that their interest lay in cooperation across ethnic lines. This second stage was the pattern of the Austrian Social Democratic Party (ASDP) founded in 1889. Its programme ringingly stated that as an international party it condemned national privilege as it did privilege based on birth, property and descent: 'the struggle against exploitation must be international as is exploitation itself'.[22] Yet Habsburg Austria showed the difficulties of implementing this principle. Not surprisingly, long-standing traditions of German hegemony were reflected in a preponderance of German-speaking organisers in the ASDP. The socialist idea tended to be brought to Balkan towns by Germans, often printers, and the socialist press appeared bilingually. Despite a Marxist rhetoric of revolution as the goal the socialist movement effectively followed a reformist course, of electoral politics aimed at improving workers' living standards. For Slovene workers, whose largest nucleus was not in Ljubljana but Trieste, this was paralleled by dominance of Italian leaders. In the spirit of internationalism, however, the Trieste Workers' Confederation was set up in 1890 as a regional organisation of the ASDP, incorporating Italian, Slovene and German sections, which retained their own identity. Slovene workers were able to found their own newspaper, the first Slovene working-class organ, with the help of funds from the central party in Vienna; the right of workers to a press in their own language was the one formal recognition of nationality in its programme. In the 1891 Austrian general election they agreed to support an Italian candidate against the sitting Slovene MP Nabergoj, whom we have met, because, unlike Nabergoj, he supported universal suffrage. This was Trieste socialists' first step into the political arena.[23] So far, so good.

However, difficulties of cooperation mounted. Italian and Slovene socialists were under pressure from their co-nationals in a general atmosphere of contestation and wished to avoid the charge of national betrayal. The Italian leader, himself a convert from the famous Garibaldi's radical republicanism, hoped to win more recruits for socialism from that quarter. He was prepared to allow Slovene separate organisation only if it were subordinate to Italian regional leadership. Slovene socialists were afraid of the Slovene mainstream daily *Edinost*, which resented their opposition to Nabergoj and withdrew aid for their efforts for Slovene workers' education. There were deeper-seated tensions. Italian socialists inherited views of Slovenes as backward country folk due to assimilate to the higher Italian culture, a culture feeling under threat from ever-growing Slav numbers. Slovenes were hypersensitive to being demeaned on these lines. Their leaders were incomers from Carniola who were horrified at their migrant compatriots' parlous circumstances at the bottom of the pile in rampant early capitalism, usually without adequate housing and language skills. Language became a neuralgic point, alongside squabbles over Italian or multinational control of local organisation. Slovene calls for conference papers to be in Slovene and German as well as Italian led to an Italian walk-out on one occasion. Such matters could not really be controlled by the central party's fiat. Eventually, the Trieste Italians' socialist leader burst into denunciations of nationalism on the Slovenes' part and assertions that richer Italian culture had always prevailed over Slavs, whose backwardness unfitted them for socialism.[24] Matters were patched together somewhat when he retired.

Outside Trieste, tensions long remained mild. Slovene workers mixed with Germans in workers' associations in Carniola, Styria and beyond in ways which are not easy to trace, but in leadership and ideas largely followed German norms as reflected in the German socialist press they mainly read. Ideological issues did not loom large and Karl Marx was overshadowed by another German socialist, Ferdinand Lassalle. Towards the end of the century, however, a Slav sense of underrepresentation in the common party, particularly among the Czechs, spurred the ASDP to take the bull by the horns, initiating a third phase when socialists confronted the national question directly. Two congresses (1897–9) reorganised the party on a federal basis, proposing a centralised state to build the prospective socialist economy, alongside full national cultural autonomy. This was not be organised territorially for workers of different nationality often lived side by side, but by the 'personality principle'. Individuals would opt for the nation of their choice – it was assumed this would be by mother tongue – and the resulting bodies would finance their schools and other cultural needs as they chose. This ingenious approach met with some Slav criticism because traditionally richer communities had deeper pockets. Eventually, most Czech workers split off to found a party of their own

(1913), but the effect in Slovene lands was more a gradual strengthening of ethnic consciousness among Slovene workers and decline of common activities with Germans, yet continued allegiance to the ASDP, the Yugoslav Social Democratic Party, a largely Slovene body set up in 1896, operated in this spirit, and its Slovene organ *Rdeči prapor* (The Red Flag) became the preferred reading for workers in Carniola. Socialist federalism was to be discredited by its subjection to central communist party control in the Soviet Union, but it remained the most far-reaching socialist approach to the national question.

Welsh experience matches the first two stages of the Austrian pattern fairly well. Early responses to incoming English workers were often ethnocentric, as in clashes in the north Wales coalfield, and in the Scotch Cattle movement of the 1830s. Alongside the latter, though, Robert Owen's early trade union movement with its bilingual paper already showed signs of second stage collaboration. Owen's hostility to religion sapped its influence, however, and unionism came into its stride only later in the century. Yet the Welsh movement grew more strongly and was a more native affair than in the south Slav world. The remarkable William Abraham (Mabon, 1842–1922), leader of the 150,000-strong south Wales miners in the last decades of the century (doubling to 250,000 in the pre-war decades, half of them unionised), presided over a course of conciliation in employer–worker relations of distinctly Welsh stamp. A devout Calvinistic Methodist chapel elder who went down the pit at ten years of age, Mabon was also a keen, prizewinning eisteddfodwr, a fine singer and a powerful speaker in both languages whose course was eased by the hegemony of Welsh nonconformity. His belief that strike action brought more harm than good was influenced by Christian principle and his experience of the short-lived attempt of an Englishman Thomas Halliday (which he loyally supported), to build up a more militant trade union presence, only to be broken by failed strikes in the 1870s. Popularity as a skilled organiser and negotiator led to his election as the first Welsh working-class MP for Rhondda in 1885, against the opposition of Liberal middle-class leaders. In fact, his own principles did not differ much from theirs (his first speech in parliament was on Welsh disestablishment), he was a great friend of Gladstone, eventually a Privy Councillor, and he operated through the Rhondda Lib-Lab Council. Chris Williams has argued persuasively, however, that the appellation Lib-Lab conventionally applied to him underplays his insistence on being the representative of the working man.[25] Mabonism, with its reliance on cooperation of local unions reflecting the narrow mining valleys' geography and a Welsh community ethos, was increasingly challenged by proponents of more centralisation and greater willingness to strike. Mabon's popularity eventually declined along with support for the Sliding Scale he supported. A means of fixing wages according to the price of coal, it came to be felt more beneficial to employers than workers, particularly as Mabon opposed a minimum wage level. The failure of a great strike in 1898 led to the formation of the South Wales Miners' Federation (SWMF) which joined the Miners' Federation of Great Britain in 1907, both moves which Mabon initially opposed. In 1912 he resigned as president of the SWMF, a position which had been one of honour rather than power for some time.

It is possible to see the stormy events of Mabon's twilight years as an echo of the third phase of the socialist movement in the Habsburg Monarchy as depicted above. If so, it was a distant echo, in which ethnic motifs were rapidly declining in importance rather than growing. Though Mabon's funeral in 1922 was the most impressive the Rhondda has ever seen, his last message to the miners reminding them that 'the workman's best friend is Jesus of Nazareth' was a world away from central Europe and the Wales he left.[26] After another big failed strike centred in Tonypandy, Rhondda, in 1910–11 a group of young miners, some of whom had been educated in the Marxist-orientated Labour College in London, issued a challenge to the SWMF executive. Called 'The Miners' Next Step' (1912), their pamphlet mixed Marxist and syndicalist ideas. Employer power was to be broken by eroding profit and shareholder value and replacing them by pits run by the men themselves. Immediate aims were a minimum wage and seven-hour working day. This programme required for success the systematic creation in the longer term of a united industrial workforce of the whole country. The pamphlet was written in a terse, brilliant, quite literary style exemplifying the confidence and dignity it sought to evoke. It climaxed with a picture of the 'pitilessly exploited' slave of antiquity, 'the medieval serf bound to the soil' and 'the modern wage slave with nothing but his labour to sell ..., in the world's market place for a mess of pottage'. 'The possibilities of slavery' having been exhausted, the former wage slaves would finally ensure that mankind could 'live as men and not as beasts'.[27] After the use of Military Police against Tonypandy demonstrators, with army troops standing by, and a man died, it was said, of wounds from a police baton, 'The Miner's Next Step', to which a session of Parliament was devoted, consolidated the image of the Rhondda in the wider public's mind as an epicentre of working-class and specifically miner militancy. The image was of Welshness but a British Wales. Actually, the two men shot dead by troops in Llanelli in 1911, were striking railwaymen.

In comparative terms the key differentiation from a Slovene context was that the latter was part of a multinational state whose operation heightened the salience of nationality. In the case of the south Wales workers, the chief aspect of that was language. A high proportion of Welsh speakers were now functionally bilingual which eased problems of internal, not to say foreign, migration (for the Welsh emigrated to English-speaking lands), and diminished levels of alienation. It made the speaking of Welsh a personal rather than a social matter. The state was institutionally English, to borrow a term, so that expressions of love for Welsh, however sincere, had next to no impact on its actual use. Mabon is a good example of this syndrome. He was undoubtedly a Welsh language patriot, who consistently sided with it in individual cases and got away with speaking it several times in parliament because of popularity and personality. But like his professions of 'Welsh nationalism', as in his parliamentary addresses of 1909 and 1910, such engagements lacked a centre. This was legitimate because it was not his priority. He had been suspicious of Cymru Fydd because he felt it risked neglecting working-class concerns central to him. Similarly, Austrian socialists treated the national question initially with cliches until circumstances forced them to address it seriously. They then came up with a body of quite sophisticated work on the operation of multicultural societies and the balancing of economic and cultural priorities reflecting Marxist theories but also the central position of national feeling in public consciousness, the most famous being Otto Bauer's classic work of 1907, regrettably only fully translated into English in 2000.[28] This was not conceived of in Britain where nothing constrained mainstream socialists to concern themselves with this quite intellectually taxing matter. But a crucial factor in the Welsh experience is that, as we have seen, neither Welsh Nonconformists, nor before them the Morris circle, addressed the core of the language question either: the question of making the language fit for internal sovereignty. Hence the limited and often petty British level of discussion of such matters: on one side socialist talk of Welsh patriotic cant and, on the other, the anti-socialist polemics of the Revd W. F. Phillips in his book of 1913 with the loaded title, *Y Ddraig Goch ynte'r Faner Goch* (The Red Dragon or the Red Flag, Cardiff, 1913).

Slovene socialists' discourse offered rather more, drawing on debates on orthodox or 'revisionist' Marxism, the 'personality principle' and culture, and the radical democratic ideas of the Prague professor Thomas Masaryk under whom some of them had studied. The leader of the Yugoslav Social Democratic Party, Etbin Kristan, in his enthusiasm for the south Slav idea was even prepared to reopen the old question as to whether the Slovene language should attempt to cover the whole range of knowledge. A playwright himself, he thought Croat might be used for technological matters. This was the sort of thinking Ivan Cankar's patriotic persona excoriated.

These last themes reflected central European concerns. They did not arise in Wales. The Welsh language did not figure materially in SWMF debates on centralisation. The sending out of a conference agenda on this matter in 1913 bilingually after years of using English only appears a tactical move by opponents of change rather than a significant commitment to Welsh.[29] However, it raises an issue of social rather than political history, which merits some attention. Plainly, the decline of the traditional language was not without personal heart searchings, Jack Jones (1884–1970), who ended a colourful career as collier, miner's agent, communist, journalist and brief associate of Oswald Mosley by becoming a very popular novelist of valleys experience, litters his pages with characters resentful of the displacement of their mother tongue. That this undercurrent of the industrial south-east has aroused little attention from its historians reflects an understandably greater interest in the building of a vibrant new society. Yet it has meant in some cases an exaggerated desire to cut off that society from the chapel-ridden, puritanical, 'Nonconformist nation' (here used derisively) which in this view preceded it. References to that society's 'organic' conception of itself or to a 'Nonconformist Gaeltacht' are intended in this discourse to contrast with what Chris Williams has called Rhondda workers' 'collective, universalist definition of working-class and indeed Welsh identity that defied the linguistically exclusivist Welshness of a privileged minority'.[30] Williams justifies his exalted view of the Rhondda Labour movement basically on its power to inspire an entire community over a long period. This mirrors Welsh Nonconformists' sense of their movement too closely not to suggest the implicit rivalry. There is much again here of sons and fathers.

Of course, the reaction against Nonconformism could be a reaction against aspects of Welsh identity itself, like deliberate rejection of the Welsh language; but this should not be pre-dated. The Glamorganshire

valleys were still substantial seats of Welsh culture in 1914; O. M.
Edwards's editions of Welsh classics enjoyed some of their best sales in
them, attendances at visits by the National Eisteddfod were massive, as was
participation in the 1905 religious revival. Besides, English workers shared
much of the religious culture. Noah Ablett, drafter of 'The Miner's Next
Step', born in the Rhondda of English parents, had at one time thought of
entering the Nonconformist ministry; English-born A. J. Cook, another
associated with it and later secretary of the British Miners' Federation,
had been a young Baptist preacher. What Chris Williams heralds in the
Rhondda as 'A Labour People' was equally a Welsh one.

It remains to recall working-class and socialist experience in solidly Welsh-speaking Wales. In 1902 the Caernarfon *Herald Cymraeg*
printed a telegram from North Walian slate quarrymen based in Porth
in the Rhondda, which declared: 'We exalt Snowdonia, our country,
ourselves, our race and our Welsh pulpit by keeping our oath and standing like men. Better death than betrayal.'[31] The cause they trumpeted
was that of their comrades in Snowdonia who had been locked out by
Lord Penrhyn, the greatest landlord in Gwynedd, whose annual rental
from his Caernarfonshire estates totalled £63,000. They had taken temporary refuge in the south from a struggle which had already lasted two
years and would continue for a third, then the longest industrial dispute
in British labour history. *Undeb Chwarelwyr Gogledd Cymru* (The North
Wales Quarrymen's Union) had been founded in 1874 and had varying
fortunes under middle-class radical liberal leaders. The privations of the
almost wholly monoglot community (Bethesda) and the rift that ensued
between striker and blackleg families are the moving subject of one of
the best-selling Welsh-language novels of the twentieth century,[32] but the
workers' crushing defeat had diverse outcomes. As well as the defiance
of the quotation above was disappointment at the limited support from
Welsh leaders and surprise at that from English trade unionists, which
contributed to the spread of Independent Labour Party branches in north
Wales. Jim Griffiths (1890–1975), coalfield-born British Cabinet member
and Labour deputy leader, has recorded how helpful it was to him in his
youthful journey to the new socialist faith to hear it preached in Welsh by
the well-known north Walian Methodist poet-pastor Revd Silyn Roberts
before the First World War.[33]

The fullest treatment nascent socialism received in Welsh came from
a teacher of rural Montgomeryshire background, David Thomas, who

lived most of his life in Gwynedd. His book's title, *The Common People and their Kingdom*, with its triple internal division between darkness, light and the breaking of the dawn betrays at once the religious culture in which it is steeped.[34] It shows the overpowering sense of the time that because of past struggles the common people of Britain have come into their own. They are Kings and this is their Book of Kings. Thomas's 'our country' is Britain in discussing issues of poverty, housing and health, his main concern, but plainly Welsh in the context of past oppressions and emotional appeal. His background shows in his concern to stem rural depopulation through state aid for small land units farming intensively, if necessarily by compulsion. Ruskin's influence is marked as are advanced liberal nostrums on drink, women's rights and war. But what impresses is the extremely detailed statistical knowledge, drawn from all parts of the world, of wealth inequalities and all kinds of cooperative-rooted but also state-aided social reform initiatives. In the last section Thomas shows his hand and outlines a history of socialism and socialist parties, where Marx has a paragraph but is oddly said to advocate the parliamentary path. The writer sees knowledge as expanding horizons and peaceful cooperation between nations. Socialism and Christianity must go together, but references to the latter suggest cultural heritage rather than a driving religious motivation. Plainly, full success requires changes in human acquisitiveness but Thomas has his society's boundless faith in the power of education. His book shows a set of attitudes and motivations individually by no means unique but in their combination and framing uniquely the result of the experiences of the Welsh national community shaped over the previous century and a half. It ends with two lines of *cynghanedd*: Dyna wlad wen, ysblennydd/O feirdd, wele Gymru fydd. (Behold a shining, splendid country/O poets, see the Wales that is to be.)

This treatment suggests the bigger role overall that socialism played in Wales than Slovenia in the period up to 1914. This is unsurprising in view of the different social structures of the two countries by this time. Yet it was far from upsetting the Liberal Nonconformist hegemony we have described. The handful of Lib-Lab MPs in Mabon's mould formally took the Labour whip from 1910, but in the context of junior partnership with the Liberal government. Labour did not defeat the Liberals in open conflict in any parliamentary seat before the war and even at county council level barely figured. The popularity in the valleys of the pioneer Scottish socialist Keir Hardie, one of Merthyr Tydfil's two MPs, owed something to his linkage of socialism with Welsh values. Increased labour representation at the district council level, as in the Rhondda, indicates an underlying shift in attitudes, certainly in hindsight, though the intellectual influence of overt socialism on the lines of 'The Miners' Next Step' or Rhondda-centred Pleb Clubs was less in evidence.[35] In the Slovene lands the balance was different. The weaker working-class base, except in Trieste, made the issue more marginal. Socialism came on the agenda because of its appeal to the intelligentsia tradition we have noted in central Europe, but this made much debate an extension of student youth's engagement with radical ideas rather than a product of class consciousness on the part of workers themselves. It continued to express participants' sense of the masses' backwardness and the lag in development behind stronger societies which had characterised the Slovene modernisation movement from the start. An admirable representative of the type might be Anton Dermota, a Prague law graduate, and tireless organiser from secondary school days, active also in Czech and Croat circles and co-founder of *Naši zapiski* (1902–22), a radical journal moving to socialism. Dermota, influenced by Thomas Masaryk, believed the essence of socialism to be knowledge. Knowledge of the workings of capitalism was essential to the overwhelmingly proletarian Slovene people; so was solidarity as opposed to the selfishness of the bourgeoisie. Nationality and internationalism complemented each other in a 'solidarity of interest of autonomous nations'.[36] *Naši zapiski* brought occasional articles on strike action but rather more on the problems of teachers and university education. Its tone was often despondent – the position of Slovene teachers and schooling had got worse, if anything, over previous decades was one complaint – and there was a strong sense of Slovene powerlessness, abetted by lack of organisation and clear goals. Calls for improvement in these respects were a constant of radical periodicals which sound eerily similar to their counterparts today in awareness of marginality in a conservative society.

Yet one is impressed by the intellectual range of the best of the young writers in *Naši zapiski* and another monthly *Veda*, founded in 1911. Surveying Slovene development over the century of rebirth to the 'crisis' of the present, *Veda* set itself the task of reporting on developments in all the fields of modern 'positive knowledge', carrying forward the intellectual 'laicisation' almost all other nations had undergone. This meant concentrating the slender resources of Slovene expertise in these fields and seeking compromises between Slovenia's hitherto 'rather primitive' circumstances

and those of western culture.[37] One critique of views on contemporary
democracy commented on fourteen books in German, French and English
including Lionel Hobhouse's famous updating of Liberalism, which the
author later translated into Slovene. He also critiqued contemporary
theories of jurisprudence and 'neo-mercantilism' of the new age of car-
tels which made 'Manchester school' free market economics outmoded.
Another young writer, Bogumil Vošnjak, who on European travels had
visited Tolstoy, specialised in constitutional law, a third in the psychology
of nationalism. The cohort of educated Slovene commentators was small
but all published in German, Czech, Serbo-Croat and sometimes French,
as well as digesting foreign materials for Slovene readers. German-language
work was the first reference point for all specialist fields, particularly on
the key issue of education, while German creative literature was passed
over. It was the historical weakness of liberalism and the crucial role of the
Gymnasium in Germanic central Europe which helped foster such patterns among Slovenes and other Slavs in the region and could give relations
between liberals and socialist intellectuals potential importance. Elements
among the liberals hoped thereby to refresh their cause. Such relations
were developing in western Europe too, as witness shifts in Britain from
Gladstonism and then Hobhouse's left liberalism towards radicalism and
socialism. But the tradition of student politics from 1848, the Marxist cast
of socialism with its ostensible revolutionary goals and emotive nationality
issues combined distinctively to make for the distinctively heady atmosphere in the Habsburg Monarchy common to the pre-war years. The future
leading literary critic Ivan Prijatelj wrote in 1906 of the new turn from
the dreamy preoccupations of Slovene students in Prague, Vienna and
Graz to a harder-headed positivism, orientated to socio-economic questions with a sociological, statistical approach to national problems. Would
positivism be absorbed in a bland bourgeois politics, he asked, or could its
radicalism be blended with an idealist superstructure as revisionist Social
Democrats in Germany were speculating?[38] The context was an inaugural
congress of Slovene radical students in Trieste. The writer Ivan Cankar, a
socialist and nationalist, may be placed in this atmosphere of intellectual
ferment on the fringes of Slovene life. As a member of the mainly Slovene
Yugoslav Social Democratic Party which in 1909 called for a united south
Slav state he was naturally drawn to the Yugoslav question. His fringe
party's stance was a new departure, conceived in the framework of the
Austrian Social Democratic Party's professed nationality policy, which

envisaged a great restructuring of the Monarchy, harmonising centralist economics and free national cultures. Of course, the ASDP's programme was a utopia, designed to defuse the nationalist imbroglio; the Yugoslav Social Democratic Party was a mere fraction and the brilliant Cankar a quite unrepresentative figure. But the sense of stasis in the Monarchy fed also into elite insecurities and popular disconnection from government. Slovenia's placid politics were being steadily drawn into the most disruptive zone of European politics. The anthropologist Niko Zupanič expressed the frustrations which led young intellectuals like himself towards a Yugoslav position when he wrote that the individual south Slav peoples were nullities, but together they could count for something.[39] Exploring this issue must be the final twist in our tale.

SLOVENIA AND THE SOUTH SLAV QUESTION: TO 1914

In most ways the 'Yugoslav question' remained marginal to the mass of Slovenes. A largely pious peasant society, now in great majority literate and 'nationally conscious', remained loyal to the Habsburg connection. Yet there was a widespread feeling of living as a minority under supercilious, increasingly aggressive Germans. The German nationalist society Südmark was attempting to shift the ethnic balance in mixed areas in their favour by buying up farms, taking over inns, founding hotels for ethnic tourism and the like. Concretely, the Südmark wished to strengthen German rural communities around Maribor, so as to buttress this largely German town against absorption by its Slovene-speaking hinterland. In the event it seems these nationalist manoeuvres failed in their purpose. Recent American historiography has explained this by the concept of 'national indifference', the rejection of nationalist activists by local people, often bilingual and resistant to national labelling. While accepting the criticism of old stereotypes stressing inflamed rival communities, Slovene historians have been chary of making interaction across national divides tantamount to indifference to national feeling. They ascribe the failure of German propaganda to the negative reaction it roused among Slovenes.[40] This is an interesting part of recent debate on the Habsburg Monarchy, where objections to nationalism can involve questioning the role of nationhood itself. Revisionists are right to point out that outright secessionism was weak in the Monarchy. But nationalist bickering in its last decades did weaken its international prestige and contribute to a sense of crisis in governing circles, leading to a wish in some quarters for strong action to demonstrate Austria-Hungary's continued vitality. It undoubtedly contributed to the decision to annex Bosnia-Herzegovina in 1908 which the Monarchy had administered under nominal Turkish sovereignty. This unilateral annexation aroused hostility in the international community and infuriated the Serbs, who had always laid claim to Bosnia. It heightened pressures for south Slav unity in the Monarchy – and more covert support for one outside it in an independent Yugoslavia.

In the same month a serious outbreak of German-Slovene hostility occurred when disturbances in Ptuj, another mainly German town in a Styrian Slovene countryside, led to counter-demonstrations by Slovenes in Ljubljana. Windows were smashed, property of German businesses damaged and, when police and military were called in, two Slovenes shot dead. At the next meeting of the Carniolan Diet the provincial governor was greeted with cries of Germaniser, lackey, traitor, ingrate, murderer, oppressor of the Slovene nation etc. and could not make himself heard amid 'indescribable noise'; the session was suspended.[41] This was par for the course for late Austrian parliamentarism, indeed mild. The Diet later thanked the Emperor for his gracious acknowledgement of their loyal address and approved the annexation, though the national liberal leader, from whose ranks the abuse had mainly come, warned that without changes in nationality policy the south Slav issue could become the Monarchy's Piedmont. This was an allusion to the role of the little kingdom of Piedmont-Sardinia in Italy's unification, ending Austrian rule in north Italy in the 1860s. Serbia was the potential south Slav Piedmont.

We have seen that playing the south Slav card was a possible Slovene gambit when dissatisfied with politics in the Monarchy. It was not a strong card. A liaison with the Croats, similar in language and religion, might potentially give the little Slovene nation more weight in the scale of things, but Croatia was weak itself and more interested in relations with Serbs. Slovene Catholics, who were stronger politically than their Croat co-religionists, were less happy with an orientation towards Orthodox Serbs.

The response of the Slovene conservative Catholic majority was thus to press, not very dynamically, for closer ties with Croatia on 'trialist lines', that is a south Slav third unit in the Monarchy alongside Austria and Hungary. In 1912 the All-Slovene People's Party even united formally with right-wing Croats, though a real fusion did not come about in practice. When the Hungarian government suspended the Croatian Diet and imposed a Commissioner in its place, mass sympathy protests broke out in other south Slav lands, and a Croatian student tried but failed to assassinate the Commissioner. But the real game-changer was the Balkan wars of 1912–13. The independent Balkan states together defeated Ottoman Turkey and pushed it out of Europe except for the hinterland of Constantinople. Serbia's prestige and Slovene Serbophilia were greatly enhanced from these events. Yugoslav unity, at least cultural, was thrust onto the agenda. Slovene periodicals filled with reviews of Serbian history and culture. In an enquiry organised by *Veda* into attitudes to language and nationality in the new situation, the majority of respondents declared themselves for closer relations with other south Slavs, for standardisation of Slovene and Serbo-Croat technical vocabulary and for a drive to expand study of that language by Slovenes. A number agreed that Slovene could not cover the full range of modern experience, for which Slovenes should adopt Serbo-Croat.[42] It was this echo of old debates about Slovene linguistic viability that infuriated Cankar, but he was one of many now avowing the political goal of national unity as Yugoslavs, if not, like Cankar, *outside* the Monarchy. That explicitly anti-Austrian position was attractive to a section of student radicals, however. Several congresses of south Slav student youth had been held since one in Belgrade in 1904. In the aftermath of the suspension of Croatia's constitution a programme agreed between Croat and Serb students affirmed the goal of 'the unification of the Serbo-Croat nation, together with the Slovene nation'.[43] Justification for the inclusion of Slovenes here lay in the activity of the magazine *Preporod* (Rebirth), five numbers of which appeared in 1912–13, and the propaganda of the tireless Ivan Endlicher who organised a union of Slovene student youth to agitate for the cause in their summer holidays. Endlicher's own work in Croatia and visits to Sarajevo made him a significant figure in the circles of Young Bosnia, from which the assassins of Franz Ferdinand came. After this fateful act of 28 June 1914, twenty-six Slovene secondary school students were put on trial in Ljubljana in December for their propaganda work, six more accused having fled. Their extreme youth mirrored that of the Bosnian conspirators. Endlicher himself died in prison awaiting retrial to lengthen the court's sentence the next year.[44] Several dozen Slovenes meanwhile had enlisted in the Serbian army, joining those who had already gone to

Serbia to fight in the Balkan wars. With Austria-Hungary's declaration of war on Serbia (28 July 1914) began the move to a general conflict which Britain entered a week later

WORLD WAR AND DÉNOUEMENT: TO 1918

In both our countries the war was greeted with patriotic enthusiasm. Mainstream Slovene opinion had blamed Serbian terrorism for the assassination of Franz Ferdinand. In Britain Lloyd George, who had not wanted war, threw his activist spirit into its promotion, urging London Welshmen to support the 'little five-foot-five nations' (Serbs and Belgians) against German bullies. Nonconformist ministers, editors and intellectual leaders like Henry Jones and John Morris-Jones denounced German authoritarianism and militarism; the Revd John Williams, Brynsiencyn, a prestigious Calvinistic Methodist and former pastor of Princes Road Chapel, Liverpool, cut a particularly surprising figure as the belligerent honorary chaplain of the new Welsh regiment formed as a result of Lloyd George's push for a 'Welsh Army'. Lloyd George's role was important in overcoming pacifist reservations. His hand was behind Brynsiencyn's innovatory appointment as a Nonconformist army chaplain, part of a design to strengthen Welsh and Irish identity in the British army, reflected also in distinctive uniforms and flags.[45] The founding of a new Welsh Guards' single battalion-regiment to represent Wales in the Guards Division was part of the same thinking. Such signals and initial positive effects of the war economy on Welsh workers' living standards helped sustain support for the war effort. Criticism was confined to elements in the Welsh-language press, which defended the civil rights of conscientious objectors to military service.

In the Slovene lands initial backing for the war was more sorely tried by heavy-handed government policy. Constitutional government along with parliament was suspended, censorship strengthened and some prominent nationalists like Cankar and the ex-mayor of Ljubljana, Ivan Hribar, put in jail. Hundreds of peasants were arrested in the Styrian areas where national indifferentism has been claimed by later historians. Religious leaders urged patriotic commitment for the Catholic monarchy against the 'Masonic' Italian secular state, but as in Wales had to negotiate the tension between religious precepts and militarism. Anton Jeglič, bishop of Ljubljana, evaded army pressure for a home guard-type civilian role in border areas, knowing that peasants were more reserved towards the war effort than enlisted youth. An Italian invasion from the west which sent eighty thousand refugees into the interior in 1915 helped motivation. The Church's hope was that sufferings in the Habsburg cause could fuse with Catholic themes of sacrifice, but as the war progressed it became clear that peasant soldiers saw themselves as victims rather than martyrs. Their over-riding existential concern was survival.[46] The committed Yugoslav Bogumil Vošnjak had meanwhile joined a Yugoslav Committee formed by Croats and Serbs in exile to work for an independent south Slav state. By the time Franz Joseph died and his young successor allowed parliament to reconvene in 1917, Slovene opinion had gone beyond old Croat-Slovene calls for trialism to favour including Serbs too in a Yugoslav state within a federal Monarchy. Slovene participation in the 'May Declaration' of South Slav MPs calling for this brought no concessions, however, but rather signs that the Monarchy's leaders would yield to German pressures for recentralisation and rolling back rights granted. Mutinies and mass demonstrations rocked an Austria suffering the privations of an Allied blockade. The Habsburgophile leader of the All-Slovene People's Party withdrew, discredited, and the May Declaration was increasingly pre-sented as a minimum programme. In August 1918 a national committee was formed in Ljubljana, then a united one with Croats in October which entered into negotiations with the exiled Yugoslavs and the Serbian gov-ernment over the future common state.[47]

If this sounds complicated to unfamiliar readers, it was barely less so for participants. The narration above shows how rapidly in shifting contexts horizons can alter and perspectives previously only dimly appre-hended stand out in heightened clarity. The articles of a young geographer, Anton Melik, in *Ljubljanski zvon* in 1918 are a good example. Laying bare the situation in western Europe where a few powerful nations had formed fully consolidated states, assimilating (nameless) minor groupings, he contrasted it with the east of the continent. There a more complex ethnic mix, invasions and other factors had thwarted the sociological ten-dency towards assimilation so that its logical opposite, fragmentation, had occurred; disjointed regimes of ethnic domination held in thrall non-dominant peoples wrongly deemed incapable of forming states on their own. But now the modern forces of democracy and nationalism were working to replace chaos with consolidation, through the rise of united Slav states to challenge empires like the Habsburg Monarchy and displace the ruling elites which had frustrated this natural development. With state power in democratic hands the Slovene countryside would assimilate the German towns. Melik's articles showed how a young generation of Slovenes had assimilated a pragmatic, not to say hard-nosed sociology, illustrating the conviction of Slovene patriots that unlucky fate had subjected Slavs to alien rule and division. They illustrated too an oversimplified, if understandable, view of western Europe which continues to hold sway.[48] Slav language and identity had been key to the concerns of steadily widening circles of Slovene people from the onset of the national revival. Ideas of nationhood had awoken them to their position and enabled them to improve it. The course of the First World War rendered their accommodation to a German-dominated world more burdensome but also made the alternative Slav perspective more plausible than before. In grasping towards it, most had not gone as far as intellectuals like Melik towards full conversion to the Yugoslav national idea but saw it basically in terms of their own national hope of autonomy in an order free from German hegemony. Yet the circumstances which had brought them thus far also faced them with the aspirations of Serbs, Croats and Italians and with the Great Powers' ideas for an international settlement. In the event, up against Italian pressure both Slovenes and Croats had to accept a Yugoslavia shaped by the stronger Serbs and the British and French Allies. That meant that Slovenes did get the removal of the German ruling elite and its language, but nearly one-third of the Slovene people lay outside the new state: mainly in the western regions of Italian social dominance, including Trieste, but also the great bulk of Slovene Carinthia, whose population voted 60:40 in a referendum to stay in Austria. These were certainly new directions, but with history's usual ironies and equivocations. Yet history does not rest and there is no point at which national history, in particular, can plausibly claim a decisive end point and declare 'job done!'

This was true of Wales too. A very overtly Welsh-speaking Welshman presided over a British Cabinet containing a highly successful minister for Food Control and fellow countryman David Thomas (Lord Rhondda), and served as deputy Cabinet Secretary by a Welsh confidant, Thomas Jones. The disestablishment of the state Church in Wales, held over for the duration of the war, was duly implemented in 1920, completing the dismantling of the alien ascendancy of landowners and clergy which the Welsh *gwerin* had battled against at every level of local power. The irony was that Lloyd George's Liberal Party had been torn apart by wartime feuds and after his fall in 1922 was never to hold power again; that during the war working-class militancy had flared repeatedly in south Wales and the Labour Party was poised to take over its Welsh hegemony; that the religious values so many Welsh spokesmen had vaunted were severely shaken by the war; and that the Welsh language was about to undergo a steady decline not just relatively but in absolute numbers.

That said, and leaving further remarks to the conclusion, one can at least affirm that the two stories told here have all history's power to excite wonder and reflection. Who could have imagined at the eighteenth-century outset that the dialects of Slovene peasants would produce the sophisticated discourses cited above or that Cardiff, the 'poor starveling place' of contemporaries in 1800 would become in a century a metropolis of 200,000 and the greatest coal-exporting port in the world?[49] True, our peoples' stories contained nothing as epic as those of larger nations or as dramatic as many smaller ones. The two Slovenes shot by Austrian police in Ljubljana in 1908 and Welsh workers killed in Tonypandy and Llanelli in 1910–11 were small beer to the hundreds of Bosnian Serbs lynched or executed in revenge for Gavrilo Princip's shots at Sarajevo in 1914, let alone the blood-letting thereafter. Yet Slovene and Welsh experiences do not thereby lack the power to move and motivate. There is testimony from a figure of this period, the mayor of Ljubljana Ivan Hribar, whom we have encountered. Summoned by Italian occupiers who partitioned Slovenia with the Nazis in 1941, Hribar refused their demand to come out of retirement in his ninetieth year to be mayor once more. He returned to his home, draped himself in the Yugoslav flag, walked to a bridge over Ljubljana's river, and plunged to his death. He left a farewell letter containing Prešeren's lines: 'night wrapped in death's black earth is less terrible than days of slavery in the sun'. A political allegiance is indicated by the Yugoslav flag, but the national inspiration was plainly Slovene. I allow myself a vignette from my own country, less striking, but evocatively Welsh. A victim of the First World War was the young Welsh shepherd poet, Hedd Wyn (Ellis Evans), whose dream was to compete successfully in the National Eisteddfod with the 'college boys'. He achieved it but was not to know, his victory being announced before an empty chair after his death in Passchendaele, the subject of a moving film which figured for a foreign-language Oscar at Hollywood. Such things are important for nationhood, at least for small nations.

NOTES

1 J. Roth, *The Radetsky March*, trans. by Eva Tucker (London, 1974), p. 222.

2 O. M. Edwards, *A Short History of Wales* (3rd impression, London, 1913), p. 126.

3 W. Rees, *Cardiff: A History of the City* (2nd rev. edn, Cardiff, 1969), pp. 276–96.

4 Theatre information is mainly based on individual town and theatre websites, and the 'Music Hall and Theatre History site dedicated to Arthur Lloyd, 1839–1904', which is detailed for Cardiff, Swansea and Newport.

5 Gwenfair Parry, '"Queen of the Welsh Resorts": Tourism and the Welsh Language in Llandudno in the Nineteenth Century', *Welsh History Review*, 22 (2001), 118–48.

6 E. D. Lewis, *The Rhondda Valleys: A Study of Industrial Development from 1800 to the Present Day* (London, 1959), pp. 220–2.

7 D. Ben Rees, *Chapels in the Valley: A Study in the Sociology of Welsh Nonconformity* (Upton, Wirral, 1975), pp. 9, 75–8.

8 Paul O'Leary, 'Processions, Power and Public Space: Corpus Christi at Cardiff, 1872–1914' (*Welsh History Review*, 24 (2008), 77–101.

9 Thomas Bowen, *Dinas Caerdydd a'i Methodistiaeth Galfinaidd* (The City of Cardiff and its Calvinistic Methodism) (n pl 1927), pp, 95–6; *Y Bywgraffiadur Cymreig hyd 1940* (London, 1954), p. 765 (Pugh).

10 Bowen, *Dinas Caerdydd*, pp. 89, 92.

11 Arthur Herbert Jones, *His Lordship's Obedient Servant: Recollections of a South Wales Borderer* (Llandysul, 1987), p. 26.

12 B. Rees, 'Sport, Coal and Identity in Swansea, 1870–1910', *Welsh History Review*, 29/4 (2019), 594–623.

13 Rhiannon Mason, *Museums, Nations, Identities: Wales and Its National Museums* (Cardiff, 2007), pp. 107–47.

14 H. Teifi Edwards, *Codi'r Hen Wlad yn ei Hôl 1850–1914* (Putting the Old Country Back on its Feet) (Llandysul, 1989), p. 240.

15 Edwards, *Codi'r Hen Wlad*, p. 250. He used this term in connection with the Investiture of the Prince of Wales in 1911. For Rhoscomyl, see also Neil Evans and Huw Pryce, 'Outlaw Historian and Popular History in Edwardian Wales', in Evans and Pryce, *Writing a Small Nation's Past: Wales in Comparative Perspective, 1850–1950* (London, 2012), pp. 111–26.

16 Edwards, *Codi'r Hen Wlad*, p. 310.

17 Neil Evans, 'The Welsh Victorian City: The Middle Class and Civic and National Consciousness in Cardiff, 1850–1914', *Welsh History Review*, 12/3 (1985), 350–87 (377–80).

18 Evans, 'Welsh Victorian City', 375.

19 Ioan Williams, *Y Mudiad Drama yng Nghymru 1880–1940* (The Drama Movement in Wales 1880–1940) (Cardiff, 2006).

20 Edwards, *Codi'r Hen Wlad*, p. 302.

21 M. Ballin, *Writers of Wales: Welsh Periodicals in English, 1882–2012* (Cardiff, 2013); M. Wynn Thomas, *In the Shadow of the Pulpit: Literature and Nonconformist Wales* (Cardiff, 2010), chs 2 and 3.

22 See Hans Mommsen, *Die österreichische Sozialdemokratie und die Nationalitätenfrage im habsburgischen Vielvölkerstaat* (Austrian Social Democracy and the Nationality Question in the Multiethnic Habsburg State) (Vienna, 1963), for the overall argument; p. 153 for the quotation.

23 For the Trieste socialist experience: Boris M. Gombač, 'Slovenska socialdemokracija v Trstu 1889–1900' (Social Democracy in Trieste 1889–1900), *Zgodovinski časopis* (2006), 95–121.

24 Gombač, 'Slovenska socialdemokracija', 118.

25 Chris Williams, *Democratic Rhondda: Politics and Society, 1885–1951* (Cardiff, 1996).

26 Eric W. Evans, *Mabon (William Abraham 1842–1922): A Study in Trade Union Leadership* (Cardiff, 1959), p. 101.

27 Unofficial Reform Committee, 'The Miners' Next Step' (Tonypandy, 1912), p. 30.

28 Otto Bauer, *The Question of Nationalities and Social Democracy*, trans. by Joseph O'Donnell (Minneapolis, MN, 2000).

29 Hywel Francis and David Smith, *The Fed: A History of the South Wales Miners in the Twentieth Century* (London, 1980), p. 19.

30 Williams, *Democratic Rhondda*, p. 212.

31 R. Merfyn Jones, *The North Wales Quarrymen 1874–1922* (Cardiff, 1982), p. 282.

32 T. Rowland Hughes, *Chwalfa* (Upheaval) (Aberystwyth, 1946). The novel is set in an imagined locality but faithfully reproduces the events in Bethesda.

33 D. Thomas, *Silyn (Robert Silyn Roberts) 1871–1910* (Liverpool, [1956]), p. 77.

34 D. Thomas, *Y Werin a'i Theyrnas* (The Common People and Their Kingdom) (Liverpool, 1910). The traditional Welsh sermon was commonly constructed around *tri phen* (three heads, or themes). The prominent Welsh-language novelist and activist of today, Angharad Tomos, is David Thomas's granddaughter.

35 Williams, *Democratic Rhondda*, pp. 47, 215, plausibly argues for the significance of growing district representation.

36 Dragotin Lončar, *Dr Anton Dermota (1876–1914)*, *Naši zapiski*, 11/7–8 (1914), 179–86.

37 *Veda*, 1/1 (1911), pp. 1–4: editors' programmatic statement.

38 Ivan Prijatelj, 'Iz naroda za narod. 1. shod narodno-radikalnega dijaštva v Trstu' (From the Nation for the Nation, The First Meeting of Slav Students in Trieste), 26, *Ljubljanski zvon* (1906), 184–6.

39 N. Zupanič, 'Ilirija', *Ljubljanski zvon*, 27 (1907), 486.

40 See Pieter M. Judson, *Guardians of the Nation: Activism on the Language Frontiers of Imperial Austria* (Cambridge, MA, 2006), ch. 4. For a Slovene view: J. Cvirn, 'Nacionalizam in nacionalno koeksistence', *Zgodovinski časopis*, 63 (2009), 228–38.

41 *Slovenski narod*, 2 January 1909.

42 Odgovori na 'Vedino' anketo o jugoslovanskem vprašanju, *Veda*, 3/2 (1913), 97–113.

43 Printed in D. Ljubibratić, *Gavrilo Princip* (Belgrade, 1959), pp. 102–5.

44 Carol Rogel, 'Preporodovci: Slovene Students for an Independent Yugoslavia', *Canadian Slavic Studies*, 5, no. 2 (1973), pp. 196–212.

45 John Ellis, 'National Armies in the Field: National Identity and Recruitment in Ireland and Wales, 1914–1916', paper given at a Conference on Ireland and Wales in the First World War at Cardiff University, 11 Sept. 2014.

46 P. Bobič, *War and Faith: The Roman Catholic Church in Slovenia and the First World War, 1914–1918* (Leiden, 2012), pp. 34–7; 241–6.

47 Walter Lukan, 'Habsburška monarhija in Slovenci v prvi svetovni vojni' (The Habsburg Monarchy and the Slovenes in the First World War), *Zgodovinski časopis*, 62 (1908), 91–149.

48 See Melik's articles, under the pseudonym Anton Loboda, in the January and September/October numbers of *Ljubljanski zvon* (1918): respectively 'Misli o slovanskih narodnostnih problemih' (Thoughts on Slav Nationality Problems), 64–73 and 'Vprašanje narodno mešnih ozemelj' (The Question of National Mixed Areas), 637–50.

49 Geraint H. Jenkins, *Bard of Liberty: The Political Radicalism of Iolo Morganwg* (Cardiff, 2012), p. 218.

RETROSPECT AND PROSPECT

This book has sought to 'place' the development of Wales as a small nation in the modern period. Though planned before the current Covid crisis, it has been completed at an intriguing juncture, when the British media have regularised as never before the expression the 'four nations of the UK'. The acceptance of Wales as a nation has never been doubted by the Welsh themselves or been called in question in conventional parlance in their own British context, perhaps because it had rarely been a politically contentious issue since the fifteenth-century rising of Owain Glyndŵr. The obvious ethnic distinctiveness of the Welsh made the term 'nation' with its long pedigree in the sense of 'people' a natural term, with a touch more substance than the modern expression 'ethnic group' with its wide range of applications. The increased politicisation of ethnicity which has been such a feature of European and then global life in recent centuries has made for ambiguity, however. Outside the British Isles, or 'these islands' in the convenient Irish term, the Welsh are largely invisible to the wider world. Are they a 'modern nation' among the many which have emerged to general view in our complex global society? This comparison of their experience with that of a clearly established small modern nation, the Slovenes, has looked at the period most significant for the crystallisation of European nations in their modern form, from the Enlightenment to the First World War. Other kinds of comparison could be made, with the Scots and Irish or with smaller west European peoples like the Bretons and Basques. The approach here arises from the writer's interest in east-central Europe and the Habsburg Monarchy. Since this book has as prime aim the elucidation of the Welsh experience, its conclusion concentrates on the Welsh side of the story.

The last chapter closed by pointing up the ambiguities of the situation in 1918 and the open-endedness and hopefully the interest of the two national stories told. Here more concrete conclusions are in order, where the hindsight of a further century may be called on for further perspective. Already it was clear that Welsh national consciousness, more in evidence in than Slovene in 1750, had fallen behind by 1918. In that year Slovenes left the Habsburg Monarchy to become a constituent people of the new state of Yugoslavia,with the Slovene language taking over in Slovene areas the leading public role that German had played under the old Monarchy. In 1919, the Slovene-language University Slovenes had been vainly demanding opened its doors. At the same time, it is symptomatic of the lack of a Welsh political programme that no representations on behalf of Wales were made at the Paris Peace Conference as they were, for example, by Bretons and Slovaks; by this time, the Welsh language was spoken by somewhat less than half the population of Wales. The underlying situation was, to be sure, not as sharply distinct as this. The Slovene dream of an autonomous Slovenia was far from fulfilled. Besides the huge loss of Slovenes in Trieste, Gorica province and Carinthia, the remaining lands did not formally constitute Slovenia in the new unitary state, which was based on the theory of a common south Slav nationality. On the other hand, Wales *was* present at Versailles in the person of the British prime minister, David Lloyd George, an unparalleled elevation to the highest office in Britain or the Monarchy of a speaker of a minority language, formerly harbouring nationalist sympathies. This was not a fluke. Lloyd George was the star of a pleiade of young Welsh-speaking Nonconformist politicians, a mark of the energy of this community at the zenith of its influence. He has been eclipsed in English memories by Churchill, though Churchill himself said on his death that he had been the leading figure in British life in the first half of the twentieth century both in peace and war. Welsh memories of him are shadowed by a national sense of shortfall after the enthusiasm of Cymru Fydd. A radical Liberal whose party was replaced by Labour after his fall from power, distrusted by English Conservatives and harshly criticised by later nationalists for failing to do more for Wales, this dynamic figure has suffered from the Welsh lack of confidence. His path-breaking social reforms as Chancellor of the Exchequer stemmed directly from his background as champion of the Welsh Nonconformist *gwerin* against privilege; his resourcefulness and willingness to compromise with former enemies has too often been written off as opportunistic, even Celtic deviousness. Kenneth Morgan has argued for the ongoing importance of Wales in his concerns.[1] His condemnation from Jamaica of the treatment of three Welsh nationalists for arson of a military site erected in a place of Welsh cultural importance in 1937 – putting Wales on trial at the Old Bailey, as he called it – is an intriguing echo of his younger self: 'I should like to be there and I should like to be forty years younger'.[2]

AFTERMATH

Wales's inter-war experience aided the disillusionment brought by the frustration of Cymru Fydd and war. Industrial depression, leading to mass emigration from a blighted coalfield, together with language decline, changed the terms of the Welsh scene. Talk of home rule waned as preoccupations shifted with the rise of Labour. The Welsh Nationalist Party (later Plaid Cymru) formed in 1926 with a programme for a Welsh-speaking Wales and 'Dominium Status' on Canadian/Australian lines, polled a mere six hundred votes in its first campaign in 1929 and only slowly began to make headway with overtures to English speakers and the formulation of economic policies. The 1937 protest against official neglect of Wales mentioned above inspired a rise in its popularity but wartime crisis intervened to cut this short. It is fair to point out the continuing modernisation of Welsh-language culture. The son of Sir O. M. Edwards founded a successful, still existing, youth movement, *Urdd Gobaith Cymru*, in 1922, whose eventual fifty or so thousand members swore to be loyal to Wales, to fellow man and to Christ. *Y Llenor* (1922–51), a literary review of modern stamp and high quality, achieved some eight thousand subscribers between the wars, Welsh language poetry reached a high standard and an anglophone Welsh literature made strides towards maturity.

Meanwhile, inter-war Yugoslavia's fortunes tottered as a backward state relative to Austria, riven by Serb-Croat discord.[3] Split between pro-autonomy Catholics and liberals who favoured a unitary state, Slovenes tended to align with the Belgrade government when they could: the Slovene Catholic leader, a priest, Anton Korošec, served briefly as prime minister as a kind of neutral. When Yugoslavia was attacked by the Nazis in 1941 the Slovene lands were divided between the Nazis and Fascist Italy and exposed to prospective de-nationalisation. The Slovene Left and a section of liberal Catholics eventually sided with the communist-led

Partisans; conservatives abstained or in some cases collaborated. These experiences show the shadow side of Slovenia's position in a turbulent multinational region, exposed to malign neighbours as much as potentially positive cultural contacts. But the Gorica region was regained from defeated Italy and Slovenes secured minority rights in Trieste; Carinthia remained in Austria with a gradually dwindling Slovene population. Overall, despite any greater success of the Slovene national programme, it seems likely that the Welsh in Great Britain continued to be more contented with their lot than the Slovenes, as had been the case in the nineteenth century.

The post-1945 years are now a lengthy era in themselves. Slovenia gained autonomy as one of communist Yugoslavia's six Republics, a formal status at first in a centralised Marxist regime which gained in substance as the state began to liberalise from the 1960s. It had a markedly higher standard of living than the rest of Yugoslavia and was the only Republic where All Saints Day was a public holiday, though Marshall Tito's ideological henchman was a Slovene. Slovenes were prominent in the pressure for further freedoms in the later 1980s. A major episode was the trial of some young radicals – one the current right-wing prime minister Janez Janša – for insulting the Yugoslav National Army, which was held in the Army's official language, Serbo-Croat. This was a much-resented breach of custom. In 1991, Slovenia voted overwhelmingly for independence and is now a member of the European Union. This was in part a replay of the development in the First World War: the degeneration of the Yugoslav Federation was the trigger for a quite rapid change of heart by Slovenes who had previously been prepared to live with a seemingly unassailable status quo.

Wales's post-war history falls in a number of parts: some economic recovery in the relatively optimistic initial decades, followed by continuous decline of heavy industry; first concessions to devolution and identity – Cardiff as capital (1955), followed by administrative devolution through the Welsh Office (1964); the rise of Plaid Cymru and the devolution referenda of 1979, 1997 and 2011; the role of the Senedd from 1999; and, throughout, the travails of the Welsh language and the many efforts, not all unsuccessful, on its behalf. The result has been the emergence of Wales as a political nation and component part of the British political process, not in the semi-disguised form of Church disestablishment but acting independently on such key current issues as health and education.

Yet Wales remains shadowed in the 'four nations' framework by the Scottish and Irish problems, and the sense that the English majority, particularly the triumphant Brexiteers, are waiting the opportunity to check and roll back the devolution project.

RETROSPECT

Thus the Welsh historiography which has blossomed in the post-war period continues to reflect uncertainty as far as Welsh nationhood is concerned. Its strength lies in an efflorescence of research on the labour movement and the moving life experiences behind it, broadening into other fields, including religion and the press, but also literature, with due attention to literature in English. Of many books assessing modern Wales as a whole only a few can be mentioned here. Those written between the failed referendum of 1979 and its successful successor in 1997 could be stark, like Gwyn A. Williams's view of the Welsh as 'now nothing more than a naked people under an acid rain' or John Davies's question, in view of the decline of both Welsh and Anglo-Welsh culture, as to whether the nation itself was coming to an end. Both, though, invoked Wales's ability to recover from past crises. Geraint H. Jenkins in 2007 contrasted evidence of more people viewing their identity as Welsh rather than British with the modern trends working against 'a coherent sense of identity' and making for 'a diverse, fragmented and multi-faceted' community. Russell Davies at the end of his multi-volume social history in 2018 is more upbeat in seeing a people 'vastly varied' and 'utterly different from each other' living nonetheless in a 'context of cultural unity'. His widely researched and colourful presentation, however, treats anyone with a connection to Wales as grist to its mill and does not really define in what the cultural unity consists. Of all these accounts the most suggestive is Kenneth Morgan's *Rebirth of a Nation: Wales 1880–1980*, though published some time back in 1981. Morgan discusses in detail the shift from the pre-1914 Nonconformist hegemony to the Labour Wales, with re-emergent nationalist fringe, of the later twentieth century, noting in conclusion another shift, in the Wales–Britain relationship as British self-confidence declined. Morgan also regularly notes the decline of the Welsh language and is ready to make comparisons. The decline he implicitly ascribes to modernisation and the comparisons are with minority national movements like the *Québécois* and Catalan. A key finding of the present book's discussion of Slovenia is that modernisation need not work against lesser used languages, and Morgan's sophisticated appraisal might benefit from comparisons with small nations (and former minorities) in east-central Europe.[4] But in this respect the work has since been done, in by far the most original recent book touching on Welsh history, though written by a literary critic, Simon Brooks's *Why Wales Never Was: The Failure of Welsh Nationalism*.

Brooks compares the fortunes of Welsh with those of non-dominant languages in the Habsburg Monarchy. His excoriating attack on nineteenth-century Welsh liberals denounces their complicity in the individualistic approach to rights of English thinkers of the time, which paid no attention to the rights of communities like Welsh speakers and left them bereft of the kind of support which language legislation was providing non-dominant groups in the Habsburg Monarchy. The argument strikes home to students of the Monarchy, but it is to Simon Brooks's great credit that he has explored the situation in both locales with such thoroughness and introduced into Welsh historiography the note of challenging polemic which any culture needs for its health. His argument focuses on the mid-nineteenth-century turning-point when, as we have seen, the introduction of constitutionalism in Austria (1848, 1860s) granted the principle at least of national and language equality, at the same time that Hugh Owen's generation were committed to progress for Wales through the embrace of world-conquering English.

Powerful arguments spoke for his strategy in the eyes of contemporaries. How could a tiny people neglect the vast cultural and practical resources for progress opened up by a world language? This was, after all, the argument of Dežman in Slovenia. It did not have to mean the abandonment of the mother tongue in daily life. As the Carniolan German poet Anton von Auersperg put it in 1863: 'May the melodious, beautiful provincial language be cultivated, developed, enriched, built up, may it be secured its rights in school, church and public office ... but let the German language retain its importance, its great task, its destined role also for this land.'[5] The role Auersperg claimed for German was to be the medium through which Slovenes accessed the wider world and international culture. But the quotation shows the great difference between the Slovene position in the Habsburg Monarchy and the Welsh in Great Britain. What accounted for this disparity, at a time when social and political development made the politicisation of Welsh and Slovene identity plausible and set patterns for the future? The first half of this book has shown how the 'awakenings' of our two countries had gradually diverged since their eighteenth-century origins. The Slovene movement evolved on linguistic lines, seeing in the advancement of the mother tongue the key to the 'progress' both countries' leaders emphasised. This went with the grain of the multi-ethnic Habsburg society, suffused with Herderian notions of the importance of language, but where none of its many peoples, was able to impose its own as overriding medium, as Dežman and Auersperg urged for German. In the context of the overwhelmingly English-speaking and successful British state, however, the argument for English was much stronger. Besides, Welsh leaders like Gwilym Hiraethog and Lewis Edwards, inspired by the religious revival, held that the key to progress lay in the energising power of their Nonconformist version of Christianity, whose remarkable rise had already become identified as a national movement. The acquisition of English seemed to them a desirable, practical goal and well within the capacities of an awoken people. As argued in chapter four, priorities have a way of winning out, and both had a logic in their respective situations. The Slovenes succeeded in making Slovene a potential medium of all spheres of life – 'cultural sovereignty'. The mass of the Welsh people succeeded in learning English without abandoning their Welsh nationality. The force of context in life is such that societies commonly take their own experience for granted and cannot easily conceive of the other. This is the case in Slovenia and Wales in the case of language. It is the role of comparative study to bring overlooked possibilities to their attention.

Let us summarise the Slovene course first, as it has been described in successive chapters above. Continuing to react to the atmosphere of cultural and linguistic renewal which had surrounded them from the late eighteenth century and taking advantage of the opportunities afforded by Austrian constitutionalism, albeit still limited and grudging, they continued as far as they could to emulate the path followed by stronger cultures, shape their language into an instrument for this by extending its vocabulary, venturing into new literary forms, forming their own cultural societies alongside existing ones in German, founding book clubs, cultural umbrella societies and Slovene cooperatives, while pushing for further recognition of Slovene in public life and the schools. Progress appeared agonisingly slow to activists: the only all-Slovene state Gymnasium was not complete till 1912, while the economic life of Slovene people was dogged by agricultural crisis, heavy emigration and continued subordination to the German-speaking minority in their own land. Nonetheless, Slovene culture, language and literature did take on the lineaments of nationhood as understood by their neighbours, if looked down on by them, certainly by non-Slavs. This record makes it easy to understand why Slovenes and small peoples with similar experience in eastern Europe may cavil with Welsh pretensions. The parallel drawn by a Carinthian Slovene cited above between Slovene decline in his province and Welsh identity deserves note, though the difference in scale makes the analogy difficult and the comparison overlooks the phenomenon of English-speaking Welsh identity.

Indeed, the failure of a language movement to develop in Victorian Wales inevitably set bounds on the use of Welsh which till mid-century had advanced at least as strongly as Slovene and more so in quantitative terms. It confirmed a compartmentalisation which associated the public sphere with the dominant language to a far greater extent than in the Slovene case. The energy Slovenes put into extending the native vocabulary in all sorts of fields had some counterpart in Wales through the vigorous Welsh press, but it was more fitful. Much technical vocabulary did not establish itself and oral discussion simply used English words. The habit of corresponding in English remained quite common, as it had been in the Morris Circle; in Slovenia this phenomenon steadily declined. Welsh was gradually diminished in its own speakers' eyes. An interesting comment from the early twentieth century was that people had not lost their love for their language but their respect for it. In 1931 only 109 new books were published in Welsh as against 10,174 in England.[6]

Nonetheless, the Welsh experience of national revival is not to be gainsaid. More diffuse than the Habsburg Slav or Baltic linguistic path, and springing from a religious movement, it involved also the force of language and history to achieve the same process of social mobilisation. The intensity of this mobilisation in terms of chapel building, the Sunday School movement, ministerial training, the extensive press network and ancillary organisations mirrored patterns of associational development in other national revivals and resulted in a take-over of social leadership in all fields, undermining the traditional structures of landlord and Church power both locally and nationally. The operational language of this movement and its voluminous literature was Welsh. While its underlying ideology was religious, its popular social composition, energy and success inevitably stimulated national feeling and self-confidence, fostering a kind of 'chosen people' mentality. True, its puritanism, which targeted the theatre, deprived the Welsh language of a field of activity important in Slovenia, and towards the end of our period could fuse with the respectability which had been achieved to distance Nonconformity from its radical roots. The emphasis on Welsh/Celtic spirituality as a defining national characteristic became in many cases Pharisaical and a thinly disguised coolness to the rising socialist movement. How far hindsight colours later charges of being stuck in old radical causes (temperance, disestablishment) to the neglect of problems of industrial labour is difficult to judge from anecdotal evidence.[7] It is not easy to reconcile ideas of an embourgeoised ministry with the meagre salaries of most Nonconformist ministers. Probably chapel elders are most open to the charge, as the democratic self-image of miners sitting alongside colliery officials in the deacons' *set fawr* became less true of chapel life. A subtler criticism of the Nonconformist tradition is that it lacked sociological awareness. Lewis Edwards's surmise that Welsh religion would sustain Welsh as a community tongue for centuries to come overestimated religion's power in the face of change, and blinded him to the risk for religion's prestige that the language of its services should be deemed unfit for the day school and modern civic life.[8] The well-organised press and cooperative network developed in their own language by Slovene Catholics could provide for most practical needs of the population. In many ways the Welsh approach reflected the ambition and energy underlying Protestant individualism. At the grass roots level Welsh communities threw themselves into the task of creating their own institutions even if in the case of the secondary school network that sprang up so densely after the 1889 Intermediate Education Act this was not underpinned by sophisticated notions of developing a national culture. The result in practice often served the cause of Anglicisation and substantial dispersion of the newly educated outside Wales, but its popular support was sapped rather than eroded in our period. As long as it retained its vitality, Welsh religion invested patriotism with something of the aura of moral value. Linguistic nationalism powerfully accessed a general sense of grievance among Habsburg Slavs about subaltern status vis-à-vis an arrogant Germandom could lack something of this allure, as could its generalised Slav orientation, whether Panslav or Yugoslav. Though extremely effective in the fight for national goals, it has often proved to have less force when these are achieved.

The reference to the Catholic cooperative movement is a reminder that religion played a considerable role in Slovenia also, however. The rhythm of religious developments varied inversely in the two countries. Catholic clergy were quietly important in pre-1848 Slovenia, because of their supportive role in the national revival and the absence of church division on Nonconformist-Anglican lines in Wales. From the later nineteenth century the Slovene Church became more politically active and anti-liberal, while a less fervent Welsh religion softened its Calvinist edges as, for example, Welsh theologians moderated their opposition to Darwinism.[9] Thus, on religion, a potential stumbling block in society's accommodation to modernity, Wales emerged relatively united, while a divide opened up in Slovenia between liberal and fundamental Catholic world-views which took ugly form in the Second World War.

The third in the triad of Welsh building blocks was history. The long period of effective Welsh independence has been a vital component of Welsh nationality. It has meant that at no time since the word Cymry (fellow countrymen) was first used in the sixth century – though the older name of Britons rivalled it for several more centuries – have people not been aware of a common history. This powerful fact has not, arguably, been an unmixed blessing – again complexity. A sense of rivalry with the English has never died but also the memory that in these encounters the Welsh were valiant losers. They see themselves as an ancient people with a deep past, which can militate against notions of a Welsh future. Likewise, pride in a long literary heritage has been important in Wales. It has made for undue detachment from outside influences and at times tension between bardic tradition and would-be modernisers, though the generation before 1914 saw an opening up of Welsh literary culture to wider influences which has continued. The sense of nationhood among Slovenes and several other historically peasant peoples in east-central Europe came more recently and with it something of the freshness of youth and an instinct for emulation of elder nations. The nearest to this in Welsh experience was the late nineteenth-century movement of Cymru Fydd, with its English title, 'Young Wales'. Surprisingly, to Welsh eyes, the relative absence of such traditions has not lessened the use of history in the Slovene revival and Slovene literature. The misty period of Slav settlement, the role of Byzantium, medieval magnates, the Reformation (with more substantial material), the peasant folk tale: these and other topics have all been fields for the literary imagination to a greater extent than in Wales. This has something to do with the conscious (re)creation of nationhood by a patriotic intelligentsia with a strong youth component, very often sons of the soil but products of a secondary education, exposed to a regionally common ideology of linguistic and national rebirth. The Welsh equivalent, the *gwerin* ideology of O. M. Edwards, came later in Wales and infused with the religious legacy of Welsh Dissent. The Welsh Language Society was founded fifty years after similar bodies in central Europe, while Welsh economic development had come fifty years before. The pressures this put on the Welsh language community come out in an impressive recent biography of O. M. Edwards, its most iconic champion, which shows the complexity of this brilliant, imaginative and intellectually receptive man, passionately engaged with his own people, but also so deeply influenced by the pervasive English culture of his education that much of his voluminous diaries is in English. Towards the end of his life he wrote that Wales had a soul which she could lose and, an insight into the age, become a dead body with nothing to contribute to the empire.[10] Language was at the heart of this soul for him but not necessarily for all. However, we must remember that others, in their frequent passivity on the language, also never doubted that a Welsh nation already existed. It is too much part of the Welsh inheritance.

We must return to the issue of context. If the regional and Habsburg context made language the obvious operative field for Slovene nation building, the British context made for the conjunction of religion, language and history in Wales. Religion, not language, has most marked the character of the four component peoples of the British Isles in their modern development and offered the Welsh a chance for some kind of recognition. Modern Scottish identity arguably began when Jenny Geddes, a market trader, threw a stool at the Dean as he started to read from the Anglican Book of Common Prayer in St Giles' Cathedral in 1637, setting a spark for the civil wars which followed. Catholicism and Irish peasant poverty together mobilised Irish alienation from British rule. Their Nonconformity gave the Welsh majority both pride and a spurring (but supportable) alienation of their own, as they celebrated the structures they had created and moved towards the demotion of the state church. The equation of language and nationhood, so powerfully displayed in the Slovene example, fits eastern Europe's experience perfectly but is open to question as a universal model. Besides religion, history and the gradual effect of territorial separation have also played a role in identity formation. For Wales, so far from God and so near to England as the old joke has it, isolation cannot take the part it has had for an Iceland or a Malta.

History and the incomplete Anglo-Saxon conquest of southern Britain set in train a millennium-and-a-half of separate existence, however, a reality which is malleable with every turn of events but has remained till now in some form or other ineradicable.

Time's effect weakens with passing. There is no equivalent in modern Welsh history to the revolutions of 1848 when youthful Slovene aspirations were first voiced. Only a few spoke at that time but the episode greatly advanced Slovene political thinking. A feature of the Slovene experience from a Welsh point of view is how early ambitions were breathed which outran apparent possibilities – Čop's hopes for an infant literature which could match the world in poetry, the passion of young patriots in the dark years of neo-absolutist reaction, the confidence of some – few indeed for a time – to challenge the dominance of the mighty German culture. This had much to do with the atmosphere of cultural Panslavism but also to European-wide literary awareness which the slim band of educated Slovenes had acquired through that remarkable German culture. One feature it shared with that German culture was the (in nineteenth-century terms) medium-sized provincial capital (Ljubljana) with its theatre, opera and wide variety of secondary educational institutions, providing the Slovene linguistic heartland with an urban cultural centre lacking in Wales. It was one of a number of ways in which Slovenes had links with the dominant culture in a way Wales did not, another being the Catholic hierarchy in which latterly Slovene bishops could hold places at the heart of the establishment. Both our peoples, however, prided themselves on being sprung from common stock – the Slovene peasantry or Welsh *gwerin*. Conventionally, alertness of the common man to culture and aspiration became part of the Welsh patriotic self-image, so that the frequent laments of 'nationally conscious' Habsburg Slovenes at peasant passivity and backwardness ring oddly in Welsh ears. This probably reflects cultural difference between the central European intelligentsia/gymnasium tradition and that of British dissent. Both movements were those of subaltern societies, from below.

This summary reveals the working of 'soft power' in the making of modern Slovenia and Wales. In various ways and with varying emphases the language and religion of the common people shaped a course for two small entities in a democratising world, yes, but one of hard power, political and economic. This discussion has paid due attention to the neglected issue of language change in Wales, which Simon Brooks has set on the agenda. It has been necessary to point out that the decline of Welsh was less a matter of the 'Providence', of nineteenth-century Nonconformists or the 'modernisation' of conventional later historiography, than of priorities shaped by Welsh leaders in the context of Victorian Britain. But no discussion can conclude without weighing the yet greater rift in Welsh society of industrialisation in this formative age. This can be seen as a factor of hard economic power where immigration of industrial workers changed the face of a culture, but the discussion above suggests something subtler than that. The dramatic industrialisation of significant parts of the country was not just loss of a traditional heritage. It produced, in conjunction with a continuing role of religion and language, a unique society and vitality in the teeming valleys of the south-east which raised Wales's profile as a whole and created over time a new dimension to national life and pride. The coalfield, largest in Britain, with its memorable history, touched with tragedy, its radical traditions, including the best-known left Labour leader of twentieth-century Britain, Aneurin Bevan, its iconic singers and brass bands, its sporting heritage as the spawning ground of Welsh rugby, deserves, after all, its clichés. In this wider sense, Brinley Thomas's thesis of the benefits of industrialisation for Wales has more force than its specifically linguistic claims. Demographically, it leapfrogged Slovenia in the modern era though at the cost of uneven development. The integration of large numbers of immigrants in the industrial valleys into this distinctive community was becoming clear by 1914 and has found eloquent testimony in *Llafur, the Society for the Study of Welsh Labour History*.

Initially, this integration often included language but this soon became negligible in the east of the coalfield (Monmouthshire) and went into reverse. From the 1890s in east Glamorgan English was becoming the language spoken by most children among themselves, a process which seems to be reaching the west of the coalfield in our days. The recession of the Welsh language might be considered part of the theme of absorption of weaker cultures by dominant ones in western Europe. This would not be wholly accurate. Language change had already been occurring in eastern border areas before industrialisation and was aided by the lack of any intellectual language defence movement in mid-century. Welsh soft power relying on religion, tradition and the cohesion of working-class life rather than language alone ensured survival of a strong Welsh consciousness in the coalfield, which therefore shows a different pattern from Gellner's model of the clash and languages and nationalisms of east-central Europe.

Which language individuals spoke in the coalfield area did not become a political matter, resembling perhaps what is said of Ljubljana before 1848. As a social matter it does come up in fiction (Jack Jones; T. Rowland Hughes) and in reminiscence, but this has not been systematically studied.

With the later rise of political nationalism, tensions between the different aspects of Welsh identity can come to be reflected historiographically, as in Chris Williams's polemical contrast between the working-class culture of the Rhondda and the 'Welshness of a privileged minority' (see Chapter 8). This book argues against such polarisation and suggests the multiple connections between the Liberal Nonconformist and Labour hegemonies in Welsh history. Warnings have been raised against turning the Welsh miners' story into a myth.[11] This term can be used negatively to mean something not grounded in reality, or more positively to suggest something carrying a powerful significance. It seems to me it can bear the latter meaning in the context of Welsh history, but only when these two aspects, the Welsh and Labour, are combined and not opposed to each other. A fuller argument rests on study of the period after 1918, which is not the direct concern here, but it is there to be made. Add to this that the large populations of Cardiff, Swansea and Newport with the urban coastal belt and Wrexham in the north were already apparent in Victorian times and that the Nonconformist hegemony was stronger and longer lasting in this third, broadly commercial Wales than that of Labour was to be, and one has a picture of the dramatic transformation of the remote, thinly populated countryside of eighteenth-century Wales in the dynamic Victorian age; but also of the connections that linked it through the repeated conferences in Llandudno, Aberystwyth, Llandudno and Cardiff in which the issues of disestablishment, schooling, temperance and the University were thrashed out by delegates of a nascent polity. Wales was now considerably richer and more populous than Slovenia but less cohesive, lacking the driving force which linguistic nationalism and a political goal can give. But without the formative processes she had already experienced she could not have become, a century later, after all the travails between, one of the constituent blocks, the 'four nations', of the United Kingdom.

This term, anticipated in the national sporting teams of the late nineteenth century, indicates that Wales belongs to one of the many zones of inter-national contact in the world other than east-central Europe, whose fraught twentieth-century stories have conspired to give the idea of the nation an ominous ring in much modern discussion. The British,

British imperial and English-speaking worlds have their own rhythms and diversity of nationhood, with distinctive problems. In them devolved Wales has achieved its own small place as a political nation, just as one may say the Slovenes did with their revived language as password in late Habsburg Austria.

PROSPECT

Historians should eschew speculation beyond their specific topic of study. Yet the nature of my theme, Welsh nationhood, suggesting some settled disposition and durability, invites a testing of my claims on its behalf. True, the claim made in the Introduction was for a Welsh national identity, not necessarily a strong one. It is tempting to see parallels between the rise in interest in Wales as nation in the build-up to Cymru Fydd and to devolution in our own day. If enthusiasm for Cymru Fydd has often been criticised as superficial, how much more might this be said of Welsh nationhood now, when many of the objective factors behind it earlier, like the Welsh language, Welsh Nonconformity and Welsh industrial strength, are now much weaker? Three explanations, which do not exclude each other, are possible for the continued salience of a Welsh question, nonetheless. One of them was suggested in the Introduction: once a national consciousness is established it can survive weakness in the factors which gave it birth. A second relates to the decline in British self-confidence and the attractiveness of the British system to an admiring Welsh opinion. A third is the attractiveness of the national idea itself.

The first needs little further elaboration than that given in the narrative. A great deal was achieved in the period covered by this book. The powerful force of religious awakening, which penetrated deep into the heart of the common people, the movement for mass education reaching to the highest, University level, the massive infrastructure of Sunday Schools and chapel associations, capped by National Library and Museum, the development of a press at the level of every little town, the eisteddfodic and choral singing movements, the spread of all these from the countryside to the hugely developing industrial and commercial sectors as the population nearly quadrupled (though quite often these processes developed almost simultaneously), the overthrow of a centuries-old domination of squire and parson. These were amply recorded as heroic times, not likely to be so easily lost from social memory. These are the conventionalities of anyone familiar with Welsh history. One can, though, say without too much distortion that the Welsh experience has engaged, in quick succession, with two very powerful hegemonic movements: evangelical Christianity and the socialist search for justice. Constrained by smallness and their situation side by side with the phenomenon that is Anglo-British culture, Welsh people have not wholly come to terms with a third force, their own identity. That is a pity because together the three make for a rich inheritance. The wonder is that so many in the circumstances have been able to make the connection.

The second explanation is that a small people's consciousness is determined as much by their relation to others as by their own objective circumstances: a theme stressed throughout this book. It has been used to explain the rapid spread of Herderian cultural nationalism in the small, weak Slovene society as part of a general Slav revival movement in the conflicted Habsburg Monarchy. Welsh development took place in a very successful British society where the Welsh were a small minority. The effect was described by Lewis Edwards's son, Thomas Charles Edwards, first Principal of Aberystwyth University College: 'We Welshmen must acknowledge the greatness of the English nation. They are a greater people than we are. They are so much greater that if we live among them before our mental character is fairly formed, we are crushed or absorbed.'[12] It was harder for Welsh leaders to achieve psychological independence from this society than it was for Habsburg Slavs or the Irish, for much of the period far more numerous than the Welsh and cut off from the British success story. Many early leaders of the Indian Congress movement were likewise impressed by the British achievement, as were English leaders themselves. In pressing Britain's role as mediator in the Sudeten German question in 1938, Neville Chamberlain commented on her long history of success in dealing with nationality problems. In fact Britain's record on this score was already not so brilliant, and outcomes at Munich, in Ireland, in apartheid South Africa, the million massacred on departure from partitioned India and the mess left in Palestine and Cyprus following British rule there undermine notions of a special political wisdom. This is not to deny many fine things in the British record, just to say that its capacity to inspire awe and loyalty has declined with imperial power.

Independence of spirit emerges from this story as a key requirement of Welsh nationhood, as it proved to be in Slovene. The Brexit episode has quickened this. By imperilling the UK's economy and its own union in Scotland and Northern Ireland in return for nebulous 'global Britain' trade deals, it speaks for an irresponsible populism rather than the sober rationality which could be posited for Britain in its pomp. The Brexit vision is more fanciful than any small nation enthusiast, free from imperial illusions, would dare dream up. Its likely consequences for Wales should alert thoughtful Welsh people to the need to respect Wales's still young political autonomy as a valuable safeguard, rather than assume Whitehall knows best. Seen in broader terms, one can say that the stress of context in this book need not relegate west European minorities to inevitable assimilation or subordination, as appeared the case in the nineteenth century. Contexts change and with them mentalities, if people take the chance to look afresh at old assumptions. That is what is entailed in the independence of spirit referred to above.

Yet the continued relevance of Welsh nationhood need not be affirmed only in negative terms. There is a positive force in nationality itself. The number of nation-based states in Europe in 1900 was some fifteen (five of them empires), plus three enjoying national autonomy. Today there are around thirty nation states plus eight with elements of autonomy, including Scotland and Wales. That is prima facie evidence for the power of national sentiment, which growing with the growth of democracy has allowed more and more peoples to assert their identity. The aspiration to nationhood has been posited here as one of the three main factors in modern history, alongside the religious and the social. It is a source of pride and identity for most ordinary people which sits alongside other aspects of identity, though it needs the ability to take hard knocks and avoid hubris. Even in its national aspect, it can be plural in acknowledging matters of ethnic origin and cultural and historical affinity, as in the Welsh/British nexus. Its claims are mostly muted in modern discourse, at least in large countries. To the charge that nations and nationalism are divisive and can lead to aggressive authoritarianism and 'Balkanisation', the answer must be that these are real problems but problems are common to all major belief systems and small states on the whole have a better record than large ones, because less subject to remote bureaucracies and delusions of grandeur. All political systems can be subverted in the cause of power and ambition. Religion and socialism show in addition the inherent difficulties produced in practice by universalist claims. Such are the oppression which followed religious orthodoxy's insistence on uniformity of the true faith in the state and the inability of communism in power to accommodate political pluralism. Historically, the political solution to ethnic diversity was often multinational empires under a dominant dynasty and nationality, with local autonomies and rights, like the use of local languages. Quite an efficient method of rule in undeveloped societies with limited resources, empires are, however, dependent on hierarchies which are irksome to modern people who have developed a sense of their own worth. This seems to have been forgotten in revaluations of the Habsburg Monarchy, which rightly criticise nationalist stereotypes only to replace them with an unlikely world of loyal subjects of the dynasty.[13] The rise of the national principle was a natural development, though the hardening of notions of absolute national sovereignty since 1918 has caused unnecessary problems for cooperation. Coolness to the principle out of discomfort for an imperial past or exaggerated view of its role in international conflict – which arose in the twentieth century from a host of factors – is often felt by liberal-minded English people in particular. Welsh people should not be swayed by it to deprecate what in their case has a powerful positive role to play. Simon Brooks has shown the destructive effect on Welsh language communities, for example, of British identification of civic rights with the individual alone.

These reflections have strayed too far into speculation. They should resume their due historiographical course. If the bid to offer a view of Wales as nation has any traction, where might more qualified hands take it? There are several areas where research would be of benefit on issues inadequately addressed here. A link between social and national themes is the unexplored nature of the Welsh middle class. Slovene experience and that of the small Baltic nations show the importance in the development of the modern nation from peasant and artisanal ranks of what has been called a national bourgeoisie. The development of the middle class in Swansea, where Joseph Harris's *Seren Gomer* was published in the early nineteenth century, would make an interesting study, to parallel work on Thomas Stephens and the middle class of Merthyr Tydfil. Swansea is not included in the volume on the 1891 language census in the richly informative *Social History of the Welsh Language* published in 1998–2000. Nineteenth-century periodicals, their editors and readerships, a topic much studied by central European historians, are also open for more study. The Welsh landed class in the first part of the period studied, and Professor R. J. W. Evans's question: 'Was there a Welsh Enlightenment in the Eighteenth Century?' further expand the theme of the links between social and intellectual history in new areas. Here the issue of Welsh national unity or lack of it, raised by the authors cited above, comes to the fore. Plainly, the formation of the industrial working class in south-east Wales had a national dimension. How different was this from the putative Welsh-speaking nationality of the north-west, or from the dissenting traditions that lay behind both north and south Wales forms of Welshness? Here the issue of Welsh national unity or lack of it, raised by the authors cited above, comes to the fore.

That these two versions of Welsh nationality followed each other into being is the thesis of this book. That they are compatible despite the language shift is a plausible hope. The issue is intriguing academically but potentially something more, as a severe test of the British political system looms. Concrete ground for the hope is what was achieved in the second devolution referendum of 1997. As counting proceeded and only two of Wales's twenty-two regions remained to declare, the devolutionist cause lagged behind by almost fifty thousand votes. One of the regions was the iconic heartland of Welsh and British Labour, centred round the Rhondda valley; the other was the largely rural, Welsh-speaking county of William Williams Pantycelyn, the hymnist of the eighteenth-century religious revival. Between them, by ballots of two to one, they overturned the deficit and delivered devolved government by less than seven thousand votes. The 2011 referendum which endorsed substantial legislative power for Wales passed by nearly two-thirds. All this is not necessarily an assurance of Welsh nationhood's survival but certainly a necessary condition. The Slovene case shows how in a sophisticated modern society it is perfectly possible to combine a national life with participation alongside others in the global community, for all the less attractive features of individual leaders. Modern technology has made access to the world's cultures available to all, making the reconciliation of the national and the international possible beyond the imagination of previous generations. If discourses of multiculturalism and the value of diversity are more than slogans, making them work for Wales is surely a worthy and exciting goal in today's world.

A last word should recall that this book's discussion of Wales has been conducted in a context of comparison. Both our countries experienced a strong drive to social mobilisation in the period studied, from which the modern nations emerged, more emphatically in the Slovene case. The balance of factors involved varied, not least because of the circumstances of the two framing states. The Slovene example shows the powerful role language can have in nation-building. Linguistic patriotism was part product of the co-existence of many peoples in the empires of east-central Europe, which could pose problems for democratisation, relatively benign as the late Habsburg monarchy was. Nationhood outspans language, just as it itself is only one of a triad of interrelated issues, involving also social justice and religious beliefs, which have helped shape the modern world. This book has sought to show how our two small peoples, each with its own story, played a far larger and more interesting role in this process than was anticipated at its outset.

NOTES

1 Kenneth O. Morgan, *David Lloyd George: Welsh Radical as World Statesman* (Cardiff, 1964). It is interesting that as President of the Welsh Baptist Union in 1908–9, still a time of habitual nods towards the English language, he saw to it that the proceedings of its Annual Conference were held entirely in Welsh (p. 40).

2 Ned Thomas, *The Welsh Extremist: A Culture in Crisis* (London, 1971), p. 56.

3 For this paragraph, see *Slowenische Geschichte*, pp. 311–96.

4 Gwyn A. Williams, *When Was Wales? A History of the Welsh* (Harmondsworth, 1985), p. 305; John Davies, *Hanes Cymru* (History of Wales) (London, 1990), p. 661; Geraint H. Jenkins, *A Concise History of Wales* (Cambridge, 2007), p. 305; Russell Davies, *Sex, Sects and Society, 'Pain and Pleasure': A Social History of Wales and the Welsh, 1870–1945* (Cardiff, 2018), p. 366.

5 V. Melik, *Auersperg in Slovenci* (Auersperg and the Slovenes) (Maribor, 2006), p. 139.

6 K. Morgan, *Rebirth of a Nation: Wales 1880–1980* (Oxford, 1981), p. 245.

7 For abundant evidence of traditional Nonconformist positions on these issues, see W. R. Lambert, *Drink and Sobriety in Victorian Wales c.1820–c.1895* (Cardiff, 1983).

8 See Chapter 5, note 41 for D. Densil Morgan, *Lewis Edwards* (Cardiff, 2009), p. 219.

9 Harry Williams, *Duw, Daeareg a Darwin: yn bennaf ar dudalennau'r Traethodydd 1845–1900* (God, Geology and Darwin: chiefly in the pages of *Y Traethodydd* 1845–1900) (Llandysul, 1979). Interestingly, the contemporary Slovene response to Darwinism, alongside Catholic opposition, stressed the implications of the 'survival of the fittest' for nationality relations: Oskar Habjanič. 'Darwinizam na Slovenskem' (Darwinism in Slovenia), in *Zgodovinski časopis*, 70/1–2 (2016), 98–126.

10 Hazel Walford Davies, *O. M. Cofiant Syr Owen Morgan Edwards* (Life of Owen Morgan Edwards) (Llandysul, 2019). For the Welsh soul, see O. M. Edwards, *Er Mwyn Cymru* (Wrexham, 1922), pp. 11–14.

11 For example, in Steven Thompson's review article, 'Class Cohesion, Working-class Homogeneity and the Labour Movement in Industrial South Wales', *Llafur*, 9/3 (2006), 81–91.

12 R. Tudur Jones, *The Desire of Nations* (Llandybie, 1974), p. 161.

13 As is the case, to some extent, in Pieter M. Judson, *The Habsburg Empire: A New History* (Cambridge, MA, 2016). For a Slovene review unsympathetic to Judson's position see: Maček, Jože, Review of Pieter M. Judson, *Habsburg. Geschichte eines Imperiums 1740–1918*, in *Zgodovinski časopis*, 74 (2020), 278–83.

BIBLIOGRAPHY

The bibliography provides translations of non-English titles where they are deemed helpful to the reader. It observes the common use of pseudonyms in Welsh public, particularly literary, life due to the paucity of Welsh surnames.

'Addysgiad y Genedl' / The Education of the Nation, *Y Traethodydd*, 3 (1847).

Aaron, Jane, *Nineteenth-Century Women's Writing in Wales: Nation, Gender and Identity* (Cardiff, 2010).

Acton, Baron John E. E. Dalberg-Acton, 'Nationality' in *The History of Freedom and other Essays*, ed. and intro. J. N. Figgis and R. V. Laurence (London, 1907), pp. 270–300.

Additional Letters of the Morrises of Anglesey (1735–1786), transcribed and ed. Owen, Hugh, in *Y Cymmrodor*, vol. XLIX, Part I (London 1947); Part II (London, 1949).

Addysg Chambers i'r Bobl: Cyfieithiad o'r argraffiad Seisnig diweddaraf, cyfrol 1 / Chamber's Education for the People: Translation of the most recent edition, vol. 1 (Pwllheli, 1851).

Baar, Monika, *Historians and Nationalism in East-Central Europe in the Nineteenth Century* (Oxford, 2010).

Ballin, M., *Writers of Wales: Welsh Periodicals in English, 1882–2012* (Cardiff, 2013).

Bauer, Otto, *The Question of Nationalities and Social Democracy*, trans. Joseph O'Donnell (Minneapolis, MN, 2000).

Bibliografsko kazalo Ljubljanskega zvona / Bibliographical Index of Ljubljanski zvon, compiled by J. Munda and N. Rupel (Ljubljana, 1962).

Bobič, P., *War and Faith: The Roman Catholic Church in Slovenia and the First World War, 1914–1918* (Leiden, 2012).

Borrow, G., *Wild Wales: Its People, Language and Scenery* (London, c.1862).

Bowen, Thomas, *Dinas Caerdydd a'i Methodistiaeth Galfinaidd* / The City of Cardiff and its Calvinistic Methodism (n.p., 1927).

Brooks, Simon, *Pam na fu Cymru: Methiant Cenedlaetholdeb Cymraeg* (Cardiff, 2015). For a revised English edition, see Brooks, Simon *Why Wales Never Was: The Failure of Welsh Nationalism* (Cardiff, 2017).

Brown, Roger L., *John Griffith: The unmitred bishop* (Welshpool, 2007).

Bruk, S. I. (ed.), *Naselenie mira: etnodemograficheskii spravochnik / World Population: An Ethnodemograhic Handbook* (Moscow, 1982).

Brutus (David Owen), 'Y Gymraeg'/The Welsh language, *Seren Gomer* 7 (1824), 80–4, 369–73.

Bulmer-Thomas, Ivor, *Top Sawyer, A Biography of David Davies, Llandinam* (London, 1938).

Y Bywgraffiadur Cymreig hyd 1940 / Welsh biographical dictionary up to 1940 (London, 1954).

Cankar, I., *Martin Kačur, The Biography of an Idealist* (Budapest and New York, 2009).

Cankar, Ivan, *Materialen und Texte*, assembled by Erwin Köstler (Klagenfurt / Celovec, 1999).

Carr, Glenda, *William Owen Pughe* (Cardiff, 1983).

Cattaruzza, M., 'Slovenes and Italians in Trieste, 1850–1914', in Engman M. (ed.), *Ethnic Identity in Urban Europe, 1850–1914* (New York, c.1992), pp. 189–220.

Černik, B., 'The Role of Dr Janez Evangelist Krek in the Slovene Cooperative Movement', *Slovene Studies*, 11 (1989), 75–81.

Chłebowczyk, J., *On Small and Young Nations in Europe* (Wrocław, 1980).

Cofiant, a gweithiau barddonol a rhyddieithol Ieuan Gwynedd / The Life and Poetical and Prose Works of Ieuan Gwynedd (Wrexham, c.1880).

Colyer, R. J., 'The Gentry and the County in Nineteenth-Century Cardiganshire', *Welsh History Review*, 10 (1980), 498–535.

Cooper, H. R. Jr., *France Prešeren* (Boston, 1980).

Cragoe, Matthew, *Culture, Politics and National Identity in Wales, 1832–1886* (Oxford, 2004).

Croll, Andy, *Barry Island: The Making of a Seaside Playground c.1790–c.1965* (Cardiff, 2020).

Cvirn, J., 'Med nacionalizmom in nacionalno koeksistence'/Between Nationalism and National Co-existence, *Zgodovinski časopis*, 63 (2009), 228–38.

Darlington, T., 'Iaith Cymru Fydd' / The Language of Wales to be, *Y Geninen*, 11 (1893), pp. 224–31.

Davies, Catherine Glyn, *Adfeilion Babel, Agweddau ar syniadaeth ieithyddol y ddeunawfed ganrif* / The Ruins of Babel. Aspects of linguistic thought in the eighteenth century (Cardiff, 2000).

Davies, Charlotte Aull, 'Welsh Nationalism and the British State', in Glyn Williams (ed.), *Crisis of Economy and Ideology: Essays on Welsh Society 1840–1980* (Bangor, 1983).

Davies, Hazel Walford, *O.M: Cofiant Syr Owen Morgan Edwards* / O.M: The Life of Owen Morgan Edwards (Llandysul, 2019).

Davies J., *Bywyd a Gwaith Moses Williams 1685–1742* / The Life and Work of Moses Williams (Cardiff, 1937).

Davies, J. H. (ed.), *The Letters of Goronwy Owen, 1723–1767* (Cardiff, 1924).

Davies, John, *Cardiff and the Marquesses of Bute* (Cardiff, 1981).

Davies, John, *Hanes Cymru* / History of Wales (London, 1990).

Davies Russell, *Hope and Heartbreak: A Social History of Wales and the Welsh, 1776–1871* (Cardiff, 2005).

Davies, Russell, *People, Places and Passions, 'Pain and Pleasure': A Social History of Wales and the Welsh, 1870–1945* (Cardiff, 2018).

Davies, Russell, *Sex, Sects and Society, 'Pain and Pleasure': A Social History of Wales and the Welsh, 1870–1945* (Cardiff, 2018).

Davies, T. Eirug (ed.), *Y Prifathro Thomas Rees: Ei Fywyd a'i Waith* / Professor Thomas Rees: His Life and Work (Llandysul, 1939).

Denning, R. T. W. (ed.), *The Diary of William Thomas of Michaelston-super-Ely near St. Fagans, Glamorgan 1762–1795* (Cardiff, 1995).

Detholiad o Erthyglau a Llythyrau Emrys ap Iwan / Selected Articles and Letters of Emrys ap Iwan (3 vols, Denbigh, 1937–1940).

Dežman Jože; Hudalec, Jože; Jezernik, Božidar *Slovensko meščanstvo od vzpona nacije do nacionalizacije (1848–1948)* / The Slovenian bourgeoisie from the rise of the nation to full nationhood (Klagenfurt, 2008).

Dickson, P. G. M., *Finance and Government under Maria Theresa 1740–1780*, 2 vols (Oxford, 1987).

Dimitz, August, *Geschichte Krains von den ältesten Zeiten bis auf dem Jahr 1813* / History of Carniola from the Earliest Times to the Year 1813 (Ljubljana, 1876).

Dolenec, I., 'Krek, Janez Evangelist (1865–1917)', *Slovenska Biografija* (ZRC SAZU, 2013).

Dolinar, F. M., Mahnič, Jože and Vodopovič, Peter (eds), *Vloga Cerkve v slovenskem kulturnem razvoju 19. stoletja* / The role of the Church in Slovene cultural development in the nineteenth century (Ljubljana, 1989).

Edwards, Lewis, 'Barddoniaeth y Cymry' / The Poetry of the Welsh, in Edwards, *Traethodau llenyddol* / Literary Essays (Wrexham, *c.*1867), pp. 153–66.

Edwards, Alfred George, Archbishop, *Memories* (Cardiff, 1927).

Edwards, H. T., *The Church of the Cymry: A Letter to the Right Hon. W. E. Gladstone* (Aberdare, 1869).

Edwards, Hywel Teifi, *Codi'r Hen Wlad yn ei Hôl 1850–1914* / Putting the Old Country Back on its Feet (Llandysul, 1989).

Edwards, Hywel Teifi, *Gŵyl Gwalia: Yr Eisteddfod Genedlaethol yn Oes Aur Victoria 1858–1868* / Welsh Festival: The National Eisteddfod in the Victorian Golden Age (Llandysul, 1980).

Edwards, J. Hugh, MP, *The Life of David Lloyd George with a Short History of the Welsh People*, 4 vols (London, 1916).

Edwards, Lewis, 'Addysg yn Nghymru' / Education in Wales, in *Traethodau Llenyddol* / Literary Essays (Wrexham, 1867), pp. 374–405.

Edwards, Lewis, 'Adroddiadau y Dirprwywyr' / Reports of the Commissioners in *Traethodau Llenyddol* / Literary Essays (Wrexham, 1867), pp. 406–21.

Edwards, O. M., *A Short History of Wales* (London, 1906).

Edwards, O. M., *Er Mwyn Cymru* / For the Sake of Wales (Wrexham, 1922).

Edwards, T. C., *Bywyd a Llythyrau y diweddar Lewis Edwards* / Life and Letters of the late Lewis Edwards (Liverpool, 1901).

Ellis, John, 'National Armies in the Field: National Identity and Recruitment in Ireland and Wales, 1914–1916', paper given at a Conference on Ireland and Wales in the First World War at Cardiff University, 11 September 2014.

Ellis, T. E., *Speeches and Addresses by the late Thomas E. Ellis, M.P.* (Wrexham, 1912).

Ellis, T. I., *The Development of Modern Welsh Secondary Education* (London, 1934).

Ellis, T. I., *Thomas Edward Ellis: Cofiant* / Thomas Edwards Ellis: A Life, 2 vols (Liverpool, 1944–8).

Erjavec, F., *Zgodovina katoliškega gibanja na Slovenskem* / History of the Catholic movement in Slovenia (Ljubljana, 1928).

Evans, Caradoc, *My People: Stories of the Peasantry of West Wales* (London, c.1915).

Evans, D. Silvan (ed.) *The English Works of the Revd Walter Davies* (Carmarthen and London, 1868).

Evans, Eifion, *Bread of Heaven: The Life and Work of William Williams Pantycelyn* (Bridgend, 2010).

Evans, Eric W., *Mabon (William Abraham 1842–1922): A Study in Trade Union Leadership* (Cardiff, 1959).

Evans, Herber, 'Cymru Fydd' / Young Wales, *Y Geninen*, 11 (1893), 93–5.

Evans, J. J., *Morgan John Rhys a'i amserau* / Morgan John Rhys and his times (Cardiff, 1935).

Evans, Neil, 'The Welsh Victorian City: The Middle Class and Civic and National Consciousness in Cardiff, 1850–1914', *Welsh History Review*, 12/3 (1985), 350–87.

Evans, Neil and Pryce, Huw, *Writing a Small Nation's Past: Wales in Comparative Perspective, 1850–1950* (London, 2012).

Evans, Neil and Sullivan, Kate, '*Yn Llawn o Dân Cymreig: Yr Iaith Gymraeg a Gwleidyddiaeth yng Nghymru 1880–1914*' / Full of Welsh Fire: The Welsh Language and Politics in Wales, in Geraint H. Jenkins (ed.), *Gwnewch bopeth yn Gymraeg. Yr Iaith Gymraeg a'i Pheuoedd 1801–1911* / Do everything in Welsh. The Welsh Language and its Domains 1801–1911 (Cardiff, 1999), pp. 527–52.

Evans, R. J. W., 'The Origins of Enlightenment in the Habsburg Lands', in Evans, R. J. W., *Austria, Hungary and the Habsburgs: Essays on Central Europe, c.1683– 1867* (Oxford and New York, 2006), pp. 37–56.

Evans, The Revd J., *Letters written during a tour in North Wales in the year 1798, and at other times* (London, 1804).

Evans, The Revd J., *Letters written during a tour in South Wales in the year 1803* (London, 1804).

Evans, Trebor Lloyd, *Lewis Edwards: Ei fywyd a'i waith* / Lewis Edwards: life and work (Swansea, 1967).

Fisher, H. A. L., *An Unfinished Autobiography* (Oxford, 1940).

Foulkes, E. F., 'Diwylliant llenyddol yng Nghymru' / Literary Culture in Wales, *Y Geninen*, 3 (1885), 271–6.

Francis, Hywel and Smith, David, *The Fed: A History of the South Wales Miners in the Twentieth Century* (London, 1980).

Gellner, Ernest, *Nations and Nationalism* (Oxford, 1983).

Gombač, Boris M., 'Slovenska socialdemokracija v Trstu 1889–1900' / Slovene Social Democracy in Trieste 1889–1900, *Zgodovinski časopis* (2006), 95–121.

Gow, James and Carmichael, Cathy, *Slovenia and the Slovenes: A Small State and the New Europe* (Bloomington, 2000).

Gramich, Katie, *Twentieth-Century Women's Writing in Wales: Land, Gender, Belonging* (Cardiff, 2007).

Griffiths, Gwyn, *Henry Richard: Heddychwr a Gwladgarwr* / Henry Richard, Pacifist and Patriot (Cardiff, 2001).

Gruden, J. J., *Zgodovina slovenskega naroda* / History of the Slovene Nation (Celovec, 1912).

Gruffydd, W. J., *Hen Atgofion* / Old Memories (1936; Llandysul, 1964).

Gurden-Williams, Celyn, *Lady Llanover and the Creation of a Welsh Cultural Utopia* (PhD thesis, Cardiff University; Pro-Quest Dissertations Publishing, 2009).

Gweithiau awdurol y diweddar Barch. Joseph Harris (Gomer) gyda Chofiaint yr awdur a'i deulu / Works of the late Revd Joseph Harris (Gomer) with the life of the author and his family, ed. D. ap Rhys Stephen (Llanelli, 1839).

Habjanič, Oskar, 'Darvinizem na Slovenskem' / Darwinism in Slovenia, in *Zgodovinski časopis*, 70/1–2 (2016), 98–126.

Hacin, Marina Lukšič, et al., *Socialna, gospodarska in kulturna zgodovina slovenskega izseljenstva, 1870–1945* / Social, economic and cultural history of Slovene emigration (Ljubljana, 2018).

Harris, Joseph, 'Nodiadau ar Ysgrif y digyffelyb Brutus' / Notes on the Article of the Ineffable Brutus, in *Gweithiau Awdurol y Diweddar Parch. Joseph Harris (Gomer)* / Works of the late Revd Joseph Harris (Gomer), (Llanelli, 1839), pp. 343–53.

Hechter, M., *Internal Colonialism: The Celtic Fringe in British national development, 1536–1966* (London, 1975).

Historija naroda Jugoslavije / History of the Nations of Yugoslavia, vol. 2 (Zagreb, 1959).

Hladnik, M., *Trivialna literatura* / Popular literature (Ljubljana, 1983).

Hočevar, Toussaint, *The Structure of the Slovene Economy, 1848–1963* (New York, 1965).

Hösler, J., *Von Krain zu Slowenien: Die Anfänge der nationalen Differenzierungsprozesse in Krain und der Untersteiermark von der Aufklärung bis zur Revolution 1768 bis 1848* / From Carniola to Slovenia. The Beginnings of the National Differentiation Process in Carniola and Lower Styria from Enlightenment to Revolution: 1768–1848 (Munich, 2006).

Howell, D. W., *Patriarchs and Parasites: The Gentry of South-West Wales in the Eighteenth Century* (Cardiff, 1986).

Howell, D. W. *The Rural Poor in Eighteenth-century Wales* (Cardiff, 2000).

Howell, D. W., *Land and People in Nineteenth-Century Wales* (London, 1977).

Hroch, M., *European nations: explaining their formation* (New York, 2015).

Hroch, Miroslav, *Social Preconditions of National Revival in Europe* (Cambridge, 1985).

Hughes, J. Elwyn, *Arloeswr Dwyieithedd:. Dan Isaac Davies 1839–87* / Pioneer of Bilingualism: Dan Isaac Davies (Cardiff, 1984).

Hughes, R. Elwyn, 'Yr Iaith Gymraeg ym Myd Gwyddoniaeth a Thechnoleg' / The Welsh Language in the World of Science and Technology, in Jenkins, Geraint H. (ed.), *Gwnewch bopeth yn Gymraeg: Yr Iaith Gymraeg a'i Pheuoedd 1801–1911* / Do Everything in Welsh: The Welsh language and its Domains 1801–1911 (Cardiff, 1999), pp. 375–98.

Hughes, T. Rowland, *Chwalfa* / Upheaval (Aberystwyth, 1946).

Humphreys, E. Morgan, 'Y Ddau Gymro' / Two Kinds of Welshman, *Y Traethodydd*, 62 (1907), 13–20.

Humphreys, M., *The Crisis of Community: Montgomeryshire, 1680–1815* University of Wales Press (Cardiff, 1996).

Hunangofiant John Elias / The Autobiography of John Elias, ed. Goronwy P. Owen, (Swansea, 1974)

Hunter, Jerry, *Llwch Cenhedloedd. Y Cymry a Rhyfel Cartref America* / The Dust of Nations. The Welsh and the American Civil War (Llanrwst, 2004).

Immigration History From Wales to Victoria, Australia: *https://origins. museumsvictoria.com.au/countries/wales.*

James, Allan, *John Morris-Jones* (Cardiff, 2011).

James, E. Wyn and Jones, Bill (eds), *Michael D. Jones a'i wladfa Gymreig* / Michael D. Jones and his Welsh colony (Llanrwst, 2009).

James-Davies, H., 'The History of the Agricultural Movement in Carmarthenshire', *The Carmarthenshire Antiquary*, 1 (1942), part 2.

Jarman, A. O. H., *'Lewis Morris a Brut Tysilio'* / Lewis Morris and Brut Tysilio, *Llên Cymru*, 2 (1953), 161–83.

Jenkins, David, *Thomas Gwynn Jones: Cofiant* (Denbigh, 1973).

Jenkins Geraint H. (ed.), *A Rattleskull Genius: the many faces of Iolo Morganwg* (Cardiff, 2005).

Jenkins, Geraint, *A Concise History of Wales* (Cambridge, 2007).

Jenkins, Geraint H., 'Na wadwch eich iaith: y cefndir hanesyddol i gyfrifiad 1891' / Don't deny your language: the historical background to the 1891 census, in Parry, Gwenfair and Williams, Mari A. (eds), *Miliwn o Gymry Cymraeg! Yr Iaith Gymraeg a Chyfrifiad 1891* / A million Welsh speakers! The Welsh language and the 1891 census (Cardiff, 1999).

Jenkins, Geraint H., '"Horrid unintelligible jargon": the case of Dr Thomas Bowles', *Welsh History Review*, 15 (1990–1), 494–523.

Jenkins, Geraint H., *Bard of Liberty: The Political Radicalism of Iolo Morganwg* (Cardiff, 2012).

Jenkins, Geraint H., *The Foundations of Modern Wales: Wales 1642–1780* (Cardiff, 1987).

Jenkins, R. T., *Hanes Cymru yn y Ddeunawfed Ganrif* /History of Wales in the Eighteenth Century (1931; Cardiff, 1972).

Jenkins, Roy, *Gladstone: A Biography* (New York, 1997).

Jones, Aled, 'Yr Iaith Gymraeg a Newyddiaduraeth' / The Welsh Language and Journalism, in Jenkins Geraint H. (ed.), *Gwnewch bopeth yn Gymraeg: Yr Iaith Gymraeg a'i Pheuoedd 1801–1911* / Do Everything in Welsh: the Welsh Language and its Domains (Cardiff, 1999), pp. 353–74.

Jones, Aled, *Press, Politics and Society: A History of Journalism in Wales* (Cardiff, 1993).

Jones, Arthur Herbert, *His Lordship's Obedient Servant: Recollections of a South Wales Borderer* (Llandysul, 1987).

Jones, D. Ceri, Boyd Schlenther, and Eryn White, *Elect Methodists: Calvinistic Methodism in England and Wales, 1735–1811* (Cardiff, 2012).

Jones, Dafydd Glyn, *Agoriad yr Oes: Erthyglau ar Lên, Hanes a Gwleidyddiaeth Cymru* / Unto the Age: Articles on Welsh Literature, History and Politics (Talybont, 2001).

Jones, Dafydd Glyn, *Un o Wŷr y Medra: Bywyd a Gwaith William Williams, Llandegai 1738–1817* / One of the Men of the Medra. Life and Work of William Williams, Llandegai, 1738–1817 (Denbigh, 1999).

Jones, David, *Before Rebecca. Popular Protests in Wales 1793–1835* (London, 1973).

Jones, Dot (ed.), *Statistical information relating to the Welsh Language, 1801–1911* (Cardiff, 1998).

Jones, Frank Price, *Radicaliaeth a'r werin Gymreig yn y bedwaredd ganrif a'r bymtheg* / Radicalism and the Welsh common people in the nineteenth century (Cardiff, 1997).

Jones, Gareth Elwyn, *Controls and Conflicts in Welsh Secondary Education 1889–1944* (Cardiff, 1982).

Jones, H., *Y Soned Gymraeg hyd 1900* / The Welsh-language sonnet before 1900 (Llandysul, 1967).

Jones, Henry, 'Anghenion Cymru' / The needs of Wales, *Y Geninen*, 8 (1890), 209–14.

Jones, I. G., 'Henry Richard ac Iaith y Gwleidydd yn y Bedwaredd Ganrif ar Bymtheg' / Henry Richard and the Language of the Politician in the Nineteenth Century, in Geraint H. Jenkins (ed.), *Cof Cenedl*, 3 (1988), 117–49.

Jones, Ieuan Gwynedd, *Mid-Victorian Wales: The Observers and the Observed* (Cardiff, 1992).

Jones, Iorwerth, *David Rees, Y Cynhyrfwr* / David Rees, the Agitator (Swansea, 1971).

Jones, J. R., *Ac onide : ymdriniaeth mewn ysgrif a phregeth ar argyfwng y Gymru gyfoes* / And is it not so: a moral tale on the crisis of Wales today (Llandybie, 1970).

Jones, J. R. Kilsby, 'Pa un ai mantais neu anfantais i Gymru fyddai tranc yr iaith Gymraeg' / Would the death of the Welsh Language be an advantage or a disadvantage to Wales?, *Y Geninen*, 1 (1883, 18–23).

Jones, Jack, *Unfinished Journey* (London, 1937).

Jones, Jonathan, *Cofiant y Parch. Thomas Jones, o Ddinbych* / The Life of Thomas Jones of Denbigh (Denbigh, 1897).

Jones, Katharine Viriamu, *Life of John Viriamu Jones* (London, 1915).

Jones, Marian H., 'Wales and Hungary', *Transactions of the Honourable Society of Cymmrodorion* (1969), 1–27.

Jones, Mark Ellis, '"Dryswch Babel": Yr Iaith Gymraeg, Llysoedd a Deddfwriaeth yn y Bedwaredd Ganrif ar Bymtheg' / The 'Confusion of Babel', The Welsh Language, Courts and Legislation in Wales in the

Nineteenth Century, in Geraint H. Jenkins (ed.), *Gwnewch bopeth yn Gymraeg: Yr Iaith Gymraeg a'i Pheuoedd 1801–1911* / Do Everything in Welsh the Welsh Language and its Domains (Cardiff, 1999), pp. 553–80.

Jones, R. Cefni, *Gwili: Cofiant a Phregethau* / Gwili: Life and Sermons (Llandysul, 1937).

Jones, R. Merfyn, 'The Mountaineering of Wales 1880–1825', *Welsh History Review*, 19/1–2 (1999), 43–67.

Jones, R. Merfyn, *The North Wales Quarrymen 1874–1922* (Cardiff, 1982).

Jones, R. Tudur, *Ffydd ac Argyfwng Cenedl: Hanes Crefydd yng Nghymru 1890–1914* / Faith and Crisis of a Nation: The History of Religion in Wales 1890–1914, 2 vols (Swansea, 1982).

Jones, R. Tudur, *Hanes Annibynwyr Cymru* / A History of Welsh Congregationalists (Swansea, 1966).

Jones, R. Tudur, *Yr Undeb. Hanes Undeb y Annibynwyr Cymraeg* / The Union. A History of the Union of Welsh-language Congregationalists 1872–1972 (Swansea, 1975).

Jones, R. Tudur, *The Desire of Nations* (Llandybie, 1978).

Jones, Revd W., *A Prize Essay in English and Welsh on the Character of the Welsh as a Nation in the Present Age* (London, 1841).

Jones, Sir Henry CH, *Old Memories*, ed. Thomas Jones, MA, LLD (London, *c.*1923).

Jones, T. Gwyn, *Cofiant Thomas Gee* / Memoirs of Thomas Gee (Denbigh, 1913).

Jones, T. M., (Gwenallt), *Cofiant Y Parch. Roger Edwards* / Life of The Revd Roger Edwards (Colwyn Bay, 1908).

Jones, T. R. *Y Parchedig J. J. Roberts (Iolo Caernarfon)* / The Revd J. J. Roberts (Iolo Caernarfon) (Caernarfon, n.d.).

Jones, W. Glasnant, *Cyn Cof Gennyf a Wedyn* / Before memory and thereafter (Swansea, 1949).

Judson, Pieter M., *Guardians of the Nation: Activism on the Language Frontiers of Imperial Austria* (Cambridge, MA, 2006).

Judson, Pieter M., *The Habsburg Empire: A New History* (Cambridge, MA, 2016).

Jutikkala, E., *A History of Finland* (London, 1962).

Koht, Haldan, 'The Dawn of Nationalism in Europe', *American Historical Review*, 52/2 (1947), 266–80.

Kolarič, Rudolf, 'Cigale, Matej 1819–89', *Slovenska biografija*, ZANU ZRC SAZU, 2013, *http://www.slovenska biografija.si.*

Kotnik, V., *Small Places. Operatic Issues: Opera and its Peripheral Worlds* (Newcastle upon Tyne, 2019).

Krek, J. E., 'Materialistično modroslovje' / Materialist philosophy, *Katoliški Obzornik*, 1 (1897) 37–50, 2 137–56.

Kublar, F., 'Toman, Lovro (1827–1880)', *Slovenska biografija*, ZRC SAZU, 2013, http://www.slovenska-biografija.si.

Lake, E. Cynfael, *Huw Jones o Langwm* (Caernarfon, 2009).

Lambert, W. R., *Drink and Sobriety in Victorian Wales c.1820–c.1895* (Cardiff, 1983).

Lampe, E., 'Leposlovje fin de siècle' / Literature of the fin de siècle, *Katoliški Obzornik*, 1 (1897), 63–78.

Lampe, E., 'Giordano Bruno in svobodna misel' / Giordano Bruno and free thought, *Dom in svet*, 13 (1900) 188–91, 220–3.

Lenček, R., 'Kopitar's Place in the Evolution of Slavonic Philology', in Lenček R., Cooper H. R. and Kopitar, B (eds), *To Honor Jernej Kopitar (1780–1980)* (Ann Arbor, MI, 1982), pp. 1–25.

Lenček, R. L. *The Structure and History of the Slovene Language* (Columbia, OH, 1982).

Levi, T., 'Lle Cymru fel rhan o ymerodraeth Prydain' / The Place of Wales as part of the British Empire, in *Y Traethodydd* (1901), 460–71.

Lewis, E. D., *The Rhondda Valleys: A Study of Industrial Development from 1800 to the Present Day* (London, 1959).

Lewis, J. Saunders, *A school of Welsh Augustans, being a study in English Influences on Welsh Literature during part of the eighteenth century* (Wrexham, 1924).

Light, Julie, 'The Middle Classes as Urban Elites in Nineteenth-Century South Wales', *Welsh History Review*, 24/3 (2009), 29–55.

Linhart, Anton, *Versuch einer Geschichte von Krain und den übrigen südlichen Slovenen Oesterreichs* / Towards a History of Carniola and the Other south Slavs of Austria (Nuremberg, 1796).

Ljubibratić, D., *Gavrilo Princip* (Belgrade, 1959).

Lloyd, J. E., *A History of Wales: From The Earliest Times to the Edwardian Conquest* (2 vols, London, 1911).

Lloyd, Morgan, QC, 'Dyfodol y Cymry' / The future of the Welsh, *Y Geninen*, 4 (1886), 91–2.

Loboda, Anton (Melik, V), 'Vprašanje narodno mešanih ozemelj' / The Question of National Mixed Areas, *Ljubljanski zvon*, September–October (1918), 637–50.

Loboda, Anton (Melik, V), 'Misli o slovanskih narodnostnih problemih' / Thoughts on Slav Nationality Problems, *Ljubljanski zvon*, January (1918), 64–73.

Lončar, Dragotin, 'Dr Anton Dermota (1876–1914)', *Naši zapiski*, 11/7–8 (1914), 179–86.

Lukan, Walter, 'Habsburška monarhija in Slovenci v prvi svetovni vojni' / The Habsburg Monarchy and the Slovenes in the First World War, *Zgodovinski časopis*, 62 (1908), 91–149.

Malkin, B. H., *The Scenery, Antiquities and Biographies of South Wales*, 2nd edn, 2 vols (London, 1807).

Marn J. (ed.), *Kopitarjeva spomenica* / Festschrift for Kopitar (Ljubljana, 1880).

Mason, Rhiannon, *Museums, Nations, Identities: Wales and Its National Museums* (Cardiff, 2007).

Masterman, N., *The Forerunner: The Dilemmas of Tom Ellis 1859–1899* (Llandybie, 1972).

Matić, Dragan, *Nemci v Ljubljani 1861–1918* / Germans in Ljubljana 1861–1918 (Ljubljana, 2002).

Melik V. and Vodopivec, P., 'Slovenski izobraženci in austrijske više šole 1848–1918' / Slovene students and Austrian university-level institutions 1848–1918, *Zgodovinski časopis*, 40 (1986), 269–82.

Melik, V., *Auersperg in Slovenci* / Auersperg and the Slovenes (Maribor, 2006).

Mikša, Peter, '"Da je Trigav ostal v slovenskih rokach je največ moja zasluga": Jakub Aljaž in njegovo planinsko delovanje v Triglavskem pogorju' / 'That Triglav remained in Slovene hands was mainly thanks to me': Jakub Aljaš and his mountaineering activity in the Triglav highlands, *Zgodovinski časopis*, 69/1–2 (2015), 112–23.

Mill, John Stuart, *Utilitarianism, Liberty, and Representative Government* (1861; London, Toronto and New York, 1910).

Miskell, L., *'Intelligent Town': An Urban History of Swansea 1780–1855* (Cardiff, 2006).

Mollé, V., 'Umetnost in narava' / Art and nature, *Ljubljanski zvon*, 30 (1910) 27–34.

Mommsen, Hans, *Die österreichische Sozialdemokratie und die Nationalitätenfrage im habsburgischen Vielvölkerstaat* / Austrian Social Democracy and the Nationality Question in the Multiethnic Habsburg State (Vienna, 1963).

Morgan, D. Densil, *Lewis Edwards* (Cardiff, 2009).

Morgan, D. Densil, *Theologia Cambrensis, Protestant Religion and Theology in Wales, Volume 2: 1760–1900. The Long Nineteenth Century* (Cardiff, 2021).

Morgan, Geraint Dyfnallt, *Ysgolion a Cholegau yr Annibynwyr* / Schools and Colleges of the Independents (Llandysul, 1939).

Morgan, J. J., *Hanes Dafydd Morgan Ysbyty a Diwygiad 1859* / The Story of Dafydd Morgan and the Revival of 1859 (Mold, 1906).

Morgan, J. Vyrnwy, *Welsh Political and Educational Leaders in the Victorian Era* (London, 1908).

Morgan, Kenneth O., 'The Realist: Henry Richard', in Morgan, Kenneth O., *Revolution to Devolution: Reflections on Welsh Democracy* (Cardiff, 2014), pp. 75–100.

Morgan, Kenneth O., *David Lloyd George: Welsh Radical as World Statesman* (Cardiff, 1964).

Morgan, Kenneth O., *Rebirth of a Nation: Wales 1880–1980* (Oxford, 1981).

Morgan, Kenneth O., *Wales in British Politics 1868–1922* (Cardiff, 1970).

Morgan, Prys, 'The Emergence of Empire 1750–1898', in Morgan, Prys (ed.), *The Tempus History of Wales 25000 BC–AD 2000* (Stroud, 2001).

Morgan, W., *Cofiant, neu hanes bywyd y diweddar Barch. Christmas Evans* / The Life of the late Revd Christmas Evans (Wrexham, 1883).

'Nodiadau llenyddol a diwinyddol' / Literary and Theological Notes, *Y Traethodydd*, 57 (1902), 68–80.

O'Daunt, W. J., *Personal Recollections of the late Daniel O'Connell* (London, 1849).

O'Leary, Paul, *Immigration and Integration: The Irish in Wales 1798–1922* (Cardiff, 2002).

O'Leary, Paul, 'Processions, Power and Public Space: Corpus Christi at Cardiff, 1872–1914', *Welsh History Review*, 24 (2008).

Odgovori na 'Vedino' anketo o jugoslavenskem vprašanju / Answers to Veda's enquiry on the Yugoslav question, *Veda*, 3/2 (1913), 97–113.

Okey, Robin, 'Religija, zezik in narodnost: primer modernega Walesa' / Religion, language and nationality: the case of modern Wales, *Zgodovinski časopis*, (2012), 1–2, 116–43.

Okey, Robin, 'Wales and Eastern Europe: Small Nations in Comparison', in T. M. Charles-Edwards and R. J. W. Evans (eds), *Wales and the Wider World* (Donington, 2010).

Orožen, M., 'Uredovalna slovenščina v drugi polovici osemnajstega stoletja' / Official use of Slovene in the second half of the eighteenth century, in *Obdobje razsvetljenstva v slovenskem jeziku, književnosti in kulturi* / Slovene Language, Literature and Culture in the Period of the Enlightenment, ed. Boris Paternu (Ljubljana, 1979), pp. 155–82.

Owain, O. Llew, *Hanes y Ddrama yng Nghymru 1850–1943* / A history of drama in Wales (Liverpool, 1948).

Owen, Pierce, 'Cenadwri o'r Eidal' / A Message from Italy, *Y Traethodydd* (1913), 107–20.

Pantheologia, sef Hanes Holl Grefyddau'r Byd, in *Holl Weithiau, Prydyddawl a Rhyddieithol, y diweddar Parch. William Williams, Pantycelyn* / A History of All the World's Religions, in The Complete Works, Poetry and Prose, of the late Revd William Williams, Pantycelyn), ed. J. R. Kilsy Jones (London, n.d.), p. 529.

Parry, Gwenfair, '"Queen of the Welsh Resorts": Tourism and the Welsh Language in Llandudno in the Nineteenth Century', *Welsh History Review*, 22 (2001, 118–48).

Parry, Thomas (ed.), *The Oxford Book of Welsh Verse* (Oxford, 1962).

Paternu, Boris, 'Francoska revolucija in slovenska literatura' / The French Revolution and Slovenian Literature), in Kmecl, M. (ed.) *Obdobje slovenskega narodnega preporoda* / The Period of the Slovene National Revival (Ljubljana, 1991), pp. 51–72.

Phillips, Sir Tomas, *Wales: the language, social condition, moral character and religious opinions of the people* (London, 1849).

Pleterski, J., 'Die Slowenen' / The Slovenes in *Die Habsburgermonarchie 1848–1918*, vol. 3, *Die Völker des Reiches* / The Peoples of the Empire, ed. A. Wandruszka and P. Urbanitsch, Part 2, pp. 801–38.

Pleterski, J., *Narodna in politična zavest na Koroškem* / National and Political Consciousness in Carinthia (Ljubljana, 1965).

Pogačnik, J., *Kulturni pomen slomškovega dela* / The Cultural Significance of Slomšek's Work (Maribor, 1971).

Pogačnik, Jože, 'Pojem naroda v slovenskem razsvetljenstvu' / The Concept of the People in the Slovene Enlightenment, in Kmecl, M. (ed.), *Obdobje slovenskega narodnega preporoda* / The Period of Slovene National Revival (Ljubljana, 1991), pp. 87–96.

Pope, Robert, *Building Jerusalem: Nonconformity, Labour and the Social Question in Wales, 1906–1939* (Cardiff, 2007).

Pohlin, Marko, *Grammatik der crainerischen Sprache* / A Grammar of the Carniolan Language (Ljubljana, 1768).

Poniž, K. N., 'The Representations of Slavic nations in the writings of Josipina Turnograjski', in Amelia Sanz et al. (eds), *Women Telling Nations* (Amsterdam and New York, 2014), pp. 169–90.

Prijatelj, Ivan, 'Iz naroda za narod. 1. shod narodno-radikalnega dijaštva v Trstu' / From the Nation for the Nation, The First Meeting of national radical Slav Students in Trieste, *Ljubljanski zvon*, 26 (1906), 184–6.

Prijatelj, Ivan, 'Več Prešerna!' / Let's have more of Prešeren!, *Ljubljanski zvon*, 20 (1900), 724–32.

Prijatelj, Ivan, *Slovenska kulturnopolitična in slovenstvena zgodovina 1848–95* / Slovene cultural-political and literary history 1848–95, 6 vols (Ljubljana, 1955–85).

Prunk, J., *Slovenski narodni vzpon* / The Rise of the Slovene Nation (Ljubljana, 1993).

Pryce, Huw, *J. E. Lloyd and the Creation of Welsh History: Renewing a Nation's Past* (Cardiff, 2011).

Pwyll, 'Y Beirdd a Beirniadaeth' / The Poets and Criticism, *Y Geninen* (1907), 11–14.

Ravenstein, E. G., 'The Celtic Languages in the British Isles', *Journal of the Royal Statistical Society* (1879), 579–636.

Rees, B., 'Sport, Coal and Identity in Swansea, 1870–1910', *Welsh History Review*, 29/4 (2019).

Rees, Caleb, 'Addysg a'r Genedl' / Education and the Nation, *Y Traethodydd*, 62 (1907), 241–9.

Rees, D. Ben, *Chapels in the Valley: A Study in the Sociology of Welsh Nonconformity* (Upton, Wirral, 1975).

Rees, D. Ben, *Hanes Rhyfeddol Cymry Lerpwl* / The remarkable history of the Welsh in Liverpool (Talybont, 2019).

Rees, D. Ben, *Pregethwr y Bobl: Bywyd a Gwaith Owen Thomas* / The People's Preacher. The Life and Work of Owen Thomas (Liverpool, 1979).

Rees, T., 'Diwinyddiaeth yr Eglwysi Rhyddion' / The Theology of the Free Churches, *Y Traethodydd*, 62 (1907) 300–7.

Rees, T., *Miscellaneous Papers on Subjects Relating to Wales* (London, 1867).

Rees, W., *Cardiff: A History of the City*, 2nd rev. edn (Cardiff, 1969).

Reports of the Commissioners of Inquiry into the State of Education in Wales ... in three parts (London, 1848).

Roberts, T. and Roberts, D., *Cofiant y Parch: W. Rees, D.D. (Hiraethog)* / Life of the Revd W. D. Rees (Hiraethog) (Dolgellau, 1893).

Roberts, Eleazer, 'Isaac Roberts DSc, FRAS', *Y Geninen*, 22 (1904), 276–82.

Roberts, Enid P., *Detholiad o Hunangofiant Gweirydd ap Rhys* / Selection from the Autobiography of Geweirydd ap Rhys (Llandysul, 1949).

Roberts, Gwyneth Tyson, *The Treason of the Blue Books* (Cardiff, 1998).

Roberts, P. R., 'Tudor Legislation and the Political Status of "the British Tongue"', in Geraint H. Jenkins (ed.), *The Welsh Language before the Industrial Revolution* (Cardiff, 1997), pp. 123–52.

Rogel, Carol, 'Preporodovci: Slovene Students for an Independent Yugoslavia', *Canadian Slavic Studies*, 5/2 (1973), 196–212.

Rogel, Carol, *The Slovenes and Yugoslavism 1890–1914* (Boulder, CO, 1977).

Roth, J., *The Radetsky March*, trans. Eva Tucker (London, 1974).

Rozman, F., 'Deutsche und Slowenische Arbeiter in der Arbeiterbewegung in Slowenien / German and Slovenian workers in the working-class movement in Slovenia, in P. Vodopivec and F. Bister (eds), *Kulturelle Wechseltätigkeit in Mitteleuropa: Deutsche und Slowenische Kultur im Slowenischen Raum vom Anfang des 19. Jahrhundert bis zum zweiten Weltkrieg* / Cultural interchange in Central Europe: German and Slovenian culture in Slovenian territory from the beginning of the nineteenth century to the Second World War (Ljubljana, 1995), pp. 165–71.

Rustja, Peter (ed.), *Med Trstom in Dunajem: Ivan Nabergoj v avstrijskem državnem zboru (1873–1897)* / Between Trieste and Vienna. Ivan Nabergoj in the Austrian Reichsrat (Trieste, 1999).

Saurer, E., *Die politischen Aspekte der österreichischen Bischofsernennungen 1867–1903* / Political aspects of Austrian episcopal appointments 1867– 1903 (Vienna, 1968).

Schmidt, Vlado, 'Šolstvo na Slovenskem v buržoaznodemokratični revoluciji (1848–51)' / Schooling in Slovenia in the Bourgeois Democratic Revolution, 1848–51), *Zbornik za historiju školstva i prosvejete*, I (1964), 41–76.

Schorske, Carl, *German Social Democracy, 1905–1914* (Cambridge, MA, 1955).

Šenoa, August, 'Karanfil s pjesnikova groba' / A Carnation from the Poet's Grave, in Nazečić, Anka (ed.), *Kameni svatovi i druge povjestice* (Sarajevo, 1962), pp. 49–119.

Shuttleworth, J. N. (ed.), *The Life of Edward, First Lord Herbert of Cherbery, written by himself* (London, 1976).

Simoniti, P., *Humanizam na Slovenskem i slovenski humanisti do XVI stoletja* / Humanism in Slovenia and Slovenian Humanists to the Sixteenth Century (Ljubljana, 1979).

Slanovič, Branko, *Blaž Kumerdej* (Kranj, 1997).

Slodnjak, A., 'Fran Levstik (1831–87): the first representative of radicalism in Slovene literature', *Slavonic and East European Review*, 15 (1956–7), 24–39.

Smith, Anthony D., *The Ethnic Origin of Nations* (Oxford, New York, 1988).

Smith, D. (ed.), *A People and a Proletariat: Essays in the History of Wales 1780– 1980* (London, 1980).

Sommer, J., 'A Step away from Herder and the Question of National Language', *The Slavonic and East European Review*, 90 (2012), 1–32.

Šorn, J. and Adamič, F. 'Terpinc, Fidelis' (1799–1875); Gorup, Josip wikipedija, prosta enciklopedija, *http//www.slovenska-biografija.si*.

Southall, J. E., 'A ydyw y Gymraeg yn marw?' / Is Welsh dying? *Y Geninen*, 16 (1898), 242–5.

Southall, J. E., *Bilingual Teaching in Welsh Elementary Schools, or minutes of evidence of Welsh witnesses before the Royal Commission on Education in 1886–7* (Newport, 1888).

Štih, P., Simoniti V., and Vodopivec P., *Slowenische Geschichte. Gesellschaft-Politik-Kultur* / A History of Slovenia: Society, Politics, Culture (Graz, 2008).

Štuhec, Marko, 'Iz Lesc v Ljubljano po francusko. K poznavanju jezikove rabe krajnskega plemstva v prvi polovici osemnajstega stoletja' / From Lesec to Ljubljana in French. Towards an understanding of the linguistic usage of Carniolan nobles in the first half of the eighteenth century, *Zgodovinski časopis*, 20/3–4 (2006), 327–44.

Šunalić, Zlata, 'Pojem naroda u Vodnikovoj poeziji' (The concept of the people in Vodnik's poetry), in M. Kmecl, *Obdobje slovenskega narodnega preporoda* (The period of Slovene national revival), pp. 209–18.

The Torrington Diaries containing the tour through England and Wales of the Hon. John Bynge between the years 1781 and 1795, vol. 1 (London, 1807).

Thomas, D., *Silyn (Robert Silyn Roberts) 1871–1910* (Liverpool, *c*.1956).

Thomas, D., *Y Werin a'i Theyrnas* / The Common People and Their Kingdom (Liverpool, 1910).

Thomas, John, *Cofiant y Parchedig T. Rees, D.D. Abertawy* / Life of the Revd T. Rees D.D. Swansea (Dolgellau, 1888).

Thomas, M. Wynn, *In the Shadow of the Pulpit: Literature and Nonconformist Wales* (Cardiff, 2010).

Thomas, Owen *Cofiant John Jones Talsarn* / The Life of John Jones Talsarn (Wrexham, *c*.1874; facsimile reprint Whitefish, MT, 2010).

Thomas, R. Brinley 'Pair Dadeni: Y Boblogaeth a'r Iaith Gymraeg yn y Bedwaredd Ganrif ar Bymtheg' / Cauldron of rebirth: population and the Welsh language in the nineteenth century, in Geraint H. Jenkins (ed.), *Gwnewch Bopeth yn Gymraeg: Yr Iaith Gymraeg a'i Pheuoedd 1801–1911* / Do Everything in Welsh: The Welsh language and its domains (Cardiff, 1999).

Thompson, Steven 'Class Cohesion, Working-class Homogeneity and the Labour Movement in Industrial South Wales', *Llafur*, 9/3 (2006), 81–91.

Ušeničnik, Ales '"Leonovo Društvo": Boj véde zoper vero' / The Leo IX Society: The Struggle of Science against Faith, *Katoliški Obzornik*, 1 (1897), 1–9.

Ušeničnik, Ales 'Ideali slovenske mladine' / Ideals of Slovene Youth, *Katoliški Obzornik*, 5 (1901), 126–38.

Ušeničnik, Ales '*Naš čas*' / Our epoch, *Čas*, 1 (1907), 1–4.

Ušeničnik, Ales 'Starost človeskega roda' / The age of the human species, *Katoliški Obzornik*, 5 (1901), 145–8.

Valvasor, J. W. *Die Ehre dess Hertzogthums Crain* / The Renowned Duchy of Carniola (Ljubljana, 1689).

Vertous, M, 'Ilirske dezhele nekadaj in sada' / The Illyrian Lands then and now, in *Kmetijske in rokodelske novize*, 1 (1843), 16–30, VIII.

Vodopivec, P., 'Die sozialen und wirtschaftlichen Ansichten des deutschen Bürgertums in Krain vom Ende der 60-er bis Anfang der 80-er Jahre des neunzehnten Jahrhunderts' / Economic and Social Views of the German Bourgeoisie in Carniola from the end of the End of the 1860s to the Beginning of the 1880s, in H. Rumpler and A. Suppan (eds), *Geschichte der Deutschen im Bereich des heutigen Slovenien, 1848–1941* / A History of Germans in the Area of Present-Day Slovenia (Munich, 1988), pp. 85–119.

Vodopivec, P., *O gospodarskih in socialnih nazorih na Slovenskem v 19. stoletju* / Economic and Social Thought in Nineteenth-Century Slovenia (Ljubljana, 2020).

Walters Huw, 'Y Gymraeg a'r Wasg Gylchgronol' / The Welsh Language and the Periodical Press, in Jenkins Geraint H. (ed.), *Gwnewch Bopeth yn Gymraeg: Yr*

Iaith Gymraeg a'i Pheuoedd / Do Everything in Welsh: The Welsh Language and its Domains (Cardiff, 1999), pp. 327–52.

Wilks, I., *South Wales and the Rising of 1839: Class Struggle as Armed Struggle* (London, 1984).

Williams, Chris, *Democratic Rhondda: Politics and Society, 1885–1951* (Cardiff, 1996).

Williams, D., *A History of Modern Wales* (1950; London, 1969).

Williams, D., *The History of Monmouthshire* (London, 1796).

Williams, David, *The Rebecca Riots: A Study in Agrarian Discontent* (Cardiff, 1955).

Williams, G. A., *The Search for Beulah Land* (London, 1980).

Williams, Gwyn A., *When Was Wales? A History of the Welsh* (Harmondsworth, 1985).

Williams, Harry, *Duw, Daeareg a Darwin: yn bennaf ar dudalennau'r Traethodydd 1845–1900* / God, Geology and Darwin: chiefly in the pages of *Y Traethodydd* 1845–1900 (Llandysul, 1979).

Williams, Hettie, 'Yr Iaith Gymraeg yn yr Ysgolion' / The Welsh language in the schools, *Y Geninen*, 23 (1905).

Williams, Ioan, *Y Mudiad Drama yng Nghymru 1880–1940* / The Drama Movement in Wales 1880–1940 (Cardiff, 2006).

Williams, J. Gwynn, *The University Movement in Wales* (Cardiff, 1993).

Williams, Peter (Pedr Hir),'Y Cymry yn Genedl' / The Welsh as a Nation, *Y Geninen*, 11 (1893), 76–9, 154–8.

Wyn, Eifion, *Telynegion Maes a Môr* / Lyrics of Land and Sea (n.p., n.d.).

Wyn, Watcyn, 'Cymru ar ddiwedd y bedwaredd ganrif ar bymtheg' / Wales at the end of the nineteenth centry, *Y Geninen*, 11 (1893), 182–7.

Zupanič, N., 'Ilirija', *Ljubljanski zvon*, 27 (1907), 486, 554, 615.

INDEX

A

Abbey Theatre, Dublin, 246
Aberdare, 265, 272
Aberdare Committee, 199–200, 201
Abergavenny, 96, 109
Abergavenny Welsh society, 96
Aberystwyth, 149, 165, 175, 178, 193, 198, 199, 211, 249, 269, 308
Aberystwyth University College, 178, 197, 199, 200, 211, 310
Ablett, Noah, 281
Abraham, William *see* Mabon
absolutism, 5, 25, 27–8, 45, 74, 81, 92, 123, 134, 147, 155, 157–8, 161, 168, 306
Act of Union, 25, 216
Acton, John Dalberg-Acton, Lord, 4, 5, 7
Adams, David, 233, 250
advertising, 198, 264
African Steamship Company, 202
agricultural cooperatives, 189
agriculture, 31, 62, 89, 92, 93, 112, 127, 136, 177, 180, 188, 212, 282, 301
Almanac y Miloedd, 235
almanacs, 26
alphabets, 52, 72, 84, 85–6
Alun *see* Blackwell, John
amateur dramatics, 159, 169, 198, 245–6, 272
America *see* United States
American Civil War, 150

Amserau, 95, 101–2, 140, 175, 202
Anglesey, 26, 56, 72–3, 150
Anglican Church
  and the 'Blue Books' report, 128–9, 131–2
  disendowment, 207, 212, 214, 215
  disestablishment, 135, 175, 207, 211, 212, 214, 216, 217, 277, 290, 303, 308
  and education, 128–9, 133
  hegemonic position of, 6
  in Ireland, 135
  and Methodism, 74, 131
  Nonconformity breaks from, 65–6
  numbers of adherents, 106, 265
  periodicals, 97, 101
  revival, 182, 205, 265–6
  in Scotland, 305
  and the Welsh language, 26, 36, 94, 97, 116, 182
  and Welsh literature, 36
Anglo-Saxon invasions, 22, 38, 57, 59, 116–17, 139, 252–3, 306
Anglo-Welsh literature, 247, 272–3, 297
anti-landlordism, 94, 188
antiquarians, 22, 35, 36, 56–9, 71
anti-slavery movement, 63, 110, 117
anti-tithe riots, 176
Aquinas, St Thomas, 174, 236
Archaeologia Britannica (Lhuyd), 35
archaeology, 171, 181, 224, 252
architecture, 25, 33, 198, 202, 212
Arfonwyson, 101, 136

aristocratic courts, 23
Aristotle, 236
Arminian Methodism, 107; *see also*
    Wesleyanism
Arnold, Matthew, 225
art, 33, 212, 226–7, 248
Arthur, King, 36–7, 249, 253
artisans, 62, 75, 127, 152, 188, 196, 197,
    244, 274, 312
Aškerc, Anton, 227, 250
Asquith, Herbert, 214
assimilation, 2, 4, 91, 139, 166, 192, 289,
    311
Association for the Promotion of Social
    Science, 163
Association of Welsh Clergy in the West
    Riding of Yorkshire, 95, 199
astronomy, 99, 101, 224
Athanaeum, 164
atheism, 45, 212
Auersperg, Anton von, 191, 300
Auersperg family, 190–1
Augustinian order, 46, 47
Australia, 79, 118, 150
Australydd, 150
Austrian Civic Code, 117
Austrian German Alpine Club, 181
Austrian legal system, 28, 29, 104, 157
Austrian parliament, 124–5, 127, 147,
    158, 171, 191, 204, 239, 286
Austrian Social Democratic Party
    (ASDP), 275–7, 284–5
Austro-Slav tendency, 54, 126
authoritarianism, 4, 104–5, 166, 288, 311
autonomy, 124, 141, 157, 206–7, 218,
    276, 290, 297, 298, 311
Avars, 22

B
backwardness, 4, 5, 41, 83, 138, 171, 195,
    222, 276, 283
Baine, Edward, 153
Bala, 109, 165, 173, 174
Balkan wars, 287
Balkans, 21, 51, 82, 140, 210, 223, 275,
    277, 287

ballads, 56, 226, 250
Baltic states, 82, 104, 136, 312
Band of Hope, 153
Baner ac Amserau Cymru, 154, 175,
    176–7, 182, 235
Bangor, 176, 198, 199, 253
Bangor Normal College, 199
Bangor University College, 176, 199,
    253
banking, 83, 136, 189–90
baptism, 66
Baptist Church, 64, 65, 67, 74, 98, 106–7,
    109, 110, 131, 152, 246, 281
bardic tradition, 35–6, 57, 63–4, 100,
    163, 304
Baroque architecture, 25, 33
Barry Island, 177, 264
Basque country, 11, 295
Bauer, Otto, 279
Beardsley, Aubrey, 237
Beaumarchais, Pierre, 50, 54
Beddau'r Proffwydi (Gruffydd), 246–7,
    271, 272
Beirniad, 241
Bel, Mátyás, 37
Belgium, 288
Belgrade, 287, 297
Bell, Alexander Graham, 223
Bergson, Henri, 234
Bethesda, 281
Bevan, Aneurin, 307
Bible, 24–6, 34, 36, 50, 62, 66, 70, 75,
    103, 153, 223, 232, 236, 242
bilingualism
    language census data, 192–4
    Slovene, 39–40, 49, 84, 90, 93, 106,
        158, 172, 193–4, 285
    Welsh, 39–40, 64, 90, 112, 165, 187,
        192–3, 230–1, 235, 240, 244, 255,
        264, 271, 279
Bill of Rights, 28
Bird, Robert, 214
Blackwell, John, 105
Blaenafon, 100, 191
Blanc, Louis, 102
Bleiweis, Janez, 88–9, 93, 98, 124, 125,
    127, 155, 158–62, 167, 171, 239

'Blue Books', 79, 112, 128–34, 139, 151, 154, 163, 222
Blumen aus Krain (Linhart), 49, 50
Boer War, 228, 235, 262, 270
Bohemia, 22, 28, 32, 38, 104, 190, 274
Bois, Henri, 233
Bonomi, Petrus, 24
Borrow, George, 141, 167, 172
Bosnia, 140, 261, 286, 287
Bosnian Serbs, 291
Bourget, Paul, 226
Bowles, Thomas, 60, 72–3
Bowring, John, 87
boxing, 268
Bradfield, John, 64, 72
Brecon, 33, 109
Breconshire, 65, 73, 76, 193
Breton language, 11, 72, 86
Brexit, 310–11
Bridgend, 150
bridges, 149, 177
Brigstocke, W. A., 189
Brissot, Jacques Pierre, 64
Bristol, 33, 215
Britannia Bridge, 149
British and Foreign Bible Society, 66
British army, 288
British culture, 11, 71, 227, 310
British Empire, 1, 2, 40, 45, 79, 123, 163, 166, 180, 186, 218, 228, 235, 254, 261–2, 265, 270, 310
British identity, 186, 218, 299
British legal system, 28, 29, 40, 45
British Miners' Federation, 281
British Museum, 269
British Navy, 149
British parliament, 27–8, 29, 62, 79, 112, 114, 167–8, 207, 212, 214, 217
British Society for Nonconformists, 133
Brittany, 4, 11, 91, 164, 238, 266, 295
Brooks, Simon, 13, 166–7, 179, 300, 306–7, 312
Brud a Sylwydd, Y, 101
Brunel, Isambard, 149
Bruno, Giordano, 237–8
Brutus, 99–100, 105, 133, 164
Brython, 202

Buddhism, 68
bukovniki, 34
Bulkeley, William, 26, 75
'Bully, Taffy a Paddy' (Emrys ap Iwan), 213
burial law, 175, 176
Bute, John Crichton-Stuart, 2nd marquess, 97, 149
Bute, John Crichton-Stuart, 3rd marquess, 150
Byron, George, Lord, 170

C
Caernarfon, 163, 193, 281
Caernarfonshire, 30, 60, 281
Calvin, John, 24
Calvinistic Methodism, 66, 95, 102, 106–10, 131, 151–3, 160, 166, 173–7, 202, 225, 233–4, 266, 277, 288
Cambrian Archaeological Society, 181, 252
Cambrian Combine Company, 215
Cambrian Register, 272
Cambrian Visitor, 272
Canada, 45, 79, 215
Cankar, Ivan, 196, 228, 247–8, 250, 251, 280, 284–5, 287
Cannwyll y Cymry (Pritchard), 26
Canterbury, 23
Cape *see* South Africa
capitalism, 3, 111, 148, 188–90, 207, 215, 237, 276, 283
Capuchins, 25, 35
Cardiff, 1, 39, 90, 103, 115, 149, 150, 177–8, 187, 193, 198–200, 263–4, 266, 268–71, 291, 298, 308
Cardiff City Library, 269
Cardiff Civic Centre, 269
Cardiff University College, 199–200, 269
Cardiganshire, 31, 36, 59, 72, 75, 178, 190, 241, 273
Carinthia, 22, 23, 31, 32, 33, 40, 53, 125, 162, 194–5, 290, 296, 298, 302
Carmarthen, 31, 35, 90, 109, 115

Carmarthenshire, 67, 107
Carnhuanawc, 96, 97, 99, 100, 253
Carniola, 22, 24–7, 29, 31–5, 39, 46–53,
    69, 71, 83–4, 88–90, 93–4, 125,
    147, 154, 158–9, 161, 171, 187–8,
    191, 194–5, 207–9, 252, 262,
    276–7
Carniola, 90
Carniolan Agricultural Society, 83, 89,
    93–4
Carniolan Constitutional Party, 172
Carniolan Cooperative Union, 208
Carniolan Historical Association, 90, 252
carting, 31, 83, 147
Čas, 236, 237
catechisms, 25, 84, 85
Catherine the Great, 71
Catholicism
    in Austria, 45, 47–8, 74, 127–8
    Catholic emancipation, 80, 177
    and the cooperative movement, 187,
        208, 303
    Counter-Reformation, 25, 29, 33, 34,
        47, 74
    in Croatia, 286
    and education, 25, 34, 105, 127–8,
        137, 209
    and the Enlightenment, 45, 47
    and the First World War, 288–9
    in Ireland, 80, 92, 131, 140, 177–8,
        266, 268, 305
    and liberalism, 142, 204, 207–10, 216,
        231, 297, 304
    monasteries, 33, 47, 49, 74
    newspapers and periodicals, 126, 155,
        224, 236–7, 303
    pilgrimages and processions, 25, 34,
        47, 266
    political representation, 13, 204, 207–8
    reform Catholicism, 47, 137
    and the Second World War, 297–8,
        304
    in Slovenia, 13, 25, 34, 47–9, 74,
        92, 105, 126–8, 137, 155, 204,
        207–10, 216, 224, 231, 236–7,
        250, 251, 286, 288–9, 297–8,
        303–4, 306

in the United States, 189
    in Wales, 266, 268
Ceiriog *see* Hughes, John Ceiriog
Čelakovský, František, 87
Celje, 23, 24, 207, 267
Celovec, 33
Celt, 223
Celtic languages, 35, 80, 180, 207
Celtic Remains (Morris), 57
Celts, 21–2, 59, 139, 229, 266
censorship, 46, 47, 94, 117, 239, 288
Central Welsh Board, 201, 271
centralisation, 5, 28, 45, 81, 126, 156, 232,
    278, 280
centralism, 147, 158, 285
Cerddor Cymreig, Y, 153
Chalmers, Thomas, 80, 173
Chamberlain, Neville, 310
Chamber's Encyclopedia, 95, 102, 133
Change (Francis), 270, 272
Charles I, 81
Charles, Thomas, 66–7, 75
Chartism, 112, 114–15, 129, 131
child labour, 111
China, 45, 260, 274
choral societies, 153, 158, 160
Chrétien de Troyes, 36
church building, 25, 33, 182, 198, 202, 302
church courts, 28
Church of England *see* Anglican Church
Churchill, Winston, 202, 296
Cigale, Matej, 239–40
Cilmeri, 240
circulating school movement, 34, 65, 67,
    69
Cistercian order, 49
'City, The' (Parry-Williams), 250
civil society, 44, 55, 72
class *see* elites; middle classes; working
    classes
cloth production, 31, 62, 83, 97
coal, 31, 95, 97, 111, 149, 150, 154–5,
    177, 187, 189, 215, 263–5, 277–8,
    307–8
colonisation, 45, 79, 130
Colwyn Bay, 149
common man, cult of, 73, 196, 306

Common People and their Kingdom, The (Thomas), 282
communism, 189, 238, 277, 280, 297–8, 312
Cobbett, William, 113
Congregationalism, 65, 67, 74, 95, 101, 107, 109, 110, 234, 253
Congress of the European Powers, 83
Conservative Party, 131, 135, 148, 154, 188, 195, 207, 214, 216, 262
constitutionalism, 2, 3–4, 27–8, 74, 118, 123, 157–8, 300, 301
Cook, A. J., 281
Cooper, James Fennimore, 244
cooperative societies, 136, 189, 190, 208–9, 218, 301, 303–4
Čop, Matija, 86–7, 90, 105, 125, 179, 306
copper, 31, 149
Corn Laws, 80, 102
Cornish language, 73, 86
Cory, John (of Cory and Bros. Ltd), 263
Cory, John (of John Cory and Sons Ltd), 263
Costa, Heinrich, 158
cottars, 30, 31
Council of Wales and the Marches, 28
Counter-Reformation, 25, 29, 33, 34, 47, 74
Court of Great Sessions, 28, 45
Cranogwen, 245
credit cooperatives, 189, 209
Crefydd a Bywyd (Edwards), 234
Crimean War, 141
Critique of Pure Reason (Kant), 102
Croatian literature, 226
Croats, 51–3, 82, 88, 92–3, 126, 140, 157, 159–60, 206–7, 210, 261, 283, 286–90, 297
Cronicl yr Oes, 153
Cross Commission on Education, 240
cultural associations, 158–60, 225, 301
cultural nationalism, 5–6, 48, 82, 137, 158–60, 183, 215, 225, 239, 310
cultural sovereignty, 6, 10, 12, 14, 137, 206, 218, 301
culture
    British culture, 11, 71, 227, 310
    English culture, 99, 174, 305
    folk culture, 23, 27, 33, 44, 56, 82, 156, 164, 169, 304
    German culture, 26, 71, 117–18, 159, 171, 301, 306
    high culture, 33, 116, 158, 160, 179, 196, 222, 243
    Hungarian culture, 71
    and identity, 37, 70–1, 218, 269–71
    Italian culture, 276
    and language, 37, 41, 82–106, 136, 137, 158–65, 178–82, 218
    low culture, 196, 243
    Nonconformist culture, 9, 10–11, 98–102, 110–11, 140, 151–4, 181–2
    revival of, 57, 82–106, 229
    Russian culture, 71
    Serbian culture, 287
    Swedish culture, 71, 196
Cwyn yn erbyn Gorthrymder (Richards), 62
'Cyflafan Morfa Rhuddlan' (Evans), 116–17
Cylchgrawn Cynmraeg, 62–3
Cymmer mining accident, 155
Cymmrodorion Society, 56–8, 69, 136, 271
Cymro, 202
Cymru Fydd movement, 186, 211–16, 230, 233, 239, 245, 254, 269, 279, 296, 297, 304, 309
Cymru'r Plant, 235
cynghanedd, 105, 163
Cynon valley, 265
Cyprus, 310
Cysondeb y Ffydd (Jones), 234
Czech language, 38, 55, 82, 104, 226, 284
Czech literature, 226–7
Czechs, 2, 7, 11, 55, 82, 87, 93, 124–5, 156–9, 162, 189–90, 196, 204, 206, 262, 276–7, 283

D

Dafydd ap Gwilym, 38, 57, 58, 179
Dafydd ap Gwilym Society, 240–1
Daily Telegraph, 164

Darwinism, 15, 225, 304; *see also* evolution
Davies, Sir Alfred T., 202
Davies, D. T., 270
Davies, David, Llandinam, 150, 177–8, 197, 199, 263
Davies, Griffith, 101
Davies, J. Glyn, 202
Davies, John, 299
Davies, Richard, 150
Davies, Russell, 299
Davies, Walter, 70, 95–6, 97, 105, 116
Ddraig Goch ynte'r Faner Goch, Y (Phillips), 279
democracy, 6, 7, 8, 29, 91, 168, 180, 186, 209, 210, 252, 255, 284, 289–90, 311, 314
Denbigh, 175, 182
Denbighshire, 172, 176
department stores, 198, 263
'Departure of Arthur' (Jones), 249
Dertel, R. J., 132, 167
Dermota, Anton, 283
Descartes, René, 47
Deschmann, Karl *see* Dežman, Dragotin
devolution, 8, 216, 298–9, 309, 313; *see also* home rule
devolution referenda, 298, 299, 313
Dežman, Dragotin, 158, 171–2, 194, 252, 300
dialects, 7, 38, 53, 84, 87–8
dictionaries, 47, 49, 51, 66, 72, 169, 234, 239–40
Diets, 24, 25, 29, 81, 94, 125, 158, 161
diocesan structures, 23, 34, 74
diplomacy, 24
disendowment, 207, 212, 214, 215
disestablishment, 135, 175, 207, 211, 212, 214, 216, 217, 277, 303, 308
Disraeli, Benjamin, 80, 178, 264
Diwygiwr, 101, 103, 115, 131, 136
Dobrovský, Jozef, 52
Dom in svet, 222–8, 229, 237, 247
Donetsk, 149
Dowlais, 111, 112
Doyle, Arthur Conan, 244
Driscoll, Jim, 268

droving, 31
druids, 63
Drws y Society Profiad (Pantycelyn), 67
Drych y Prif Oesoedd (Evans), 36, 53
Drysorfa, Y, 66, 101, 153, 223
Dualist constitution, 162, 194, 197, 267
Dublin, 197, 212, 246
Dyfed, 22
Dysgedydd, Y, 101

E

East India Company, 149
economic growth, 79, 81, 187
Edinburgh Review, 102
Edinburgh University, 80, 131, 173, 182
Edinost, 202, 204, 205, 276
education
    in Austria, 46, 48–9, 70, 82, 104, 198–9
    'Blue Books' report, 79, 112, 128–34, 139, 151, 154, 163
    circulating school movement, 34, 65, 67, 69
    discussion in periodical press, 223, 225
    of elites, 14, 29, 157
    in English language, 34, 70, 109, 128, 133–4, 136, 174, 201, 255, 271
    in German language, 70, 82, 84–5, 135, 136, 161, 172, 194, 201, 255
    in Germany, 104
    grammar schools, 34, 56
    humanistic education, 201
    intermediate schools, 200–1, 225, 303
    in Ireland, 118
    in Latin, 34
    and Nonconformity, 9, 102, 109, 110, 128–34, 154, 165, 216–17
    non-denominational schools, 154, 176, 216
    primary education, 34, 46, 48, 52, 70, 82–5, 91, 127, 136–7, 161, 190, 195, 201, 231, 240
    reform of, 48–9, 130
    and religion, 9, 14, 25, 33–4, 45, 47, 85, 105, 109, 110, 127–34, 154, 216–17, 232

in Scotland, 34
secondary education, 34, 52, 84–5,
    104, 125, 136, 157, 197–201, 207,
    231, 240, 303, 306
seminaries, 34, 105
in Slovene language, 24, 34, 47–50,
    52–3, 69–70, 82–6, 91–2, 104,
    125, 127–8, 135–6, 157, 161, 172,
    191, 194–5, 199, 201, 203–4, 207,
    240, 296, 301
in Slovenia, 24–5, 29, 33–4, 47–50,
    52–3, 69–70, 82–6, 91–2, 104,
    125, 127–8, 135–7, 157, 161, 172,
    191, 194–5, 198–9, 201, 203–4,
    207, 240, 255, 283–4, 296, 301,
    306
Sunday schools, 67, 69–70, 107, 110,
    129–30, 137, 152, 232, 302
teacher training, 48, 84, 127, 199
textbooks, 69, 84–6, 92, 99, 100, 103,
    133, 137, 271
travel abroad for, 24, 34
tutoring, 157, 168, 251
universities, 24, 80, 83–4, 128,
    159–60, 161, 165, 198–200, 212,
    225, 296
voluntarist principle, 128, 132–3
in Wales, 9, 34, 62, 65, 67, 69–70, 79,
    84–5, 97, 99, 100, 102–3, 128–34,
    136–7, 142, 152, 154, 165, 190,
    197–201, 212, 216–17, 231, 240,
    242, 245, 255, 271, 303
in Welsh language, 34, 62, 69–70,
    84–5, 97, 99, 100, 102–3, 133–4,
    136, 142, 152, 165, 201, 231, 240,
    242, 271
women's education, 245
Education Act (1870), 154, 165, 195,
    199
Education Act (1902), 216–17
Edward VIII, 262
Edwardian conquest, 8, 22, 38
Edwards, H. T., 154
Edwards, Hywel Teifi, 162
Edwards, Lewis, 80, 95, 102, 117, 131,
    134–6, 139, 160, 165, 173–4, 177,
    183, 197, 213, 301, 303

Edwards, Miall, 234, 237
Edwards, O. M., 8–9, 197, 201, 229, 239,
    241–2, 245, 254, 263, 281, 297,
    305
Edwards, Roger, 152–3
Edwards, Thomas Charles, 310
Eiddil Ifor, 100, 138
Eifion Wyn, 232
1848 revolutions, 4, 79, 94, 123–8, 140,
    141, 156, 171, 206, 306
1867 settlement, 147
Einspieler, Andrej, 194, 195
eisteddfodau/eisteddfods, 58, 63–4, 72,
    94–6, 100, 102, 153, 162–4, 179,
    182, 191, 202, 225, 230, 241, 249,
    281, 291
Elfennau Rhifyddiaeth (Arfonwyson), 101
Elias, John, 102, 108, 110, 131, 177
elites, 6, 10, 14, 21, 22, 23, 26–7, 29,
    40, 45, 82, 96, 116, 157, 190–1,
    195–6, 262–3
Elizabeth Church settlement, 26
Ellis, Robert, 152
Ellis, Tom, 211–12, 213–14, 216, 235,
    239, 242
Ellis-Griffith, Sir Ellis Jones, 197
emigration, 9, 57, 63, 80, 148, 150–2,
    188–90, 201, 245, 248, 251, 279,
    297, 301
Empire Palace, Newport, 263
Emrys ap Iwan, 160, 169, 212
enclosures, 112, 115
encyclopaedias, 95, 102, 133, 175
Endlicher, Ivan, 287
Engels, Friedrich, 91
English culture, 99, 174, 305
English exceptionalism, 148
English language
    Anglo-Welsh literature, 247, 272–3,
        297
    bilingualism, 39–40, 64, 90, 112, 165,
        187, 192–3, 230–1, 235, 240, 244,
        255, 264, 271, 279
    and the British Empire, 40, 180
    and commerce, 178
    discussion of in periodical press, 98–9,
        134, 136, 230–1

English language (continued)
  education in, 34, 70, 109, 128, 133–4,
    136, 174, 201, 255, 271
  and eisteddfod, 163–4
  in Ireland, 80, 140
  language borders, 39
  language census data, 192–3
  and law, 25–6, 40, 62, 134, 164
  literature in *see* English literature
  monolingualism, 60, 112, 176, 187,
    193, 260–1, 264
  newspapers and periodicals, 95,
    111–12, 115, 118, 226, 231, 242,
    252
  and Nonconformity, 109, 110
  ordinary people's knowledge of, 41,
    73, 112, 113, 116, 137, 176,
    192–3, 216, 238, 240, 264, 268–9,
    301
  public use, 25–6, 40, 180, 181, 271
  publishing in, 60, 95, 253–4
  religious texts in, 25
  and socialism, 13, 280
  and sport, 268, 271
  and theatre, 247
  use for correspondence, 58–9, 76, 165,
    174, 302
English literature, 22, 136, 170, 180, 223,
  224
English nationalism, 16
Enlightenment, 14, 37, 44–8, 52, 67–8,
  71–3, 82, 84, 104, 116, 141, 198,
  243
epic poetry, 164, 165, 230
'Essay on Man' (Pope), 49
European Union, 1, 298
Evans, Beriah Gwynfe, 246
Evans, Caradoc, 272–3
Evans, Christmas, 110, 111
Evans, Ellis *see* Hedd Wyn
Evans, Evan, 57, 105, 116–17
Evans, J. J., 59–60
Evans, John, 63
Evans, Neil, 271
Evans, R. J. W., 312
Evans, Sir Samuel T., 197
Evans, Theophilus, 36, 38, 53

Evans, Thomas, 64
evolution, 233, 239, 250; *see also*
  Darwinism
exceptionalism, 130, 138, 148
exploration, 63

F
famine, 31, 45, 83, 118
Faner, Y see Baner ac Amserau Cymru
farming *see* agriculture
fascism, 205, 251, 297
Faust (Goethe), 102, 249
federalism, 147, 158, 277
feminism, 4, 225, 245
feudalism, 5, 23, 28–9, 40, 41, 50, 127,
  134, 137
Finland, 10, 82, 87, 104, 196, 197
Finnish language, 10, 87
First World War, 7, 187, 203, 215, 251,
  260, 261, 270, 288–91, 298
Fisher, Herbert, 242
Flintshire, 29, 39, 155
folk culture, 23, 27, 33, 44, 56, 82, 156,
  164, 169, 304
folk music, 82, 164
folk poetry, 87, 88, 223
folklore, 23, 44, 51, 156, 169, 243, 304
Fonmon estate, 29
food prices, 30, 112, 113
food riots, 112
football, 267–8
Football Association of Wales, 267
foreign policy, 28, 157, 218
Forward Movement, 266–7
Foulkes, Edward, 224
fragmentation, 289
France, 5, 6, 28, 45, 47, 51–3, 55, 61, 62,
  64, 69, 81, 82, 141, 224
Francis I, 83
Francis, J. O., 270, 272, 273
Francke, A. N., 65
Frankfurt, 124, 125
Frankfurt parliament, 124, 125
Franks, 22
Franz Ferdinand, 287, 288
Franz Joseph, 147, 148, 210, 261, 269, 289

Frederick the Great of Prussia, 45
free markets, 148
freedom of assembly, 123
freedom of movement, 30, 46, 93
freedom of press, 62, 123, 124
freedom of religion, 9, 62, 80, 107
freedom of speech, 123
freedom of thought, 83, 237–8
Freising manuscripts, 52
French language, 40, 54, 56, 226, 249,
  284
French literature, 170, 226
French Revolution, 5, 6, 55, 61, 62, 82,
  224
friendly societies, 94, 100
Frost, John, 112, 114, 118
Froude, James Anthony, 164

G

Gair yn ei Amser (Jones), 65
Galsworthy, John, 246
game laws, 29
Garibaldi, Giuseppe, 275
Geddes, Jenny, 305
Gee, Thomas, 175–7, 182, 188, 211, 214
Gellner, Ernest, 196, 222, 243
Geninen, 223–4, 228, 230–1, 235
Geoffrey of Monmouth, 23, 36, 59, 72,
  252, 253
geology, 44, 51, 95, 163, 224
George II, 29
George IV, 58
German culture, 26, 71, 117–18, 159,
  171, 301, 306
German language
  education in, 70, 82, 84–5, 104, 135,
    136, 161, 172, 194, 201, 255
  influence on Slovene language, 14
  language borders, 39
  language census data, 192, 194
  and law, 104
  literature in *see* German literature
  nemškutarji, 126, 142, 158, 161, 167,
    210
  newspapers and periodicals, 81, 252,
    276

official language of Habsburg
  Monarchy, 5, 21, 49
public use, 125, 158, 300
publishing in, 46, 52, 239–40, 284
German literature, 49, 88, 90, 159, 170,
  224, 227, 249, 284
German nationalism, 91, 126, 156, 181,
  194, 206, 207, 285
German Social Democratic movement,
  194, 232, 284
Germans
  commerce and industry, 188–9, 192
  dominant position in Habsburg
    Monarchy, 5, 46, 91, 117–18, 161,
    172, 188–90, 194, 255, 285, 302
  education, 104
  and the First World War, 288, 290
  Frankfurt parliament, 124, 125
  economic dominance, 188–90, 262
  Kočevje enclave, 262
  liberalism, 232
  mountaineering, 181
  nationalism, 91, 126, 156, 181, 194,
    204, 206, 207, 285
  newspapers and periodicals, 81
  social democracy, 194, 232, 284
  socialism, 91, 274–7
  sport, 267
  tensions with Slovenes, 286
  theology, 224
Gibbon, Edward, 52
Gildas, 253
Giraldus Cambrensis, 23
Gladstone, William, 135, 151, 154, 177,
  207, 211, 223, 264, 277, 284
Glamorgan, 30, 32, 39, 41, 62, 64, 72, 81,
  107, 111, 113, 192, 193, 215, 233,
  271, 280–1, 307
Glasbena matica, 195, 202
Glasgow University, 239, 241, 254, 255
Glasnant Jones, W., 234–5
Glorious Revolution, 148
Glyndŵr, Owain, 22, 23, 38, 199, 253–4,
  295
Glyndŵr revolt, 38, 295
Gymraes, 156
Gododdin, 57–8

Goethe, Johann Wolfgang von, 102, 170, 225, 249
Golden Bull, 28
Goldsmith, Oliver, 170
Golyddan, 182–3
Gomer *see* Harris, Joseph
Good Templars, 153
Gorchestion Beirdd Cymru (Evans), 57
Gorica, 32, 33, 83, 250, 296, 298
Gorizia, 32, 33, 194, 195, 250
Gorsedd of Bards, 63–4
Gorup, Josip, 188, 189
Gothic architecture, 198, 202
Gottschee, 39, 262
Govekar, Fran, 247
Gower peninsula, 39
Graham, Sir James, 118
Grammar of the Slav language in Carniola, Carinthia and Styria (Kopitar), 52
grammar schools, 34, 56
grammars, 24, 46–7, 52, 53, 72, 92, 241
Grammatik der crainerischen Sprache (Pohlin), 46–7
Grand Theatre, Cardiff, 263
Grand Theatre, Llandudno, 264
Graz, 28, 33, 53, 83–4, 93, 124, 198, 239
Graz University, 198, 239
Great Disruption, 80
Great Exhibition, 79
Great Reform Act, 79–80
Great Western Railway, 149
Greece, 212
Greek, 51, 87
Green, T. H., 239
Greenly, Elizabeth, 97
Gregorčič, Simon, 188, 189, 250–1
Griffith, John, 182
Griffith, Robert Arthur, 246–7
Griffiths, Ann, 75, 117
Griffiths, Jim, 281
Gruber brothers, 48
Gruden, Josip, 253
Gruffydd, Owen, 35
Gruffydd, W. J., 244, 246–7, 249, 271, 273
Guest, Lady Charlotte, 97
Gutsman, Ožbalt, 53

Gweirydd ap Rhys, 253
Gwent, 107
gwerin, 9, 14, 55, 73, 102, 103, 196, 206, 211, 241, 296, 305, 306
Gwilym Hiraethog, 24, 95, 101–2, 105–6, 117, 140, 151–2, 155, 16–6, 175, 183, 202, 301
Gwladgarwr, 97
Gwyddoniadur, 175
Gwyliedydd, 97
Gwynedd, 22, 39, 40, 187–8, 281–2
Gwyneddigion Society, 58, 61–2, 63–4, 69, 95
gymnastic societies, 158–9, 181, 198
Gymraes, Y 245

H
Hacquet, Balthazar, 52
Hall, Benjamin, 97
Halliday, Thomas, 277
Hamilton, William, 174
Hanes Cymru (Carnhuanawc), 96
hard power, 4, 306
Hardie, Keir, 282–3
harp music, 58, 96
Harris, Howel, 65, 66, 76, 110
Harris, Joseph, 94, 98–100, 102, 106, 312
Hart, Brett, 244
Haul, 101
Hechter, Michael, 11
Hedd Wyn, 291
Hegel, G. W. F., 239
Heine, Heinrich, 224, 227, 249
Hen Wlad fy Nhadau, 153
Herald Cymraeg, 281
Herberstein, Johann Karl von, 48, 75
Herberstein, Sigismund von, 24
Herbert, Edward, Lord of Cherbury, 26
Herder, Johann Gottfried, 5–6, 10, 48, 82, 87, 92, 137, 183, 228, 301, 310
High Calvinism, 107–8, 174
high culture, 33, 116, 158, 160, 179, 196, 222, 243
Hindusim, 68
Historia Regum Britanniae (Geoffrey of Monmouth), 36, 253

historic rights, 162, 210
historical pageants, 269–70
historiography, 8–10, 36, 50, 53, 59, 60, 89–90, 93, 96, 148, 202, 251–6, 299–300, 308
History of Modern Wales (Williams), 2
History of Protestant Nonconformity in Wales (Rees), 153
History of the Slovene Nations (Gruden), 253
History of Wales (Edwards), 8–9
History of Wales (Lloyd), 254
History of Wales (Warrington), 59
Hobhouse, Lionel, 284
Hočevar, Toussaint, 190
holocaust, 3, 7
Holy Roman Empire, 22
Holyhead, 108, 193
home rule
    Hungary, 147, 206
    Ireland, 80, 177, 207, 211, 214, 217
    Wales, 177, 186, 216, 297
    see also devolution
Hösler, Joachim, 90–1
House of Commons *see* British parliament
House of Lords *see* British parliament
housing, 31, 41, 81, 111, 129, 178, 202, 237, 276, 282
Howard de Walden, Lord, 270, 272
Howell, David, 41, 182
Hribar, Ivan, 197, 198, 209–10, 288, 291
Hroch, Miroslav, 10, 54, 127, 137, 139
Hughes, John Ceiriog, 155, 165, 172
Hughes, R. Elwyn, 103
Hughes, Thomas, 149
Hugo, Victor, 170
humanism, 24, 201
Humphreys, E. Morgan, 228, 246
Hungarian culture, 71
Hungarian nationalism, 156
Hungary, 4, 11, 28, 45, 74, 81, 82, 140, 147, 156, 206, 267, 287
hunting, 29
hymns, 67, 75, 110, 117, 153, 155, 233, 265
Hywel Dda, 113

I
Ibsen, Henrik, 246
Icelandic literature, 22, 58
identity
    British identity, 186, 218, 299
    and class, 280
    and culture, 37, 70–1, 218, 269–71
    and history, 252
    Irish identity, 266, 288, 305
    and language, 10, 135, 139–40, 218, 229, 231, 280–1, 302
    and nationalism, 311
    and religion, 10–11, 76, 140, 231, 238, 265–7, 280–1
    Scottish identity, 305
    Slovene identity, 38–9, 41, 195, 231, 239, 252
    and sport, 267–8
    Welsh identity, 37–9, 41, 70–1, 76, 135, 139–40, 186, 229–31, 238, 252–3, 265–71, 280–1, 288, 299, 302, 309–10
Idrija, 31
Ieuan Glan Geirionydd *see* Evans, Evan
Ieuan Gwynedd, 117, 130–1, 132–3, 135, 156, 245, 265
Illustrated London News, 164
Illyria, 38, 51–2, 54, 61, 88, 126
'Illyria Enhanced' (Vodnik), 51
'Illyria Revived' (Vodnik), 51
Illyrian movement, 88
immigration, 154, 187, 194, 203, 262–74, 307
In the Blood (Govekar), 247
independence of spirit, 310–11
India, 45, 79, 140, 206, 310
individualism, 3, 104, 225, 229, 300, 303, 312
Indo-European languages, 45
industrial decline, 298
industrial relations, 113–15, 154–5, 188, 277–9, 281
Industrial Revolution, 55, 148–9
industrialisation, 11, 55, 62, 69, 79–81, 100, 107, 111–16, 137–8, 141, 148–50, 154–5, 182, 187–90, 254, 263–4, 274–5, 307–8

Innsbruck, 83
intelligentsia, 14, 82–4, 94, 104–5, 116,
    126, 141–2, 159–60, 181, 196,
    198, 207, 225, 246–7, 283–4,
    304–6
Intermediate Education Act (1889),
    200–1, 242, 245, 303
intermediate schools, 200–1, 225, 303
Internal Colonialism (Hechter), 11
International Federation of Association
    Football (FIFA), 267
internationalism, 168, 249, 275, 283
Iolo Caernarfon, 205–6
Iolo Morganwg, 49, 63–4, 71, 72, 113
Ipavec, Benjamin, 229
Ireland
    Anglican Church, 135
    Catholic emancipation, 80, 177
    Catholicism, 80, 92, 131, 140, 177–8,
        266, 268, 305
    cooperative movement, 189
    education, 118
    emigration, 80, 191
    famine, 118
    home rule, 80, 177, 207, 211, 214, 217
    immigration to Wales, 266, 268
    land reform, 175–6, 190, 212
    nationalism, 186, 189, 206, 207,
        211–12
    parliament, 28, 45
    theatre, 246
Irish identity, 266, 288, 305
Irish language, 22, 80
Irish literature, 22, 58, 246, 249
iron, 31, 83, 97, 111, 148–9, 150, 187, 263
Israel, 140
Islam, 68, 140
Islwyn, 172–3, 268
Italian culture, 276
Italian language, 54, 84, 203, 204, 226,
    276
Italian literature, 51, 170, 237, 249
Italian nationalism, 4, 123–4, 156, 206
Italy, 4, 24, 51–2, 123–4, 156, 203–4,
    206, 251, 275–6, 286, 288–9, 290,
    291, 297–8
itinerant preachers, 109

J
Jac Glan-y-gors, 61–2, 65, 69
Janša, Janez, 298
Jansenists, 47, 48, 75
Jarnik, Urban, 53
Jefferson, Thomas, 4
Jeglič, Anton, 288–9
Jenkins, Geraint, 39, 299
Jenkins, John Gwili, 233–4
Jenkins, Philip, 41
Jenkins, R. T., 56, 57, 73
Jesuit college, Ljubljana, 25, 48
Jesuit order, 25, 34, 47, 48
Jesus College, Oxford, 24, 241
Jewin Church, London, 131
Johann, Archduke, 84
Johanneum, Graz, 84
Johnson, Samuel, 58
Jones, Alfred Lewis, 202
Jones, Arthur Herbert, 267
Jones, Cynddylan, 234, 236, 237
Jones, Dafydd, Trefriw, 58–9
Jones, Dafydd Glyn, 253, 254
Jones, David, 9
Jones, Edward, 58
Jones, Evan *see* Ieuan Gwynedd
Jones, Griffith, 34, 41, 45, 65, 67, 85
Jones, Henry, 239, 240, 254–5, 288
Jones, Ieuan Gwynedd, 9, 130
Jones, Ifano, 246
Jones, J. R., 12–13
Jones, J. Tywi, 272
Jones, Jack, 193, 280
Jones, John *see* Jac Glan-y-gors
Jones, John, Talsarn, 108, 109, 110, 165,
    203
Jones, Kilsby, 230
Jones, Mark, 103
Jones, Mary, 75
Jones, Merfyn, 181
Jones, Michael D., 213
Jones, Robert Ambrose *see* Emrys ap Iwan
Jones, T. Gwynn, 224, 237, 248–50, 251
Jones, Thomas (almanacist), 26, 35
Jones, Thomas (Cabinet Secretary), 290
Jones, Thomas (Denbigh, Methodist),
    64–5, 66, 110

Jones, William, 45, 138, 229
Joseph II, 5, 46, 47, 49–50, 71, 74, 81, 93
Josephinism, 47, 70, 74, 92, 137
Joshua, Seth, 267
journals *see* periodicals
Judaism, 68, 261
Jurčič, Josip, 160, 179
Justices of the Peace (JPs), 25, 29, 46

K
Kant, Immanuel, 49, 102
Karadžić, Vuk, 52
Katoliški Obzornik, 236–7
Kay-Shuttleworth, James, 132
Klagenfurt, 32, 33, 83, 106, 169, 194, 225
Kmetijske in rokodelske Novice, 88–9, 93, 98, 100, 125–7, 154, 155, 157, 158, 160, 171, 179
Kollár, Jan, 87, 169
Kopitar, Jernej, 52, 54–5, 72, 81, 87, 105, 239
Korošec, Anton, 297
Koseski, Jovan, 160
Kossuth, Lajos, 11, 140, 202
Krek, Janez Evangelist, 208–9, 210, 237
Kristan, Etbin, 280
Kumerdej, Blaž, 48–9, 51, 55

L
labour movement, 9, 260, 262, 274–83, 299, 303; *see also* socialism; trade unions
Labour Party, 16, 149, 193, 195, 281–3, 291, 296, 297, 299, 307, 308, 313
Ladislas Posthumus, 23–4
laissez-faire politics, 15, 46, 81, 104, 117, 128
Lampe, Evgen, 237–8
Lampeter, 97
Land Commission, 190
Land League, 212
land ownership, 23, 30–1, 40–1, 93–4, 117, 127, 175–6, 188, 190, 212

land reform, 81, 93–4, 127, 175–6, 190
landlordism, 9, 60, 62, 93–4, 118, 133–4, 154, 175–6, 188
Landsker, 39, 262
language borders, 39
language censuses, 192–4, 216, 312
language movements, 5–6, 10, 46–55, 69–70, 82–106, 137, 156–67, 239–41, 301–2
Lassalle, Ferdinand, 276
Latin, 22, 23–4, 34, 35, 47, 51, 54, 56, 249, 253, 268
Latvia, 82
law
    Austrian legal system, 28, 29, 104, 157
    British legal system, 28, 29, 40, 45
    burial law, 175, 176
    Corn Laws, 80, 102
    and the English language, 25–6, 40, 62, 134, 164
    equality before the law, 28, 216
    game laws, 29
    and the German language, 104
    Hungarian legal system, 28
    property laws, 29, 127
    Roman law, 28
    Scottish legal system, 28
    and the Slovene language, 104
    in Wales, 22, 25–6, 29, 38, 40, 45, 62, 94–5, 100, 103, 164
    and the Welsh language, 22, 25–6, 38, 40, 94–5, 100, 103, 134, 139
learned societies, 6, 33, 56–8, 61–2, 63–4, 69, 136
lectures, 64, 101, 163, 214, 229
Lendava, 267
Leo XXIII, 236, 237
Leon Society, 236
Lermontov, Mikhail, 160
Lessing, Gotthold, 168
Levi, Thomas, 218
Levstik, Fran, 160–1, 168–72, 179, 180
Lewis, J. Saunders, 57, 203
Lewis, Sir John Herbert, 197
Lewis, Richard, 114
Lewis, W. T., 150
Lewis, William, 197

Lhuyd, Edward, 35, 36, 56, 72
Liberal Party, 135, 148, 151, 176–7, 190,
   195, 197, 207, 211, 214–15, 217,
   277, 282, 291, 296, 308
liberalism, 79, 104, 123, 132, 137, 142,
   166, 207, 209–10, 232, 237,
   250–1, 274, 284, 297, 304
libraries, 50–1, 249, 269, 271, 309
life expectancy, 32
Light, Julie, 150
Lingen, Ralph, 112, 129–30, 216
linguistic nationalism, 142, 151, 252, 263,
   303, 308
linguistic standardisation, 38–9, 70, 84,
   85–8
linguistics, 45, 72, 240–1
Linhart, Anton Tomaž, 49–50, 54–5, 64,
   71, 105, 116, 252
Lisburne, Ernest Vaughan, Lord, 190
literacy, 34, 41, 48, 69, 84, 102, 107, 137,
   190, 285
literary criticism, 87, 152, 160, 170, 212,
   224, 247, 284
literary language, 3, 7, 24, 26, 38–9, 53,
   74, 87, 139, 156, 157, 242–3
literature
   Anglo-Welsh literature, 247, 272–3,
      297
   Croatian literature, 226
   Czech literature, 226–7
   discussion of in periodical press,
      223–5, 226–7
   drama, 33, 50, 51, 54, 56, 69, 132,
      159, 168, 169, 170, 226, 245–7,
      251, 270–2
   English literature, 22, 136, 170, 180,
      223, 224
   French literature, 170, 226
   German literature, 49, 88, 90, 159,
      170, 224, 227, 249, 284
   in Greek, 51
   Icelandic literature, 22, 58
   Irish literature, 22, 58, 246, 249
   Italian literature, 51, 170, 237, 249
   in Latin, 22, 23–4, 51, 54
   novels, 170, 179, 223, 227–8, 244–5,
      247, 249, 261–2, 272, 280, 281

   poetry *see* poetry
   Polish literature, 226
   popular literature, 14, 179, 244–5,
      255
   Russian literature, 226
   serialisation of, 153, 223, 227–8,
      244–5
   short stories, 88, 156, 168–9, 170,
      179, 208, 223, 247, 273
   Slovene literature, 14, 23–4, 49–52,
      54, 69, 86–8, 90, 116, 155–6,
      159–60, 168–70, 179, 191, 227,
      229, 242–4, 247–8, 250–1, 301,
      304–6
   translations of, 6, 97, 102, 136,
      157, 159, 170, 180, 227, 243–4,
      249
   travelogues, 58, 59, 169, 241
   Welsh literature, 22, 35–8, 57–8,
      60, 70–1, 95, 97, 101, 105,
      116–17, 129, 136, 139 163–4,
      179, 212, 230, 242–50, 255, 281,
      297, 304
   women authors, 245, 247
   world literature, 136
   see also publishing
Liverpool, 101, 108, 131, 148, 150, 174,
   181, 202–3, 205, 214, 234, 249,
   288
Liverpool University, 202, 203
living standards, 41, 75, 275, 288
Ljubljana, 21–6, 32–5, 48–53, 61, 83, 88,
   90, 93, 106, 124–5, 147, 158–60,
   168–72, 180–1, 189, 195–8, 209,
   225–6, 247, 250, 255, 267–8,
   286–7, 291, 306
Ljubljana Casino, 90, 180
Ljubljana Credit Bank, 189
Ljubljana Dramatic Society, 246
Ljubljana Gymnasium, 159–60, 168, 169,
   171, 197
Ljubljana Shooting Society, 90
Ljubljana Slovene Society, 125
Ljubljanski Zvon, 223–7, 229, 235, 237,
   247, 250, 289
Llafur, 307
Llandovery College, 97, 133

Llandudno, 149, 150, 182, 264, 308
Llanelli, 115, 269, 279, 291
Llanidloes, 193
Llanover, Augusta Hall, Lady, 94, 96–7, 133
Llenor, Y, 297
Lloyd, John Edward, 202, 253–4
Lloyd, Morgan, 228
Lloyd George, David, 154, 197, 202–3, 210–11, 213–17, 235, 262, 270, 288, 290–1, 296–7
Llwyd, Morgan, 26
Llwyfo, Llew, 164
Llythyr i'r Cymry (Owen), 133, 163
Llywarch Hen, 58
Llywelyn ap Gruffydd, 240
Llywelyn the Great, 214
Locke, John, 112
London, 35, 36, 56–7, 59, 61–4, 69, 72, 95, 100–1, 108, 118, 131, 151, 173, 181, 214, 278, 288
London University, 173
low culture, 196, 243
Lublanske Novice, 51
Lutheranism, 5, 24, 65, 82
Lycée, Ljubljana, 48, 83, 86

M

Mabinogi, 22, 37, 97, 228
Mabon, 277–8, 279, 282
Macaulay, Thomas, 148
Mácha, Karel Hynek, 87
Madog, 63–4, 95, 172
Maesteg, 235
Magna Carta, 28
Magyars, 22, 140, 147, 180
Mahnič, Anton, 208, 250
Manchester, 148
manuscripts, 22, 35, 36, 47, 52, 56–7, 64, 72, 96, 253, 269
Maria Theresa, 28, 46
Maribor, 32, 159, 250, 285
Marles, Gwilym, 75
marriage, 30, 61, 66, 111, 269, 273
Marriage of Figaro, The (Beaumarchais), 50, 54

Marx, Karl, 3, 91, 276, 282
Marxism, 274–5, 278, 279–80, 282, 284, 298
Masaryk, Thomas, 280, 283
Masterman, Neville, 211
materialism, 48, 207, 230, 237
'matter of Britain', 36, 59, 72
Matthias Corvinus, 23
May, Karl, 244
May Declaration, 289
Mazzini, Giuseppe, 235
Melik, Anton, 289, 290
Merionethshire, 117, 132, 212
Merthyr riots, 112, 113–14
Merthyr Tydfil, 9, 40, 55, 97, 111–12, 113–14, 149, 155, 167, 264, 282–3, 312
Metelko, Franc Serafin, 170
Methodism, 9, 57, 61, 64–9, 74–6, 95, 101–2, 106–10, 131, 151–3, 160, 167, 172–7, 202, 205, 213, 233, 254, 266, 277, 288; *see also* Nonconformity
Metternich, Clemenz, 81, 83, 117, 124
middle classes, 14, 71, 94, 104, 125, 128, 135, 142, 150, 164, 186, 196–9, 202–3, 225–6, 247, 264, 272, 277, 281, 312
Middlesborough, 149
Miklošič, Franc, 239
Mill, John Stuart, 4–5, 6, 7, 91, 173–4, 178
Milner, Arthur, 262
Milton, John, 72
'Miner's Song, The' (Ieuan Gwynedd), 117
'Miners' Next Step, The', 278–9, 281, 283
mining, 31, 41, 112–13, 117, 133, 149, 154–5, 177, 187–90, 235, 264–7, 274, 277–81, 307–8
Missia, Jakub, 208
missionary work, 95, 110, 186, 202
Mississippi River, 63
Missouri River, 63
modernism, 15, 249, 250, 251
Mold strike, 245

Molé, Vojislav, 227
monasteries, 33, 47, 49, 74
Monmouthshire, 31, 41, 62, 73, 81, 96,
  111–13, 117, 133, 138, 172,
  191–3, 215, 233, 235, 264, 267–8,
  307
monolingualism
  English, 60, 112, 176, 187, 193,
    260–1, 264
  language census data, 192–4, 216
  Slovene, 39–40, 193–4
  Welsh, 39–40, 68, 73, 80, 99, 108,
    165, 176, 192, 193, 216, 230–1
Montenegrins, 89, 169
Montgomeryshire, 29, 73, 75, 178, 193
Moravia, 22
Morgan, Eluned, 245
Morgan, J. Vyrnwy, 205
Morgan, Kenneth, 9, 16, 168, 176, 215,
  216, 297, 299–300
Morgan, Prys, 70–1
Morgan, William, 24
Morgans of Tredegar, 30, 111
Morris, Lewis, 55–9, 64, 65, 71, 72, 230
Morris, Richard, 55–6, 57, 59, 72
Morris, William, 29, 55–6
Morris circle, 29, 55–9, 70–3, 76, 95, 110,
  116, 138, 166, 279, 302
Morris Jones, John, 169, 240–1, 249,
  288
Morys, Huw, 172
Moscow, 24
Mosley, Oswald, 280
mountaineering societies, 181
mountains, 44–5, 172, 181, 242; *see also*
  Snowdonia
multiculturalism, 7, 91, 226, 279, 313
museums, 35, 63, 83, 171, 172, 178, 269,
  271, 309
music, 58, 60, 67, 72, 81, 96–7, 115, 153,
  155, 158, 164, 195, 202, 229, 307
music hall, 263
My People (Evans), 273
Myfyr, Owain, 61
myth, 36–7, 63, 95, 141, 163–4, 183, 251,
  252, 253, 308
Myvyrian Archaiology, 58

N

Nabergoj, Ivan, 204, 206, 275–6
Napoleon, 45, 51, 81
Napoleonic wars, 53, 61, 69, 81, 141
Narodni Dom, Trieste, 204–5
Naši zapiski, 283
nation-building, 2–3, 7, 13, 139, 314
national anthems, 153
national costume, 97
National Eisteddfod, 63, 162–4, 182, 191,
  202, 225, 230, 241, 249, 281, 291;
  see also eisteddfodau/eisteddfods
national indifference, 285, 288
National Library of Wales, 249, 269, 271,
  309
National Museum of Wales, 178, 269,
  271, 309
National Progressive Party, 208
National Society for Anglicans, 133
nationalism
  British attitudes towards, 3–5, 166
  and the cult of the common man, 73
  cultural nationalism, 5–6, 48, 82, 137,
    158–60, 183, 215, 225, 239, 310
  English nationalism, 16
  German nationalism, 91, 126, 156,
    181, 194, 204, 206, 207, 285
  Hungarian nationalism, 156
  and the intelligentsia, 104–5, 126–7
  Irish nationalism, 186, 189, 206, 207,
    211–12
  Italian nationalism, 4, 123–4, 156,
    206
  and liberalism, 123–4, 166, 297
  linguistic nationalism, 142, 151, 252,
    263, 303, 308
  psychology of, 284
  and racism, 7, 91
  romantic nationalism, 88, 96, 156–7,
    171
  Slav nationalism, 206, 243, 288–90
  Slovene nationalism, 46–8, 88, 90–1,
    156–7, 162, 180, 276, 288–90
  and socialism, 284–5
  Welsh nationalism, 9, 249, 296–7,
    299, 308
natural rights, 162, 194

Nazism, 7, 291, 297
Neath, 31
Negri, Anna, 237
nemškutarji, 126, 142, 158, 161, 167, 210
Nennius, 253
neo-absolutism, 134, 147, 155, 157, 158,
    161, 168, 306
neo-Hegelianism, 239, 254
neo-Nazism, 195
neo-Slav movement, 210
neo-Thomism, 236
New Theatre, Cardiff, 263–4
Newcastle Commission, 216
'Newcastle Programme', 211
Newport, 9, 90, 112, 114–15, 118, 131,
    193, 214, 263, 268, 308
Newport rising, 114–15, 118
newspapers
    American, 166, 189
    Catholic press, 126, 155, 224, 236–7,
        303
    closure of, 126
    daily, 180, 195, 202, 225, 255, 276
    diaspora newspapers, 150, 166, 189
    English, 111–12, 115, 118
    and Nonconformity, 98–102, 152–3,
        181, 302
    press freedom, 62, 123, 124
    Slovene, 51, 69, 88–9, 93–4, 100,
        125–7, 154–5, 157–8, 160–1,
        171, 180, 189, 194, 195, 202, 225,
        255, 275–6, 277
    socialist press, 275, 276, 277, 283–4
    weekly, 51, 88–9, 94–5, 98–100, 272
    Welsh, 60, 94–5, 98–102, 115, 129,
        130–1, 137, 150, 152–4, 166,
        175–7, 202, 272, 277, 302, 312
    see also periodicals
Newton, Isaac, 47
Newtown, 73
Nicholas, Thomas, 164
Nietzsche, Friedrich, 237
Nonconformity
    becomes dominant form of worship,
        106–7, 117, 138
    break from Anglican Church, 65–6
    burials, 175, 176

chapel activities, 153
decline of, 12, 15
doctrinal disputes, 107–8
and education, 9, 102, 109, 110,
    128–34, 154, 165, 216–17
and emigration, 63, 150–2
and the English language, 109, 110
and the First World War, 288
hegemonic role of, 110–11, 142,
    265–7, 277, 282, 299, 308, 310
and identity, 10–11, 76, 265–7,
    280–1
and journalism, 97–102, 152–3, 181,
    302
in Liverpool, 131, 174, 202, 203,
    234
ministers, 108–9, 110, 130, 152–3
Nonconformist culture, 9, 10–11,
    98–102, 110–11, 140, 151–4,
    181–2
Nonconformist movement, 9, 10–11,
    55–6, 65–9, 74–6, 106–11, 115,
    117, 130–4, 137–8, 182, 205–6,
    301–3, 310
    organisational and infrastructural
        development, 6, 66–7, 106–10,
        130, 150, 152
    political representation, 148, 150, 154,
        167–8, 211
    revivals, 55, 66, 104, 205–6, 232–5,
        254, 281, 301
    and social unrest, 115
    and socialism, 280–1, 303
    and theatre, 246, 271–2, 302–3
    and the Welsh language, 98–102,
        110–11, 151, 154, 181–2, 279,
        302–3
    see also individual denominations
non-denominational schools, 154, 176,
    216
Norman conquest, 38
Norman French, 40
North Wales Liberal Federation, 214–15
Northern Ireland, 16, 311
novels, 170, 179, 223, 228–9, 244–5, 247,
    249, 261–2, 272, 280, 281
Novice see *Kmetijske in rokodelske Novice*

O

O'Brien, William, 212
O'Connell, Daniel, 80, 140
Offa's Dyke, 39, 95
Ohio, 63, 189
old Dissent, 107, 108–9, 131
Old Slav, 51, 52–3
Old Slovenes, 160, 172, 208
Old Welsh, 22
open-air preaching, 65, 66, 110, 111
opera, 164, 190, 226, 227, 306
'Oriau'r Hwyr' (Hughes), 155
Orthodox Churches, 140, 210, 286
Ottoman Empire, 140, 212, 260, 287
Owen, Daniel, 244–6
Owen, David *see* Brutus
Owen, Goronwy, 57–8, 73, 105, 179
Owen, Hugh, 133, 163, 199, 202, 300
Owen, Robert, 212, 277
Oxford University, 24, 36, 72, 95, 211,
        240–1, 249

P

Padua University, 24
paganism, 68
pageants, 269–70
Paine, Thomas, 62
Palacký, František, 23, 82, 123
Palestine, 310
Panslavism, 87, 88, 125, 169, 194, 210,
        303, 306
Pantheologia (Pantycelyn), 67–9
Pantycelyn *see* Williams, William,
        Pantycelyn
Paradise Lost (Milton), 72
Paris, 62, 169, 251
Paris Peace Conference, 296
parliaments
        Austrian parliament, 124–5, 127, 147,
                158, 171, 191, 204, 239, 286
        British parliament, 27–8, 29, 62, 79,
                112, 114, 167–8, 207, 212, 214,
                217
        Frankfurt parliament, 124, 125
        Hungarian parliament, 28, 81, 147
        Irish parliament, 28, 45

        parliamentary reform, 62, 112, 114
        Scottish parliament, 45
Parnell, Charles Stewart, 207, 211–12
Parry, Blind John, 58
Parry, Joseph, 164
Parry, Robert Williams, 250
Parry-Williams, Thomas, 249–50
Patagonia, 151, 213
patriarchy, 32, 127, 160, 245
Peace Society, 167
peasant calendars, 26
peasant revolts, 30, 41, 45
Pembrokeshire, 39, 64, 262, 266, 267
Pennal Letter, 199; *see also* Glyndŵr,
        Owain
Pennsylvania, 63, 149
Penrhyn estate, 60, 188, 281
Penrhyn lockout, 188, 281
Penydarren, 148
'People's Budget', 217
periodicals
        Anglican, 97, 101
        Catholic, 126, 155, 224, 236–7,
                303
        German, 81
        Nonconformist, 97–103, 152–3, 181,
                302
        Slovene, 69, 83, 100, 126, 155–6, 157,
                170, 222–32, 236–8, 250, 252,
                283–4, 287, 303
        socialist, 275, 276, 277, 283–4
        Welsh, 57, 60, 61–3, 66, 94–5,
                97–103, 112, 136, 152–3, 173–4,
                179, 181, 222–32, 235, 238, 245,
                252, 272, 297, 302
        see also newspapers
Persia, 260
Persian language, 249
Pezron, Paul-Yves, 72
Phillips, Sir Thomas, 131–2, 133, 151
Phillips, W. F., 279
philology, 72, 241
philosophy, 34, 45, 49, 56, 83, 99, 173–4,
        224, 234, 236, 239
physiocracy, 47
Piedmont, 286
pilgrimage, 25, 26

Pius IX, 236
Plaid Cymru, 297, 298
Plans of Harbours, Bays and Roads
    (Morris), 56
Pleb Clubs, 283
Pleterski, Janko, 218
Plunkett, Sir Horace, 189
Poe, Edgar Allen, 244
Poems, Lyric and Pastoral (Iolo
    Morganwg), 64
poetry
    bardic tradition, 35–6, 57, 63–4, 100,
        163, 304
    Czech, 87
    eisteddfodic poetry, 95, 101, 117, 179,
        249–50, 291
    epic poetry, 164, 165, 230
    folk poetry, 87, 88, 223
    German, 88, 90, 224, 227
    Latin, 54
    Slovene, 22, 49, 51–2, 54, 69, 86–90,
        116, 168, 169–70, 223–4, 226,
        227, 250–1, 306
    Welsh, 22, 35–6, 38, 57–8, 60, 67, 95,
        101, 105, 116–17, 165, 172–3,
        179, 182–3, 224, 230, 249–55,
        291, 297
Pohlin, Marko, 46–7, 48, 50, 52, 53, 55
Poles, 82, 88, 91, 140, 147, 157
policing, 112, 118, 278, 286, 291
Polish language, 226
Polish literature, 226
political reform, 5, 7, 62, 79–80, 112,
    114
Political Register (Cobbett), 113
Pontardawe, 193
Pontypool, 150
Poor Law, 32, 128
Pope, Alexander, 49
population growth, 30, 62, 80, 81, 83,
    111, 115, 148, 149, 187, 188, 263
portraiture, 33
ports, 149, 150, 177, 187, 202, 263, 291
positivism, 229, 239, 284
poverty, 30–2, 40, 62, 81, 83, 108, 112,
    118, 152, 191, 203, 248, 251, 282,
    305

Powel, David, 253
Powys, 22
Prague, 83, 125, 196, 197, 198, 227
Prague University, 198
preaching festivals, 110
Preporod, 287
Presbyterianism, 34, 75, 80, 131
Prešeren, France, 22, 86–90, 105–6, 116,
    125, 157, 160, 170, 179, 191, 223,
    272, 291
press *see* newspapers; periodicals
press freedom, 62, 123, 124
Price, Thomas *see* Carnhuanawc
Prijatelj, Ivan, 284
primary education, 34, 46, 48, 52, 70,
    82–5, 91, 127, 136–7, 161, 190,
    195, 201, 231, 240
Primitive Methodism, 266
Princip, Gavrilo, 291
printing, 35, 44, 83, 175; *see also*
    publishing
Pritchard, Rhys, 26, 41
Pritchard, T. J., 242
progress, 76, 98, 152, 186, 204, 233, 239,
    301
propaganda, 51, 63, 171, 285, 287
property laws, 29, 127
Protestantism, 24–5, 29, 34, 45–6, 59,
    65–6, 74, 84, 98, 108, 140, 166–7,
    186, 197, 224, 234, 237, 266,
    303
Provincial Theatre, Ljubljana, 226,
    251
Prussia, 45–6, 148
Pryse, John Robert *see* Golyddan
Ptuj, 39, 286
publishing, 24–5, 34–5, 51, 57–8, 61–2,
    100, 135–6, 153, 159, 175, 180,
    194, 243–5, 302
pubs, 100, 103, 109, 154, 235, 265
Pugh, John, 266–7
Pughe, William Owen, 72, 87, 105, 138,
    241
Punch, 179
puritanism, 26, 34, 75, 246, 264, 271, 280,
    302–3
Putin, Vladimir, 3

R

racism, 3, 4, 7, 91, 118
Radetzky March, The (Roth), 261–2
radicalism, 16, 49–50, 55, 61–5, 113–15,
   126, 188, 274, 283, 284, 287, 298
Radnorshire, 39, 73, 95, 193, 256–6
railways, 83, 148, 149, 175, 177, 178, 182,
   187, 264
Raumer, Rudolph von, 166
Ravenstein, E. G., 192
Rdeči prapor, 277
reading societies, 158, 159, 169, 194, 198,
   202, 301
Rebecca Riots, 9, 115, 118, 129
Rebirth of a Nation (Morgan), 9, 16,
   299–300
Red Dragon, The, 272
Rees, David, 103, 115, 131
Rees, Henry, 154, 165
Rees, Sarah Jane *see* Cranogwen
Rees, Thomas (Congregationalist
   minister), 135
Rees, Thomas (historian and editor), 152,
   153
Rees, Thomas (theologian), 234
Rees, William *see* Gwilym Hiraethog
reform Catholicism, 47, 137
Reformation, 24, 25, 33, 66, 304
religious freedom, 9, 62, 80, 107
religious movements, 9, 10–11, 55–6,
   65–9, 74–6, 106–11, 115, 117,
   130–4, 137–8, 182, 301–3, 310
religious processions, 25, 34, 47, 266
religious reform, 47, 108, 141
religious revivals, 55, 66, 104, 205–6,
   232–5, 281, 301
religious tolerance, 46, 61, 74, 141
Renaissance, 24, 36, 51
Renan, Ernest, 229
resorts, 33, 149, 264
revolutions of 1848, 4, 79, 94, 123–8, 140,
   141, 148, 156, 171, 206, 306
Revue des deux Mondes, 115
Rhiwbina garden village, 273
Rhodes, Cecil, 262
Rhondda valley, 1, 149, 155, 177, 187,
   265, 277–9, 280–1, 283, 308, 313

Rhoscomyl, Owen, 270
Rhyl, 149
Rhys, John, 241
Rhys, Morgan John, 62–3, 69, 70, 107
Rhys Lewis (Owen), 245–6
Richard, Edward, 56, 57
Richard, Henry, 131, 155, 167–8, 199
Richards, Brinley, 164
Richards, Thomas, 62, 69
Riga, 82
roads, 31, 73
Roberts, Isaac, 232
Roberts, J. J. *see* Iolo Caernarfon
Roberts, Robert Silyn, 249, 281
Roberts, Samuel, 166–7
robota, 30, 83, 127
Rolph, Heinrich, 166
Roman Empire, 21
Roman law, 28
Romania, 82
romantic nationalism, 88, 96, 156–7, 171
Romanticism, 33, 45, 58, 59, 96
romanticism, 73, 87, 156–7, 249
Rome, 26
Rot, Johannes, 23–4
Roth, Joseph, 261–2
Rousseau, Jean-Jacques, 170, 224
Rowland, Daniel, 65–6, 110
Royal Music Academy, 164
Royal Society, 35, 36, 64, 101
Rubaiyat of Omar Khayyam, 249
rugby, 267–8, 307
Ruskin, John, 212, 282
Russia, 3, 4, 71, 82, 104, 124, 149, 210,
   223, 260, 274
Russian culture, 71
Russian language, 210, 223, 226
Russian literature, 226

S

St David's, 23, 182
St David's theological college, 97
St Hermagoras Society, 170, 194, 225,
   244, 253
Salesbury, William, 24
Samo, 22

sanitation, 111, 175
Sarajevo, 261, 287, 291
satire, 56, 99, 179
'Satisfied Carniolan, The' (Vodnik), 54
Schiele, Egon, 237
Schiller, Friedrich, 170, 225
Schlegel, Friedrich von, 86
Schopenhauer, Arthur, 170
Schorske, Carl, 232
science, 44, 49, 101, 102, 103, 163, 182,
    223, 224, 236, 237
scientific revolution, 44
Scotch Cattle movement, 113, 114, 115,
    277
Scotland, 16, 28, 34, 45, 80, 131, 140,
    192, 207, 266, 295, 305, 311
Scott, Sir Walter, 80, 170
Scottish identity, 305
Scottish parliament, 45
Second World War, 238, 297–8, 304
secondary education, 34, 52, 84–5, 104,
    125, 136, 157, 197–201, 207, 231,
    240, 303, 306
self-assertion, 13, 73, 140, 211
seminaries, 34, 105
Serbo-Croat, 52–3, 88, 89, 156, 226, 229,
    280, 284, 287, 298
Serbs, 52–3, 82, 88, 126, 140, 159, 206,
    210, 261, 286–8, 289, 290, 291, 297
Seren Gomer, 98–100, 103, 105, 110–11,
    138, 152, 179, 312
serfdom, 30, 79, 83, 89
serialisation, 153, 223, 227–8, 244–5
Seven Years' War, 76
Shakespeare, William, 37, 49, 136, 180
Shaw, George Bernard, 246, 270
shipping, 150, 189, 202, 263
short stories, 88, 156, 168–9, 170, 179,
    208, 223, 247, 273
Shrewsbury, 33, 35
singing festivals, 153
slate quarrying, 60, 155, 187–8, 281
slavery, 4, 62, 68, 110, 117, 150, 166, 278
Slavonic tribes, 21, 22
Slomšek, Anton Martin, 92–3, 167
Slovene Bee (Prešeren), 86
Slovene Dramatic Society, 169

Slovene identity, 38–9, 41, 195, 231, 239,
    252
Slovene language
    absence from medieval public life, 23
    alphabet and orthography, 84, 85–6
    bilingualism, 39–40, 49, 84, 90, 93,
        106, 158, 172, 193–4
    dialects, 7, 38, 53, 84, 87–8
    dictionaries, 47, 49, 51, 169, 239–40
    diplomatic use, 24
    discussion of in periodical press,
        223–4
    early documentation, 23
    early Slovene-speaking Slavs, 22–3
    education in, 24, 34, 47–50, 52–3,
        69–70, 82–6, 91–2, 104, 125,
        127–8, 135–6, 157, 161, 172, 191,
        194–5, 199, 201, 203–4, 207, 240,
        296, 301
    grammars, 24, 46–7, 52, 53, 92
    language borders, 39
    language census data, 192, 193–4
    language movement, 46–55, 69–70,
        82–94, 137, 156–62, 239–40,
        301–2
    literature in *see* Slovene literature
    monolingualism, 39–40, 193–4
    and nationalism, 46–7, 156–7, 252,
        303, 308
    newspapers and periodicals, 51, 69,
        88–9, 93, 125–7, 136, 155–8,
        160–1, 169, 171, 179–80, 194–5,
        202, 222–32, 250, 275–7, 283–4,
        287
    numbers of speakers, 192, 193–4
    peasant calendars, 26
    public use, 125–6, 141, 157, 161,
        227–8, 239, 255, 296, 301
    publishing in, 24–5, 35, 51, 100, 136,
        159, 194, 243–4
    reading societies, 158, 159, 169, 194,
        198, 202, 301
    religious texts, 24, 25, 50
    revival, 10, 13, 46–55, 69–70, 82–94,
        137
    songs in, 81, 155, 158, 229
    standardisation, 38–9, 84, 85–8

Slovene literature, 14, 23–4, 49–52, 54, 69, 86–8, 90, 116, 155–6, 159–60, 168–70, 179, 191, 227, 229, 242–4, 247–8, 250–1, 301, 304–6
Slovene music, 81, 155, 158, 195, 202, 229
Slovene Music Society, 181
Slovene nationalism, 46–8, 88, 90–1, 156–7, 162, 180, 276, 288–90
Slovene People's Party, 208, 210, 286–7, 2899
Slovene Reformation, 24–5
Slovene societies, 124–5, 126, 158–9, 180–1, 194, 205
Slovenian National Museum, 172
Slovenija, 125, 126, 171
Slovenska bčela, 156
Slovenska matica, 159, 160, 169, 180, 189, 191, 225, 244
Smith, Anthony D., 3
Snowdonia, 45, 60, 61, 181, 264, 272, 281
Soča region, 250–1
social Darwinism, 166
social democracy, 194, 232, 248, 275–6, 280, 284–5
social mobilisation, 10–11, 14, 91–2, 147, 188, 302, 313
social reform, 5, 282
social unrest, 60, 62, 81, 93–4, 111–15, 118, 286, 289
socialism, 13, 91, 104, 167, 186–7, 207–9, 212, 225, 232, 237, 248–9, 260–1, 274–85, 303, 310
socialist press, 275, 276, 277, 283–4
Societas Operosum, 33
Societas Philharmonica, 33, 180, 195
Society for the Promotion of Christian Knowledge (SPCK), 34, 65
Society for Utilising the Welsh Language, 240
soft power, 6, 13, 306–7
Solferino, battle of, 261
songs, 81, 82, 155, 158, 229; *see also* music
South Africa, 45, 79, 112, 310
south Slavs, 7, 50, 51, 187, 209, 210, 261, 280, 284–8, 289
South Wales Daily Post, 270

South Wales Liberal Federation, 214–15
South Wales Miners' Federation (SWMF), 278, 280
Southampton, 33
Southey, Robert, 72
Soviet Union, 3, 10, 277
Spain, 4, 149
'Speak them both' (Ceiriog), 165
Specimens of the Poetry of the Ancient Welsh Bards (Evans), 57
spirituality, 230, 254, 303
sport, 265, 267–8, 271, 307, 308
Sri Lanka, 140
statues, 269
steam power, 83, 148, 149, 182, 187
steel, 149
Stephens, Thomas, 312
Stevenson, Robert Louis, 244
Stowe, Harriet Beecher, 243–4
strikes, 113, 155, 245, 277, 278–9, 281, 283
Strindberg, August, 246
Stritar, Josip, 160, 169–70, 179
student movements, 159–60, 198, 283–4, 287
Styria, 22, 28, 30, 32–3, 53, 83–4, 88, 93, 125, 159, 162, 167, 187, 194–5, 207, 225, 229, 276, 288
Sudetenland, 310
Südmark, 285
suffrage, 114, 209, 216, 274, 275
suffragette movement, 260, 262
Sunday schools, 67, 69–70, 107, 110, 129–30, 137, 152, 232, 302
Šušteršič, Ivan, 210
Svetokriški, Janez, 35
Swedish culture, 71, 196
Swedish language, 87, 196, 197
Swansea, 31, 33, 90, 98, 103, 106, 149, 187, 193, 198, 264, 268, 269, 308, 312
Swansea Metal Exchange, 149
Swift, Jonathan, 244
Syllabus of Errors, 236
Symons, Jelinger C., 129
syndicalism, 278
Széchenyi, István, 82

Index

Index

T

tabori gatherings, 158, 159, 162, 197, 199
tai unnos, 31, 112–13
Tarian y Gweithiwr, 272
Tarw Scotch movement *see* Scotch Cattle
   movement
Taufferer, Siegfried von, 64
taxation, 29, 30, 52, 93, 98, 115, 175
teacher training, 48, 84, 127, 199
teetotalism, 117, 153, 178, 245, 267; *see
   also* temperance
Telford, Thomas, 149
Telynegion (Gruffydd and Roberts), 249
temperance, 110, 153, 175, 178, 202, 214,
   303, 308; *see also* teetotalism
tenant rights, 29, 40–1, 60, 154, 175–6
Tennyson, Alfred, Lord, 123, 223, 224
Terpinc, Fidelis, 189
textbooks, 69, 84–6, 92, 99, 100, 103,
   133, 137, 271
textile production, 31, 62, 83, 97
theatre, 33, 50, 51, 54, 56, 69, 81, 83, 137,
   159, 170, 190, 226, 245–7, 251,
   263–4, 270–2, 302–3, 306
Thirlwall, Connop, 133
Thomas, Brinley, 191–2, 307
Thomas, David (teacher and author),
   281–2
Thomas, David (Viscount Rhondda), 149,
   197, 215, 263, 290
Thomas, Dylan, 75
Thomas, John William *see* Arfonwyson
Thomas, Owen, 203, 234
Thomas, William *see* Islwyn
Thomas, William Thelwall, 202
Times, 164
tithes, 62, 115, 175, 176, 212, 214, 249
Tito, 53, 298
Tocqueville, Alexis de, 3
tolls, 115
Tolstoy, Leo, 136, 284
Toman, Ivan, 197
Toman, Lovro, 156–7, 188
Tonypandy, 278–9, 291
tourism, 58, 59, 149, 181, 264
Toynbee, Arnold, 70
trade, 31, 80, 187–8, 218, 312

trade unions, 114, 235, 262, 277–8,
   280–1
Traethodydd, Y, 95, 102, 106, 131, 134,
   136, 153, 173–4, 218, 222–5, 226,
   231, 232, 235
travelogues, 58, 59, 169, 241
'Treason of the Blue Books' (Derfel),
   132
Treason of the Long Knives, 38, 132
Tredegar, 117
Tredegar estate, 30, 111
Trieste, 31, 32, 55, 83, 158, 169, 189, 194,
   202, 203–5, 275–6, 283, 284, 290,
   296, 298
Trieste Workers' Confederation, 275
Trinitarianism, 107
Triglav, 44, 181
Trstenjak, Davorin, 93, 171
Trubar, Primus, 24, 25, 38–9
Tudor dynasty, 25, 59, 61, 253
Tudur Aled, 35
Tudur Jones, R., 232, 233, 234, 238
Turkey, 23, 89, 169, 286, 287; *see also*
   Ottoman Empire
tutoring, 157, 168, 251
Tysilio, 59, 72

U

Učiteljski tovariš, 161
Uncle Tom's Cabin (Stowe), 243–4
Undeb Chwarelwyr Gogledd Cymru, 281
unemployment, 113
Unitarianism, 64, 75, 107, 167
United Nations, 2
united Slovenia, 127, 162, 172, 194, 239
United States, 3, 45, 57, 62–3, 140, 148,
   149, 150, 152, 166, 187–9, 213,
   215, 227, 245, 262, 270
universal suffrage, 209, 216, 274, 275
universalism, 4, 8, 166, 167, 171, 311
universities, 24, 80, 83–4, 128, 159–60,
   161, 165, 198–200, 212, 225,
   296
University of Wales, 199–200, 212, 225,
   241
Urdd Gobaith Cymru, 8, 197, 297

'useful knowledge', 89, 94, 100–1, 102,
    108, 136
Ušeničik, Ales, 236–7, 238
utilitarianism, 163, 182, 243

V
Vale of Clwyd, 176, 182, 249
Valvasor, Johann Weichard, 26–7, 35,
    37, 252
Vatican, 26, 204
Vaughan, Arthur Owen *see* Rhoscomyl,
    Owen
Vaughan, Gwyneth, 245
Vavák, František Jan, 75
Vazeh, Mirza Shafi, 160
Veda, 283–4, 287
Vega, Gerog, 48
Vicar of Wakefield, The (Goldsmith),
    170
Victoria, Queen, 96, 269
Vienna, 22, 24, 28, 48–9, 52, 64, 81, 83,
    123–7, 159–61, 168–9, 171, 191,
    197–8, 204, 239, 251, 275
Vienna University, 24, 159–60, 161, 169,
    171, 191, 197, 198, 239, 251
Viriamu Jones, John, 199–200, 201
Vodnik, Valentin, 51–2, 54–5, 69, 116,
    169, 179
Voltaire, 45
voluntarist principle, 128, 132–3
Vošnjak, Bogumil, 284, 289
Vraz, Stanko, 87–8, 230

W
wages, 113, 115, 155, 278
Walters, John, 64
Warrington, William, 59
Watcyn Wyn, 231, 235
Waxenstein, Barbo von, 191
Waxenstein, Joseph Anton von, 191
Welsh, Freddy, 268
Welsh chronicles, 22
Welsh Department of the Board of
    Education, 193, 201, 202, 242,
    271

Welsh exceptionalism, 130, 138
Welsh Guards, 288
Welsh identity, 37–9, 41, 70–1, 76,
    135, 139–40, 186, 229–31, 238,
    252–3, 265–71, 280–1, 288, 299,
    302, 309–10
Welsh language
almanacs, 26
    bardic tradition, 35–6, 57, 63–4, 100,
        163, 304
    bilingualism, 39–40, 64, 90, 112, 165,
        187, 192–3, 230–1, 235, 240, 244,
        255, 264, 271, 279
    and the 'Blue Books' controversy, 79,
        112, 128–34, 139, 151, 163
    decline and erosion, 11, 40, 73, 166,
        191–2, 238, 291, 297, 299, 307
    dictionaries, 66, 72, 234
    discussion of in periodical press,
        229–31
    education in, 34, 62, 69–70, 84–5,
        97, 99, 100, 102–3, 133–4, 136,
        142, 152, 165, 201, 231, 240, 242,
        271
    grammars, 72, 241
    and internal sovereignty, 279
    language borders, 39
    language census data, 192–3, 216, 312
    language movement, 8, 94–106,
        162–7, 240–1
    and the law, 22, 25–6, 38, 40, 94–5,
        100, 103, 134, 139
    literature in *see* Welsh literature
    monolingualism, 39–40, 68, 73, 80,
        99, 108, 112, 165, 176, 192–3,
        216, 230–1
    newspapers and periodicals, 57, 61–3,
        66, 69, 94–5, 97–103, 112, 129,
        130–1, 136–7, 150, 152–3, 165,
        173–7, 179–80, 202, 222–32,
        235, 245, 272, 297, 302, 312
    and Nonconformity, 98–102, 110–11,
        151, 154, 181–2, 279, 302–3
    numbers of speakers, 12, 192–3, 216,
        291, 296
    opera in, 164
    orthography, 241

philology, 72, 241
public use, 139, 162
publishing in, 34–5, 57, 58, 61–2,
    135–6, 153, 175, 180, 243–5, 302
religious services in, 25, 58, 97, 134,
    151
religious texts in, 25, 26, 36, 66, 70,
    108
and social and industrial unrest,
    111–15
and socialism, 277, 279, 280–2
and sport, 268
standardisation, 70
Welsh Language Society, 253, 305
Welsh laws, 22, 38, 113
Welsh literature, 22, 35–8, 57–8, 60,
    70–1, 95, 97, 101, 105, 116–17,
    129, 136, 139, 163–4, 179, 212,
    230, 242–50, 255, 281, 297,
    304
Welsh Manuscripts Society, 96
Welsh music, 58, 72, 96–7, 164
Welsh national costume, 97
Welsh nationalism, 9, 249, 296–7, 299,
    308
Welsh Nationalist Party, 297
Welsh Office, 298
Welsh Renaissance, 24
'Welsh Revolt', 214, 215, 217
Welsh Rugby Union, 267
Welsh societies, 94, 96, 99, 100, 101, 103,
    133, 181
Welsh Trust Schools, 34
Wesley, John, 65, 66, 107
Wesleyanism, 106–8, 109–10, 230,
    266
West Indies, 45
Whitefield, George, 66
Why Wales Never Was (Brooks), 13, 300
Wilde, Jimmy, 268
Williams, Chris, 277, 280, 281, 308
Williams, David, 2, 9, 41, 130
Williams, Edward *see* Iolo Morganwg
Williams, Eliseus *see* Eifion Wyn
Williams, Gwyn Alf, 62, 65, 299
Williams, Hugh, 112, 115
Williams, Ioan, 246, 271–2

Williams, Jane, 96
Williams, John, Brynsiencyn, 288
Williams, Moses, 36, 41
Williams, Owen, 150
Williams, Peter, 228
Williams, William, Llandegai, 60–1, 70,
    71, 72
Williams, William, Pantycelyn, 65, 66,
    67–9, 76, 102, 153, 165, 313
Williams, Zephaniah, 112, 115
woollen industry, 97, 149, 178
workhouses, 32
working classes, 107, 149, 203, 232, 264,
    268–9, 274–83, 291, 307–8,
    313
workshops, 100, 138
'Wreath of sonnets, A' (Prešeren), 86, 89,
    105
Wrexham, 31, 308
Williams-Wynn, Sir Watkyn, 29, 176
Wynne, Ellis, 26
Wynnstay estate, 29, 30

Y
Young Bosnia, 287
Young Slovenes, 160, 169, 172, 189, 208,
    225
Young Wales *see* Cymru Fydd movement
Yugoslav Committee, 289
Yugoslav National Army, 298
Yugoslav Social Democratic Party, 248,
    277, 280, 284–5
Yugoslavia, 1, 3, 15, 53, 170, 189, 194,
    209, 210, 216, 251, 260–1, 284–9,
    291, 296–8

Z
Zagreb, 53
Zgodnja Danica, 155
Živnostenska Banka, 189
Zois, Žiga, 50–2, 54, 96, 105–6, 116, 179
Zola, Émile, 226
Župančič, Oton, 251
Zupanič, Niko, 285
Zvon, 170